Critical Incidents

in

School Counseling

Edited by

VINCENT F. CALIA
Rhode Island College

RAYMOND J. CORSINI
Family Education Centers of Hawaii

Prentice-Hall, Inc., Englewood Cliffs, New Jersey

**PRENTICE-HALL SERIES
IN COUNSELING AND HUMAN DEVELOPMENT**
NORMAN R. STEWART, *Consulting Editor*

ADAPTIVE COUNSELING IN SCHOOLS
ROTHNEY

CHANGING CHILDREN'S BEHAVIOR
KRUMBOLTZ AND KRUMBOLTZ

COUNSELING STRATEGIES AND OBJECTIVES
HACKNEY AND NYE

CRITICAL INCIDENTS IN SCHOOL COUNSELING
CALIA AND CORSINI

THE HELPING RELATIONSHIP: PROCESS AND SKILLS
BRAMMER

MAKING VOCATIONAL CHOICES
HOLLAND

© 1973 by Prentice-Hall, Inc.
Englewood Cliffs, New Jersey

ISBN: 0-13-193946-7

Library of Congress Catalog Number: 74–37639

10 9 8 7 6 5 4 3 2

Printed in the United States of America

Prentice-Hall International, Inc., *London*
Prentice-Hall of Australia, Pty. Ltd., *Sydney*
Prentice-Hall of Canada, Ltd., *Toronto*
Prentice-Hall of India Private Limited, *New Delhi*
Prentice-Hall of Japan, Inc., *Tokyo*

Contents

part **I**

The Counselor and the Counselee

part **II**

The Counselor and the Family

Preface

It took three years from the time of our agreement to produce *Critical Incidents in School Counseling* to the time we finally sent the manuscript to the publisher. Only at the conception and at the completion were we, the editors, in the same place at the same time. The rest of the time we were separated by some five thousand miles—and the volume of our correspondence exceeded the manuscript.

The basic idea of a critical incident book is simple: obtain sample incidents in any field and then obtain comments on these incidents from a variety of qualified people. The actual process of coordinating the one hundred or more people involved in this process as contributors, consultants, advisers, and typists is quite complicated and calls for a great many editorial decisions about what to use or not use in the case of incidents; who to invite as a consultant; what to do when a consultant does not contribute what he promises, or worse, when what he produces is unacceptable.

During our three years we had many problems, a number of disappointments, and considerable fun in editing this book. Now that it is finally completed, we breathe a sigh of relief, feel thankful for all those who helped us in one way or another, and we hope that *Critical Incidents in School Counseling* will begin to do its intended job: improve the art of counseling in the schools.

Many people in addition to those listed as consultants and contributors have helped us in one way or another. The list would be too long were it to be complete. The senior editor's secretary, Mrs. Sherry Hanoian, who kept order despite the confusion and who performed miracles of typing should get special notice.

VINCENT F. CALIA
RAYMOND J. CORSINI

Contributors
of Critical Incidents

The incidents in this book were selected from contributions generously supplied by counselors and former counselors from all parts of the country. A list of these contributors and their locations is given below.

John H. Bauer   Elkton, South Dakota
Henry J. Bertness   Tacoma, Washington
Dr. William Beucler   New Haven, Connecticut
John H. Bruno   Trumbull, Connecticut
Richard L. Bruce   Seattle, Washington
Patrick R. Bunten   Port Orchard, Washington
Gary D. Carlson   East Greenbush, New York
Irene Cleworth   Fairbanks, Alaska
Deborah Clough   Kansas City, Kansas
Nora Dafoe   Valley City, North Dakota
Dominic J. DiMattia   Amherst, Massachusetts
Joseph F. DiPietro   Bellingham, Massachusetts
Austin Donnelly   Providence, Rhode Island
Mary Moore Downey   Smyrna, Georgia
Sydney R. Eltringham   Newtown, Pennsylvania
Virginia Emmert   Providence, Rhode Island

Bailey M. Faile   Camden, South Carolina
Darrell Finley   Honolulu, Hawaii
Dr. Donald L. Frye   Radford, Virginia
Jim D. Gower   Fairbanks, Alaska
Jean Greenleaf   Fredonia, New York
Dr. Clarke Hess   Huntington, West Virginia
Dr. George Hill   Athens, Ohio
Joan Hingston   La Mesa, California
Dennis A. Houston   Minden, Nebraska
James W. Iovino   Newfields, New Hampshire
Marguerite Johnson   Casper, Wyoming
Peter Kanarian   Barrington, Rhode Island
William J. Lagreid   Seattle, Washington
Barbara Jane Luke   Honolulu, Hawaii
Roger S. Nichols   Sioux City, Iowa
Martin Pierce   Westerly, Rhode Island
Ron Pozzo   Brockton, Massachusetts
Muriel T. Robinson   Cedar Rapids, Iowa
Kevin H. Rose   Beaver Falls, New York
Dr. James T. Rudolph   Glen Ellyn, Illinois
Joseph Salvatore   Warwick, Rhode Island
Stanley Shuman   Sharon, Massachusetts
Wayne Stevens   Mountain Home, Idaho
Mary Jane Strause   East Moline, Illinois
Rhoda B. Tillman   Providence, Rhode Island
Thomas R. Vitola   Denver, Colorado
Naomi D. Vogel   Coolidge, Arizona
Gearline Young   Seattle, Washington

Commenting Consultants

THOMAS W. ALLEN, Ed.D., director of the Student Counseling Service, is assistant professor of education and psychology, Washington University. He has taught at Stanford and Roosevelt Universities, been a counselor in the public schools, and a psychologist in a university, in hospital settings, child guidance clinics, and private practice. He designed the Diagnostic and Adjustment Center in the St. Louis public schools and was research evaluator for the Center. He is the coauthor of *Dimensions of Effective Counseling* and *The Role of the Counselor in the School*.

MARY A. BARBER, M.A., is a counselor and director of testing at Elk Grove High School, Elk Grove, Illinois. She has worked in experimental projects involving talented underachieving students and work-oriented students. She was formerly a research assistant at the University of Iowa and a high school teacher.

BENJAMIN C. BELDEN, M.S., C.S.W., is a teacher in Chicago. He has taught extensively in the inner city. Mr. Belden has held positions in industry as a personnel and training manager and has been chief of an alcoholism treatment center for a Chicago hospital.

DONALD H. BLOCHER, Ph.D., is professor of educational psychology at the University of Minnesota. He has been a high school teacher and counselor, and a counseling psychologist in a veterans' hospital. Dr. Blocher has trained counselors and counseling psychologists at the University of Minnesota for the past ten years. He has been concerned with the creation of counseling treatment models based upon concepts of human effectiveness rather than pathology. Dr. Blocher is the author of *Developmental Counseling* and *Guidance Systems*. He has published articles in the area of vocational development, counseling theory, and counselor education.

EDWARD S. BORDIN, Ph.D., is professor of psychology at the University of Michigan, chief of the Counseling Division, Bureau of Psychological Services, and director of counseling in the Office of Student Affairs. He has held positions at the University of Minnesota and Washington State University. He is a past president of the Division of Counseling Psychology of the American Psychological Association and a past editor of the *Journal of Consulting and Clinical Psychology* (1959–1964). He is the author of *Psychological Counseling* (2d ed. 1968) and of many research and theoretical articles on counseling, psychotherapy, personality, and vocational choice.

ANGELO V. BOY, Ed.D., is professor of education in counselor education at the University of New Hampshire. He has been a visiting professor at Boston University, Suffolk University, and the Universities of Arizona, Hawaii, Toronto, and Colorado. Dr. Boy has been a public school teacher for four years, a school counselor for nine years, and has been affiliated with counselor education since 1958. He has published extensively in journals devoted to counseling and is the coauthor of two books: *Client-Centered Counseling in the Secondary School*, and *The Counselor in the Schools: A Reconceptualization*.

GEORGE J. BREEN, Ed.D., is an assistant dean at Worcester (Mass.) Junior College and director of counseling services at Worcester Hahnemann Hospital School of Nursing. He also has a private counseling practice. Dr. Breen was a member of the study team investigating guidance and pupil personnel services in Massachusetts, and is a fellow of the Institute for Rational Living.

NATHAN T. CHERNOV, M.Ed., is an elementary school counselor in Providence, Rhode Island. He has been involved extensively with the inner city where he worked both as a teacher and counselor. He views himself as an eclectic with a leaning towards Adlerian counseling.

DWAYNE COLLINS, Ed.D., is professor of educational psychology at the University of Hawaii and chief of party of the USAID/Laos/University of Hawaii Contract Team. His experience includes training public school counselors in several universities, as well as counseling in elementary, secondary, and university institutions. He has contributed to several professional journals and is the author of the series of slide lectures, "Considerations in Personal Planning."

DON C. DINKMEYER, Ph.D. is professor of educational and counseling psychology at DePaul University, Chicago, and also serves as a school consultant and private practice psychologist. He has taught in elementary and senior high schools and has written widely in professional journals. He has served as author and coauthor of several texts, including: *Encouraging Children to Learn: The Encouragement Process, Child Development, The Emerging Self, Guidance and Counseling in the Elementary School,* and *Developmental Counseling and Guidance* (with Edson Caldwell).

RUDOLF DREIKURS, M.D., is professor emeritus of the Chicago Medical School and director of the Alfred Adler Institute of Chicago. Dr. Dreikurs is the author of more than two hundred articles and chapters in books as well as a contributor to *Critical Incidents in Psychotherapy* and *Critical Incidents in Teaching.* His major books are: *Fundamentals of Adlerian Psychology, Children: The Challenge* (with Vickie Soltz), *Psychology in the Classroom,* and *Logical Consequences* (with Loren Gray).

JAMES DONOVAN, M.A., is a counselor in Setauket, New York. His specialty is group counseling.

MARSANNE C. EYRE, M.Ed., program director, Susannah Wesley Center, Honolulu, is a former assistant director of the Beaupré School and has several years of teaching experience in the public school systems of New York and Hawaii. She has served as project writer-teacher in special education for the expansion of reading comprehension and verbal communication for the economically deprived.

DANIEL W. FULLMER, Ph.D., is professor of educational psychology at the University of Hawaii. Dr. Fullmer was an elementary school and junior high school teacher, and secondary school counselor in Illinois and Colorado. In 1962–63, Dr. Fullmer was a specialist in counseling and guidance in the U. S. Office of Education. In 1963, the American Personnel and Guidance Association's Nancy C. Wimmer Award was conferred on Dr. Fullmer for outstanding contributions to guidance. He has served as coauthor of the following books: *Counseling: Content and Process, Principles of Guidance,* and *Family Consultation.*

ALLEN E. IVEY, Ed.D. and diplomate in counseling psychology, is professor of education and psychology at the University of Massachusetts. He has served as director of university counseling centers at Bucknell and Colorado State Universities and as visiting lecturer at numerous universities. He has published extensively in student personnel and counseling journals and is author or coauthor of several monographs including *Micro-counseling and Attending Behavior* and *Administering College Counseling Centers.*

ORVAL G. JOHNSON, Ph.D., is an associate professor at Southern Illinois University. He is a visiting professor at the University of Colorado, and has taught at the University of Michigan, Michigan State University, University of Vermont, and Idaho State College. He was school psychologist at Jackson, Michigan; director of Special Education and Psychological Services in Lewis County, Washington; and senior psychologist at the Wisconsin State Reformatory. He is the author of numerous professional articles. He has been a consultant on evaluation and school psychology for many school districts and preschool projects.

C. GRATTON KEMP, Ph.D., is professor of education at the Ohio State University. He is an assistant examiner of the New York City Board of Examiners. He is a Fellow of the American Association for the Advancement of Science, a member of the Ohio Central Ministerial Association, and the author of over thirty articles and chapters in several books. He wrote *Perspectives of the Group Process, Intangibles in Counseling,* and the *Foundations of Group Counseling.*

BARBARA A. KIRK, M.A., is director of the Counseling Center at the University of California, Berkeley. She is a vocational consultant to the Bureau of Hearings and Appeals (HEW), as well as a consultant in counseling psychology to the Vocational Rehabilitation Board. She is a past president of the American College Personnel Association, and she has contributed over sixty articles to professional journals, as well as coauthoring *Occupational Information in Counseling: Use and Classification.*

WALTER G. KLOPFER, Ph.D., is professor of psychology at Portland State University, executive editor of the *Journal of Projective Techniques and Personality Assessment,* and psychological consultant for the Parkrose School District in Portland, Oregon. He is coauthor of: *Advances in Personality Assessment, Advances in Projective Techniques, Handbook of Clinical Psychology,* and author of *The Psychological Report, Use and Communication of Psychological Reports,* and *Use and Communication of Psychological Findings.*

HAROLD K. KOZUMA, Ed.D., is an assistant professor in the Department of Educational Psychology at the University of Hawaii. He has been an instructor at the California State College at Long Beach and at Pepperdine College in Los Angeles. Prior to his present position he was with the guidance section of the Hawaii State Department of Education. His experience in education also includes teaching elementary school and extensive consultation work in the area of the multiple handicapped, classroom management, family counseling, compensatory education, and classroom group dynamics.

PHYLLIS M. MARTIN, M.Ed., CAGS (Certificate of Advanced Graduate Specialization), is an elementary guidance counselor and school psychologist in the Portsmouth, Rhode Island schools.

JOHN D. MULLEN, M.Ed., is a high school counselor in Honolulu, Hawaii. He was a former elementary principal, high school teacher, and pastor.

HOWARD J. PARAD, D.S.W., is professor and dean of the Smith College School for Social Work. He edited *Ego Psychology and Dynamic Casework, Crisis Intervention,* and with Roger Miller *Ego-Oriented Casework: Problems and Perspectives.*

C. H. PATTERSON, Ph.D., is professor of educational psychology at the University of Illinois. He is a Fellow in the Division of Counseling Psychology and the Division of Psychological Aspects of Disability of the American Psychological Association and a past president of the American Rehabilitation Counseling Association. In addition to numerous articles in the professional journals and chapters in books, he is the author of: *Counseling the Emotionally Disturbed,*

Counseling and Psychotherapy: Theory and Practice, Counseling and Guidance in Schools, and *Theories of Counseling and Psychotherapy.*

JAMES N. PEPPER, Ed.D., is the area superintendent of the Department of Defense Overseas Dependents Schools. He has had over thirty years experience as teacher, principal, and superintendent of public schools in Michigan. He was associate professor of education in the School of Education at Miami University in Ohio. He has been a frequent contributor to professional journals.

HERMAN J. PETERS, Ph.D., has worked as a teacher, counselor, and school administrator. He is now professor of education at Ohio State University. He is a past president of the Association of Counselor Education and Supervision. Some of his major books are: *Guidance: Program Development and Management* (with B. Shertzer), *Guidance: Techniques for Individual Appraisal and Development* (with B. Shertzer), *Pupil Personnel Services: Selected Readings* (with G. A. Saltzman), *School Counseling: Perspectives and Procedures* (with M. J. Bathory).

GERALD J. PINE, Ed.D., is associate professor of education at the University of New Hampshire and staff associate at the New England Center for Continuing Education. Since 1967 he has been the director of the Experienced Teacher Fellowship Program for the preparation of elementary school counselor-reading specialist teams. His experience includes ten years of public school teaching and counseling. He has been a summer school visiting professor at the Ontario Institute for Studies in Education, University of Toronto. Dr. Pine has coauthored two books: *Client-Centered Counseling in the Secondary School* and *The Counselor in the Schools: A Reconceptualization,* and has written over thirty articles dealing with counseling and delinquency.

E(WING) LAKIN PHILLIPS, Ph.D., is director of the George Washington University Psychological Clinic and Professor of Psychology. He is also director of the School for Contemporary Education (for disturbed and handicapped children) in McLean, Virginia. He is the author of *Psychotherapy: A Modern Theory and Practice; Educating Emotionally Disturbed Children; Discipline, Achievement and Mental Health;* and *Short-term Psychotherapy and Structured Behavior Change.*

T. ANTOINETTE RYAN, Ph.D., is a researcher/professor at the Education Research and Development Center, University of Hawaii. She has been active in professional organizations concerned with counseling, has conducted many research investigations dealing with counseling, counselor education and supervision, and has been awarded an American Personnel and Guidance Association citation for outstanding research in counseling. Dr. Ryan is a contributor to professional journals, and coauthor of the book *Guidance for Emerging Adolescents.*

MITCHELL SALIM, Ed.D., is coordinator of Pupil Personnel Services at West Irondequoit Central School District (New York). Previously he was engaged as a counselor educator at the University of Rochester and at Pennsylvania State University. Dr. Salim has written a number of articles and has conducted studies in various areas of pupil services. Current interests include use of support personnel, and computerized information systems in pupil services.

PAUL W. SCHMIDCHEN, M.Ed., is superintendent of schools, Cape May, New Jersey. He is an editor of *The Clearing House* and of *Hobbies Magazine.* He is a former teacher, coach and high school principal. His publications include journal articles as well as a contribution as a consultant to *Critical Incidents in Teaching.*

BRUCE SHERTZER, Ed.D., is professor of education ,and chairman of the counseling and personnel services department at Purdue University. He has held positions as school counselor, director of guidance and state director of guidance, visiting professor of educational psychology at the University of Hawaii, Fulbright Senior Lecturer at the University of Reading, England, and is past president of the Association for Counselor Education and Supervision.

MANFORD A. SONSTEGARD, Ph.D., is professor of guidance and counseling at the College of Human Resources and Education, West Virginia University. He has taught elementary and secondary school and was an elementary and secondary school principal for several years. For two years he was educational advisor to the Ethiopian Administrator of Education and director of the Harra Teacher Training School in Ethiopia. He has served as a child guidance consultant in Jamaica, West Indies, is a consultant to Family Education Centers and has been a visiting professor at several universities.

STEVEN H. STEIN, Ph.D., is a staff and supervisory psychologist at the Brooklyn Veterans Administration Hospital. He is also in private practice in individual and group psychotherapy in New York City, and has conducted workshops for guidance counselors on group process techniques. He has written articles in professional journals concerning emotional arousal, psychological defensive operations, and innovative techniques in psychotherapy.

CHARLES B. TRUAX, Ph.D., is professor of Educational Psychology at the University of Calgary, Alberta, Canada. He has been codirector of the Postdoctoral Training Program at the University of Wisconsin and has held positions at the University of Iowa, the University of Kentucky, the University of Arkansas, and the University of Florida. Dr. Truax was formerly consultant at Mendota State Hospital and research consultant for the Kentucky Department of Child Welfare. His major interests are psychotherapy, counseling, and human behavior change. Among his publications as coauthor are *Toward Effective Counseling and Psychotherapy, The Therapeutic Relationship with Schizophrenics,* and *Handbook of Psychotherapy and Behavior Change.*

E. G. WILLIAMSON, Ph.D., is professor emeritus and formerly director of the University Testing Bureau, coordinator of Student Personnel Services, and dean of students at the University of Minnesota. Dr. Williamson is the author of more than four hundred papers and articles. His major books are: *How to Counsel Students, Counseling Adolescents,* and *Vocational Counseling: Some Historical, Philosophical and Theoretical Perspectives.* He is past president of the American Personnel and Guidance Association.

Introduction

Although many texts in educational counseling and guidance discuss problems of professional role and function, these books often fail to generate in the student counselor a feeling of confidence and increased knowledge. A sense of precisely what the school counselor does, how he fits into his role, and how he uses theory in specific incidents, is typically lacking. Such books often seem *impractical*. Something seems to be missing. They don't quite relate to how life really is.

At least this is what we have heard a generation of neophyte counselors complain about. This complaint is probably justified. Writers of textbooks are usually theoreticians who see the big picture rather than practitioners interested in specific events and cases. The college professor, whether lecturing or writing, tends to deal with generalizations rather than specifics. In this manner, he hopes his students will apply general theory to specific problems.

Professional learning has a *supra-deductive* aspect (learning first the theory and interpreting experience in terms of the theory) and an *infra-inductive* aspect (learning by experience and developing ideas based on the experience). In general, school counselors learn the first way in universities and the second way on the job. What a shock it is for a person to find that what he has learned in a university seems to have no relation to reality. One postgraduate student stated that he was sent out armed with the knowledge of how to administer an individual intelligence test and some information about a variety of personality theories, but that these seemed to have little relation to the real problems he encountered.

The problem in school counseling is that pedagogically it is in the Dark Ages to some extent. We teach it the way law and medicine were taught in the Middle Ages, deductively, talking about principles, using case histories which have little import for practice rather than the way law and medicine are taught now from observations of real problems and from clinical experience.

The counseling practicum course does represent progress by relating classroom learning to reality in a viable and meaningful way. Its exclusive preoccupation with problems involving the one-to-one counseling relationship restricts its usefulness, however, as a learning vehicle for the gamut of situations the counselor encounters in his daily work.

It was this feeling of a lack of meeting real needs of school counselors, relating theory to reality, principles to experiences, that led to the concept of the "critical incident" as a teaching device. Critical incidents were solicited from school counselors.

Critical Incidents in School Counseling is a case book. The incidents we finally selected from those submitted were those that (a) presented relevant problems, (b) did not duplicate each other, and (c) covered a variety of *common* problems faced by school counselors. Incidents involving problems in ethics, theory, and proper role behavior were submitted to people we considered competent to comment on them—college professors, school administrators, school counselors, supervisors of counselors and assorted professionals—for their ideas on the issues and their reactions to the counselor's methods of handling them.

Each consultant commented independently. In this way the reader has access to a variety of authoritative opinions and perspectives. When the same incident is examined from a variety of viewpoints, the reader is made aware of the richness and complexity of problems, and more importantly, how theories can be applied *in practice*. We note how an apparently simple case, when analyzed in some depth, yields a complex array of techniques, philosophies, possibilities, and solutions.

And now a comment about the general philosophy of *Critical Incidents in School Counseling*. The school counselor's life is a difficult one. He often is forced to tolerate all kinds of stupid minor irritations: tending to cumulative records, scheduling, programming, filing, and answering the same questions over and over again. But counselors must also cope with difficult problems or people. Even when it is the firm intention of the counselor to handle them at a safe distance, it is not unusual for situations to erupt suddenly into powerful dramatic events with profound consequences for the student, the teacher, and the parent. Such crisis situations call for action, initiative, judgment, and fast and sure handling. The worth of a counselor is measured by how he views and how he handles a new problem.

Critical Incidents in School Counseling is composed of a sampling of significant problems which have confronted counselors. Both aspiring and experienced counselors should find these incidents useful and meaningful. We trust they will raise questions of how the problem occurred and what to do about it. The reader is alerted to the particular problem in the incident and placed in a situation of trying to plan solutions. He is then presented with a series of independent solutions and comments by a number of consultants whose experiences and backgrounds vary considerably.

In reading this book we trust that you will read actively rather than passively. The following guidelines should prove helpful:

1. While reading each incident ask yourself how *you* would have viewed and handled the situation.

2. Then "tell" the writer of that incident how *he* should have handled it. "Explain" to him as carefully as you can how he should have viewed and dealt with the problem. "Compliment" him on what he did right and "criticize" him for what he did wrong.

3. Having yourself served as a "consultant" to that contributor, now turn to the first of the consultants, and "listen" to what he says, and be ready to agree or to disagree with him, but have the courtesy to listen carefully to his ideas and suggestions. Then, enter into a "debate" with that consultant, explaining, if you will, once again how he should have conceptualized the situation.

4. Now go on and read the comments made by the other consultants and, in each case, be ready to argue with them.

As a result of this "schizophrenic" type of behavior, you will have managed, especially if you "listened" carefully to the "authorities," to have made this reading a live and dynamic experience. This experience should eventuate in progressively richer insights for you and more accurate estimates of the explanations posed by the various consultants.

From our privileged position as editors, having the prerogative to see and hear all, we have some comments to make about the overall problem of the role of school counselors.

1. The school counselor is often involved in difficult and conflicting situations. There are five influences which contribute to his dilemma:

a. his need to please individuals in positions of power and influence for reasons of self-interest

b.   the expectations and demands of faculty and colleagues
c.   the counselor's theoretical-philosophical orientation
d.   the wants and the needs of the student
e.   the demands of parents and others outside the school system.

The good judgment of the counselor must be relied upon in the event there are conflicting and contradictory demands among these vectors. Ultimately, the counselor must always consider whether his behavior will measure up to the standards of his professional peer group, and his own sense of ethics and integrity.

Counselors' solutions must always be viewed in light of these five vectors of influence and demands. Any judgment of their worth will be a function of our own vectors, including our sense of professional and personal morality.

2.   We have little respect for those counselors who assume that children must always adjust to the school. This mentality, appropriate to a less enlightened age, is the root cause for a great deal of the problems of the schools. Some school situations are deplorable and to demand that children adjust to them willy-nilly, without reason or explanation "because that is the way things are," does little to enhance the credit or image of school counselors. The counselor should not be an apologist for the school or the system or the school hierarchy. He must value his independence and he must always do what he thinks is right. In this way he can best serve his clients, whoever they may be: child, teacher, parent, or principal.

3.   In our judgment, the understanding and insights of the counselor should be made available to all members of the educational institution, staff and pupils alike. Perhaps when we have arrived as a profession and are strong and skilled enough to have earned the respect of our colleagues, our expertise will be more actively sought and valued. Hopefully, consideration of the incidents which follow will serve to inch us along the road to increased confidence and competence.

part **I**

The Counselor

and the Counselee

Naturally, the most important part of a school counselor's work has to do with his relations with his clients, students who come to him for counseling. Some come reluctantly, some are forced to come, and a few come voluntarily, often out of desperation, knowing nowhere else to turn. Most often the problem the counselor faces is simple, but once in a while, what happens is unexpected.

What can a counselor do if a student comes in voluntarily and then is unable to talk? In the "Silent Partner," a counselor, newly trained in Rogerian client-centered counseling, faces this problem with an unusual solution.

It is very difficult for a person to act as both an individual and as a role model, but when serving as a role model his slightest comment may have the most unusual and peculiar effect. In "The Counselor Shoots from the Hip," a harried school counselor has a short interview with a worried mother. The counselor, without much thinking about the problem, makes a half-humorous suggestion that is taken at face value by the mother with a somewhat surprising result. This incident should help counselors realize the way comments can be interpreted and misinterpreted by parents.

5

In "Helping the Disadvantaged," a most dramatic situation occurs illustrating the possible value of schools in dealing with real-life problems, and how schools can become instruments of social change. It also illustrates how often the influence of other children can be more important in changing children than the efforts of adults. This incident is an example of the school dealing with quasi-therapy issues that cannot be put in the curriculum and of dealing with the child as an entity. The title is somewhat ironic in that the "disadvantaged" may really be the school itself rather than Violet, the heroine of the incident.

"Stop! I'll Help You" is perhaps not as controversial today as it was yesterday, but the major issue to which our consultants address themselves has to do with working outside the system and dealing with real problems emotionally rather than intellectually. We doubt that anyone can really fault the counselor, although calm reflection would show that he did not operate according to the rules.

In "Drugs in the School," we see the dangers of a counselor not being true to herself and, consequently, making a mess of a counseling situation. However, the alert reader should notice how she got sucked into an untenable position with the very best intentions.

In "Cry Rape," we have an example of a careless and irresponsible counselor who was lucky to get out of difficulty as easily as he did. This is another illustration of the importance of professional attitudes when operating with students.

And yet in the next incident, "The Counselor Blows Up," we see the importance of being true to oneself even if one's actions are "unprofessional," in the limited sense of the word. The counselor abandoned an artificial attitude of reserve and, as a result, was able to relate to a troubled child.

In "Mother————!" we see how a counselor successfully treated a very difficult problem in a unique manner. However, our consultants go beyond the outcome of the specific incident to debate the issues of goals and means, a problem of continuing significance.

In this section, we also run into the general problem of the relationship of the counselor to the counselee.

Our main hope is that by presenting these incidents and the comments by our consultants, we can help the school counseling profession develop realistic standards of behavior which will make counselors more effective in meeting real-life problems and still enable them to function in a system that tends to restrict the freedom of those within it.

1

The Silent Partner

Background

Last year I was appointed a counselor in a high school. This is a very good school with an excellent principal and staff, located in a high income community. My own training was directed by a professor who was highly nondirective, and being the kind of person who believes in following rules strictly, I also became nondirective in any situation in which I didn't know quite what to do, or in any situation in which the individual was exploring his individuality.

One day a girl came to see me and told me she had "problems." I had no time to see her just then, but asked her to make an appointment at a suitable time so that I could give her a full half-hour of my undivided attention. We set a time for the next day at our mutual convenience. I wondered what was troubling her for she showed evidence of being greatly agitated.

Incident

In a manner of speaking the incident was nothing, for the girl said nothing when she came in. I mean this literally. She knocked on the door, and I went to open it, and greeted her pleasantly. At my invitation she sat down, and we looked at each other. I waited for her to say something, to explain, complain, or ask questions. I looked at her trying to be as pleasant and as accepting as I could. Her eyes filled with tears and the tears rolled down her face, but she said nothing. I wondered what I should do. The simplest and most natural thing might have been to say, "What is bothering you?" But it must be remembered that I had been trained precisely not to ask questions or to give advice, and so, feeling quite foolish, I just kept looking at the girl. For half an hour, nothing happened. I then said to her, "It is time to end our session. Would you like to see me again?" Somewhat to my surprise and relief, she nodded, and when I suggested another appointment at the same time next week, she nodded again, and went out without having said a single word.

The following session was a repeat of the first one. We looked at each other, she cried silently, I waited, and then she once again accepted my invitation for another session without a word being said. Not to weary the reader, we had two more sessions and they were all exact duplicates of the first two, though several times I thought that the student was about to talk. At the end of the fourth session, when I again asked if she wanted to have another session, she shook her head, and walked out.

Discussion

I was really puzzled about this and wrote to my professor. He was kind enough to respond, telling me that I had misunderstood the theory and philosophy of nondirective counseling and that I could have either shown some expression of sympathy or given the girl some indication about my own feelings. I didn't know what to do after I got this letter and considered calling in the girl and making a full confession that I had been following the book and that I really was interested in her. I wondered whether she thought there was something wrong with me. However, things were very different from what I suspected because during the last week of the semester I got another request from Jill, and I saw her immediately. Her statement was a critical incident for me.

"I want to thank you very much for what you did for me, Mrs. —"

"But I did nothing!" I impulsively cried out. "I wanted to so much help you, but I just did nothing but look at you."

"You did a great deal. You changed my whole personality. That you had the kindness and love to wait for me to talk, to just be there, and not to ask me questions, or try to make me talk, that you were willing to just be there, and not be critical, and not complain that I was wasting your time was the best and most wonderful thing. While we were looking at each other I was thinking how wonderful the silence was, how good it was for you to understand me, and make me feel good and important. I felt you were loving and comforting. I just couldn't talk, and if I had it would have been banalities. Because you valued me so much, that you just were willing to be with me, I realized that my crazy thoughts that no one loved me or cared for me, were all wrong. You loved me and you cared for me and you were patient and kind and understanding and warm, and you didn't put any pressure on me or try to get me to talk or to manipulate me. I felt so comfortable with you, and the relationship was so real. No, you did a great deal for me, and as a result I decided I was worthwhile and I was a good person and I was one to be respected, and I was able to solve my problems which I had sorely exaggerated."

After this long statement, we talked a bit and indeed she seemed to have really changed from the girl she told me she had been prior to the counseling to the girl she was now. She insisted that the four sessions with me had represented a turning point in her life.

I just wonder what the principal or the girl's parents or any member of the school board would have thought of my behavior during the sessions. I can imagine them thinking that there was something wrong with the counselor. However, during the half-hour, or those four half-hours, I really worked hard, even though it may have appeared that I did nothing. I was very restless, and wanted to read or to do something. I did think of saying to her: "If you have nothing to say to me, why don't you return when you do?" Or, "Just sit there and when you feel you can talk let me know" and I would have done some reading or writing. However, my training told me to be alert to her, watch her, and give her silent support by giving her my full attention.

I must confess that by the end of the second session I wondered if I had not made a serious mistake in my procedure and wondered how long this would go on, and what I would say if someone found out about our strange interaction and were to ask me for its rationale. However, I am very happy that I acted in a consistent manner and I can now see how Jill could have felt loved and valued by my behavior or nonbehavior. Words aren't everything.

Questions

1. What do *you* think of my behavior? Suppose that I had come to you at the end of the first session and said to you that a student came to see me and that I waited for her to say something and she said nothing for the whole half-hour? Suppose I asked what I should do if she repeated this behavior another time?

2. Why do you think Jill really felt appreciative of me and believed she improved?

3. Do you believe it is wise to follow some theory even if one doesn't understand it? I did what I did because I felt that my professor would have wanted me to. At times I felt annoyed and foolish, and yet, once having started acting in one way I felt that I had to continue in the same manner. It all worked out well, however, and I wonder if it is because of my allegiance to client-centered theory that I was successful.

4. Suppose I had changed my approach in midstream, as it were, and suppose I had intervened and asked her questions? Do you think that progress might have been made anyway? That is, if a student improves, does this mean that what one did was the right thing to do?

COMMENTS ON THE INCIDENT

THE EDITORS

Is counseling just common sense? Is the ideal counselor a warm and friendly person with considerable knowledge about school systems and understanding of the world of work? Or is the counselor a junior psychiatrist, dealing with complex human problems? If the former is true, then common sense and knowledge may be enough. But if the counselor is to act as a psychotherapist, what may be needed is a theory of personality and an institutionalized mode of operation which differs from common sense. For the counselor *qua* therapist often works in unfamiliar territory, and cannot depend solely on his own experiences and thinking. He must operate according to certain rules dictated by theory.

However rigid adherence to a theory may precipitate problems. The client may be puzzled and threatened by the counselor's atypical responses and not know what to do or say. The counselor, in turn, may find himself dealing with material and problems that are beyond the scope of his skills and understanding and having no one to turn to for guidance or for direction. This is one of the hazards of using a system of therapy without adequate training and knowledge.

In this fascinating incident a counselor relentlessly employed, perhaps unwisely, an unfamiliar procedure. Once started, she grimly decided to stay with it. The process of counseling was distinctly unusual, and so too, perhaps, was the outcome.

Our consultants seem to indicate that theory and procedure are secondary to good intention and humane consideration. But what does the reader think?

MARY A. BARBER

My first reaction to this incident was amazement that the counselor was able to maintain such a nondirective stance during not just one but four complete sessions with the counselee. It sounded like one of the caricatured incidents that have been described to most of us during counselor training as examples of misuse or misunderstanding of a theory. One has to admire the extent of the counselor's self-discipline and depth of commitment to her interpretation of a technique, however misunderstood it might be. In spite of this counselor's behavior and misunderstanding of her training, perhaps her sincere wish to help was somehow communicated nonverbally to the student.

I rather doubt that such an extreme nondirective approach would have the desired effect with many young people and suspect that this counselor modified her approach in dealing with other students as a result of this experience. Since there are so many forces of influence in any young person's environment and since school counselors' contacts are necessarily limited in time and number, I think they often overestimate their impact on their counselees. Perhaps the technique itself is not so important as the sincerity and consistency of the counselor and his degree of comfort in using the technique. This young girl may have been subconsciously groping to find some person, some adult, who acted consistently, however strangely, and in finding one she was able to use her discovery as a basis for renewing or rebuilding her own integrity.

If I had been asked for advice after the first session, I probably would have suggested that the counselor's interpretation of the nondirective approach was quite extreme but that if she were sincerely committed to this nondirective attitude and felt comfortable using it, she should continue to do so. She should, however, examine her own feelings carefully and be sure that her commitment was made on the basis of understanding acceptance rather than the blind pursuit of a doctrine espoused by her professor. Following a course of action simply because it has been didactically imposed on you, however much admired and respected its source, is not the mark of professional maturity. Neither should the beginning counselor expect to be absolutely and completely competent. Is anyone? As in any profession, especially those involved with people and personalities, the first years necessarily include a certain amount of experimentation and some degree of failure. I do not believe that a dedicated counselor ever stops questioning his own competence or trying new ways to improve himself. I expect the counselor in this case to become more eclectic with added experience since her very questioning of the handling of this case suggests openness to other approaches. My advice to her would be to do your own thing as soon as you find out what it is!

However, I think after several sessions with no apparent movement, the counselor could very easily have modified her approach without destroying the relationship. If the counselor really had a sincere desire to help this girl I don't see how she could have let her terminate the relationship after four sessions of just crying. Obviously the girl was seriously disturbed and if the counselor had been more concerned about her and less concerned about technique, the client might have been less enigmatic and more responsive. The counselor should have shifted gradually into a more verbal approach. It is recognized that a great deal of communication is possible through posture, gestures and facial expressions, but verbal communication must accompany or follow such interaction in order to get accurate feedback and clarify whatever messages are being sent. In this case, which seemed rather to solve itself, the counselor might have facilitated the resolution of the girl's problems sooner if she had not left her in an emotional limbo for several months.

EDWARD S. BORDIN

The description of the incident represents a fragment of what is needed to decide what changes have occurred and to what they can be attributed. The counselor assures us that the girl had indeed changed but no evidence of this is offered. The statement of the student refers to a lack of self-acceptance but there is little on which to differentiate an existentially normative crisis of transitory character from the more enduring malignant external circumstances or personality malformations. We must always allow for the possibility, unpalatable though it may be, that the counselor's interventions were irrelevant to the change. Both counselor and client have a need to account for the change in terms of their joint effort. The counselor wants to feel that she has been useful and that her ideas about how to help have been vindicated. The client gains greater security in her change by being able to assign rational meaning to it.

"Intervention" must appear to be a strange term when applied to saying nothing. But that is not the same as *doing* nothing. Keeping silent for a half-hour, as the counselor noted, requires a great deal of effort. I am convinced that she did more, just as I believe the girl did more. Both were expressing in nonverbal terms—facial expressions, tears, body positions, and intentness of gaze—what they were experiencing in the situation and, no doubt, this was being communicated. Counselors can become overdependent on verbal communication. Counseling is more than a conversation; it is a relationship, an interaction between two persons.

I must share the professor's dismay. A teacher in any field seeks more than a mere reproduction of a specific set of words or actions. In counseling and psychotherapy, the use of theory as a stimulus to understanding cannot hope to take the place of the counselor's capacity to respond as an integrated person, sensitive to the needs of others, flexibly able to give of himself as the occasion demands. Perhaps, in the nonverbal behavior already mentioned, the counselor transcended her rote version of nondirective counseling. There are suggestions that part of what she acquired was an attitude which surely will be useful to many clients.

If in fact the crucial factor in the situation was the counselor's willingness to allow the client to use the time in whatever way she saw fit, even if it meant being silent, there is no reason to suppose that some parts of the message could not have been effectively conveyed in words. Both the verbal messages the counselor considered and rejected were inconsistent with such a willingness. The first told the client not to come unless she was willing to talk and the other said that she could not have the counselor's attention unless she talked. But I am inclined to believe that a message such as: "You seem to be feeling very deeply. Sometimes it is useful to try to express it in words. At others it is more important to express it without words," would not have interfered and would be helpful for those clients who need encouragement toward more verbal communication of their feelings.

If a counselor is to act by any rule, I would prefer the rule that understanding determines one's action. If the search for understanding requires that we ask a question, then the question must be asked. I believe modern proponents of client-centered counseling would accept this statement. The client-centered counselor would, of course, hasten to add that the central part of the understanding he seeks is an empathic view of the other person. This further specification I can accept as long as it is taken to include understanding of a depth that goes beyond the client's immediate awareness. The counselor must be able to distinguish a silence which must be participated in at a distance, from one reflecting fear approaching panic, for which the client needs to feel the counselor's willingness to help more actively when the need arises.

This incident demonstrates clearly that in some counseling situations the content of the communication is irrelevant, while the feeling is crucial. It is my impression that most situations involving human interaction are like this. Here was a girl who obviously needed to know that someone cared for her and understood her. Because the counselor was nondirective, the girl was able to project onto her whatever image suited the girl's strong emotional needs at the time. The counselor was therefore perceived as kind, loving, and understanding, and the situation came off well.

For most children, having the undivided attention of an adult outside the family for half an hour is a unique experience. Frequently, the client does not know what to do with the opportunity, so he just sits until the adult initiates a dialogue. If the adult does not speak, clients will interpret the silence in different ways. Some will see the counselor as playing it cagey, not committing himself any more than necessary. Others perceive the silence as a challenge, a contest to see who can outlast the other in maintaining the silence. Some will perceive it, as this client did, as an act of love and concern, a manifestation of the counselor's positive regard for the client.

Clearly, the procedure followed by the counselor was comfortable to this girl, since she chose to return for further sessions. Some clients would feel most uncomfortable in a similar situation, and would not choose to continue the counseling relationship. There are some actions that the counselor could take which would remove the marked discomfort that many clients feel during extended silence and still remain within the framework of nondirective therapy. In this case, for example, the counselor, being a woman, could go over to the girl, sit beside her, hold her hand, give her a handkerchief, put her arm around her, and in numerous other ways show her compassion and understanding. There are much more "natural" responses in our culture than sitting behind a desk and looking or attempting to look understanding and compassionate. Another course of action, consistent with the client-centered approach and more comfortable to most clients, would be to reflect the feelings that are being so clearly manifested. The client in this case did not have to tell the counselor in words that she was unhappy or upset, that she felt she had a problem. If the counselor had said, "You are feeling terribly unhappy now," would she have appeared any less understanding? Might this not have encouraged the client to discuss and ventilate her feelings in words so that she would understand herself better?

My point here is that client-centered counseling can be approached in various ways, some of them more and some less comfortable to the client, without violating the theoretical principles on which this form of therapy is based. If an approach to therapy involves procedures that make the client uncomfortable over an extended period of time, and consequently less likely to remain in therapy, the technique is to that extent less effective.

A theoretical position, in counseling as well as in other pursuits, has value because it provides some guidelines. These guidelines are of particular importance in counseling, where each case is different so that a "cookbook" approach is not feasible. Every counselor has a theory of counseling, although he may not be able to articulate it, and often does not understand his own theoretical position.

BARBARA A. KIRK

The counselor had great good fortune in the case of the "Silent Partner." Whereas it is often wise and useful to do nothing when one doesn't know what to do, it would seem that it was a high-risk undertaking to remain as silent as the counselor did in this case. Silence can be quite threatening and even punitive and, therefore, it was most fortunate that the projections of the counselor were positive and helpful to the student.

This may not be so in other cases. The counselor might help the student to talk, that is, help her genuinely have the option of whether she wished to talk or not. Perhaps the counselor could ask if the student wanted help in being able to talk while making it quite clear that she didn't need to talk if she didn't wish to. The counselor could perhaps have asked the student if she wanted the counselor to do anything, and if so, what. A clarification and structuring of the context in which the two are working can also be very comforting to the counselor, by giving her more confidence that she is behaving in a helpful way. In other words, she communicates and thus clarifies what she's doing in relation to what is being asked of her. This takes a good deal of the guesswork out of the encounter. The counselor is thus enabled to better understand what she is doing in relation to what is wanted.

The professor who told the counselor she did not fully understand the theory of nondirective counseling was addressing himself to the issue of following rules strictly. Counseling cannot be done by rigid adherence to rules. Perhaps it would have been helpful to this counselor if she had been well-supervised in translating theory into practice during her original training. Any general approach to counseling requires considerable skill in its adaptation to individual cases. There can be no substitute for really well-supervised practice in the activity.

One more point deserves comment. There is nothing sacred about the period of time assigned for a counseling interview. The counselor could have altered or adjusted the half-hour appointment according to her needs or feelings about the student, with, of course, some helpful interaction and feedback from the student. In this case, however, it was desirable not to alter the regular period because it served a particular need of the student, as she so beautifully expressed it when she was finally able to speak.

C. H. PATTERSON

It is interesting how the term "nondirective" persists when, since 1951, it has been superseded by the term "client-centered." In my experience, those continuing to use the former designation, even though they may be counselor-educators, are in the 1942–1951 era of client-centered counseling. This certainly seems to apply to the counselor-educator involved in this incident. I am continually amazed at the misconceptions about client-centered counseling that persist and which are being taught in counselor education programs. The only system of counseling or psychotherapy that is more misunderstood than client-centered counseling is psychoanalysis. Well-known psychiatrists and psychologists continue to refer to the passivity and inactivity of the client-centered counselor and his technique of "merely" or "simply" listening and reflecting.

While I deny that client-centered counseling is inactive, passive, and unresponsive—a "grunt-and-groan" technique—I would continue by saying that listening empathically is a major—the major—technique of every good counselor and that it is by no means a passive technique. Respecting the desire or need of the client for silence and his simply valuing the presence of the counselor is an important aspect of any approach to counseling.

The counselor in the present instance learned well the first requirement of any counseling approach—to keep one's mouth shut, at least most of the time, particularly in the early stages of a relationship. Some counseling students never seem to learn this. They cannot tolerate a silence, but must fill it up with their own chatter if the client is less verbal than they are.

But not all clients want or need silence or can tolerate long periods of it. It can be perceived as evidence of lack of interest on the part of the counselor. Thus the counselor needs to know how the client is feeling about this and the simplest, most direct, and most honest method is to ask. This counselor, in her misperception of client-centered counseling, felt she could not do this. But once the client indicated that she wished to return, it was no longer necessary to wonder or to ask, since the client was indicating that she wanted more of the same treatment. In effect, the counselor stumbled into an appropriate relationship with this client.

The first session might have been more comfortable for the counselor (though, perhaps, not the client) if the counselor had, through some simple interchange, ascertained that the girl did not wish to talk or to be talked to. In spite of the counselor's discomfort, she did communicate to the girl her interest, concern, and respect. Simply giving her time, as the girl reported, conveyed this.

The pressure for activity, for filling up every interpersonal relationship with talk, is a characteristic of our Western society. We abhor silence in a social situation as nature abhors a vacuum. The concern of the counselor in this incident about what others would think of her behavior is of interest. It led me to recall a situation in my early work as a counselor, where, in a less than completely soundproof office, an administrative superior—anti-client-centered in attitude—"overheard" a long silence in an interview. Apparently feeling that I was not earning my salary, this inactivity was reported to my professional superior in Washington.

The occupation—or preoccupation—of the counselor during long silences has been of some concern. Rogers once said, if I remember correctly, that he would engage in work at his desk, telling the client to speak when he wanted to. I have never been able to do this, but I have done a lot of thinking, sometimes mentally drafting papers I have been working on. One cannot stare fixedly at a client for the full hour—or at least one should not with some clients, who may be uncomfortable in this situation, as one client once told me.

A final comment: It was not because the counselor followed a theory that she was successful. She was successful in spite of her adherence to a (misconception of) theory, because of the person she was—a person who showed herself to the client without need of verbalization.

E. LAKIN PHILLIPS

This is a very interesting case and raises a lot of theoretical and procedural problems in therapy or counseling. I am not a Rogerian, but I try to recognize the fact that all procedures in therapy may have rewarding or gainful consequences.

My impression here is that the counselor's accepting attitude (and therefore, by implication, nontalking attitude) was needed to help the client face up to some issues of moment to her. One can have confrontations with oneself from reading a book, hearing a speech, listening to others talk, or a "silent counselor." What the girl evidently needed at this juncture in her life was simply an opportunity to sit down in a quiet place and come to grips with herself. The counselor's role here may have been most superficial.

We have all faced people who tried to ask too many questions, who did not perceive accurately our problem, or who tried to talk us into a solution that was no solution. Verbal interaction in therapy is not necessarily productive; sometimes knowing when to leave, or when to keep still, is more important. This does not necessarily mean that the Rogerian position is the only workable one in such cases. In dealing with adamant patients among hospitalized psychotics, autistic children in school and clinic settings, or very disturbed "normals," one has to be very careful to let the patient state his position in terms of his behavior. In effect, the counselor's response should reflect an awareness of *all* the cues (both verbal and nonverbal) emitted by his patient.

CHARLES B. TRUAX

It is easy to be theory-bound and to look for answers in a book or to follow a professor's instructions literally. It is much different to be real and to sit and to share—even in silence—another's fears and hurts. In considering this case, it seems to me that what the counselor did—waiting to listen to the girl, being alert to her, watching and giving silent support through full attention—was quite sound. This means the counselor set aside her own need system, for she considered those half-hours as belonging to the client.

In the same situation, I think I might have sat silently as long as I could, and at most have said, "It's just too troubling to put into words . . ." or something of the sort. But in any event, in this case, the girl, I believe, could sense the attentive silence which communicated warmth and understanding.

Starting out in counseling, one feels self-conscious and even annoyed in practicing what one has learned, just as in learning how to drive a car or how to play bridge. One can even feel foolish in following the rules. Yet, once one has mastered the art of driving or playing bridge, it seems second nature to do what is right.

In considering the observed improvement, it seems to me that we should assume that changes can be attributed to counseling. While it is undoubtedly true that everyday events have their impact on clients, we should accept responsibility for the consequences of our counseling, and this means sharing the credit or the blame for changes in each and every client. I think there is no doubt that this counselor significantly affected this girl.

E. G. WILLIAMSON

What a honey of a case this is! And how beautifully the counselor handled it! Even though I consider myself a directivist, I have sat through many interviews of silence, being empathetic and exuding sympathy. I remember one case, if no one minds my reminiscing, of a poor girl who tried for two years to come in and talk to me, and when she finally had the courage, found that she was unable to speak. She disappeared for two years, and then one day a psychiatrist called me and said that she finally was able to come to him and was able to talk, and that she wanted to come back and see me. I never did know all the circumstances, but apparently she had a very traumatic experience with a gang of boys in another city which so affected her that she simply could not talk to me or anyone else about it.

I think the counselor did exactly what needed to be done. There is no question that in these circumstances the individual does feel fully accepted, buoyed up, and dignified just because someone sits and listens in silence. It is a great joy to have such an individual come back, as happened in my case years later, and to learn that the individual recovered, and that one was a factor in the recovery. This incident gives one confidence in the value of silence. But this doesn't mean that silence is the universal panacea. One must know how to use words, but words are not everything. There are all forms of communication without words, by means of gestures, facial expressions, and the like. We counselors must be adept and skillful in knowing the technique appropriate for the situation. Many times we blunder in trying to help.

I think the counselor did precisely what was indicated in this case because here silence was a form of acceptance, and can be with many individuals under certain traumatic circumstances. Let me express my own bias by saying, with a little bit of resentment, that I am as client-centered as anyone else; otherwise, I would have given up counseling years ago. I just happened to have developed a style appropriate to me and to my clients. In general, if the individual is helped in solving his problems then that is the criterion by which we must judge the counselor's method.

2

The Counselor Shoots
from the Hip

CRITICAL INCIDENT

Background

The school secretary called me while I was busy with some paper work to tell me that a Mrs. Morales had come in to ask for the name of a doctor because she was sure her son Ramon was crazy. Would I want to see her? Intrigued by this, and not knowing either the mother or the child, I said I would come down to the office and see the mother, intent on conducting a "standup" interview. When I came to the front office I noticed Mrs. Morales seated, nervously fingering a paper bag on her lap. I looked at the secretary who nodded confirmation to me. I introduced myself to Mrs. Morales, and she looked so worried that I decided to see her in my office.

From her I learned the following: she had become convinced that there was something seriously wrong with Ramon, her ten-year-old son, who was in the fourth grade in our school. Mrs. Morales's brother had assured her that Ramon was probably crazy. Mrs. Morales, a fairly recent Puerto Rican immigrant, was also a recent widow. Of six children that had been born to her, two were living. The younger, Araldo, went to a nursery school, and she had no problem with him. The older boy, Ramon, was impossible to awaken, she told me. She would yell at him, pinch him, put ice cubes in his mouth, but at times he just wouldn't awaken. At other times he would awaken easily. She had told this story to her brother who informed her that Ramon was just faking. A couple of days ago, her brother came to the house, picked up the sleeping boy, and put him down on the sidewalk. Some fifteen minutes later the uncle brought the boy back and declared, "He is really sleeping. He just didn't wake up. Even when people came by and walked over him." At this point the uncle gave his pronouncement that Ramon was "crazy." I also learned from the mother that she went to work as a cleaning woman and that she was worried about leaving Ramon at home since she didn't know what he might do. Some neighbor had suggested that Ramon might have sleeping sickness; other diagnoses had also been advanced.

Incident

I should explain that I am well-versed in Adlerian theory and am convinced that children generally behave in clever ways that enable them to gain their goals. While Mrs. Morales talked, I looked over Ramon's record and noticed that it was completely unremarkable, except for some absences. He had been with us for about a year, and there was nothing in the record to indicate any problem. I was suspicious about the diagnosis of sleeping sickness or of craziness.

I mentioned to Mrs. Morales that I would have been much more convinced about Ramon's condition if the uncle had brought him into the street nude. I also suggested she take her son to a doctor for an examination. After some discussion she left, and I put the matter out of my mind and into my tickler file. Some weeks later, I called her, and learned that Ramon was doing fine, getting up every morning, and coming to school. She thanked me for my help and told me that I had been completely right. Somewhat puzzled, I asked her for more information, and was shocked to learn that she had told her brother that I had told her to have him bring Ramon out in the street naked. He had undressed Ramon and had put him on his shoulder and brought him out into the street. The boy squirmed, escaped from the uncle, and ran back into the house and when the uncle returned, the boy was back in bed and "asleep." The uncle again picked him up and started out into the street with him, but the boy screamed that he was awake and would go to school. The uncle, still keeping him on his shoulder the way he would carry a log, had a talk with him. I can see it in my mind's eye—the uncle carrying a naked squirming boy of ten on his shoulder, meanwhile asking him questions and getting answers. The boy confessed that he always was awake and only "made out" that he was asleep because he was afraid to go to school when he hadn't done his homework. He promised never to pull this trick again. And he didn't.

Mrs. Morales was very thankful that I had given her this idea of how to handle the problem which was now completely solved because of my perceptive understanding of children.

Discussion

I enjoyed this little incident for several reasons. First, I think I was right in my diagnosis of the problem, but didn't really have enough confidence to make a definite suggestion. When I more or less casually replied, "I wonder if your brother had brought him out naked whether Ramon would wake up," I said it as a kind of side remark, and would not have dared present this as a formal suggestion, the kind I would record in my notes. Second, supposing the situation had not worked out as it did, what if Mrs. Morales had charged me with telling her to do this? This points out the importance of saying things one doesn't mean, since relatively unsophisticated people, such as Mrs. Morales, might take such notions literally and act upon them. Third, I suppose there is a discrepancy between my theory and my behavior. Now that I think back on it, I really don't think that given an identical situation, I would really suggest what Mrs. Morales and her brother did, even though it worked. The last issue has to do with the matter of symptoms and underlying causes. Apparently, Ramon had discovered a good method of handling a problem when he didn't do his homework. I wonder if an uncovering or nondirective approach would really have been any better than this direct action on the part of the brother of Mrs. Morales.

Questions

1. How far can a counselor go in making suggestions? In a case like this would a counselor be ethically and professionally wise to have suggested that the child be taken out naked to test the theory that he was faking?

2. Cannot more elaborate methods, involving complete examinations, and exhausting interviews actually be harmful in comparison to the use of direct behavioral suggestions of the sort discussed here?

3. Has this been a good learning experience for Ramon or has he learned simply that he must develop more devious schemes for dealing with his frustrations and fears?

COMMENTS ON THE INCIDENT

THE EDITORS

School counselors often operate in a state of quiet and harried desperation barely managing to meet the demands for their time and services. Sometimes demands are made on them simultaneously in multiple directions, and one really has to be in more than one place at one time to satisfy everyone. Pressure on the job is responsible for many of the problems described in the various incidents and is a constant problem for counselors even when they are well accepted and their functions well understood. Because time is at a premium, the counselor may make a random remark, to which he pays little attention. However, such remarks may well have considerable impact on his listener, especially if the counselor is viewed as an expert or has prestige in the eyes of the client.

In this incident, the counselor heard a problem, apparently realized it was beyond his sphere of competence, made an offhand suggestion, which was taken literally and followed. It turned out that this instant diagnosis and the implied treatment of the problem were probably correct, and the problem disappeared as a result. However, this incident raises a number of questions which our consultants tackle.

How careful should a counselor be in making "offhand" remarks? What are the limits of his sphere of competency? Are symptom-reductions real improvements? Can such improvement actually be harmful to the general well-being of the child? Should superficial, off-the-cuff diagnoses and courses of treatment be suggested if there just isn't time and/or adequate resources available for helping the individual with his problem? These and other issues are raised and discussed by our consultants.

BENJAMIN C. BELDEN

After all, who was the client in this incident? Was it Mrs. Morales, because she is the one who came in to request help, or was it Ramon, because it was his behavior that the two were determined to change? These are not easy questions. Whom to see, who is relevant, who is the "identified patient"—these are questions every counselor must ask in each case. Interacting members of the social system are increasingly being brought together so that the treatment plan can be both relevant and effective. It is now *de rigeur* to see the whole family or the complete marriage. Unlike lawyers or physicians, the counselor's client may not be just the person who pays the bill.

This "therapy at a distance" has a further moral implication. It is not merely a question of how far to go in making suggestions. It is more a question of how far can a counselor go in manipulating the behavior of a third person, especially someone he has not even seen. Furthermore, doesn't the child have a right to an interview to determine what *he* wants? Doesn't the child have a say in whether or not his behavior should be changed? Doesn't he have a right to do mediocre work in school or, as in this case, to be a malingerer? Should the counselor automatically accept the norms and aspirations of the parents for the child? Recent legal decisions upholding the rights and responsibilities of children against the claims of their parents make these questions quite relevant. This counselor, not atypically, concluded that Ramon's behavior was faulty. The counselor could just as well have assumed that it was the mother's behavior that needed changing, not the son's. Mrs. Morales could have presented the same problem and the practitioner could have replied, in effect, "Sorry Ma'am, that isn't what your problem is about. It happens that you have an inordinate need to control. Forget about the kid and let's screw your head on right." There follows two years of client self-examination and introspection. During the interim, poor Ramon could "go to hell in a wheelbarrow" for all the counselor could care!

Thus, as in this case, when a counselor zeros in on symptoms, he is markedly deviating from the psychotherapeutic tradition of the last fifty years. Most counselors try to steer clear of influencing the client unduly. They have preferred to maintain a certain distance and anonymity, adhering to general recommendations, and playing an inactive role in the management of their client's life. They feel that they can stand aloof, summon the client's inherent resources for growth, and influence him indirectly rather than through what they see as "interference."

Such a professional distance is rarely obtained. The counselor is continually influencing the behavior of his client. Seasoned counselors have confidence in their point of view and they are not afraid to take responsibility for their actions. They know that counseling is a form of persuasion. They are not afraid to use a hard sell when they feel a "soft" approach might prove ineffective.

Reputations are made in strange ways, however. Should this counselor continue to conduct "standup" interviews with similar results he should be prepared for a reputation of considerable note with the general public while at the same time being known as a quack of the first order among his fellow professionals.

MARSANNE C. EYRE

I assume that the counselor's offhand remark, "I wonder if your brother had brought him out naked whether Ramon would wake up," was not meant as a suggestion. The fact that he appeared to have been right and the sleeping was a fake would appeal strongly to a counselor with Adlerian orientation as evidence of the validity of his view of human behavior.

What I see in this incident that is worthy of comment is the unspoken but frustrating reality of the impossibility of doing work of a professional quality. May I suggest that in the typical school we need a counselor-pupil ratio of perhaps one to a hundred to do a reasonable job. What with the enormous amount of time expended in some school systems in noncounseling work, a good and sympathetic counselor is soon swamped with demands and just cannot keep up. For this reason, the counselor sometimes relays responsibilities and makes diagnoses and decisions on the run, rather than spending the proper amount of time with his needy clients.

This particular incident surely didn't cure Ramon's problem, and I would hope some further counseling would improve communication. However, the mother saw that she need not worry about narcolepsy; the child saw that his malingering was uncovered and that he had better be honest and responsible for his homework. Hopefully, the counselor has alerted someone in the school that Ramon's homework assignments are excessive and too difficult.

But I see another hazard here. Sometimes we harm a child by over-attention! Just imagine the following: say that Ramon simply wanted to play a lot, didn't want to do homework, and developed this sleeping scheme for getting out of going to school. Ramon is taken to a doctor who finds his heart, lungs, and reflexes fine, his vision and hearing normal, and so forth. Subsequent medical tests are negative. Still, there is concern about the matter and for the sake of the story, let's assume that Ramon's mother is affluent. And so Ramon now gets EEG's, consultations with psychiatrists, and so on. Still no determining factors. In the meantime, Ramon keeps on sleeping. The next step is psychotherapy and Ramon begins play therapy while a qualified professional gives him further attention. Ramon may realize that his trick of faking sleep is really paying off —he has power! Or what is worse, he may actually start to believe he is physically "disabled" and use it as a dependency crutch.

It seems to me that we could benefit from a favorite principle of mine in dealing with common school problems: "Given a variety of possibilities to explain the behavior of children, that which assumes the child is trying to take advantage of a situation, either consciously or unconsciously, is most likely correct."

Now, to quell any anxiety over these heretical remarks, let me say that this principle implies basic respect for the child. Too frequently, counselors and parents consider the child a helpless victim mistreated by the world. I see most children as strong, intelligent, powerful, small-sized adults, packages of vitality, and naturally self-seeking. I see the child as invincible rather than inadequate. To me, and to the counselor, Ramon's way of problem-solving (regarding schoolwork) was devious and inappropriate. In any case, I think this was a valuable experience to all concerned. Had the procedure not worked, of course, then more diagnostic methods should have been tried. It *could* have been epilepsy, narcolepsy, or some other condition.

Consequently, my own reaction is that the counselor's off-hand remark showed an intuitive sense. I wish he had been courageous enough to have made such a suggestion consciously and to have recorded it in his notes. For the test of theoretical validity is in clinical experience! Some children are pretenders, maybe all are at one time or another, and perception is needed to help them *not* to fool others—or themselves.

ALLEN E. IVEY

The counselor's attitude and behavior in this case is the prime issue. A picture of the detached, "professional," and casual counselor emerges from such comments and items as his "intrigue" with the case, the casual (perhaps even flippant) comment suggesting nude therapy; after handling the matter briefly, he put the matter "out of his mind" until a tickler file reminded him to check up, and finally his comment— "I kind of enjoyed this *little* (italics the author's) incident . . ." Some satis- faction and possible smugness is indicated when his first evaluation of the case in the discussion section indicates his pleasure with his "correct" diagnosis. One sees no interest in the child himself as a person.

One cannot question the perceptiveness or potential ability of the counselor, one can only raise questions about this counselor who with deep faith in his own ability pays more attention to himself than to this client. Beyond an expression of attitudes on the counselor's part, some of the more obvious "holes" in the handling of this case include:

1. the failure of the counselor to see the boy and talk with him in an effort to discover how the boy felt and possible motivating factors underlying his "sleeping."
2. examining the boy's record, but not discussing this matter with the boys teacher.
3. letting the casual conversation with the mother close the case.

The counselor is possibly correct when he suggests that more elabo- rate methods with complete examination and interviews could be more harmful than the results apparently gained in this case. It would indeed be easy for an overly conscientious counselor to spend hours with the boy, perhaps further reinforcing the benefits of faked sleeping. However, this counselor has violated a basic principle of an interventionist approach— he has not carefully assembled sufficient data to act nor considered all alternatives. The behavior therapist, sometimes falsely maligned for his coldly mechanistic approach to counseling, spends considerable time get- ting to know the individual, identifying specific behavior in need of modification, and in clarifying what environmental events are reinforcing to the child. An interventionist approach would carefully evaluate the child and the situation before making direct suggestions or manipulating the environment.

How far can a counselor go in making suggestions? He has a respon- sibility to make suggestions and involve himself as far as he has mar- shalled the facts, understands the child and the situation, and communi- cates his suggestions clearly. At the same time, he has a professional responsibility to be humble with his data, to realize that even the clearest clinical diagnosis always contains a large margin of error, and that the environment surrounding a child contains many dimensions impossible to predict or control. While it is often useful to treat specific behavior such as the one described here, the counselor also has a responsibility to consider and treat the environment which produced this behavior. For example, the counselor could help Mrs. Morales understand how she herself has reinforced some of Ramon's behavior. The teacher's homework assignments need evaluation; how much and what type of homework should be used to help this boy learn more effectively? If he is bright enough to find such devious ways to avoid school, can these same talents be channelled into more positive directions? The counselor and teacher could use this situation (perhaps more than a "little" incident) as an entering wedge to a new relationship between the school and the child.

The last question posed by the counselor speaks of the nature of the learning experience provided for Ramon. It is believed that this rude experience is another step in teaching a small child that society is on the lookout for people who do not conform and that schools are not interested in his reasons for failing to conform. Over a period of time, this lack of concern with the individual can lead to depersonalization (note counselor's almost complete objectivity and depersonalization of Ramon), dropping out of school, and militancy against this society.

WALTER G. KLOPFER

This incident seems like a very unimpressive piece of behavioral modification to me. Granted that the boy had changed his behavior and now came to school, nothing has been done about his feelings of inferiority or his inability to feel like a competent student. Rather, he has been further humiliated by exposure of his devious ways of trying to escape blame. The counselor's question of whether more elaborate methods involving complete examinations and exhaustive interviews could be harmful seems to me to be rather absurd. I cannot imagine how understanding someone's feelings and giving him an opportunity to do some conscious problem solving on his own, could possibly be harmful. After all, human beings are not robots to be programmed, unless we want to reinforce robotism in our youth. If the counselor wanted to argue that he has time for nothing but behavioral modification in a crisis situation, he might have some ground to stand on, but his question about the possible harmful effects of a more thorough means of assessing and dealing with the problem, appears unwarranted.

Behavioral modification per se is, of course, a perfectly legitimate device. Even this particular drastic form of intervention could be quite useful if it is part of an overall strategy followed by constructive and rehabilitative methods of strengthening Ramon's ego and his interpersonal effectiveness. Also, Ramon's mother and uncle should be helped to realize that the boy really does have a lot of fears and doubts to be driven to such extremes. Rather, they were left to believe that he is a clever little devil who should never be trusted again. Unfortunately, I think that the counselor might have succeeded in establishing a permanent role for Ramon in the family, as someone who need never be taken seriously.

C. H. PATTERSON

This case is an excellent illustration of chance reinforcement. One does something on the spur of the moment, without thinking, and it happens to "work." It is then often easy to generalize—even on the basis of one "reinforcement"—and to persist in the behavior, or the class of behavior, in dealing with similar situations. It is interesting how resistant to "extinction" such behavior is. Perhaps this is influenced by the ignoring of negative results. Of course, one may question the applicability of the reinforcement model in the case of one-trial learning and its resistance to extinction, but the model has been pushed to cover all kinds of behavior. It would appear that if behavior such as this can occur, the reinforcement model is insufficient.

The Adlerian model has likewise been adopted by some of its enthusiasts as being applicable to all behavior. And, like reinforcement theory, it can be stretched to fit any incident of behavior—or the behavior can be interpreted to fit the model.

The counselor in this case wisely avoids generalizing. However, he accepts the results as validating his diagnosis. Such validation by a single spectacular case can often override many other negative results. The Adlerians, however, do not often admit to negative results. Somehow they seem to be able to rationalize any outcome into their theory, or perhaps they are successful in convincing their clients that their diagnosis is right and then create expectations which occur in the manner of the self-fulfilling prophecy. It is interesting, however, that the counselor would be reluctant to deliberately suggest or recommend such treatment in other situations where faking is considered to be present. Yet such faking, to a greater or less extent, appears to be assumed to underly all problem behavior of children from the Adlerian point of view. The beauty of the position is its simplicity. Indeed, it is so simple that little time or effort is needed to determine what the problem is—it is always the same. Perhaps this is in part why the counselor in this case gave so little time or consideration to the mother and her problem. It is rather surprising that a parent with a serious question such as Mrs. Morales had would be treated so cavalierly.

What if the problem had *not* been one of faking? Then, of course, the counselor would probably have heard nothing more about the case— and a negative result would not have been recorded. What about the question raised about alternative methods? This question, as in other instances, cannot be answered in this particular case since no other method was tried. But certainly it would appear reasonable that faking could be discovered and treated in some other way. And it is possible that another method might be preferable for Ramon's total development than a "shock treatment" which could have some deleterious results.

The question of the harmfulness of "more elaborate methods" must be considered in relation to the action to be taken in a particular case. It is certainly unprofessional and unethical to recommend or take drastic action—such as that taken in this case—without first being sure that the child was faking and was not physically ill. But it is also a tremendous waste of time and money to engage in extensive so-called diagnostic work-ups which result only in voluminous reports with no action and no counseling. In most instances it would be preferable for a professionally trained counselor to begin working with the child, and then to obtain any examinations that appeared to be necessary in order to determine the possible involvement of neurological or physiological factors.

T. ANTOINETTE RYAN

This case points out two important areas of counseling service and raises a question about the place of theory in practical counseling situations. The counseling role can be conceptualized as encompassing a set of expected patterns of behavior, implemented by specially trained professionals, to help individuals deal realistically and successfully with developmental tasks encountered in the process of becoming a fully functioning person. The primary focus of school counseling is the educational process, and the school counselor's main concern is with helping pupils realize their learning potential and achieve the objectives of the school. Counselor's training programs are designed to equip the counselor with knowledge about human behavior, and with skills in the use of counseling theory and techniques. It is presumed that such knowledge and skills are minimum requirements for the counselor to function effectively in meeting his obligations to provide consulting services to parents, teachers, and administrators, and counseling services to pupils in the school. The counselor's responsibilities encompass the individual child *and* the environment in which he is growing and developing. In counseling with the pupil, problem situations can be identified and clarified. Counselor and counselee together can agree upon goals to be reached to alleviate the identified problems, and counseling techniques can be employed to help the child in reaching these goals. In consulting with parents, teachers, and administrators, the extra-counseling environment can be taken into account, so that reinforcement can be provided for the child's progress toward the counseling goals. If home and school factors are not considered, too often the child's progress in counseling is negated by home or classroom situations which are contrary to the achievement of counseling goals.

To the extent that a counselor fails to provide consulting services to parents *or* counseling services to the pupil, he is abdicating his responsibilities. The counselor in this situation seems to have given a "half measure" of consulting to the parent, and no counseling service to the pupil. The case could be made that the counselor was interpreting the child's behavior and thereby attempting to help the mother understand her child. The failure of the counselor is that he did not go beyond this point, in either working directly with the mother to help her in figuring out ways of changing the environment to make for more positive growth of the boy, or in referring her to other agencies or professional persons better equipped for providing the services needed. The counselor did suggest that the mother take Ramon to a doctor, and this could be construed as a referral. However, it would be hoped that a counselor would demonstrate more professionalism in his use of the referral process than was evident in this instance. Referral is an important process, and deserves being handled in a serious, considered manner. The counselor should make sure at the outset that the referral does not mean rejection. The counselor has a responsibility for making a referral without raising the anxiety of the client. The counselor also has some obligation for seeing a client at least through the initial stages of coping with a problem. In this instance the counselor left the mother completely at sea. His remark about taking the boy into the street naked was not intended as advice to the mother, but rather as an aside. His vague suggestion to take the boy to a doctor was at best a poor illustration of referral.

By failing completely to provide counseling to the boy, the counselor committed a serious error of omission. The problem was essentially one of not getting his homework finished, and this, in turn, led to the truancy behavior. This could have been identified and clarified in a counseling session with the boy, specific goals agreed upon by Ramon and the counselor, and a plan for a series of counseling interviews devised. In essence, this counselor appears to have failed both the mother and the boy.

Every counselor operates from assumptions that he holds, either explicitly or implicitly. The more explicit the assumptions and the more logically they are related, the more likely it is that the counselor will achieve success in his counseling role. A counselor needs guidelines for his behavior in providing consulting or counseling services. Theory provides these guides to counseling behavior. The counselor who thinks he functions without theory, in effect, is basing his behavior on vaguely defined, loosely organized, implicit theory. In implementing his responsibilities for counseling or consulting, the counselor is in a decision-making role. Theory provides the basis for the counseling decisions. The counselor purported to subscribe to Adlerian theory. However, his failure to counsel with the child suggests he was implementing non-Adlerian principles as well. Had the counselor been more committed to a theory, he might have achieved a better understanding of the child.

The counselor raises two questions, one concerned with ethical aspects of the counselor's behavior, and the other with counseling techniques. The American Psychological Association Code of Ethical Standards (Principle 1.31.1) states that—

psychologists in all fields should recognize the boundaries of their competence and not offer services which fail to meet professional standards established by recognized specialists in particular fields.

Principle 1.11.3 also notes that—

as a practitioner, the psychologist should strive at all times to maintain highest standards in the services he offers. Because the psychologist in his work may touch intimately the lives of others, he bears a heavy social responsibility, of which he should ever be cognizant.

It appears that for the counselor to advise the parent to take the child naked into the street, to test out the counselor's hunch that the child was faking, would be a blatant violation of these principles of ethical standards. Evidence to support such an approach is lacking, and the possible effects of such action on the child are not considered.

The second issue, concerning the comparative harm of "elaborate methods" and "direct behavioral suggestions" begs the question. The issue at hand should be "what techniques and approaches" appear, on the basis of the most reliable and valid evidence available, to offer the greatest possibility of achieving clearly defined objectives. To look at "methods" without taking into account the counseling goals is to look at only half the issue.

MITCHELL SALIM

The title of this anecdote could be restated as: "Shock Therapy: For Whom?" The potential exists in all sorts of roles for workers to meet their needs in ways which are detrimental to organizational goals. Counselors, like people in general, are not immune from this occupational hazard.

The developing counselor gradually matures in self-understanding. His personal sense of security, based on self-understanding and acceptance, facilitates the sorting out of personal needs during client interaction. Through periodic self-reflection the counselor begins to establish his personal guidance system.

Ramon's counselor was expressing his needs throughout the entire anecdote. The background material indicated the need for a pupil services team conference consisting of the school nurse, social worker, psychologist, and counselor. If these resources were not in existence, then the counselor, with the permission of Ramon's mother should have contacted a community agency. Comprehensive evaluation was warranted.

The questions which the counselor presents are of concern to the writer. They appear as rationalizations rather than genuine attempts by the counselor to increase his self-understanding and professional competency. The counselor seems to be looking for support for his inadequate behavior.

The counselor inquires about limits in offering suggestions. Here, we must remember that the counselor's primary responsibility is to his client and he exists to help the client become a more fully-functioning person. The counselor is not there to make matters worse for the counselee. The counselor's offhand suggestion to Mrs. Morales was professionally unwise because of the great risk to her son. The effect of this event on Ramon's long-term psychosocial development is a critical unknown.

To the writer, it is difficult to see how this could have been a good learning experience for anyone. Mrs. Morales, Ramon, and the uncle now have a distorted perception of the counseling service. The counselor has reinforced his unwarranted positive perception of professional adequacy.

Hopefully, the counselor is an illustrative and unreal entity. To paraphrase one of Freud's earlier statements, sometimes it is hard to tell which one is the doctor.

MANFORD A. SONSTEGARD

It is difficult to be critical of something that appears to be effective; the approach used by the boy's uncle was radical, but not unrealistic. However, other approaches could have been used to produce the same result. What is amazing is that the counselor, quickly arriving at a hypothesis that appeared to be valid, did not take the time to verify his hypothesis. This is a hazardous procedure.

The mother came to the school specifically to obtain help. It was an opportune moment for an in-depth interview to discover the purpose behind the youngster's behavior. The fact that Ramon did not do his homework was symptomatic, and one can surmise what was taking place. Ramon was the only child until his brother was born. Although he had been pampered, he was dethroned by his younger brother. He, therefore, lacked courage to face the problems of everyday life, such as getting his work done. He resented the attention the baby got.

To keep his mother busy with him, Ramon resorted to useless attention-getting mechanisms. Because he did not do his homework, his mother would keep after him. Not getting up in the morning kept his mother busy yelling at him. When the uncle came into the picture, Ramon succeeded in involving him. There were undoubtedly innumerable ways invented by Ramon to keep people constantly involved with him; he succeeded most probably in involving his teacher as well. From the given information, one can hypothesize that this is what was occurring.

Regardless of the psychological orientation, the counselor did not seem aware of what constitutes systematic, professional counseling. The mother's visit was an opportune time for an interview. She might also have been asked to wait while the counselor talked with Ramon. These interviews would have enabled the counselor to verify or discount his hypothesis. Having obtained verification, he could have helped the mother institute practices to redirect Ramon's mistaken goals. A session with the teacher might have helped him understand the dynamics of Ramon's behavior and the steps involved in reeducation. These procedures would follow approved counseling methods.

Also, a medical examination is a requirement in a case like this. It is unfortunate this did not occur, and the fact that it was not needed is beside the point.

Although the method used by Ramon's uncle was effective, it is professionally unwise to make an off-hand suggestion without clearly understanding the purpose of behavior. The counselor's preoccupation with causes and symptomatic treatment could be an explanation for what happened. That a thorough, properly conducted psychological investigation could be harmful compared to the symptomatic treatment used must be rejected as not in keeping with sound counseling practices.

It may have been a good learning experience for Ramon. However, since neither the child nor the parent was helped in gaining any insight into the dynamics of the behavior and no attempts were made to redirect mistaken goals, it is not likely that substantial behavioral changes took place. Ramon probably worked out other schemes for keeping both the mother and teacher busy with him. While these might be more acceptable means, they were, quite likely, just as useless.

3

Helping
the Disadvantaged?

CRITICAL INCIDENT

Background

The drama in a critical incident can be a function of what has occurred before. Thus, for example, if a child raises his hand to ask a question in class, there is no drama in that act; but if this particular child has never before raised his hand, asked a question, or participated, this simple behavior can be most exciting to a teacher who is interested in the behavior of the whole child. The incident to be recounted becomes critical and dramatic only if one understands the total situation and the people in it.

Our school is located in a disadvantaged area. We established what we called a "discussion class," a kind of group therapy in which a nurse, a social worker, and/or a psychologist participated with the teacher, myself (the counselor), and selected students. Of the various goals we sought to accomplish in this discussion class the two major ones were:

1. to develop in the child the ability to relate to adults

2. to encourage participation by every one at least once during the proceedings.

My comments will refer to sixth-grade groups. We have found that such groups should run for about forty-five minutes. We have also found that it is important for the teacher to be present to help evaluate the session, to inform us about the behavior of the children in the class, and to make suggestions for the future development of the group.

Prior to describing the critical incident, it is necessary to understand that we have found preplanning of the discussions by adults does not often pay off. That is, one cannot operate on the basis of a curriculum. Rather, one should discuss topics meaningful to the children. This is a critical point in such discussions. If adults agree that sex is an important topic for sixth-grade children but the topic fails to interest the children, then the discussion is only a waste of time. The problem is to find topics which will move children, and this is not an easy task with disadvantaged children who are frequently nonverbal, noncommunicative, and basically suspicious of adults.

The participation issue refers to Violet, a black, sixth-grade girl whose main problem in the school was her open hostility. In our group she never participated unless directly asked to do so, and then only minimally. During the sessions she would sneer, mock others, and make comments behind her hand to her girlfriend (also black). None of her comments were ever directed to the entire group. I hoped, however, that a time would come when we would hit on a topic which would impel her to participate in the group and which would lead her to share her ideas and feelings with us. This expectation seemed hopeless, however.

Incident

A new boy came into this group and immediately began to dominate it. He was a nonstop talker. If anything was brought up, he always had some comment to make, usually involving his brothers and sister. His silly behavior was in a sense disruptive and seemed to inhibit free discussion on the part of others. His outrageous domination of the group continued for session after session. I could see the other students looking at me, wondering why I did not stop him. During one session he spoke practically all the time, but neither I nor any of the other adults interrupted. The reason, of course, was that we felt that what he had to say was important to him and that his domination of the group reflected some problem. And this theory proved to be correct when, after about three sessions of incessant talking, he suddenly became quiet. My curiosity got the better of me. In the group I asked him why he didn't have so much to say anymore. The substance of his answer was that he realized that *now* people were listening to him. It was no longer necessary for him to engage in this compulsive talking, for he realized that the audience was there, that we respected him, and that he didn't have to fight to be heard. This comment on his part was a "critical incident" in two senses: (a) he began to understand the reason for his own general verbal misbehavior in the classroom, and (b) it was the trigger that set off Violet. After this boy had made his insightful statement, there was a strained silence. Suddenly I realized that Violet was speaking. "I don't believe that blacks and whites should go to the same school," she was saying. She continued to express her ideas in a loud, almost piercing voice, as though she expected to be stopped, and she shouted a variety of "black power" slogans. All of us were surprised at this outburst, and we listened while she expounded her ideas rapidly, loudly, and belligerently. Like a little black Joan of Arc, this twelve-year-old girl stood up brazenly facing the adults, screeching a barrage of furious and jumbled remarks on the topic of race. I was tremendously excited by this outpouring and I remember saying to myself: "Pour it on, baby, get it out of your system." When she finished she looked at us defiantly, and I had the impression that she expected us to attack her physically. But to my surprise (and, I found out later, to the surprise of other adults), when the attack on her did come, it did not come from the adults nor from the white children, but from the other black children in the group. None of them agreed with the ideas of this girl. It seemed to us Violet was shocked that her black friends did not agree with her. As she listened while others explained their ideas, explained how her point of view would only harm her, explained her mistakes, she seemed to light up, and it was evident that this confrontation was helping her to reappraise her stand on these matters.

Discussion

This incident was crucial to Violet's growth and development. After this occurrence she began to participate in the group and the teacher reported that her behavior in class was much improved. As a matter of fact, Violet later commented freely on other topics discussed in the group during succeeding weeks. It was obvious to me that this incident marked the beginning of her social growth.

As I see it, the question of how to start discussions on the proper topics in group sessions depends on several things. One of them is illustrated in this incident. If we had cut off the aggressive member, then Violet would never have spoken out. Our behavior towards the boy encouraged Violet to confront us with her feelings and convictions. I believe that if group leaders can be comfortable in uncomfortable situations when there is no threat involved (as when the aggressive boy took over), then, when a tender or sensitive topic comes up, children will be brave and intelligent enough to make the generalizations necessary to solve the dilemmas of their lives.

Questions

1.   I submit that the kind of learning Violet experienced was much more important than learning how to divide and multiply and that if the school is to teach the whole child, such understanding as Violet was helped to achieve is much more important than learning the three Rs. Shouldn't all schools have therapeutic sessions of this kind for all children with behavior problems?

2.   Schools enslave children with their preplanned curricula, since it is assumed that adults know what is best for children and that children should conform. I believe this incident shows us that children must be given an opportunity to express themselves. Violet's behavior in a classroom might well have resulted in disciplinary action. Do the consultants agree that all schools should encourage students to express themselves emotionally?

3.   What general principles of group dynamics should one employ in school discussion groups? In our group the basic rule was: no interruption, no correction, hands off. What other principles will work?

4.   In all our groups we have a great deal of trouble getting discussion started. How can we "warm up" groups more quickly?

5.   Was Violet really helped or was she subtly assimilated into our middle-class culture? Is this what we mean when we speak of aiding the growth and development of the culturally disadvantaged? What has she really learned?

COMMENTS ON THE INCIDENT

THE EDITORS

What should the school teach? We often refer to "teaching the whole child," but inevitably we end up organizing regimented classes and rewarding children on their ability to remember facts. If "teaching the whole child" refers to character education and the development of good citizens, we must find ways to help children to express themselves irrespective of the mental, cultural, physical, and/or economic handicaps they may have.

Nowadays some school counselors are engaged in group psychotherapy under a variety of names, such as Guided Group Interaction, Group Counseling, Group Guidance, or Discussion Class (as in this incident). These group procedures using group dynamics and processes represent an attempt to help children with problems of living. The primary vehicle for such learning is free and open discussion. This requires a minimum or absence of limits, absence of threats, freedom of expression, and great tolerance of behavior.

In this incident a rather dramatic change occurred in a girl as a result of the permissive atmosphere of the group. Significant learning took place. However, this is not the kind of learning that can be prepared for by designing curricula, and it cannot be graded.

Our consultants agree that this type of personality change is important and that in general the counselor in this case acted wisely in her handling of the group.

BENJAMIN C. BELDEN

Was this group therapy or massive retaliation? Mind you, the adults in the group included a nurse, social worker, psychologist, teacher, and counselor. The presence of so many adults would deter young people in almost any group from feeling comfortable and expressing themselves. It is no wonder that the counselor had such difficulty in getting the group going.

How were the students selected for this group? Were they behavior problems or star students? Judging from the group's reaction to Violet, I would think that most of the kids were "good" with a sprinkling of one or two troublemakers.

The counselor's theory of permissiveness does not adequately explain his response to the boy's behavior. This counselor simply did not understand the role and function of a leader. He should have interrupted the boy soon after it was clear to him that the boy was becoming a bore. He should have asked the group how they felt about the boy's remarks. The boredom he observed in the group should have been interpreted and discussed. Boredom usually masks feelings of anger. If the counselor felt that there were negative feelings in the group he should have encouraged their expression. He should have let the kids know right from the start that this was a safe place for the expression of feelings and dissidence. The counselor makes a mistake if he concludes that he is establishing such a climate by his "noninterference." On the contrary, a more timid member would perceive him as supporting aggressive or dominating behavior rather than helping the weaker members to join in. A discussion leader in this context must be active and facilitative. A climate of trust and safety is not built by permitting a strong member to take over.

Furthermore, his belief that the children will be "brave and rise to the occasion" is patently naive. Children can be marvelous, delightful, and unforgettably endearing, but they are also quite as capable as adults at doing malicious, stupid, and inhumane things to each other, especially when they are without guidance.

I would question Violet's alleged "social growth." As a result of this session Violet did begin to conform, but is that really progress? Considered from the viewpoint of the "establishment," she did seem to be accepting the norms of the teachers. From the viewpoint of running a smooth school this certainly was "progress." But from the viewpoint of the militant black community, would it be the same? Violet got the message from the "good" black kids not to "rock the boat." The pressures upon her were great. It appears as if the "black Joan of Arc" sold out her militant principles in order to join the group. This says little about her "social growth." It does say a lot about the terrible power of group pressure.

DONALD H. BLOCHER

This incident is an example of the way in which guidance and counseling activities can have real impact on the growth and development of children when those activities are treated as a central rather than a peripheral part of the total educational process. Several aspects of the incident are important in this context.

First, the crucial learnings that were involved in Violet's experience were a vital part of her life in the classroom. The pent-up feelings, the inability to deal with them directly in expressive communication with others in the classroom represented an inhibiting factor in her total educational development. Without learning to deal with powerful feelings that were continually aroused in the classroom situation, she could not possibly learn to utilize that environment fully to meet more traditional, subject-centered tasks.

Second, in this incident the new learning occurred directly in a situation in which new patterns of behavior were needed. She was not counseled about her problem in a counseling office and then sent back to the classroom to attempt to use new behaviors there. Instead she learned new behavior in the setting where it was needed.

Finally, in this experience Violet learned to use existing classroom relationships to further her own development as a person. She experienced honest reaction to her feelings and ideas from people who cared for and respected her enough both to listen and to react honestly. The basis for further growth and development thus became visible to her as she experienced both the disagreement and concern of her fellow students and the acceptance of adults.

A very large part of the function of guidance in an educational setting is to help insure that incidents like this occur in the school environment. Guidance workers can have much more impact on the growth and development of children by helping to shape the milieu of the school than by attempting to remedy one at a time the problems that are themselves the product of an ineffective or even destructive educational system.

MARSANNE C. EYRE

What is important to me in this incident may not appear important to anyone else, including the counselor who wrote the incident. Schools should teach the whole child, not just a part of him. Our schools have been teaching two-thirds of the child: the *mental* and the *physical*. What is left out completely is the *emotional*: feelings, attitudes, and points of view. I see the kind of "group therapy" described in this incident as an example of what the schools should do for *all* students, as an incidental treatment for maladjusted children. That is, I see such content-free groups, wherein all children get an opportunity to express themselves, to explain themselves, and to interact formally with other children and with adults, as a must. Our troubled world with its problems of prejudice and fear, war and disaster needs education of a new sort—the sort exemplified by this example. And we need it damned quick!

We should be less concerned with teaching children like Violet how to divide three-eighths by seven-sixteenths and become more concerned with enabling the Violets of this world to know who they are, what they can do, who are their friends, and who are their enemies, to teach them love and compassion, to make them capable of expressing themselves, to make them lose fear, to make them understand people. Content-free therapy sessions (call them what you will) provide one of the ways to make this happen.

The elements that occurred within the group are exciting in and of themselves, but what seems of greater importance is the absolute necessity of meeting children on their own territory, as it were. Some schools are in a never-never land totally unrelated to reality. This is why there is so much hostility directed against schools, as evidenced by the frequent acts of vandalism, theft, and assault which plague the schools. This is the reason why students in some cases find it a mark of prestige to fail. Anyone can pass. All one has to do is to study. But to be bright and to taunt teachers and parents by failing, that is the thing to do. How powerful children can be when they are determined to fail in order to punish those who torment them.

In any event, it seems to me that both the long-winded boy and this sullen angry girl strongly needed the cleansing effect of the therapy group, and conventional content material would have been inappropriate and lost on them. I am impressed by the sensible handling of the group, the absence of a "curriculum," the permissive attitude shown, all of which permitted Violet's letting-go, which, in turn led her to a greater understanding of society and a loss of some of her harmful feelings. It seems to me that too many schools operate on the premise that the child must adjust to the school rather than on the premise that the school should help the child adjust to himself.

ALLEN E. IVEY

Violet's learning in this dramatic situation is indeed as valid and as important as any academic learning the school can provide. The work of the counselor with this unstructured group represents an important new direction in school counseling—that of providing children with an opportunity for personal growth and learning in a variety of contexts other than traditional ones of individual and group guidance.

One senses that the counselor in this case was especially empathic and understanding. It does not seem likely that she really maintained a hands-off policy with her groups, but rather communicated acceptance and warmth through vocal quality, nonverbal gestures, and occasional comments which served to encourage personal growth. It takes an especially talented and integrated individual to use the group procedures described herein to help students move in a positive direction.

The situation, while therapeutic, could also be discussed within a learning framework. Violet was not necessarily a disturbed child. Violet *learned* through observation that it was all right to talk out strongly about one's feelings; she learned that it might be possible for her to express herself and someone might listen; she learned that fellow black students might not agree with her, but that they would listen and respect her for her opinions. This type of learning should not be restricted to therapeutic sessions for "problem children," but should be made available to all children to aid them in understanding themselves and the processes of communication with others.

There are a variety of methods for initiating group discussions. The counselor should be skilled in several alternative methods. Role playing, structured groups of many types, value discussions led by the teacher in the regular classroom as part of subject matter discussions, filmstrips on personal or social issues, class projects, and even programmed texts can all be used to explore the affective dimension of education. Generally, less counseling skill is demanded by these more structured techniques, but the lessons taught can be equally important, though less dramatic. What seems most important is that the technique used is appropriate to the skills of the individual counselor, and to the particular moment of the child's growth.

An especially promising approach to affective or values education is the learning-objectives approach. The counselor or teacher can identify a target behavior—free expression of emotion regarding race, for example. Then, through a variety of approaches ranging from highly unstructured methods to more directly organized procedures, such as reading units in racial studies or even programmed texts, the teacher or counselor can introduce the opportunity for discussion of racial attitudes. Then, when a student makes a comment in which racial attitudes are freely expressed, the teacher or counselor can reinforce these comments. Such "pump-priming" techniques make the discussion of important issues more likely to occur. Gradually, important behavior changes can happen in the child as he learns more about himself and others. Planned experiences can reach more students if a regular part of the daily classroom experience is not held to a set guidance period or group session.

This, in turn, suggests a new and more challenging role for the counselor of the future—that of curriculum consultant in the affective aspects of education. Using strategies ranging from the unstructured methods cited in this case to techniques adapted from behavior modification, the guidance counselor of the future can help make the classroom a more exciting innovative and, most important, more humane setting.

What has Violet really learned? She has learned what it feels like to be listened to, and maybe she has learned something about listening herself. I also think that Violet has learned that many white people feel as oppressed and ignored as do black people. She also has learned that if a person speaks out there is a better chance of being heard. The boy who talked nonstop for session after session finally learned that he was being listened to and no longer felt the need to demand attention militantly. While more dramatic, Violet's outpouring of emotion is similar to the boy's cry for someone to listen to him. Both the boy and Violet heard that they were accepted, that their feelings and behavior were valid and reasonable, despite the fact that all others might disagree with them.

Will the learning last? People often learn important things about openness, listening, and emotions through nonstructured groups. Unfortunately, much of life in the "real world" of the school and community does not reward or even reinforce the important values and new behaviors inculcated by the group. Unless the school classroom and the greater society at large can offer opportunities for continued use of newly learned behaviors, they will rapidly extinguish them. Thus, it becomes incumbent upon the counselor to work with teachers, school administrators, and his home community, insofar as possible, to see that they provide an environment in which important new behaviors can be "tried on," tested, and learned thoroughly. One way of achieving this vital goal is for the counselor to work with teachers, showing them how the techniques described here can be applied in the classroom. It is the responsibility of the counselor not only to help the child to grow, but also help those who work with the child to grow.

E. G. WILLIAMSON

I shall respond to the issues presented in this incident by addressing the counselor. Your second stated objective was that everyone should participate at least once during each meeting. Why is this an objective? You are forcing some members beyond their readiness to participate. It would be wonderful if there were direct participation by everyone during every session, but I think it is a bit unreasonable. There should be sessions when students can feel that they can be silent if they don't have the urge to participate. The right to privacy includes the right of nonparticipation. I don't have the time to spell out all the implications here, but the concept of democracy means we can participate if we want to and need not if we don't.

I sympathize greatly with the problems faced by counselors and teachers who try to motivate children who are unmotivated and disadvantaged, who not only are nonverbal and noncommunicative, but are essentially suspicious of adults. Such children are often motivated toward other objectives than the ones the schools have selected. Violet is a case in point. Her defensive hostility was tragic.

The boy who dominated the group with his talking had a problem deserving of sympathy, empathy, and patience. He eventually did get a release from this particular urge. The insight gained and the improvement in him through the behavior of the group through your leadership was remarkable. You are to be congratulated that he did catch on so quickly. You are also to be congratulated that your handling of the boy triggered Violet to begin speaking, and your acceptance of her words was just beautiful. Perhaps you could have eased a bit of the shock that Violet received when her black friends began to put the brakes on her uncontrolled verbalizing. In any case you got help from her associates, and she too began to get some insights and some satisfaction from that insight.

I don't know whether your analysis of cause and effect is correct, but it doesn't make any difference. The fact is that both Violet and the talkative boy became more socialized in a way we hope will be of benefit to them as they grow and mature. You are correct that group leaders must be comfortable, or at least appear to be comfortable in uncomfortable situations. What a life of duplicity counselors must live!

Now, what did Violet learn? I think she reached the point of being ready to learn the standard preparatory curriculum. But she had to go through these therapeutic traumatic experiences before she could be ready for curriculum materials. Fortunately you were working in a school situation which permitted you to be permissive enough to forget the standard requirements of a formal curriculum, and let Violet go through the therapeutic exercise of learning to learn and wanting to learn. I don't criticize preplanned curricula (there must be some order in the universe), but I do criticize those who impose a formal curriculum with rigidity and those who cruelly demand adherence to it by students who are unready for it, rather than waiting until they can be coaxed along. Of course, students should be given the opportunity to express themselves, but we must remember that we have more than that at stake. Students have to learn to express themselves not in terms of gibberish, as I view her sloganizing to be, but in terms of what they need to learn, the more maturing kinds of experiences that schools are established for (e.g., being responsible, rational, cooperative, etc.). All this should occur in due time. Patience is needed on the part of her teachers and counselor not to discipline Violet in the fond hope of forcing her into line so that she will become a standardized well-motivated learner.

I do not agree that schools should encourage all students to express themselves at all times. Students have to learn the mature criteria of how and when and what to express and not merely to verbalize whatever nonsense comes to mind. This is the maturing process that we hope the school experience will provide. Unfortunately we don't always succeed. In this instance, I think you handled the group situation beautifully, and I suppose it was occasionally difficult for you to restrain yourself after hours of talkativeness. I won't agree that in such situations there should never be interruptions or corrections, that the policy should always be hands-off. These are good principles in group discussions, but they have to be modified in terms of situations, the nature of the participants, how much they can take in the way of distractions, and how much the school can permit in the way of digressions from regularized learning.

At times I think the counselor would find it advisable to nudge the individual gently in the right direction. The right direction is toward intellectual and social maturity. In this case, I think you, the counselor, received help from unexpected sources, and you should count yourself fortunate because you won't always be this lucky.

You ask about warming up groups, getting them to function well quickly. This is partly a function of how the students feel, their response to you, and your almost unconscious revelation to them of how you feel that day—your amount of acceptance and permissiveness. These variables are terribly difficult to regularize or control. Don't try a formula; just roll with the punches, as it were. If you don't have the patience and can't stand the group of the moment find an excuse for leaving the room for a while. Go and get a drink or something.

I don't know whether Violet was really assimilated into our middle-class culture by being helped. But she seemed to have worked out whatever problem was inhibiting her. The release of inhibitions is part of the counseling process. I wish that more school teachers would use counseling devices to cause the release of their students' inhibitions. Let us not be so concerned about whether Violet was assimilated, but rather be thankful that she now seems to be better adjusted. This means she is going a step further into maturity. I think she learned a new style of interaction with others, she learned to listen—a most urgent necessity in our kind of society. She learned that other people had similar thoughts, but expressed them differently. She learned that other people sympathized with her. She also learned, however, that other people would restrain her when she went into wild, impulsive, and emotional tirades.

Let us think what might have happened both to Violet and to the talkative boy if these incidents had not happened to them early in life. We should all be thankful they did happen. Perhaps some day we will know enough about setting up situations—I started to say "manipulate" —so that the situations will turn out this way and this well.

One does not have to go through many such extreme and traumatic experiences to realize that we don't know as yet how to manipulate situations so that they come out as we would wish. We must keep trying and experimenting. Someday we will understand better how to make ourselves more useful to students like Violet.

4

Stop! I'll Help You!!

CRITICAL INCIDENT

Background

One day, while in my office, I heard a timid knock on the door and I called out, "Come in." A small thin girl with a very pale face and big blue eyes came in hesitantly and walked unsteadily toward my desk. My first thought was that she was high on some drug. She sat down when I pointed to the chair. When I asked, "What's on your mind?" she seemed to be struggling to catch her breath and tried several times to speak but could not. Even though I was busy with some important work I could see she was terrified, and so I just looked at her as kindly as I could, waiting for her to tell me what was bothering her. Finally she said something, but perhaps because of the noise of the air conditioner in my office, or perhaps because of her low voice, I didn't catch what she said. I leaned over toward her and she moved away from me rapidly in a startled manner as though she expected me to strike her. "I'm sorry, I didn't hear you," I said. "Please tell me again." This time I heard her soft whisper: "I'm pregnant."

By the end of an hour, by insistent questioning, I learned the following. Her name was Maureen and she was a junior in the high school.

Her grades were about average. She came from a large family, relatively well-known in the community since one of her uncles was a priest and two of her aunts were nuns. Her father and mother were very devout Catholics and had brought up their children with severity and piety. Maureen had never had a boyfriend. She looked considerably younger than her true age of sixteen. About a month before she had gone to the movies with a boy who had asked her out, and while in his car he had forced himself on her, and despite her entreaties, he had penetrated and discharged.

She had never gone out with the boy again, and he, as a matter of fact, had never talked with her again. She didn't like him, and he was unaware that she was pregnant. She knew she was pregnant because although normally as regular as clockwork, she had missed two consecutive periods. She had not told anyone else about her condition. She had decided to commit suicide and had been systematically collecting sleeping pills from her parents' supply. What she really wanted to know was how many pills one should take to commit suicide. She had heard that if one took too few or too many one would not succeed.

Small and slight as she was, she had a will of iron. When I suggested that she tell her mother or her father, she said, "You don't know them." She pleaded with me, "You must not tell them. I'll throw myself out a window." Whether or not her statement was a bluff I did not know, but I believed she meant this literally. Right in front of her I called up my family doctor and told him briefly the facts of the case. His reply surprised me. It seemed that in our state there was a law that if a doctor examined a person who was technically a child and if the doctor found that the child either had venereal disease or was pregnant, the doctor had to inform the parents of the situation on pain of losing his license.

"If she comes to me, this is what I would have to do," he said. "Sure, I don't know the girl but if eventually she mentions my name as the doctor who saw her and if someone wants to make trouble for me, I'll really be in hot water." I thanked him and when I looked at Maureen I thought she was going to faint, for she had gotten even paler.

"I'll be willing to talk to your parents myself," I told her. She clutched my arm. "No!" she pleaded. "You don't know them. I'd much rather die." She got up and started to totter toward the door.

Incident

As she reached the door, my mind was spinning a mile a minute. My thoughts were, *Too bad kid that you got caught. Maybe she is a floosie and is just giving me a story. Maybe she is not pregnant and this is a plot to test me to see what I'll do. All this is no skin off my nose. I told her*

what to do. Well, I must look out for myself, and this is not my problem.
In other words I made a decision that this was not my problem, that I
wasn't getting involved, and that I had done my duty by simply telling
her to tell her parents. Consequently, I was quite surprised to hear myself
say: "Stop! I'll help you."

This made no difference, for she continued to open the door. I ran
to her, brusquely shut the door, and dragged her back to her chair. "Damn
you," I said, "I may get in trouble, I may lose my job, I may even go to
jail. I don't know why, but I'll help you. Will you give me a chance and
not do anything foolish?"

Maureen couldn't answer and she merely nodded her head. I told
her I would try to find an abortionist and take care of everything. She
just looked at me uncomprehendingly. I finally asked her how much
money she had and she told me she had seventeen dollars. And so, here
I was, a man of a different faith, working in a strongly Catholic neighborhood, agreeing to commit at least two crimes: concealing information and
getting an abortion for a teen-age girl. On top of that I had been in this
school system for less than three months, and I really didn't have a single
friend in the school or the community. To make everything worse, I was
myself only eight years older than Maureen. I sure put myself in a pretty
pickle. And there wasn't a single person in the whole community whom
I knew well enough to discuss the problem with.

I told Maureen to go home and say nothing, but to come in to see
me in a week. I assured her that a lot of girls got into this kind of trouble
and that it would soon be over. By this time she seemed more comfortable
and kept telling me, "Thank you, thank you, thank you." When she
finally left, I was weak as a dishrag and just didn't know what to do.

I opened the telephone directory to "physicians" and as I looked
down the list I saw the name of a woman physician whose last name was
the same as mine. I called the number, and when there was an answer, it
sounded like a man's voice. I asked for the physician and the voice said
it was she. I asked for an immediate appointment and was given it. I got
in my car and, within twenty minutes, I was in her office—she had an office
in her home—and I told her the whole story. She listened in silence.
Finally she spoke. "Like yourself I am more or less of an alien in this
town. I believe every word you have told me. You know that we would be
both conspiring to commit a crime. Also, you know that if anything goes
wrong, we could both go to prison. On top of that I have never done an
abortion myself, and would not do it. However, I know some people who
will do it. The question is simply how to do it and how to pay for it.
Refer the girl to me, and I'll take it over from this point."

The next day I intercepted Maureen as she came out of a class, gave
her the doctor's phone number, and asked her to call. In a sense this is
the end of the incident, since Maureen never came to see me again and

since I never had any further contact with the doctor. However, I saw Maureen from time to time and she definitely showed no signs of pregnancy. Whether the girl had been pregnant, whether she got the abortion or what, I never found out.

Discussion

What makes this a critical incident was simply my reaction to the situation. I knew well enough that I shouldn't get involved, that only a lot of trouble and no thanks could result, and I decided, even though sadly, to keep out of the situation; and yet, when she opened the door I spoke out "Stop! I'll help you," without any premeditation. It was as though my words came out by themselves. On thinking things over, I realize I did a very foolish thing and I could have gotten myself into a lot of real trouble. The woman doctor also did a foolish thing. We both broke the laws. Reflecting more deeply on this incident, however, I feel we both operated in terms of a higher set of rules than the ones made by men. In other words, as far as I am concerned, I did the right thing. My own perception at that time of the principal and other school administrative personnel was that they were so rule-bound that they would have simply told the girl's parents, had they found out.

Questions

1.   Given the circumstances as described in this incident, what do the consultants think of simply telling the girl, "It is not my problem"?

2.   Is a counselor ever justified in committing one crime (such as the one indicated) to avoid another crime (in this case possible suicide)?

3.   Should I have called the parents, or informed the school authorities; or should I have thought that this just isn't my problem?

4.   What dangers exist not only for the counselor (they are evident) for this kind of independent behavior but also for school counselors as a profession?

5.   Had you been the principal and if you had found out what I had done, how would you have regarded my behavior?

COMMENTS ON THE INCIDENT

THE EDITORS

By what standards can a counselor guide himself in those terrible moments such as when he is confronted with the anxieties of unwanted pregnancy, the threat of suicide or other contingencies having moral and legal implications? Should one base one's behavior on self-survival? Common sense? Altruism? Or on a rigid adherence to the policies of the school and/or the dictates of the law?

Sometimes it is wise to feel "It is not my problem," and pass it along —upward to one's supervisor or outward to others. At other times such behavior may be viewed as cowardly or unprofessional. The school counselor must often wrestle with this issue and decide when to stay with a counselee and when to refer "up" or "out." This is especially true of school counselors who are frequently seen as school teachers assigned to counseling in both a legal and public sense. A counselor is a teacher with a special assignment, and there is little tradition for differentiating clearly between them.

In the present case, the counselor, new to the school and an alien in a number of ways, was thrown a hot problem. He reacted by first denying the problem and then getting involved. He managed to get himself out of the situation well enough. But had he done the right thing?

Our consultants view this not uncommon problem in a variety of ways. How might you have acted if this had happened to you?

ANGELO V. BOY

In this incident, the counselor's concept of rendering therapeutic assistance to Maureen was to take direct action by contacting a local physician so that an abortion could take place. Once again, we see a situation in which counseling is conceived to be synonymous with direct action on the part of a counselor. For too many counselors counseling is a relationship in which the client presents a problem and the counselor offers a solution. It sounds logical to do this, but such a procedure indicates a glaring insensitivity to how a counselor therapeutically assists a client to solve or resolve a psychologically based problem.

When Maureen said, "I'm pregnant," the counselor apparently became unglued. But what might have happened if he, instead, had said, "Let's talk about it. You sound frightened and upset. Let's begin to talk about what happened and perhaps I can help you to decide what you should do."

Maureen first needs a therapeutic catharsis before she can begin to take a realistic look at her situation and what she should do about it. This may demand that the counselor get together with Maureen for three one-hour counseling sessions per week over a period of weeks. But Maureen needs the opportunity to blow off steam—psychologically to vomit her feelings about herself, her male companion, and the reactions of her parents. She needs this psychological cleansing before she can begin to take a rational look at what she should do. I can't determine what Maureen's solution should be, but I do know that if a solution is to make any real sense to Maureen, then it must come from Maureen. Certainly, this will be a difficult decision for Maureen—the most difficult that she will ever make. Forty years from now, however, Maureen will be able to live with that decision because she had the opportunity to think it through carefully with a counselor and because it was *her* decision.

I'm not avoiding responsibility here. To me it's a greater personal responsibility to help Maureen work out her feelings and reach toward a solution than to offer a quick solution. Such a quick solution rids me of responsibility in the shortest period of time. I unhook myself from responsibility because I've *done* something.

The skilled counselor realizes that clients can solve their own problems in a counseling relationship in which they have enough psychological elbow room to engage in catharsis. After catharsis, the potential for a personally meaningful solution is increased. But if the counselor insists on plunging ahead toward a solution, then the client is still left with the repressed feelings which must first be unclogged and released before she can ever hope to reach a personally meaningful and realistic solution to her problem.

Schools are answer-centered institutions and these answers are constructed by teachers. Within the context of learning, students present problems and teachers render solutions. In such an atmosphere, school counselors are conditioned to listen to the client's presenting problem and, after all the facts are in, to present a well packaged answer. In some cases, where the client is presenting a purely rational problem which has a rational answer, such behavior on the part of the counselor would be appropriate. But Maureen is suffering psychological pain, anguish, confusion, resentment, and culturally induced shame. She needs to get these feelings out of her system and examine them before she can reach the point where she can rationally decide what she should do.

When the counselor telephoned the local physician for help, he wasn't assuming responsibility—he was absolving himself of responsibility. He unhooked himself neatly. It became the physician's responsibility to help Maureen, not the counselor's.

What about Maureen today? Does she have a greater sense of guilt because of the abortion? Was she ever really pregnant, or was this merely Maureen's presenting problem?

DON C. DINKMEYER

I don't see how the counselor could have said to himself at any time, "It's not my problem." After all, the girl had sought him out, a counselor, for help with a personal problem. It is precisely his function to be available, to listen to, to understand, and to help with all problems, not merely to assess vocational potential or to aid in college decisions. Thus he would have been irresponsible had he rejected Maureen's problem as not pertaining to him.

The issue is what he should have done. Generally speaking, in all situations the counselor assumes a responsible attitude but demands the same from the student, or at least tries to make the student responsible. In my judgment the counselor got overly involved and assumed too much responsibility by calling a doctor and by not informing his principal or getting in touch with Maureen's parents. There are always grave dangers attending anyone whose behavior violates the law. While it is perfectly appropriate for a counselor to listen and to understand and to counsel, when he starts to act in a student's behalf he is likely to get into trouble. In my opinion the method of helping in this case was questionable, even though understandable. By calling the doctor and making a referral he showed he cared—and this could have been of value. However, I wonder if he had stopped to talk with her and to investigate other possibilities, whether (a) it may have turned out that he had only gotten part of the story, or (b) that he and the girl might have come up with more acceptable solutions. For example, it may have been that he could have convinced her to share her problem with her parents and that a solution could have been worked out in that manner. What I object to in this case is the counselor's impulsive rejection first and then his equally impulsive assumption of responsibility.

This is a good example of why school counselors need to have available supervisory resources. A good supervisor would have asked: "Why doesn't the girl assume responsibility?" or "What have you done to make her feel more responsible?" First, a boy practically raped her—if this is what really happened—and now another male, only a bit older, takes over in his masterful manner. But what of the girl? Would she not just feel used and abused, and by the counselor first rejected and then manipulated?

It is difficult to fathom the meaning of this incident. Was the girl really pregnant? Was it all a put on? Was the girl simply seeking special attention with a fanciful story?

In any event, if the school had consultative resources whereby the counselor could confer with either an older, more experienced school counselor or with a professional person, he would not have been inclined to act so hastily. I am afraid he really didn't learn much from this whole incident.

WALTER G. KLOPFER

The role of a counselor in the school is to be available for students no matter what kind of problem that they might present. The counselor who limits in any way the kinds of problems that he is willing to take on is in the wrong profession. If someone wants a job with no pitfalls, where the decisions are never ambiguous, where he never has to stick his neck out, he should avoid the field of counseling like the plague. Consequently, accepting the problem and involving himself in it was the only ethical alternative open to the counselor.

However, a serious error was made by the counselor in assuming that the girl wanted to have an abortion. A girl who is pregnant has open to her a number of alternative courses of actions. She might attempt to get the boy to marry her if he wishes to. She might go to a home for unwed mothers and have her baby, subsequently placing it for adoption. She might leave town and live with relatives, or she might decide to keep the baby and raise it herself, since sometimes that can be done. It is not the business of the counselor to decide which of these alternatives is preferable, but it is his business to discuss all of them frankly and fully with the student so that she knows she has choices and is free to make them.

The question of whether the counselor should break the law revolves around his personal hierarchy of values. Everyone breaks the law at some time and in the field of counseling it is necessary to use judgment as to what is in the best interests of both the client and society. In regard to calling the parents, I think it is general policy among school counselors not to call parents except with the consent of the student. In this case there was the apparent danger of the girl killing herself if he insisted on telling them. His decision was that the life of the girl was more important than doing the "proper thing." Whether I agree or not would depend on my estimation of the degree of sincerity involved in her threat of suicide.

It would be helpful to know something about the parents. Sometimes children perceive their parents as being more moralistic and rejecting than they are in reality. If the parents were known to myself or some other member of the staff, it would be possible to make a judgment as to whether they could be involved with impunity or not.

Last, if I were the principal, I would be very glad to have a counselor like this on the staff and I would hope that he would tell me only those things that I could officially acknowledge. As an administrator, a principal has certain duties and obligations which are not identical to those of the counselor. As long as the principal is not made aware of illegalities, he has no obligation to act. If the principal and counselor have confidence and faith in each other they can work out a relationship in which each plays a somewhat different role, but one in which the two roles complement each other effectively.

PHYLLIS M. MARTIN

What a heartbreaking situation! I feel sure every school counselor will encounter such a situation some day if she or he remains long enough in the profession. Simply telling the girl "It is not my problem" would be destructive and, even though she presents a difficult problem, no ethical counselor would make this remark. This solution just cannot be entertained. The girl has a problem. She is asking advice concerning what to do about her problem. Since the counselor is a professional, his problem is counseling and not Maureen's pregnancy. Several elements in this case question the logical thinking of the counselor. I charitably assume that he was young and inexperienced. First, it seems to me he reacted impulsively, and I get the feeling he did not think through any plan of action before he threw himself into this complicated situation. At the very least, he should have been aware of his own feelings of panic and should have made an arrangement to see her again on the next day.

He did not get facts. Some investigation of the events of the pregnancy seems indicated if only to give her a chance to talk and to calm down. He ignored her request for information about the number of sleeping pills required in order to put her "threat" into operation. The reason for discussing this would be to reduce the suicide threat. I find that if a counselor does not get rattled and can discuss suicide rationally, this calms people.

Then, of course, I feel he was completely out of line in making arrangements for an abortion when he and Maureen could not be sure of the facts of the case. Calling the doctor was premature, to say the least.

In essence, the counselor seemed to panic. No doubt he felt compassion for this young girl, but in becoming her accomplice he loses his professional status. I wonder about his view of people when he behaved as if he had no superior or colleague to discuss the matter with him or give advice and support.

Although this young counselor acted unwisely and unethically, one must feel sympathy for him and perhaps admire him. Despite his fear and anxiety, he possessed compassion and courage, and he acted independently and decisively. He was lucky, of course, to have escaped any of many possible consequences.

Some follow-up to his course of action is certainly indicated. A truly compassionate counselor would have attempted to heal her mind as well as protect her body. It could well be that Maureen would have needed him more after than she did before the abortion—if she really had one. A great opportunity for a therapeutic relationship was ignored.

He believes he did not do the right thing. *What is right? What is wrong?* How can we, as counselors, meeting problems on the firing line, ever know what is right and wrong? We must follow ethical guide lines as established by professional societies; we must listen with our hearts and use our minds. Above all, we must not panic.

JOHN D. MULLEN

This incident is an example of a counselor wrongfully imposing his set of values on a counselee. The counselor who takes it upon himself to judge another's set of values and/or establish his own set of values shows disregard for the dignity of the counselee and is in the wrong profession.

The important person in a counseling relationship is the counselee, taken as an individual with his or her set of values, such as they are, and respected as such. The counselee is not clay to be molded and shaped at will by the counselor.

The letter and the intent of the law of the state was that parents should be informed by a professional person in cases of pregnancy of a minor child. The law seems to have been violated by the counselor who did not inform the parents. It should also be remembered that counselors are not protected by law. Counselor-counselee information is accessible to a court as testimony. Common sense also would dictate in a case of this nature where suicide is threatened that the parents be notified. The girl was probably asking for this by the fact that she came to the counselor even though she protested against his informing them. Often we find ourselves in the position of being asked to "pave the way" between parents and counselees. It seems certain in this case that the girl and her parents could have found a solution together and perhaps real love and communication in the process.

There was the possibility that the girl wasn't pregnant and yet the counselor jumped to this conclusion. The counselor could have encouraged Maureen to see her family doctor. The counselor had the obligation of becoming involved only to the extent of having the girl inform her parents. His role following this could have been encouragement and information. Other school authorities need not have been consulted if the parents were informed. However, if the parents are not brought into the picture, the counselor's immediate superior, the guidance department chairman or principal, should be informed. This serves as a protection for the counselor as well as a source of judgment or advice about the counselor's action and follow-through behavior.

Had I been the principal and found out about this event I would have called the counselor to my office and informed him about the folly of giving advice that entailed violating the law. Since there was nothing to be gained by further inquiry from the girl, I would suggest he not involve himself more deeply by seeking follow-up data. If an incident of this nature should happen again, I would suggest that the counselor seek advice from the principal or one of his superiors. I think the counselor was in serious error in his behavior, but he should forget it now. He should realize that his superiors most likely would be willing to discuss problems with him in the future and that he should not engage independently in any illegal actions involving students.

5

Counselor: Advocate or Accessory?

CRITICAL INCIDENT

Background

Georgia came to me with a pass from her algebra teacher which read, "Georgia would like an appointment with you to discuss the subjects that she has chosen for the eleventh grade."

After the usual get-the-client-relaxed conversation, I asked her, "What seems to be the problem with your choices for next year?"

Georgia replied, "I have not come to you to discuss my subjects for next year. I lied to the teacher so that I would not have to tell the real reason for my request to see you." She asked me whether I would be "forced" to tell the teacher that she had lied. I assured her that no one would force me and that I felt no responsibility to tell the teacher anything.

She then described her real problem. She said, "Many students in our school have been going to the city on Saturday afternoons and are taking things from department stores without paying for them. I, myself, have stolen four blouses, two bathing suits, two sweaters, and one suit. If my parents should ever find out that I had stolen anything they would be very upset because they have taught me to know right from wrong."

I asked, "What can I do about this? You know you did wrong, what can I possibly do to help you?"

She explained there were at least fifty young people involved in stealing throughout the school year. She continued, "We are not poor. We all have enough money. I do not know why we did it. I guess for the fun of it, or to see if we could get away with it. We now want to make amends."

I thanked her for placing so much trust in me. I expressed concern that the motive of the group seemed not to make things "right" but to somehow assure themselves amnesty. She responded that this was partially true, but that their even greater concern was that they wished to atone for their wrongdoing and not steal again. However, she explained, they were afraid that a manager of one of the stores might become angry with one of them and have them arrested if they would go to each store to make things "right."

After much discussion with a group of the students—for days on end—we arrived at a solution which we felt would benefit all concerned. The group had voted on all solutions presented. The final solution was: each student would determine the value of the goods which he had stolen, then we would average all of the estimates, and come up with a "true figure." Each person would then present an envelope to me with the name of the store, its location, and the amount of money in the envelope. I would take the money to the stores and present it to each manager with a brief explanation of how I obtained the money.

Before we concluded the last group meeting, I cautioned the group that they should not feel that the matter was necessarily closed after paying back the money. I said some of them might have to tell their parents about the stealing before their consciences would be eased.

The money was deposited with me. I, in turn, deposited the money with the proper stores.

Incident

One day a police officer requested a conference with me. He asked me to tell him who the individuals involved in this incident were so that "we (the police) can help them." I answered that I had acted as a confidential mediator for some young people who recognized that they had made mistakes. The action taken was for redress, but the names of the individuals would have to remain confidential. The police officer then informed me that if I did not give him the names of the individuals I could be charged with all the crimes they had committed. I would be considered an accessory to the crimes. I was quite startled by this turn of events. I felt I had a professional obligation to protect the names of those students who had confided in me and had placed their trust in my integrity, and so I refused to divulge names.

I immediately arranged for a conference with the chief of police and explained my situation to him. My basic position was summarized in a question I put to him: "What can you gain by forcing me to release their names?" I explained the ramifications which could result from my surrendering names; namely, that the students would no longer trust me or any member of the counseling staff. Fortunately, he saw my problem and dropped the entire matter.

Discussion

Looking back I feel that I did the right thing in getting the students to make restitution, to agree to not do such things again, and in helping them make restitution without the necessity of a public scandal. However, as an employee of the state, it may have looked to some agencies of the state and, in the case cited, the police, that I was withholding information. The police rightly or wrongly felt that they should know the names of the youths involved in this series of escapades and that I should have shared this information with them. One policeman said that I should have immediately told them of the existence of this "criminal gang" on finding out about it, and that my behavior was criminal in effect even though not in intent.

I don't know whether I could have been forced to reveal names if the police or the district attorney or the principal, or all of them, had insisted. The confidential nature of the counselor's interview is not legally protected in this state. I am thankful it did not come to this and that the police chief saw it my way and didn't press the matter. I don't know what I would have done if he had. There are some additional issues for me. If I had spoken out and had given names, could I have been legally sued for "invasion of privacy" by the students or by their parents? What would have been the "image" of a school counselor who gets information after he promises confidentiality and then divulges it? And, finally, what about my meeting with various groups and discussing matters which were not strictly related to the school and neglecting to let the school authorities know what I was doing?

Questions

1. Should I have handled this matter at all, or should I have referred it to someone else? In other words, what was my responsibility or my role in this type of nonschool problem?

2.   Should I have handled the conscience money and returned it? Should I have tried to have someone else handle it?

3.   Should I have let the school or police authorities know right away what was happening?

4.   Should I have attempted to have each individual return the money on his own rather than serving as the group's agent? In other words, did I step into the situation unnecessarily?

5.   Should one maintain a confidence even though on later consideration one realizes he gave his word unwisely or even illegally?

COMMENTS ON THE INCIDENT

THE EDITORS

Every once in a while a counselor will get an unorthodox request from a student or student group. While the request may indicate that students trust him and view him as a source of help and strength, the consequences of the counselor's involvement may be hazardous and have legal, ethical, and/or professional implications. Not to become involved, however, may seriously hinder the counselor's future relations with students. A counselor cannot always be running to someone for advice or counsel. Indeed, in some cases this is the last thing that the one seeking help would want the counselor to do. Sometimes, it may seem that the right thing to do may actually run contrary to community, school, and/or legal sanctions.

This incident describes such a problem, and it might well have ended unpleasantly and perhaps even tragically. The counselor did what he thought was right and took a risk in the process. Later he wondered about the legitimacy and impact of his action.

The consultants suggest various methods of dealing with such problems. Unorthodox problems sometimes call for unorthodox solutions, but we must be careful about establishing precedents. In any case, dealing with tough problems calls for creativity and resourcefulness, especially when one has limited authority and few precedents for handling unusual situations.

WALTER KLOPFER

The counselor in this incident found himself in the tricky and delicate situation of being informed of illegal activities involving a number of students. It was not clear whether the approach to him was the result of a group consensus or the decision of an individual student. However, in my opinion, the counselor had no choice but to maintain confidentiality. It is the responsibility of a school counselor to help students in the ways in which they would like to be helped, especially when their intentions are constructive. The problem would have been different if the counselor had been told of a plan to blow up the school or to rape one of the teachers. What they were planning to do was to make restitution, and certainly this fitted in with the value system of the counselor. In agreeing to act as an intermediary, he was certainly walking the extra mile for the students, enabling them to relieve themselves of their guilt feelings without exposing themselves.

Some question might be raised as to whether letting the students get off the hook through this hidden expedient was the most beneficial counseling approach. If they really wished to make restitution and relieve their guilt feelings, it might have been more effective if as many as those who wished to, had made their restitution publicly and visibly. I am quite certain that store managers under those conditions would not have taken legal action since they naturally want to encourage restitution as much as possible. The students in question might have gotten more out of the experience if the counselor had helped them to make the liaison with the authorities rather than protecting their identity. However, I would not, as a counselor, have suggested this unless I had first gotten their consent.

One of the nebulous factors in the situation are the students who were never directly in contact with the counselor. I find it difficult to believe that fifty different students would all have arrived at the same conclusion simultaneously. I am sure that the experience meant different things to different people and that they could all have used a different kind of counseling strategem. It might have been better to encourage each of the students to come to discuss the matter with the counselor individually so that their feelings could have been expressed fully. The business of them all stealing and then all wanting to make restitution just seems a little bit too pat.

HAROLD KOZUMA

I believe this case was badly mishandled in a variety of ways, even though I can sympathize with the counselor. It is my intention to comment on a number of basic mistakes that he made.

He should have not made any quick or rash promises. In a new situation the counselor should stall for time to think things over, especially if he is not too sure of himself or what to do. I assume that, had he done this, he wouldn't have acted so impetuously. He should not have acted as the agent of this gang of crooks. He is not a liaison man between the students and the storekeepers. He is not to get involved. He is a counselor, not an advocate or an accessory. He should have informed others of the general situation and what he planned to do, or at least have asked for guidance—and at the same time gain protection. A counselor should always protect himself against unusual situations. One should never promise confidentiality! This is a very subtle point and one not too well understood. First of all, one must never promise confidentiality blindly. If a student says to me, "I want to tell you something. Do you promise to keep it confidential?" I look at him in amazement and say, "How can I promise to keep something a secret when I don't know what it is? Perhaps you are planning to blow up the administration building or to poison the dean or to kill yourself. I certainly will not promise you confidentiality about something that I don't know anything about." Now, I have found that taking this attitude (or some variation of it) almost always shocks the individual and leads him to tell me what he was going to tell me anyway. So, taking this line doesn't lose you any secrets and, for all I know, will get you some. And now, if the person does tell you his secret, you still shouldn't promise confidentiality after you know! I have been put in this position many times by a person telling me something and *then* asking me to promise confidentiality. As I say, even then I refuse it! What I say in these conditions is the following: "You told me these things because you know that you can trust me. If you didn't trust me, you certainly wouldn't have told me in the first place. I can only tell you this: I didn't promise and I refuse to promise you anything. You have to depend on my judgment and my memory. I will keep it a secret if I remember that it is a secret and if your secret should be kept secret. Let me warn you never to ask anyone to keep a secret. If you don't trust them, just don't tell them. Promises aren't worth much." The good counselor must always use his judgment; and so must the person who confides in him. To promise confidentiality is to do several wrong things:

1. You indicate that you as a professional person aren't to be trusted until you take the "oath;"
2. You promise to keep a secret when you know there are times you cannot keep the secret;
3. You actually weaken yourself and demean your profession by making such promises.

JOHN D. MULLEN

As I read the incident, it seemed to me at first that there was really no problem, since I felt that the counselor handled the situation well. But when the policeman intervened, I realized that the whole matter had very serious implications for all parties concerned. As a consequence, many questions presented themselves about the counselor's handling of this case.

First of all, the counselor became legally involved in the issue as soon as he heard about it. He became an accessory after the fact, the recipient of information about a number of crimes committed by a "ring" of thieves. Whether or not he should have been implicated is academic: he *was*, simply by listening. When we don't know what we are going to hear when someone wants to tell us something, we have no way of avoiding participation and responsibility.

While organizing the offenders and placing them all in the same boat seemed like a good solution, in the sense of providing them with a model for retribution and learning, the counselor, nonetheless, placed himself in an extremely vulnerable position. The counselor made an error in how he handled the matter, even though it was the right thing to do, since he did become the recipient of the police's attention. I believe that the counselor should not have acted unilaterally, but should have made the problem known to the school authorities, preferably with the students' approval, but certainly with their full awareness of his intentions. The counselor could still maintain his integrity by keeping the names of the students confidential.

It strikes me that the counselor might have resolved the dilemma more effectively by asking each student to make individual restitution either by returning the merchandise or its monetary equivalent to the proper stores. This could have been done by mail or by use of various delivery services. In this manner each student's anonymity would have been protected and the process would not serve to indict the whole school. Since individuals committed the misdeeds, individuals should make restitution and be held responsible, not the institution. The names of the offenders might never have been revealed to the counselor. Had the counselor been able to say to the young girl immediately, "Tell each one to either return the goods to the store anonymously or send the store money in envelopes without any return addresses," this simple advice might have prevented a great deal of trouble. The police would not have intervened. If police intervention did occur, the counselor could have honestly admitted to knowledge of the thefts on the basis of rumor. He could admit that because he believed the rumor, he had suggested to the informant that all offenders make restitution.

JAMES N. PEPPER

The counselor was right in dealing with the matter. The American Personnel and Guidance Association's ethical standards code (Section B, paragraph 1) states:

> The member's primary obligation is to respect the integrity and promote the welfare of the counselee or client with whom he is working.

Apparently the problem of stealing was a great concern to Georgia and to the other students who had stolen from the department store. Their feeling of guilt certainly would affect their school work, and so the counselor had a responsibility to the students in doing whatever he could to help them with this out-of-school problem.

Whether the counselor handled the conscience money properly by returning it in an anonymous manner is questionable. Paragraph 4 of the above section states:

> The counselee or client should be informed of the conditions under which he may receive counseling assistance at or before the time he enters the counseling relationship. This is particularly true in the event there exists conditions of which the counselee would not likely be aware.

Counselors do not generally have judicial immunity from divulging privileged information. If the police in this particular case had wanted to demand the names of members of the "criminal ring" the counselor would have had to break the confidence of the counselees. In view of this possibility, of which the counselor should have been fully aware, perhaps a better way to handle the problem would have been to contact both the school authorities and the police officials; and without divulging the names of the students involved, inform them of the matter and tell them what he was planning to do to help the students make up their wrong-doings. Another method might have been to suggest to the students that they handle the problem individually, having each student return the money to the stores on his own. Sending cash in plain envelopes might have served as a better lesson for the students than the method used.

What concerns me is that the students had someone intercede for them and that a "kid glove" treatment was employed. I am not convinced that the counselor was successful in conveying an important moral message to the students which he could have effected had he induced them to make more personal kinds of reparations.

Our code of ethical standards sheds light on the key issue of confidentiality in this incident:

> In the event the counselor's or the client's conditions are such to require others to assume responsibility for him or when there is a clear and imminent danger to the counselor or to others, the member is expected to report this fact to appropriate responsible authority or take such other emergency measures as the situation demands.

This counselor took a lot of responsibility on his own by not informing the police, the school authorities, or the parents, of the children's actions.

Overall, I feel the counselor handled the matter adequately, although the bigger issue is: could he have handled it better in the sense of teaching the students a moral lesson? In such tough situations a counselor would do well to read the ethical standards of the APGA or to consult with an older, more experienced counselor.

MANFORD A. SONSTEGARD

Experiences of other counselors in similar cases and the findings of research indicate the purpose these youngsters had in shoplifting. Students in seventh, eighth, ninth, and tenth grades are confronted with a constant struggle to find their place among their peers; this struggle begins at varying ages, depending upon the individual youngsters. Georgia had suddenly become aware of the importance of gaining a place in her peer group. In fact it was more important to gain the approval of her peers than to gain the approval of adults and follow adult standards. Members of a subgroup are assured of a place in the group to the extent that they are able to follow the subgroup's norms and behavior. Even youngsters who disapprove of this behavior are forced to conform in order to keep their place in the subgroup.

By way of explanation, two incidents may be related. In the first incident, a group of about twelve girls had been shoplifting during the time that they were in the eighth and ninth grades. One of the girls who was a friend, but not involved in the group, became concerned and was able to convey the information to the principal; thus, the rampant shop-lifting was brought to light. A number of group counseling sessions were held with the girls. What happened in the group sessions was quite revealing. First, the great desire and struggle of each of the girls to become part of a group was apparent. The pilfering was started by a few of the girls, and the rest felt that they would have to follow the norms which were set by those who appeared to be the leaders. The fear that they would be considered "chicken" unless they went along with the leaders started the practice, and then the fear that they would not be accepted as part of the group if they violated its norms continued it. Once it got underway, some of them began to have second thoughts about what they were doing, but they were at a loss about how to get disentangled. One way was to enlist the help of an adult.

Another case, by way of illustration, is a case of a ninth-grade girl who was dismissed from school for wearing a miniskirt which might be described as micro-mini. Mary was on the honor roll. She was a person who had always done the right thing and the teachers couldn't understand why Mary would do a thing like this. She had always been concerned about adult approval. In the ninth grade she suddenly became aware that having a place among one's peers was important. How to achieve this place, with her past reputation of being a good girl, required some ingenuity. Of course, her appearance at school in a very short skirt brought reports from the teacher to the principal and the principal then felt he had to take action. Mary was called to his office and informed that she could not attend school because wearing a short dress was against the rules. She was told that she could not come back to school unless she dressed more appropriately. Mary was not particularly upset about being kicked out of school. She related that she had expected something like this to happen and that she had her clothes laid out at home so that it would take her only a short time to change into proper attire and go back to school.

When asked how she felt upon returning to school, she said, "I felt better than I ever had in my life." The counselor interpreted this to mean that now she had the complete backing of the other students. She was "in," so to speak. Mary said, "By golly, that is right. I never thought of it that way." In fact, she related a conversation between two of her friends, one of whom didn't understand why she wasn't in school. The other friend said, "Oh, haven't you heard," and when she told the story of Mary's encounter with the school officials she was met with disbelief: "Oh, not Mary. She doesn't do things like that." To which her friend replied, "You don't know Mary." The implication was, "She is really one of us." In fact, Mary then related what satisfaction she got from the fact that the teachers turned against her and she was now actually a member of her peer group. The approval of her peer group was more important to her at this stage of her development than the approval of the teachers and the principal.

If the counselor had made an effort to find out what purpose the girls had in shoplifting he would have been in the position to help them understand their behavior by disclosing their purposes to them. In this incident, the counselor actually became a cat's paw for the students in getting them out of the tight situation. This does not mean that the counselor should not help them resolve the predicament in which they find themselves. But if it is to be a learning situation, the youngsters must take the action and not the counselor.

A client-counselor relationship, unlike a lawyer-client relationship, is not considered privileged. In other words, the counselor can be held as an accessory after the fact. Consequently, the counselor in this situation must be prepared to face the consequences if he refuses to divulge the names of the youngsters. Recently, in a similar situation, a young woman reporter chose to go to jail rather than reveal the names of the persons who had given her the information on which she based a feature story.

In this case, the police department would have been within their legal rights to demand that the names of the youngsters be revealed. It is true, as the counselor points out, that there would be little to be gained by this; however, state and district attorneys are not always so lenient and neither are police chiefs. Consequently, if a school counselor promises confidentiality and proceeds to be bound by his promises, he will have to be reconciled to the fact that he may be prosecuted by the authorities.

In this particular incident, the counselor's role should have been one of helping the youngsters, through group counseling approaches, to understand the purpose for their behavior. Second, he should help them to find a solution to the immediate predicament, but the solution must be the youngsters' under the guidance of the counselor, and the action that is to be taken must be pursued by the youngsters themselves. No purpose is served and no constructive learning occurs when a counselor assumes this responsibility himself.

E. G. WILLIAMSON

I think the counselor handled the situation beautifully, in exactly the proper way to maintain confidentiality, still maintain responsibility to uphold the law, and help students learn that they must obey the law. She said the right things at the right time and I think she should have no question about refusing the police officer's request to violate confidentiality.

I would have laughed at the notion that one could have been charged with the crimes as an accessory. I don't think any court would have taken any such action, particularly in Children's Court. The counselor did well in explaining his position to the chief of police who, fortunately, was a reasonable man and dropped the matter. No, the counselor should not have told the policeman, the principal, or anyone else about the individuals involved. Of course, most counselors are not covered by a privileged communication statute as are lawyers and doctors. We always operate under the risk of being haled into court, but there haven't been very many such court cases, according to my reading of the literature. Were I haled into court I would just be honest with the judge, ask to see him in chambers and tell him the story off-the-record, and appeal to his sense of humanity to give the youngsters a break. One important point: you have to keep your confidentiality but you also have to learn ways of communicating confidential information without violating that confidentiality. If this sounds contradictory, it is. But there are times when one can say; "I can't tell you the details, but this girl is having trouble and I think we can work the thing out if you will just let us alone." Now most people—adults, parents, principals, policemen—will usually respond to that kind of appeal.

6

Drugs in the School

CRITICAL INCIDENT

Background

The school in which I am the counselor is located in an urban area and serves mostly middle-class children. We have the usual problems of truancy, fighting, lateness, refusal to cooperate, and so on. A recent class of problems is the taking of drugs. Every once in a while a child comes to school "stoned"—in a state of confusion, apparently drunk, with a silly smile, unable to comprehend, and in many ways a zombie. In such cases, we call the parents, refer them to their family doctors, and place the primary responsibility on the parents for handling such cases. This problem is becoming more common and presently is the subject of considerable discussion in our school.

I run a counseling group composed of ninth-grade children, who are first referred by their teachers, administrators, and so on, but who are not compelled to attend the group sessions unless they agree to. The group meets after class, thereby avoiding conflict with other classes and responsibilities.

Incident

The incident developed in the group. A discussion occurred on drugs, chiefly about pot (marijuana), and the tenor of the meeting was that pot was not harmful, not addicting, and actually beneficial. Everyone in the group accepted the notion that pot was socially and physically beneficial and that society was hypocritical in condemning it. I entered into the discussion and took the point of view that I did not really know whether or not pot was as harmful as some people believed, that I was not a bluenose, that I smoked (I smoked in this group, by the way), and that I drank.

As I was talking, one of the group pulled out a rather large, crudely made cigarette made of bluish colored paper, and lit up, taking a deep breath of smoke and holding it. He passed the cigarette to the one next to him who imitated him and then passed it to another student who without smoking it passed it right in front of me to still another student who also inhaled the smoke deeply; it was passed along until about six of the eight students had drawn on it. One of the students, when the butt was very small, used a curious instrument (which I later learned was called a roach holder) to aid him in smoking the cigarette right down to the very end. During all this time, no one said anything and all eyes, I felt, were on me.

I kept trying to think what I should do, and when the cigarette was smoked to the end and discarded, I asked, "Was that pot?"

"I don't know," said the fellow who took out the cigarette, "but it sure felt good."

"How do you know what you smoke isn't pot?" one of the students asked.

"Yeah," another said, "maybe you smoke tailor-made pot."

"Look fellows, this is serious. This is a school, and if that was marijuana, you are violating the laws, and so am I for letting you smoke."

"Well, teacher, we aren't supposed to smoke cigarettes either in school, but you let us during the group meeting."

"That's true. I felt that since we were meeting after school, cigarette smoking would be OK, especially since I do it myself."

"But it is illegal, isn't it," another asked me, "for you, a teacher, to permit students to smoke in school?"

"Well, I don't know," I said. "Maybe with you older kids, smoking ordinary cigarettes after school even on school property isn't too bad."

We went on in this fashion, the students not wanting to admit it was marijuana they had smoked, and arguing that if I smoked tobacco they could smoke marijuana, that it wasn't too bad, and so on, when all of a sudden the tenor of the meeting changed.

"It was marijuana, and I intend to smoke it here if you intend to smoke tobacco. I have every right to smoke what I want," one of the students stated flatly.

"Well, if you do, you cannot stay in this group," I retorted. "I will not countenance violation of the law."

"I don't care about the group. You are a hypocrite. You admit that you shouldn't smoke tobacco because it is bad for your health, and that you know it isn't good for the health of those in the same room as you, and that you shouldn't allow us teenage kids to smoke cigarettes in school, and yet you draw the line at marijuana when you admit you aren't convinced it is harmful. What is your answer to that?"

The whole group was alive in the conflict, something very different and more meaningful than any prior discussion. I felt pushed to the wall.

"I don't care if I am logical or illogical. I would get into trouble if it got out that I permitted smoking pot in school. I'd be fired, be in disgrace. As of now, I am not sure that it was marijuana you smoked."

"Well, it was," my chief antagonist said, and the others who had smoked nodded. "And, like I said, I am getting fed up with being pushed around by everybody. Remember you said that in this group we could do or say what we wanted so long as we didn't hurt anyone or damage school property."

"I did say that, but I didn't mean you could break the law."

"You admit you do permit breaking the law when it comes to smoking tobacco on the school property."

"Well, I am telling all of you right here and now that you are not going to smoke pot in my group, and since you made such an issue of it, I won't smoke tobacco either and will not permit anyone else to."

One by one the members of the group got up and left. That was the end of that group. I felt as though they had punished me for mistreating them.

Discussion

The members of the group avoid me and try not to come to see me, as though I had violated their confidence. I assume that part of their attitude is attributable to their resentment of the older generation. I don't feel that they really want to smoke pot in my presence as much as they feel that I didn't handle myself properly. I still think that I did the only proper thing, although I wonder whether in my initial remarks about letting them do what they wanted I should have indicated that they could not violate the law. I wonder also whether my smoking tobacco and allowing them to, for the purpose of creating a casual and permissive climate, was a mistake.

Questions

1. How would you have handled this problem assuming that you had done what I had done initially (permitted tobacco smoking, etc.)?

2. Should I have tried to anticipate such activities and have discussed them in advance?

3. Should I have simply made no issue about their smoking that strange-colored cigarette?

COMMENTS ON THE INCIDENT

THE EDITORS

A counselor can chart two general courses: be extremely cautious and not venture into unsafe areas, or be bold and try new things. The general strategy one takes is a matter of personal choice. The latter is more exciting and more dangerous. We can accomplish more—but at the same time we can be taking greater risks. After all, pioneers did have a high death rate.

It would seem that if one tries new things and one takes risks, that one should have a good deal of confidence in oneself and a feeling of confidence in what one is doing. If one is untrue to oneself or puts on an act, or if one takes a risk but isn't willing to take the consequences, the outcome can be disastrous. That is, if you swim out from shore, be sure you know how to swim, or that you have the protection of a lifeguard, or a safety vest—otherwise you may be in for a tragedy.

In this incident, the counselor ventured out too far and didn't quite know how to handle himself when things took an unexpected turn. He got rattled, attempted to assert his authority, tried to get members of a group to go along with him, and failed. In reading this incident—as in the case of the others—the reader should attempt to empathize with the hapless counselor and see where he went wrong and what he could have done to prevent a failure.

THOMAS W. ALLEN

It seems that the counselor in this instance is like the man who, having jumped from the top of a building, changes his mind half way down. Certainly, he has managed to stack the deck against himself and the therapeutic process he hopes to foster.

First, there is the question of the mix. All the members of the group seem to have been selected on the basis of the fact that they posed similar problems for the school. Thus, the counselor has increased the probability of "contagion," the likelihood that the group members will reinforce one another's undesired behavior. He thus deprives himself of one of the most important resources that the group counselor has at his disposal, the diversity of strengths and weaknesses and styles of adjustment within the group. With such heterogeneity, the counselor can utilize the success with which some group members have met the issues that trouble others to help the latter learn to cope with them. Therefore, the more homogeneous the group, the less flexibility the counselor has and the more likely he is to face a united front dedicated to preserving the member's current mode of adjustment.

Second, there are the circumstances under which the group meets. Although we cannot be certain, it appears that the members of the group were recruited with the help of a subtle form of coercion. The least that might have been done to make the enterprise more appealing to the members of the group would have been to schedule it during schooltime so that by choosing to participate, a guy could at least find respite from the rigors and unpleasantries of the classroom.

Whatever difficulties adhere to the foregoing, it is clear that they do not present insuperable obstacles to the attainment of the counselor's objectives. Of greater significance is the counselor's failure to perceive the advantages of admitting fallibility. He is not alone in this oversight which seems endemic to our culture. Indeed, much of our so-called war of generations seems to arise from the feeling of the elders that they must maintain their authority by preserving the illusion of infallibility. The belief appears to be that unless we are seen as infallible we shall have no influence at all on the young. Quite the contrary seems to be the case.

The "doctrine of parental infallibility," in all of its forms, is frequently invoked to terminate as impertinence any line of youthful reasoning that we find unappealing. This serves, of course, to condemn us to a condition wherein our demands of, and desires for, our children must pass muster in terms of their standards. We must persuade and convince them, eschewing the convenience of *ex cathedra* ("because *I*, a school official, say so, that's why!") rule. There are, however, crucial compensations. One of these is liberation from the role of the tyrant who must be routed if the self-respect of youth is to be secured and if youth's maturity is to be validated by abstaining from pretenses to omniscience ("Father knows best"), let alone to omnipotence, we are freed from the need to be forgiven for human fallibility and the imperfection of the world. How many of us bridle at the failure of our children or our students to take *our* humanity into account, to consider *our* problems and feelings? We might feel like saying, "After all, life isn't exactly a bed of roses for us either, you know!" However, when the speaker is in a position to masquerade as some sort of demigod, this plaint loses much of its credibility, appearing to the young as yet another invidious attempt to manipulate them.[1]

In this incident, a large part of the counselor's undoing seems to have been generated by his effort to maintain his supremacy. When provoked, he feels that he must rise to meet the challenge. This seems to be precisely what his "tormentor" had in mind. By these means he apparently intended to undercut the counselor and wrest control of the group from him. It is also likely that he was bent on producing further evidence of the hypocrisy of adults and of the speciousness of their good intentions justifying his hostility toward them and their system.

The provocateur's strategy is reminiscent of that employed by Brer Fox in the Uncle Remus tale of the Tar Baby.[2] He provided the counselor with something that the latter was certain to see as a threat to his prestige and let him mire himself inextricably in difficulty to save face. Had Brer Rabbit been less concerned with his place in the forest pecking-order, with the deference that was his due, he would have easily eluded his pursuer's clutches. Similarly, had the counselor been less preoccupied with defending his special position, his authority, and his ability to control the situation, he too might have emerged from this situation relatively unscathed.

Suppose the counselor had refused to rise to the bait dangled so craftily before him? Suppose he had resisted this gilt-edged invitation to discredit himself by invoking his authority? Suppose he had met the statement, "It was marijuana, and I intend to smoke it here if you intend to smoke tobacco. I have every right to smoke what I want," with a refusal to do battle. For instance, the counselor might have terminated this confrontation by focusing on the dynamics of the situation, e.g., "Could it be, Jack, that you feel that you are entitled to do whatever you please and that it is important to prove that no one can stop you?" Of course, to be successful, such an interpretation must be delivered with unmistakable goodwill and objectivity. It must not appear to be a club with which the counselor seeks to redress his personal grievances or bring dissidents to heel.

Fortunately, there are alternative modes of implementing a refusal to do battle, other ways of evading the Tar Baby. The counselor might,

---

[1] Not long ago a sixteen-year-old girl was hospitalized in a psychiatric hospital for failure in school, undependability, "wildness," and, moreover, experimentation with drugs. There were many indications that her behavior was, in large measure, directed against her parents and the demands they made of her. She fortified her "right" to do as she pleased by construing her parents' desperate attempts to protect her as arbitrary abridgements of her freedom designed to enhance their own status. Father, a very successful man in a highly prestigious profession, was in her eyes a god, transcendent. It was then patently ridiculous to think that his behavior toward her could be influenced appreciably by his fear for her. That he might act precipitously, brusquely, or stupidly, out of terror was inconceivable to her. No, Father was olympian, exempt from the apprehensions assailing ordinary mortals. *His* actions were inevitably calculated and she was the victim of his tyranny against which she was justified in rebelling.

Thus, the ascendence, so long a heady wine for Father, turned to vinegar in his mouth.

[2] Joel Chandler Harris, *Complete Tales of Uncle Remus* (Boston: Houghton Mifflin, 1955). This story is, to my mind, essential reading for counselors.

for instance, have given voice to his feelings concerning the "sudden" turn of events with which he found himself confronted. He might have articulated his concern for the legal risks they were taking—as a concern rather than as a threat or a fact. He could have expressed his sense of helplessness in dealing with the situation, a situation in which he bore heavy responsibility but possessed little control. He could have shared the difficulty he experienced in discerning a viable course of action.

At this point he might have asked his "chief antagonist" to play his (the counselor's) role, while he or another group member assumed the part of the challenger. The drama would begin with the challenge, "It was marijuana . . ." The "counselor" would be invited to respond as he thought his character should. The group would then be invited to discuss the scene. *What happened? Was this way better? Why?* In fact, each group member could be given the opportunity to "be" the counselor. Attention might then be focused on what each member of the group felt as they played the counselor. The counselor, in turn, might relate his reactions concerning the various solutions which the group offered, e.g., "I wish I could be as calm about it as Larry was." "While I watched Mike, I started wondering. Maybe it would make sense to . . ."

A good deal might be gained, as well, by having the group play out what they think would happen if the janitor, the principal, a parent, or the cop on the corner, walked into the room while they were smoking pot. A group member could be designated to play the intruder with another, probably the counselor's provocateur, appointed as the "director." As the drama unfolds, the "director's" task is to supply the scenes which follow upon the original event. The succeeding discussion might then well consider issues such as the following:

> Would it happen like that? Why or why not?
> How does each group member feel about the various possibilities?
> How would they feel if they were in charge?
> If they were the counselor's son? His wife?

Finally, the counselor could well have analyzed the group even after his pyrrhic show of strength ("Well, if you do, you cannot stay in this group. I will not countenance . . ."). There is, after all, the fine art of disengagement, of strategic retreat, of telling it like it is when "it" is that one has blundered, of admitting with the bumper sticker wit, "I came. I saw. I blew it." Suppose, for example, events in the group had taken the following course:

> "It was marijuana . . . and I have every right to smoke what I want."
> "Well, if you do, you cannot stay in the group, etc."
> "I don't care about the group . . . etc."

with this modification—

COUNSELOR: Hmmm, you've got a point . . . I guess you've got me. It doesn't make much sense, does it? Like there are two sets of rules . . . I was playing by one and asking you to play by the other. If that happened to me, I'd be pretty teed off. . . .

Might not this have been the safety rope to halt the counselor's disastrous plunge?

BENJAMIN BELDEN

This counselor has learned the power of group revenge. It is not enough, if you wish to be a group counselor, to say that you are warm, understanding, and accepting. You have to demonstrate these qualities in your actions. Arbitrarily setting limits, preaching, and mouthing fine words are actually destructive of the intentions of group meetings. If the group members sense indecision, hypocrisy, or naivete, the false veneer of permissiveness employed by some counselors in schools gives way. This is what seems to have happened here.

I would have liked more information: Was this strictly a group of drug offenders? What was the sexual composition? What goals were stated to be the purpose of the group? How long had the group met? What issues developed? Of course, the more information that is given, the more comfortable one can be in making comments.

For example, I think the counselor was mistaken in thinking she was allowing the students to smoke as a basis for improving the psychological climate. She was really buying their approval. She thought she would gain popularity by permitting them to do this, but instead they saw her as lording it over them via her bounty. She got around the law in the same way the students got around her rules. Would she have been so "generous" in her permissiveness had she not been a cigarette smoker herself?

It seems that the students planned to make their move, perhaps to test her, during this session. Perhaps they were tired of what they saw as shallow hypocrisy. I think they felt they weren't getting anywhere. The pot was ready, we know, and the discussion about it didn't "just happen." The counselor may have headed off this confrontation incident had she actively probed the genesis of the discussion and had tried to deal with the real issues instead of just talking blandly. She seemed to be more interested in being a nice guy, hurting no one's feelings, sticking to the straight and narrow of permissive leadership rather than being sensitive to what was going on. Actually, as I read it, the group was generous. They gave her the opportunity to be a real leader. They were saying, "Help us. We have problems. We are tired of this Mickey Mouse discussion. We have real and important things to discuss. Let's get on with it." That is how I read this discussion about marijuana. It was a kind of insurance to protect themselves from possible punitive consequences, and the discussion was an attempt to get her sympathetic understanding. They talked themselves into believing that pot was "actually beneficial" and then they tested her. And she failed the test.

Now why did they light up at that time? Notice that this smoking incident occurred at the moment when the counselor entered the discussion. What a slap in the face! As I see it, they were saying, "Look, Miss Counselor, we do what we want, especially when you want us to listen to you." I believe this is an example of group punishment resulting from their feeling of betrayal.

The counselor's comments are a masterpiece of naivete. Clearly she was frightened. Her authority, her values, her friendliness, and even her "deal" (I won't bother you if you don't bother me) was attacked. "Was that pot?" she asked. I feel she tried to be a "nice guy," sweet and benign, but that is not enough in being a group counselor. Effective counseling and being "nice" are not the same thing, client-centered counseling notwithstanding.

The discussion that followed after admission that it was indeed pot is a classical example of the logical genius of the young and the gullibility and misconceptions of adults. "Look, fellows," she pleads, "this is a school . . ." Students hear this kind of plea day in and day out. To think that they should want to conform to the rules of society because of her fear is just too much to believe. She opened the door, as it were, by her apparent permissiveness but when the wild horses started to come out, she begged them to close the door. As I see it, she just doesn't understand the younger generation, or at least that rebellious portion that goes so far as to smoke marijuana, and this, fortunately or unfortunately, is a rather large group and, in some localities, a majority group.

Such kids are undergoing a painful adjustment to the adult role. They want to be heard, recognized, reckoned with. They want the world to know they exist. They reject society and its values in many cases. They may have welcomed the group as an opportunity for a real meeting with an adult. But all the counselor could see was that they were violating the laws! All the more remarkable since, in greatest probability, she, too, was violating laws by letting them smoke tobacco. One kind of plant is OK to smoke, but not another kind, she said in effect. The real issue was a power contest between students and the establishment, of which the counselor was a visible and vulnerable representative. She was drawn into a debate and, when defeated, she begged and then threatened. Her behavior created more distance, and her final denial of their right to smoke even cigarettes gave the students no option but to take revenge.

What could she have done? First, she should remember that she had no proof that what was smoked was indeed marijuana. A lot of things, including catnip and oregano have been smoked in the belief that it was *cannabis sativa*. So, of her own knowledge she did not really know what it was they were smoking and, incidentally, neither did they. Then, she could have said, armed with her knowledge of her innocence, "Beautiful, you have me over a barrel. Now you have made me powerless, unable to handle you, and at your mercy. Isn't that just wonderful, just what you would like to do to all adults?"

The counselor could then take the butt when it came around to her, hold it, smile and say something like this, "Well, you are committing a crime, and now let us try to find out why it is so important for you to do what you want when you want to." The important thing here is not to be discomfited, not to get into an argument, not to threaten, not to show fear. What she should do is probe for their motivations, the "why" behind their senseless actions. "Did you have to show that you were united against me?" she might ask, prodding them for an explanation of their behavior. "Now that you have done it, do you feel better?" she might ask. "You have proved that you can do what you want to do, that ten of you are more than one of me, that you can threaten me. You have succeeded. Now, what comes next?" The counselor should not attempt to be stern or disapproving. To play helpless might be her best strategy, or she may even laugh at their attempts to put her on the spot. Her attack might be even this: "How about taking this roach (assuming she knows the current lingo), framing it, and putting a sign under it: 'We, the biggest bunch of nitwits in this school, used this to try to upset our counselor.' "

The big concept is to appear to go along with a group that tries to put a counselor on the spot, so that they can see what they are doing. To attempt to contradict them, threaten them, or scold them is, first of all, contrary to all principles of group counseling and, second, highly likely to make the students ugly. If she cannot be smart enough, there is always the procedure of last resort: play helpless. She could admit they got to her, they were smarter than she, they trapped her, she was wrong. Such honesty, especially with the young, is always more effective than a phoney front of competence or a scared attempt to threaten.

GEORGE J. BREEN

The counselor obviously was extremely lax in his failure to establish or enforce effective ground rules for the operation of the group. The most blatant example of this poor judgment was the counselor's violation of the school's smoking policy. The issue here is not one of whether the policy was (or is) right or wrong but that the policy or rule prohibiting smoking in the school existed. Bypassing this rule, particularly as overtly as the counselor did, simply opened the floodgates for further problems in the group. It is my strong belief that school counselors all too frequently make this type of mistake especially when their motivation is to gain the unqualified approval of the group members.

The counselor's commitment to such group norms, as "Let's be buddies" and "anything goes" was clearly self-defeating. This was highlighted by the fact that the incident became critical at the very moment the counselor stated that he was "not a bluenose," and that he smoked and drank. Furthermore, the counselor made an even greater mistake by allowing to go unchallenged, especially in light of the recent objective evidence available, the statements by the group members that "pot was not harmful, not addicting, and actually beneficial." Ideas such as these are the raw data that group interaction is made of. When these ideas are clearly incorrect, or at least debatable, and are allowed to go unquestioned by a group leader, problems of the type encountered in this incident certainly come as no great surprise.

This particular incident perhaps can be seen best from the viewpoint of the counselor as a role model. If we accept the premise that *certain* distinct human behaviors, values, and attitudes can be more effective, self-enhancing, and fulfilling to an individual than others, and that a counselor can encourage the development of a saner life style by serving as a model for these positive values, we can then clearly see that the counselor in this incident overlooked this important role. For example, his behavior obviously was hypocritical when he admitted that cigarette smoking was bad for one's health yet permitted himself and the group members to smoke. In addition, he contradicted himself further when he stated that "he did not really know whether or not pot was as harmful as some people believed," yet acted as if the smoking of pot was sacrilegious when he suspected its occurrence in the group. In short, the counselor did not seem to have established a clear and consistent philosophical value system particularly with regard to vital student issues. The confrontation that the group members posed by defiantly smoking pot in his presence impresses me as an obvious test of the vague and contradictory value set of the counselor.

It is my firm belief that much of the gap that frequently and overtly exists between youth and adults originates in circumstances similar to the critical incident. Young people are searching for answers in areas of personal ethics. They look to those in positions of influence or authority for such answers but usually do not receive them because these adults themselves have not coped effectively with such problems. Or, when solutions are provided by educators or counselors, they are veiled in moral platitudes, rigid absolutes, and stereotyped responses.

Counselors should assume more responsibility for "reality issues" than they do and take stands on values supported by the objective evidence available; in short, counselors must communicate clearly to students what *is* better behavior and what the personal consequences of its denial will be.

C. H. PATTERSON

This incident might well be entitled "Tested and Found Wanting," "Mary Jane and the Counselor," or "The Phony Counselor."

Two main points are illustrated by this incident. The first is simple: no counselor should attempt to engage in group counseling without special training. It seems obvious that this counselor has had no preparation in group counseling. His early behavior represents a classic example of the misunderstanding of a "permissive" atmosphere. He is actually concerned with rules, rather than limits, but the rules are applied in terms of their effect on him. A rule can be violated "as long as it doesn't hurt me." Limits are necessary, but must be consistently adhered to with, however, the possibility of modification for good reasons after discussion with the group. The counselor, however, never met the group on the issue of limits.

Second, it illustrates the impossibility of gaining the acceptance, liking, and cooperation of clients (students) by attempting to ingratiate oneself, identify with them, or "buy" a relationship. Students recognize phoniness and are experts in handling it. The counselor ends up looking very much like the stereotype system that the students see as hypocritical.

The counselor asks how the problem could have been handled, given the fact that smoking had been permitted, which the counselor admits may have been a mistake. In the extremely unlikely event that a professionally trained counselor would have made such a mistake, it should have been handled in the way any mistake should be handled; that is, honestly admitting to the mistake and discussing its implications. Such honesty might have saved the situation. The counselor in this case departed from any semblance of a counseling relationship and destroyed any possibility of salvaging the situation.

That a drug (marijuana) was involved is irrelevant to the basic problem. In other times, students have tested counselors by smoking ordinary cigarettes (which is illegal in most schools) in the same kind of situation. The principles are the same; only the behaviors of youth today are different in their testing of limits and the honesty of human relationships.

JAMES N. PEPPER

This incident is replete with real living problems, and seems to me to be worthy of extended discussion. Almost every paragraph includes some problem or some vital issue. Let me begin with some formal matters.

Group structuring.   Every group has a purpose and has certain laws or rules, expressed or understood. I get the distinct impression that this group did not have a well-understood structure, that the purposes weren't clear, that the relationships were not understood, that the processes weren't defined, and that limitations weren't established. In such vaguely structured situations anxiety is intensified, people don't know where they stand or how to behave, confusion develops, and hostilities are unleashed. This is not necessarily bad. In some kinds of groups, extreme laxity is desired, giving individuals a chance to express themselves, their resentments, hostilities, and so on. Whether the counselor realized it or not, she failed to established a structure and thereby encouraged freedom—including freedom to rebel and attack, which is precisely what happened. And the teacher didn't like it one bit. She became privy to how those kids thought and felt—and she got scared and fell back on threats.

So, the first thing a good group worker does is to assess the individuals in the group, assess herself, assess the situation, and determine the extent of freedom she wants them to have. If, for example, she feels for one reason or another that the school policy is limiting, she must assert this right from the start so that everyone knows the rules. As I see it, she set no limits and when the kids got the spirit of the group, she changed the implied rules.

Example. I assume that it was against the school rules for a teacher to smoke in front of kids and also for the kids to smoke tobacco. When the teacher broke these rules, she was telling them loud and clear that she was violating institutional regulations. She joined them in defiance of the establishment. I read their early discussion of the values of "pot" as an attempt to get her to commit herself to their mythology. After all, who *really* knows whether tobacco and marijuana are dangerous in moderation? Who knows which of the two is the more dangerous? Suppose, as some believe, smoking tobacco is actually more dangerous than marijuana (the kids seemed to believe this), what then? I see the discussion as indicating that the children were reaching out to her, wanting her approval, needing her agreement. However, I think she did right in taking a know-nothing attitude because, after all, we still don't know. However, she should have taken a very strong negative attitude towards smoking in the school and should not have given them an example. She was saying "I don't care about rules" when she smoked and let them smoke, and they took her at her word.

Strategy. I think this counselor made a number of tactical errors. For example, she asked suddenly: "Was that pot?" If she had thought a bit more about things, she would have kept her blessed mouth shut, for what could they answer but yes? Let us suppose that in reality they were smoking tobacco or banana peelings or sage, and even let us suppose that the one who had brought in the blue cigarette knew this. Surely he would still have said yes to her question. Why should she have asked such a silly question? It would seem to me that if the counselor would have assumed that, as far as she was concerned, they were smoking tobacco and if she had said nothing, everything would have been much better. Her question was a direct provocation.

Even, let us say, if the cigarette had been marijuana and if she had been questioned by the authorities, she could answer in good conscience that she just didn't know what was in the cigarette, that she wasn't competent to analyze it—which would have been quite true.

Logic. I do wonder about the logic this counselor used. Let us examine it carefully. A student is told that if the cigarette is marijuana he is violating the laws and he responds that she too is violating the law in smoking tobacco. She admits this, saying "That's true," and then goes on, "Maybe with you older kids, smoking ordinary cigarettes after school even on school property isn't too bad." Then, after admitting that she was violating the law, she takes a stand about students violating the law. She will permit one kind of law-violation, but not another! Talk about situational ethics! And then, when the students insist they are smoking marijuana and that they intend to keep on doing so, she threatens them, telling them she will eject them from the group. In other words, "You have committed a crime, and if you continue to commit the crime, your punishment will be banishment from the group."

The students saw the illogic and the unfairness, and they rallied around on this issue, and as the counselor said, "The group was alive in this conflict." There was still time—since the counselor willy-nilly had managed to stir up a discussion—to save the day, as it were. But then the climax of the situation occurs in a most revealing (and damning) statement: "I don't care if I am logical or illogical. *I* would get into trouble . . ."

And that is the whole issue. This dumb counselor got herself into a situation that could have spelled trouble and she wanted to extricate herself. "I'd be fired, be in disgrace"—that was the real issue. She played with fire, saw herself in danger of being burned, and wanted out—at all cost.

Questions. Let me attempt to answer the counselor's three questions. First, had I gotten myself into this situation, which anyone could have done, I think the right thing would have been to be honest, confess that one had made a mistake in permitting any kind of smoking, and to say that from now on she didn't intend to smoke, and that she hoped no one else would smoke, but if they did, she would bring the matter of smoking (not mentioning what was smoked) to her superior for guidance. I would have put it something like this:

> Yes, you are right. I was wrong. I shouldn't have smoked, and I shouldn't permit you to. I want to take this up with my principal, if you don't mind, just to make certain I am not violating the law. I'll ask him whether under the circumstances if you smoke, would I be permitted *not* to discipline you or send you out of the group, but just let you stay without my express approval.

In this way she would let them know that she was not countenancing any law or rule violations, thus protecting herself and also the students. Just plain old-fashioned honesty is what was called for—not threats.

In reference to the second question, the answer is yes with a big strong exclamation point. Any counselor these days would have to assume that ninth-grade kids, given an opportunity to smoke, will smoke marijuana in a situation they see as free from threats. This is what a group counseling session is all about. In view of this likelihood, she should have actually gone to her superior and asked about permissible limits of student behavior. She might not have smoked herself, and if anyone had lit up, she could then point out that while she personally didn't disapprove of smoking, and might actually show her cigarettes to the group, that after all they were meeting on school property and they should, therefore, obey school rules or state laws, whichever the case may be.

In so far as the third question is concerned, and at the risk of sounding uncharitable, it seems to me that just because one is a teacher does not mean that one has the maturity and the judgment to counsel groups. Of course, she should not have made any issue about the cigarette. Of course, her question about it was foolish. Only one who knows what one is doing, who feels secure, who understands oneself and people, who is willing to take the responsibilities of group leadership, should assume it.

Her behavior was inadequate to say the least. She told the group implicitly that if the members acted in ways that would threaten her, she wanted
no part of them. In effect, she was inept and failed them.

STEVEN STEIN

The issue concerning one's decision to smoke either marijuana or
tobacco is a red herring in this particular incident. I see the protagonists
as fighting to achieve a core identity. The counselor laments: "I would
get into trouble if it got out that I permitted pot smoking in school. I'd
be fired, I'd be in disgrace." Therefore he is not taking responsibility as
an individual in his decision to prevent pot smoking on school grounds.
Rather, he is saying "I am trapped also, just like you are; I am a prisoner
of rules which I cannot control."

Both student and counselor are expressing feelings of helplessness.
Paralysis, impotence, weakness, and the loss of identity are the real issues
here. The dialogue expressed during this session reflects the utter hopelessness and despair that both adults and youth are experiencing in our
culture. This basic conflict revolves around forming an independent identity at the price of possible rejection from one's peers.

Instead of expressing viewpoints relating to deep, personal, individual concern, this dialogue deteriorates into an argument over which
ritual is best—mine or yours. I cannot help but agree with the students in
their allegations that the counselor is being hypocritical. Yet, it is my
opinion that the students must also fall prey to their own criticism.

We must cut through the surface ritual and jargon if our society is
going to become productive. We must learn to communicate with one
another in a more honest and authentic fashion. In our culture adolescents tend to think of adults as having vast amounts of power to control
them despite the fact that in reality rules are almost flaunted at will. Why
is so much energy used to batter down walls instead of creating new
pathways?

This is the existential trap. If the adolescent were truly free to do his
own thing, he wouldn't waste so much energy in tearing down others'
viewpoints. This tearing-down action probably protects him. It provides
the security of not facing his peers as an individual. I'm not stating that
disagreement and thirst for change are harmful; I am proposing that the
true hypocrisy and self-deluding behavior be brought to light.

Both the students and the counselor are deluding themselves. One is
a hypocrite when he hides behind a phoney role or ritual. Drug-taking is
a phony role or ritual. Drug-taking is phony since it doesn't allow the
individual to face acceptance or rejection from others without using a
marijuana, LSD, speed or hash mask. The counselor also hides behind a
mask. His mask is a phony role: "I only carry out the rules; I'm not really
a mean daddy, so give me some respect because I am so benevolent."

The counselor in this situation would be able to leave his phony
role if he were able to state the real issues in the following manner:

Yes, there are certain rules that I make here. At times they may be hypocritical. That is my responsibility. I want to face it. I can't help it if you are angry. You have a right to be angry. But stop hiding behind a phony issue. Let us make contact with one another as people. Maybe I let you smoke tobacco here because I wanted to be a good guy. OK—that's real. You have a right to attack me for being phony. But stop attacking me with all your drug talk. Be a man, tell me that you don't like to be conned, but don't try to con me in the process.

Let me learn from you and maybe you can learn from me. It is about time we started to be honest with one another.

7

Cry Rape!

CRITICAL INCIDENT

Background

I don't know whether this is a critical incident, but it sure was a problem for me and I think this problem can occur to others, too. One of the girls in the elementary school I work at liked to come into my office and kid around. I secretly enjoyed her; she was fourteen and physically very well developed, had a good sense of humor, and seemed to know everything and everybody. She would call me by my first name, and even though I would continually reprove her, she would laugh charmingly and continue to call me Charlie. She had very bad habits; her grades were poor; she smoked cigarettes and, I assumed from her free and easy way, that she was fairly accessible to the boys. I used to question her about that but her answer generally was, "Wouldn't you like to know?" When she started to sit on my desk, facing me with her legs apart, I began to realize that she was trouble—big trouble—and so I began to refuse to see her. She started following me around, calling me, and making a scene with the secretary if she couldn't see me, but I steadfastly refused to see her. I felt like a fool having gotten myself into this awkward situation. One night the phone rang at home and when I answered it, sure enough it was Merillee.

"I am going to get you, Charlie," she said, "and I'm going to get you good." I fell apart and told the whole story to my wife. She was a bit suspicious and she kept asking me whether I had encouraged her, whether I had been in any way intimate, and the more I told her the absolute truth the more I realized how foolish and stupid the whole situation was —a man of fifty being pursued and hounded by a girl of less than fifteen. The only thing that my wife could say was: "Just plain refuse to see her."

Incident

The very next day my secretary came into my office leading Merillee who was crying and shaking. Merillee sat down, and when my secretary left, I opened my door. Merillee was up like a cat and closed it and soon the two of us were fighting: I, trying to open the door and she, to close it. Afraid that the secretary would hear the commotion, I went back to my desk, sat down, and finally said, "Well, what the hell do you want?"

"This," she said, reaching into her bosom and exposing one of her breasts; and, at this, she began to scream, opened the door, and ran out. I sat in my chair, petrified, unable to believe the ghastly scene. She was seated on the floor of the outside office pulling her hair, her breast out, just screaming and screaming and calling me a "nasty old man."

At that moment I felt as though it were better if I could kill myself, certain that no one would ever believe in my innocence, and absolutely incredulous about this girl's behavior which seemed to make no sense to me at all. It wasn't that she wanted something from me, such as good grades or a good report; all I had done was to reject her when her behavior had become too intimate. The whole thing was just one big mysterious nightmare. I sat at my desk immobilized, not knowing what to do, and finally Merillee was taken away by the nurse, still crying out, "My father will get you, you nasty old man."

Discussion

I assumed that I was to be dismissed and even felt that perhaps I would be arrested and no one would believe my story. However, what happened was this: When the incident came to the principal's attention, he immediately called Merillee's mother and reported that her daughter was being taken home, and he told her what the secretary had told him. The mother said, "So, she has done it again?" The mother told the principal that this was the fourth time that Merillee had claimed she had been raped or attacked. The last time occurred several months ago. After

Merillee had gone to an eye doctor for an examination, she had gone to a police station to report that the doctor had molested her. The police had immediately gone to his office and talked to him. Luckily, several patients who were in the office had been there when Merillee came out, and each of them reported that she was friendly and calm, far different from how she had been a short time later.

The principal came in to see me some ten minutes after the incident occurred with some words of consolation! I appreciated his calling this girl's mother, which he told me he did to alert her that Merillee was on her way home and also to find out what kind of girl she was. No one can estimate the depth of my feelings of helplessness against the purposeless machinations of this little psychopath.

Questions

1. What can a counselor do to avoid such situations?

2. If one is unjustly accused of something, what is the best way of handling the problem?

COMMENTS ON THE INCIDENT

THE EDITORS

In every profession there are hazards, some physical, some emotional, some legal. In those professions where two people closet themselves from the rest of the world in a frank exchange of ideas and feelings, the possibility of misinterpretations of intentions, of the eruption of intense emotional relationships and the development of other potentially dangerous situations always exists. Part of the purpose for long term training in the professions is to weed out the unstable, the emotional exploiters, those who are likely to exploit, or be exploited by, others.

In this incident, a counselor allowed a relationship with a young female get to a point where his counselee found it possible to victimize him. Small deviations sometimes become large deviations. The power that a counselor has must be used with great discretion and with considerable caution. In this case no great harm was done: the counselor was lucky, perhaps undeservedly so.

Our consultants almost unanimously agree on the dangers of unprofessional relationships and suggest proper modes of behavior for school counselors and their counselees.

GEORGE J. BREEN

This case is an example of extremely inept counselor behavior that, if anything, encouraged the incident to occur. In the first place, the counselor had evidently permitted certain self-defeating student behaviors to take place in his office. For example, when it is openly stated that Merillee "used to like to come into my office and kid around" and, furthermore, that "I secretly enjoyed her," a wealth of possible trouble for the counselor emerges.

One of the most frequent gripes voiced by guidance counselors is the lack of time they have to counsel students. Clerical chores are usually listed as the chief obstacle for counselors, although recent studies indicate that school counselors frequently contradict themselves when asked in questionnaires to designate the actual amount of time invested in weekly clerical work (often, less than 20 percent). However, a more important example of the counselor's ineffective use of time occurs when students use the guidance office as a place to "kid around"—instead of a setting where students work at resolving their problems and concerns. There is little wonder in my mind why students often view the school counselor with little respect.

Charlie obviously recognized that Merillee had problems. "She had very bad habits: her grades were poor, she smoked cigarettes, and I assumed (a rather dubious assumption in view of the fact that there was no concrete evidence to substantiate his view!) from her free and easy way that she was fairly accessible to the boys." Yet he overlooked the obvious problems that the youngster had, thereby missing an opportunity to establish a counseling relationship which dealt with observable client issues. Instead, the counselor probed into a questionable problem of the student's sexual behavior, which he was poorly trained to cope with in the first place. In so doing, he probably encouraged Merillee's sexual provocation of him.

That the counselor "secretly enjoyed" the student is an example of an issue that, more often than not, is poorly dealt with in many counselor education programs. Instead of recognizing the reality that counselors are human and are likely to be "aware," on occasion, of members of the opposite sex, the exact opposite is frequently taught. The counselor in training would be censured if such thoughts were to occur!

Therefore, the counselor in this incident probably blamed himself severely for "secretly enjoying her." From the very beginning, he was ill-equipped to counsel Merillee because of his poor self-image, which probably stemmed from his sexual attraction to her. "I felt like a fool having gotten myself in this awkward situation" was just one of the many irrational thoughts that contributed to the counselor's ineffectiveness in the situation. Other ideas probably included: "I am no good for enjoying her," "What would my wife think of me if she discovered my thoughts?" "I should be punished for having such terrible thoughts!" These self-defeating thoughts could only create confused and highly negative feelings within the counselor, thus limiting his effectiveness at best. Finally, his means of avoiding the situation by refusing to see the student quite likely gave Merillee further evidence of the counselor's fear of her.

What could the counselor have done to avoid this situation in light of this discussion? First, he could have established a clear-cut ground rule that the counseling office was for counseling, not for "kidding around." By serving as an individual who is only there to deal objectively with specific student problems, he could have reinforced this ground rule. Second, he could have recognized his lack of expertise and judgment in dealing with matters of sexual behavior and referred the youngster to a school psychologist or some other professional who might be better equipped to deal with the problem. Third, when the situation reached the point where the student sat on the counselor's desk—which is further evidence of the counselor's inappropriate sense of permissiveness—the resulting incident could have either been thwarted or better prepared for. The principal or guidance director, for example, should have been apprised of the student's disturbed behavior and threats. Then, the parents of the youngster could have been informed immediately of their daughter's actions. Most important, however, the counselor could have recognized his earlier self-condemnation of himself for "enjoying" the youngster and followed one of two alternatives. First, he could have discouraged any kind of relationship whatsoever with Merillee from the very beginning. This probably would have not allowed the situation to develop. Second, and even more effective, he could have changed his negative self-talk, depicted earlier, to: "I am not a scoundrel for thinking such thoughts. I am human. Now, if I am truly interested in this disturbed girl, how can I best help her?" He would then have been able to accept himself in spite of his attraction and moved to the important business of dealing with the obvious school problems Merillee had.

The second question—if one is unjustly accused of something, what is the best way of handling the problem?—can be answered quite simply: honestly! Insofar as this critical incident is concerned, the counselor's reaction seems to be typical of many guidance personnel faced with crisis situations. Rather than placing their professional stature and integrity—although admittedly this may be undermined or demeaned by some school systems or communities—against what usually is the unjust accusations of a disturbed or troubled individual, the school counselor frequently hides from or avoids the situation instead of facing it. If the counselor has left himself open for such accusations by ineffective policies, practices, or the like, then the most realistic solution to the problem is to face it directly and honestly.

DANIEL W. FULLMER

Merillee is a pathetic and potentially lethal person. My very first job as a counselor in a secondary school brought one of the Merillee types into my professional experience. I was almost as vulnerable as the "nasty old man." Another young man in his first year as an English teacher was not so fortunate. He was dismissed. The charges were never formalized but, even so, he was advised to go quietly away and begin teaching elsewhere—a wiser young man. Through twenty years of teaching, I have come to expect frequent reports of the Merillee type. In all cases, as in this one, the "victim" always contributes to his own "delinquency."

The principle involved is pride—pride in being rewarded by the attention of a young female child. In no case, where the male has ignored the initial reward, has the emotional extortion game worked.

The door, whether it should be open or closed, is a familiar issue. My final solution to it has been to counsel in groups. Most things important enough to discuss should be open to at least a few confidential friends. The door should have a large clear window in it or should be entirely removed, leaving an open entrance at all times. It helps to drop the psychotherapy model for in-school work. The close, secret, confidential relationship found in psychotherapy is not necessary for almost all cases in school counseling.

The counselor was a victim of Merillee. He was lucky too, and so was the eye doctor. But "luck" cannot hope to cover the abysmal ignorance of professional survival behavior contained in this incident. Apparently it will continue in counseling; each counselor thinks "it won't happen to me"—a myth I have come to call the "Immaculate Exception" syndrome.

This incident is an example of the need for properly trained professional counselors and not just well-intentioned nice guys. The nice-guy or friendly-fellow approach to school-age youth is a poor substitute for competence.

HAROLD KOZUMA

This situation was the counselor's fault. He let the matter get out of hand by allowing Merillee to control him. From the beginning he should have known that her flirting was a clue for him to be on guard and to maintain strictly professional relations with her. He cooperated and collaborated with her in her misbehavior. He was just as guilty—perhaps even more so.

His next mistake was to attempt to end the developing relationship rapidly! He had permitted it to grow gradually, but when he got scared he panicked and attempted to end it suddenly and completely. It was a rude rejection of his previous encouragement. No wonder she reacted accordingly. He learned that hell hath no fury like a woman scorned. If, once he realized he had gone too far, he had firmly and coolly extricated himself from the relationship, the incident would not have occurred. So, in my judgment, he erred at the beginning by nurturing the relationship and then again by cutting her off abruptly.

In dealing with young females, one has to learn to develop a certain sensitivity. At times one must refuse to close the door of the interview room. One may even want to interview only in the presence of another.

Or, one may refer a student to someone else. Or, and this takes a lot of courage and self-confidence, one can tell the student: "I do not think I can help you; see someone else."

Another procedure that could be valuable would be to find out as much about a student as possible. Had the parents been interviewed before all this, this hapless counselor might have learned about her escapades before the event which, in turn, would have prevented it. Still another procedure—and I am surprised that this counselor didn't think of this—is to go immediately to a supervisor, report all the details as completely as possible, and then be advised by the supervisor.

The lesson I would suggest that the reader get out of this incident is the following: all of us have hang-ups, and all of us make mistakes. But, when we become aware of what we have done wrong, or when we see that we are in trouble, we have to learn how to get out of a situation. To panic is not the answer. To placate someone is not the answer. We have to learn to be ready to take the consequences. I think, in this case, the counselor, on being threatened by Merillee could have prevented the incident by saying something like this: "Well, it looks as though I have gotten myself into trouble with you. I meant only to be friendly. However, if we can work this out, fine; if not, I'll have to report all this to my supervisor so that he can know and so we can work out something." I suspect that something like this, both strong and confident as well as concerned, might have caused this girl to back down.

PHYLLIS MARTIN

The old saying that an ounce of prevention is worth a pound of cure holds in this case. A counselor should avoid situations such as the one that Charlie found himself in.

I see him as a spectacled, baldheaded man, secretly enjoying Merillee's provocative behavior. She teased and seduced him and he was a willing partner. Not until she sat astride his desk did he realize he had lost all control and that he was in big trouble. He may have been perceptive enough before this to see he was pursuing a dangerous path but his needs seem to have overcome his common sense. He says he felt like a fool and to that I say, "Amen." He sure acted the role of a fool.

When he started to refuse Merillee's demands he was neither consistent nor firm. Charlie had become Merillee's victim, and his ineffectual attempts to extricate himself from her power only made her more determined to play her game. Soon she was running the show and dictating the rules. By the time the "rape" incident occurred they were in a frank power contest and when, in desperation, he called out, "What the hell do you want?" she took charge.

It seems to me she moved from the stage of wanting attention to a demand for power, and when Charlie tried to extricate himself she decided to punish him. Charlie just didn't have a chance with this power-drunk child. All he could do was wonder, "How could this happen to me?"

And now to some thought about prevention. If the counselor had known himself and his sexual proclivities well, it is doubtful that he would have gotten himself into this situation, which is, I suppose, some indication that counselors should have psychotherapy, not only for better self-understanding, but for professional enhancement. When Charlie began to notice Merillee's attentions, he should have referred her if possible to a woman counselor; or, if he had felt interest in her, to limit or curtail the relationship. Had this counselor been honest and accepting, had he fully understood Merillee's problem, had he been working within the frame of reference of a theory of counseling, or had he ready consulting and supervisory relationships, or, I have to add, had he some common sense, this incident would not have happened. I think he was fortunate indeed to have escaped and I hope he learned his lesson well and that other counselors who read about this incident learn from poor old Charlie's mistakes.

GERALD PINE

After reading this critical incident, I feel its title should be changed from "Cry Rape!" to "Charlie, You Asked for It." Charlie must have time on his hands and some problems of his own if he permits the counseling relationship to become a series of bull sessions in which he satisfies his own personal needs to the detriment of the client's. Can we describe Charlie's relationship with Merillee as a counseling relationship when—

1. the client sees the counseling office as a place to come to and "kid around" with the counselor;
2. there appears to be no constructive purpose ·or goal for the client or the counselor in the relationship;
3. the counselor assumes a line of questioning which seems to reflect a prurient interest in the client's activities;
4. the counselor and the client engage in mutual psychological manipulation.

·To the more psychoanalytically-oriented reader this situation may look like a classic example of counter-transference; that is, the counselor transfers or projects toward the client revived elements of attitudes, misconceptions, fears, and impulses derived from his own emotionally significant past relationships. A client's manner, age, appearance, personality, or gestures may provoke a variety of feelings in the counselor. He may become irritated by a pupil's acting out; he may be bored by another pupil; he may be overly impressed by the ability of the client; he may wish to become very authoritarian; he may tend to overemphasize certain aspects of behavior to the neglect of other aspects; or he may become seductive. When the counselor vicariously experiences thwarted needs and drives in the client, when the counselor overidentifies with the client, or when the client openly stimulates counselor attitudes (e.g. the client who is openly hostile may stimulate counselor-hostile attitudes from the counselor), counter-transference is occurring. Depending on the intensity and the type of attitude projected by the counselor, counter-transference can arouse in the client feelings of distrust, insecurity, anger, apathy, resistance, rejection, hostility, and/or dependence.

I prefer to respond to Charlie's problem from an existential perspective. For me, this incident highlights one of the most important dimensions of counseling; that is, that counseling is a reciprocal behavioral interchange. Client behavior has a reciprocal impact on counselor behavior which, in turn, has a reciprocal impact on client behavior. The counseling relationship represents a circular flow of experience, with counselor and client behavior merging in such ways as to be at one moment cause and at the next moment effect. What this means to me is that, in the counseling relationship, the counselor cannot deny himself, he cannot do away with his personal style of existence. The humanity of the counselor inevitably shows through in the relationship, and no matter how much the counselor attempts to control the expression of his personal mode of being, it is sensed and responded to by the client. Charlie needs to become more sensitive and aware of his life style and attitudes; he needs to become more aware of the influencing aspects of his personality and how they affect his counseling function. Charlie appears to assume that Merillee's behavior emanated solely from her and independently of Charlie. I think Charlie should examine himself to determine whether his own behavior generated her reaction. There is a subliminal language in counseling consisting of subtle signals and cues conveyed through tone of voice, posture, body movement, a way of breathing, expression of the eyes, and other physical mannerisms. The counselor needs to evaluate himself continuously and thoroughly so that he can sensitize himself to the messages he may be sending to the client and so that he may become more aware of the hidden aspects of his personal existence which would have an impact on the client's behavior. In effect, the counselor's main technique is himself.

If Charlie wishes to avoid such incidents again, perhaps he should reflect upon his behavior after every session with a client. One of the ways he could become more sensitive to himself and to the signals he may be transmitting is to ask himself such questions as:

> How do I *really* feel about the client?
> Do I anticipate seeing the client?
> Do I want to protect, reject, or punish the client?
> Does the client resemble anyone I know or have known?
> What is it the client is doing to make me feel as I do?
> Am I being objective in my attitude toward the client?
> Deep down do I want to control the client?
> Do I want to manipulate his/her life?
> How do I respond?
> What do I feel?
> What do I say?

Through self-reflection the counselor can refine and sensitize the technique that he himself is. It is important that the counselor know those factors which prevent him from being effective with the client so that he can control them when they seem to unduly influence the counseling relationship.

In the counseling relationship, the counselor has perceptions of himself, the client, the problems, and the entire interaction (expectancies, roles, standards). So, too, does the client have perceptions of himself, the counselor, the problems, and the entire interaction. I wonder how Merillee perceived herself, Charlie, and counseling? Did she sense that Charlie "secretly enjoyed her"? Did she see counseling as a professional helping relationship or a situation for "kidding around"? Did she see Charlie as an authentic person, as a professionally competent counselor? Did she enjoy charming (manipulating) Charlie? Did she become angry out of a feeling of rejection when Charlie began to terminate the relationship?

In summary, Charlie could have prevented this situation from occurring if he had:

1.   oriented students carefully to what counseling is. A well planned and continuous program of orientation which spells out the role of the counselor and describes the nature and the purpose of the counseling relationship will go a long way in preventing unhealthy relationships from developing.

2.   structured and defined the relationship in the first session. Counseling while open-ended and permissive is also a structured relationship, an affectional bond with defined limits. The lack of an effective orientation program and the lack of structure often leads to unreasonable expectations and distorted perceptions on the part of the client.

3.   cooperatively established constructive goals and expectancies for the counseling relationship with Merillee.

4.   engaged in self-reflection and scrutinized the nature of his behavior and involvement in the relationship with Merillee with the aim of controlling any unhealthy attitudes and feelings.

5.   moved the relationship in a constructive direction by tuning in to Merillee, reflecting her feelings, confronting her with the reality of her here-and-now feelings and expressing a genuine interest and concern for helping her.

8

The Counselor Blows Up

Background

For the past six years I have been counseling groups. The groups are conducted in a small bookroom used only by the lady who grades papers for the English department. The room is furnished with a large table and chairs and the grader's desk. The room lends itself to informality with no classroom atmosphere. I have used various criteria for determining which students to ask to be members of the groups. However, membership is always voluntary. I meet with the students during their assigned study hall period.

This particular group met twice a week over a seven-month period. The group consisted of four ninth-grade boys, two of whom were repeating the ninth grade. These boys were selected by their teachers who identified them as having the "worst attitudes" of any of their students. Although the boys knew one another prior to the group sessions, they did not run in the same "gangs." All four of the boys had police records. It might be interesting to note that this was only my second group counseling experience and the first time I worked with boys.

The boys were told that they did not have to decide about group membership until the end of our first counseling session. If, at that time, they accepted membership, they were then committed to attend the remaining meetings. I told them there were only three restrictions that I would place on the group:

1.   No physical harm was to be done to anyone or any property in the room;

2.   What was said in the group was not to be discussed outside of the room;

3.   No one member could leave the group until we all decided to discontinue meeting as a group.

All four boys chose to continue. After explaining that I hoped the time would be spent in discussing their problems, I emphasized that it was their group and they could spend the time any way they saw fit.

I am still amazed at their ingenuity in finding so many ways of testing my commitments to them. I fought hard to keep from "correcting" their behavior as they attempted to challenge, ignore, annoy, and shock me. After many weeks of somehow living up to what I had promised, a workable group began to emerge from all the chaos. The boys slowly began to join me at the discussion table, one by one; the one exception was Danny.

Although none of the boys came from ideal home situations, only Danny lived in a fatherless home. Danny was an only child and lived with his obviously doting mother. His mother had a reputation for "covering" for Danny when the school had any occasion to check up on him. Unlike the other boys, Danny did not have to work in order to have money and clothes. In my judgment, Danny was "spoiled" but quite likeable.

While it seemed that the other boys were now ready to use the time talking seriously, Danny was still instigating various distractions. The other boys never seemed to get upset with Danny and his constant shenanigans. I soon learned that their basic philosophy was "live and let live —don't bother anyone if he is not hurting you." In trying to live up to what I had said about each member spending his time as he wished, I began to ignore Danny's behavior as he set about trying to lure other boys away from the table by engaging them in private conversations or diverting their attention in any way he could.

It had been a long frustrating wait to see the group come this far. I am afraid that my feelings were becoming rather hostile towards Danny as I watched him relentlessly trying to destroy what had taken so long to develop.

Incident

On this particular day, Danny was sitting at a desk, opening the drawers and going through the contents, while the rest of us were sitting at the table talking. I had asked him not to do this, explaining that the reader let us use the room and the desk belonged to her. Since he chose to continue, my annoyance grew until I felt I could no longer keep still. Although he was not harming or taking anything from the desk, I felt I had some obligation to the reader to protect her privacy. I was unsure as to how the group would view my censure of Danny's behavior since he was not really breaking a "group" rule.

I finally decided that if I were now accepted as a group member, then I, too, had a right to express my feelings even if they were contrary to the feelings of the group. Although I spoke calmly, my choice of words was not unladylike. "This is a place to express feelings and right now I want to express mine. Danny is making me so damn mad right now that I can't even decide how to express my anger." Danny immediately jumped up, overturning his chair, and hollered, "All right, if that's the way you feel, I'll leave!" As he went toward the door, I yelled, "You can't! You can't leave the group until we all do!" Several more words were exchanged and I remember how helpless I felt since my only defense was that he could not leave the group because of our initial contract. I hoped the group had some meaning for Danny and that it would be strong enough to hold him, but my hopes were not high since he had displayed such total disinterest. Surely Danny knew as well as I did that I really was powerless to stop him from walking out the door, and I certainly could not force him to return again. On the basis of his past behavior, Danny's walking out would have been the predicted outcome. However, something held him there that day; he did not leave, and I have always wondered why he decided to stay.

Discussion

First, let me state that I do not recommend "blowing-up" as an acceptable technique for a counselor. I consider it my weakness and my inexperience that allowed me not only to lose control when the incident occurred, but also to cloud my vision to the circumstances leading up to it. Although I feel that I was justified in being upset with Danny's efforts to sabotage the group, I know that I was wrong in getting so involved with my own anger and temporarily ceasing in the process to care about or to understand Danny's feelings. I can see how Danny might have interpreted my permissiveness as rejection. By ignoring Danny's actions, I also ignored Danny. Perhaps it was only through this incident that I was able to show Danny that I did consider him a group member and that he was not insignificant. Nevertheless, my attack might have easily placed him in a position of feeling compelled to leave in order to "save face."

Another possible explanation for his failure to leave was his perception of me as an authority figure. He stayed because he felt he had to. However, I believe that I had already passed that test and was no longer a threat to any of the boys. Also, since Danny was not adverse to being absent from school, he could have easily arranged to be absent on group days.

I feel this incident is an example of the value of group counseling, indicating the power of the peer group. Possibly, Danny was rejecting me as a group member and resented my feminine intrusion into this masculine group. Looking back at the type of distractions that Danny created, they were usually of a masculine nature, such as rough talk, "horsing around," and activities that he felt would exclude me. I feel that Danny had a strong need to belong and to identify with the masculine norms generated by his peers in the group. Perhaps he realized that to become a real member of the group, he would have to join with the others in their acceptance of me.

It appeared to me that Danny gained a great deal from his group experience. He looked up to Vik, a large well-built boy who emerged as leader of the group. I often watched Danny as Vik talked about such things as "love" and "fear," which I'm certain Danny had viewed as effeminate. Danny's concept of what one must feel or do to be masculine was obviously altered.

I have offered several ideas that I feel were factors as to why the incident occurred and as to why I believe that Danny would ultimately have chosen to remain in the group. But the question that is still in my mind is: why did a boy with a history like Danny's choose to remain when I had put him on the spot in front of his peers at a time when he was obviously operating at an emotional level rather than a rational one? I would be interested in the opinion of others.

Questions

1. How much should a counselor be an active group member? How emotionally involved should one become?

2. Was I really rejecting Danny, or was he rejecting me, or both?

3. How could I have better handled the situation?

4. Since Danny had not joined with the rest of us, was a clash of

this type inevitable, or would he have found some other way to have joined us in time?

5. Why didn't Danny walk out?

COMMENTS ON THE INCIDENT

THE EDITORS

In these incidents we, the editors, see things that especially impress us, just as we note that the consultants tend, at times, to become interested in diverse aspects of these situations. In this particular incident, we are concerned with the issue of "behavior." In most schools, at the early ages anyway, proper behavior is most important. Children are always being told what to do and what not to do. In this manner, by employing verbal reminders, issuing reprimands, and occasionally administering rewards, we try to shape children's behavior.

When troublesome children no longer respond to verbal authority and efforts to control or influence them fail, the next step often is to attempt "psychotherapy"—regardless of the label we attach to it. This is precisely what occurred in this incident.

But, "treatment" has its own rules, its own logic, and violation of this logic can lead to trouble. In treatment there is an assumption of equality. That is, there is an essential leveling off of the "therapist" and the "patient"—and the rules that apply to one often apply to the other. So, if the therapist wishes the patient to express himself freely, then, too, the therapist should express himself freely. Only when there is this essential human equality can therapy work. Too often people attempt therapy who do not understand this point.

In any event, a counselor blew up in this incident and did not get the expected consequences. Our counselors discuss this issue and present a variety of explanations.

RUDOLF DREIKURS

The counselor submitted this report for the purpose of understanding a crucial event in her work with a group. She tries to analyze the development of the group in a way which would perhaps be acceptable in a different frame of reference. From my point of view, her interpretations of the events are incorrect; I see them in a different light.

The cause of her difficulty seems to be evident on the first page. One may question the validity of an attitude merely from the words used to describe what happened; for me the words this counselor used are highly significant. She says: "The boys *were told*," "they did not *have to decide*," "they were then committed," "no physical harm *was to be done*," "was *not* to be discussed," "no one member *could* leave." It is obvious that the counselor wanted to be democratic; but the choice of her words along with her probable tone of voice indicated a rather autocratic approach. All subsequent events show clearly that she got herself into a power conflict with the boys from the first moment.

Had she recognized her involvement, she would not have been so amazed at their "ingenuity" to fight her. Since she did not realize that the boys had involved her in a power conflict, she misinterpreted their behavior as "testing my commitments." It is her involvement in a power struggle which made it so difficult for her to keep from correcting them. She tried not to respond, but obviously she was annoyed and shocked. What made it difficult for her to "live up" to what she had promised was her pretense to be democratic, a pretense which the boys easily recognized and challenged. This is the reason why it took her so many weeks to emerge from the chaos. When the boys realized that they could not succeed in defeating her, they slowly gave up the fight—except one boy.

The counselor recognized that Danny was spoiled. She refers to his status as an only child without a father, with a mother who tried to make up for that and who gave him the justification that he had a right to do what he wanted. This is the way he behaved in the group. At no point did the counselor attempt to explain to Danny the significance of his own behavior; therefore, she failed to recognize his determination to defeat her at every turn. It was almost as if she was a sitting duck at whom the boy directed his potshots. When she tried to counteract his disturbance he became only worse, instigating the other boys to side with him against her. Naturally this frustrated her because she did not know what to do with a boy in a power conflict, how to extricate herself, to help him and the others to understand his goals, and to lead him away from the power struggle. Under these circumstances it is not surprising that by "waiting" she became hostile, not merely because he tried to destroy the group, but because he continued to defeat her. That went on until finally she put the cards on the table, no longer pretending to be uninvolved.

The incident started off in the typical way such conflicts take place. She told him what *not* to do and so he decided to do it, until she could no longer stand it. When she blew her top, it was not because she tried to protect the privacy of the test reader, but because she was helpless in view of Danny's power. And in this moment, she came down from her throne and became human. But leave it to Danny to increase his pressure by jumping up, overturning his chair, and threatening to leave. She felt utterly helpless, and Danny, as well as she, knew that she was powerless to stop him from walking out. Then why did he fail to leave? Why should he leave? She revealed her defeat, and he liked it. It was only his old game of defeating her. She was a good sparring partner, an easy target for his provocations. There was now no benefit for him to leave. This is how it looks to me. But the counselor gave a number of other possible reasons for his staying which deserve closer scrutiny. The events look different from another point of view.

She considered it a consequence of her weakness and inexperience that she lost control. Actually, she gained control by admitting her defeat.

Contrary to what she assumed, she was not "getting" involved with Danny when she got angry; in this moment she extricated herself from the long-suffering involvement which she precipitated before the incident. She was right that her outburst gave Danny the realization that he was not insignificant.

In this light, the value of group counseling or the power of the peer group appears superfluous. The group actually played a very limited role in the incident. Since the counselor did not identify the power conflict in which Danny involved her, she assumed—without any justification—that the boy was "rejecting" her. Once she began this kind of speculation, she even went so far afield as assuming that Danny resented her feminine intrusion into a masculine group. Naturally, Danny's destructions were aggressive—what else would one expect from such a boy? The need for masculine identification may be correct, but it does not explain the way he dealt with the counselor. His assumed fear of being effeminate reflects, rather, the counselor's preoccupation with masculinity and femininity and her own apprehension about being feminine in a group of tough boys.

Now let us consider the questions:

1. The counselor of a group should always be an active participant. Emotional involvement is not desirable. However, the counselor was deeply involved emotionally with the group long before the incident occurred.

2. I can see no evidence for either Danny rejecting her or she rejecting him. He provoked her; but this does not mean that he did not like her at the same time.

3. The effort of the counselor to keep him in the room was only the last step in her effort to control the group. What the counselor needed was not to handle "this situation" better, but to resolve the conflict long before it came to a showdown. Contrary to what she believed, losing her temper was constructive. She admitted her defeat openly and he responded to that by not going much further.

4. The clash was inevitable when the counselor became more and more defeated in her attitude and transactions with Danny.

C. GRATTON KEMP

This incident illustrates the problem of structure in working with groups. Structure is one of the most significant and difficult aspects of group process. There are three interrelated aspects in making decisions related to structure. One element is the degree of administrative freedom in the existing situation. A second aspect is the leader's understanding of and the nature of need structure. A third factor is the members' degree of need for structure.

In this situation the administrative requirements are the following. The school administration did not permit physical attack or misuse of property. Regarding the latter limitation this could have been assumed to prohibit disturbing or examining the contents of the desk.

The leader's understanding of his need structure may be difficult for her to assess but nevertheless is extremely important. In this situation the leader was incongruent. It is evidenced in the disparity between her true psychological needs and her overt behavior. In the beginning she imposed the structure. She could have developed this cooperatively. It may have been that she perceived the members as being incapable of exerting the degree of impulse control necessary to allow cooperative planning. It may also have been a function of her own need for some certainty in direction and outcomes. The latter reason may account for her statement that she hoped they would discuss "their problems." Her incongruity surfaces when she emphasizes that "they could spend their time any way they saw fit." It appears that intellectually she desired to be permissive, tending to be group-centered, but emotionally she was not completely ready. Her inconsistency and incongruency are quite apparent in the incident with Danny. She was not psychologically ready to permit Danny to spend his time any way he saw fit. Asking the boy "not to do this" was a violation of one of the operational rules she set for the group.

The third consideration of structure refers to the leader's perception of the members' need for structure. Apparently, her knowledge of the past behavior of the boys convinced her that imposed structure was necessary. However, it may have been wiser to impose only such structure that might result in positive growth. She could have imposed the one requirement she perceived most necessary and studied the result. She may later have been able to develop other goals cooperatively. To the degree that she found this possible she would be developing an open-ended structure and encouraging impulse control by developing growth in cooperative planning.

She could have increased the possibilities for cooperative planning by the inclusion of other boys. Two or three boys who had already demonstrated that they could handle environmental demands and who had varied wholesome interests should have been included in the group. They would have added stability, purpose, and provided constructive behavioral patterns.

She needed to distinguish between the set limits of the situation and those that were modifiable. Those that were a product of the institutional setting and therefore "fixed" (e.g., place, time, care of property, and nonviolence) could be stated as such and therefore accepted by the leader and members as not matters for discussion. Other framework matters such as seating arrangement, listening, remaining with the group, could then be cooperatively decided upon in a developmental fashion in relation to the needs of the group.

Although the group met for an extended length of time, no mention is made of evaluation. Ongoing evaluation was necessary to help the boys understand the aims and possibilities of the process in which they were involved. In this manner they could establish developmental goals in relation to their progress. The activity of evaluation in which the leader asks and expects both negative and positive ideas regarding performance assists group members to become intelligent with regard to their behavior and to set individual and group goals.

The fact that the leader set the goals for the group, hoping that they would accept them, made a difference in her attitude toward the boys' behavior. She was not at ease. She was not as permissive as her original statement indicated. She could not really accept the boys' use of the time as they saw fit. In the preface to the incident with Danny, the counselor writes that it had been a long frustrating experience and that she felt hostility developing within her. She was not really genuine; her inward feelings and outward actions did not agree.

However, she finally did become genuine, and, from the boys' and Danny's point of view, masculine. When she expressed herself as she did in the incident with Danny, she revealed both her authoritarian and her unsure character. All façades evaporated. She was now a person with whom Danny could identify: spontaneous and emotional. She now represented for Danny an attractive kind of person.

The group had moved into a dependent, safe relationship with an adult. It meant: "The leader decides finally, so keep the rules and you are safe." Within that group climate, the boys apparently felt sufficiently relaxed to commence to talk in a meaningful way. They perceived the leader to be as emotional as themselves with the added power conferred on her by "the system."

The leader is critical of her behavior in this incident, recognizing that blowing-up is not an acceptable technique. In this case, however, it was not a technique; rather it was that the leader became uncontrollably real, her pseudopermissiveness not having stood the strain. The leader feels that she was justified in "being upset." She was not justified, but she was genuine.

Such an incident emphasizes the importance of the leader's self-examination of ego needs and demands along with personal fears and expectations. Knowing the boys to the degree she has indicated, it would have been possible for her to "go through" in her imagination the first few sessions. She could thus have "tried on" several approaches and recognized her own reactions to each of these. She could have determined which procedure was most consistent with her values, capabilities, and methods and, in this way, proceeded to work much more effectively with this group.

Conclusions. The development of this situation was in large part the result of poor leadership. The leader was unaware of her own need structure and its relationship to self-congruency in her leadership. She apparently did not recognize the necessity of personal assessment before undertaking group counseling and the importance of genuineness in leadership. She failed to consider the importance of peer influence and, therefore, did not include others who would have served as models to the boys with problems.

WALTER G. KLOPFER

Composition of the group is somewhat questionable. Why a group of boys, who all had very poor attitudes, should be put together requires some explanation. I have had more success by composing groups with students of equivalent intelligence who had a continuum of attitudes towards school, so that they could have some range in their discussion. Also, the concept that the group can do whatever they like is not very realistic. Obviously, the counselor is there for a reason and, if this reason is not made explicit, it is necessary for group members to project upon her what they think her reason is. The assumption that, on the one hand, she is having no influence and, on the other hand, she is being of value as a counselor seems rather paradoxical. The concept of remaining emotionally uninvolved is another source of ambiguity. If a counselor is not interested in what the boys are talking about or the feelings they are expressing then I do not know what she is doing there. If she expects them to express themselves freely and spontaneously, and describes herself as one of them, then what choice does she have other than "blowing her cool" once in a while.

Also, there is some question as to why a boy who expresses so much disinterest should remain in the group. Even though he might become involved eventually, in the meantime he keeps others from progressing. Surely there are many other boys in that particular school who could benefit from counseling but who are being neglected in favor of such "hard core" cases. Generally, I question the procedure of a counselor spending ninety percent of her time with those students who have the poorest prognosis, ignoring those many students who might benefit from a relatively small investment of counselor time.

Who was rejecting whom? It seems most likely that there was real antagonism between the counselor and Danny because they were pursuing different goals. He wanted the boys to relate to him in his way; the counselor wanted the boys to relate to her in her way. She won out and whether she won because of her authority or because Danny felt that the other boys had allied themselves with her is difficult to know. That he decided to stay in this particular situation means no more than that he decided to stay in this particular situation. Whether what went on was group counseling or just a power struggle won by the teacher is difficult to interpret.

9

Mother————

CRITICAL INCIDENT

Background

I was appointed as a counselor in an integrated school where the student population was about eighty percent white and twenty percent black. The teacher population was the other way around: twenty percent white and eighty percent black. Since this may be important in the incident which follows, I should report that I, myself, am black.

One of the kids about whom I got reports was Kenneth, and the reports were all the same: *filthy language*! Never did he use this language with teachers, but rather in the yard, in the playground, in the auditorium, and in the classes with other children. His favorite term was "mother————."

I called the boy in to find out what I could. He was just nine years old, very dark, quite small. He seemed cowed, and when I began asking him about his language, he showed resignation, as though saying, "Oh, this again." I tried to be neutral but he didn't want to discuss the matter. He expected me to warn him not to use such language or to give him a lecture on its impropriety. All I did was ask him if he could tell me why he used such language. I could get no satisfactory reply. I dismissed him without extracting any promises, but at the same time I made it quite clear that I did not think his language represented acceptable behavior. I assumed that he probably heard such language in his neighborhood—but then so did all the kids in that school. I also assumed that he had been warned repeatedly. Well, that wasn't an assumption—he had been seen on this matter several times, and I could well imagine that he had been advised many times to stop using such language. I also assumed that his foul language provided him with a secondary gain, namely attracting the attentions of others in this useless manner. After all, he had gotten to see me because of his language. Using such language obviously conferred some status on him. At the same time, being a little fellow, he probably felt that he couldn't be outstanding in any useful way.

Several weeks later, the vice-principal, the school psychologist, and I met to discuss a number of problem referrals and, sure enough, one of these was Kenneth, our foul-mouthed boy. We reviewed his problem and discussed various solutions. We agreed that all the usual methods of dealing with him were likely to fail. Then the psychologist, a blonde middle-aged woman, made an extraordinary suggestion.

"Look," she said, "this can be the beginning of a very bad pattern. I think that something has to be done. I have a suggestion. It comes from a theoretical position that I have. Instead of trying to stop him, which hasn't worked so far, let us encourage him to use such language."

"How is that?" asked the vice-principal who was black. She and the psychologist were friends.

"I suggest that we call him in and encourage him to use this kind of language with us. I think that he will resist and that we should urge him to use it, and that the more we insist the more he will resist. This could do it."

We discussed this unusual suggestion and, after a while, we agreed to act on it. Moreover, we also agreed on how to do it, the procedure being described in the incident which was certainly critical in a lot of ways.

Incident

The next day, Kenneth came in for a conference with us, and I can still see his big black eyes looking at us over the table. The vice-principal started off by saying that we wanted to have a nice talk, and in the second sentence she used *shit*, one of Kenneth's favorite words. Then the psychologist began to talk sweetly to him and she used *nigger*, another of his favorite words. And when it was my turn, I used *mother———*, his favorite-of-favorite words. His eyes looked as if they might pop out. He got up and backed away from us toward the door, putting his hand on the knob. At this point, the psychologist used all three of his favorite words in one sentence, which ended in a question mark. The vice-principal, using several more expletives, asked him to come back to the table, which he did, slowly, with his mouth open. Then we began to discuss him and his language among ourselves, freely using his own terminology. Our sentences went somewhat like this: "Can you figure out why this little p———, this f——— b——— uses such mother——— language?" "I just think the little s——— doesn't know any f——— better, that's all."

The session lasted no longer than three minutes since the psychologist had warned us that Kenneth might not get the shock of the intended session if we overplayed our hand. We finally told him to get his "f——— b——— a———" out of the room, and he left, not having said a single word during the entire session.

The consequences were dramatic indeed—in a behavioral sense. The boy's verbal misbehavior stopped immediately and completely. I checked with his teacher who reported that his foul talk had stopped completely.

Questions

1. A number of teachers, counselors, and administrators with whom I have discussed this incident have stated that the ends do not justify the means, and that it was wrong in every sense, regardless of results, to do wrong things to get good results. What do you think of the propriety of what we did?

2. If someone, say Kenneth's mother and father, preferred charges against us on the grounds that we used unacceptable language in front of a young child and if we had admitted doing so, would you think that some sort of reprimand would have been justified?

3. How far can a counselor go in doing what is ordinarily unacceptable behavior? In one instance, a counselor in a therapy group actually pulled out his penis to show it to his group. He was immediately dismissed. I believe this would be an example of completely unacceptable behavior. He argued that in his judgment what he did was proper at the time and in the circumstances. What guides, besides common sense, can one have in such matters?

4. Do you think we harmed Kenneth in any way? Or, if the students had heard about the incident (they hadn't), would it have affected them adversely in any way?

COMMENTS ON THE INCIDENT

THE EDITORS

How far can a counselor go in her attempts to improve or rectify a situation? Suppose what she intends to do is illegal or immoral? Should she take the chance? Would she be better off not to do what she believes will work if it may endanger her? Should she push forward, committed to her counselee's welfare, no matter what the personal cost, and be ready to take the consequences? Is she a professional person who must be given respect and a wide latitude in her behavior to achieve her ends with difficult students or must she always operate in a circumspect manner?

Of course, there are no definitive answers to these philosophical questions. From time to time, however, these issues become real. There are occasions when the counselor and counselee have to decide whether some unusual behavior that may skirt the edge of propriety will work, and whether it should be used.

Dunlap had developed the notion that one of the ways to learn to give up errors is to practice them. Frankl has discussed the value of the use of paradoxical intention in psychotherapy. This means encouraging a patient to indulge in his erroneous behavior or to express an undesired emotion. In this incident a school psychologist made a rather extraordinary suggestion for the treatment of a behavior problem which has elements of Dunlap's and Frankl's procedures. However, as carried out, the suggestion presents a variety of ethical and social issues.

Our consultants take various stands relative to the wisdom of the procedures used. We come more or less to the recurring philosophical issue: Do the means justify the ends? This is an issue that will demand more attention as the technology and potency of school counseling evolves.

RUDOLF DREIKURS

The technique suggested by the psychologist is not as unusual and "extraordinary" as the counselor assumes. I have described a similar approach many years ago as "anti-suggestion" and Viktor Frankl utilizes "paradoxical intention" as a major part of his therapeutic procedures. When one asks a person to deliberately increase his symptoms or misconduct, he will stop it. A stutterer cannot continue his stutter if he deliberately tries to produce it.

However, the application of this method, as described here, is not quite acceptable. One could get the same results by inviting the boy to several counseling sessions, asking him to repeat all the dirty words he knows, and encouraging him to find new and stronger ones. That, too, would stop him cold, but without the necessity for the adult's using these words.

It is interesting to speculate as to why this particular tactic was so effective. In a sense, it goes beyond the application of paradoxical intention. It is usually quite effective when a mother of a thumb-sucking child puts her thumb in her own mouth as soon as the child does it. Usually, the child gets furious. Why? *He* has the right to suck the thumb, but mother hasn't. The child feels justified in stealing, but would object violently if somebody would take what belongs to him. In other words imitating the child's misconduct gives him a new perspective of what he is doing. It is an invasion into his domain.

However, one wonders why the counselor did not discuss with the boy the reason for his misconduct, helping him to become aware of his goals. This question is particularly justifiable since the counselor became aware of them. It is not a "secondary gain," as the counselor who apparently has been trained in other approaches assumes. He is probably right about the boy using his language to get special attention, to gain status among his friends as a compensation for his being small for his age. It might have given him a feeling of masculinity particularly among his peers, because it is primarily with them that he felt compelled to use his language.

Of course, the counselor was ill-advised to ask the boy to tell him why he used such language. The child never knows why he does something wrong—the trained counselor or teacher has to help him to understand it, so that he can see alternative forms of behavior for feeling important and significant. Therefore, the counselor should not have been surprised when he got "no satisfactory reply" to his question. Instead of dismissing him, telling him that his language did not represent "acceptable behavior," something that he already knew, the counselor should have disclosed the goals to the boy, a process by which one gets a "recognition reflex" if the disclosure is correct. In other words, the counselor succeeded in changing the child's behavior without uncovering his goals and intentions.

These are the questions which this incident raises and which the counselor does not take into consideration. To repeat, applying this particular form of paradoxical intention or "anti-suggestion" is quite improper and unnecessary. As to the "propriety" of such action, one can expect to find angry reactions. On the other hand, one can use "unacceptable behavior" if it is understood to be part of a game. When a child lies, one can make agreement with him that everyone in the family could do the same, so that he realizes the futility of his conduct. Obviously, the limits to which one can go in changing behavior might be defined by common sense and propriety. It is precisely common sense that provides some guidelines for how far one can go. Exposing one's penis, for example, certainly goes far beyond acceptable behavior. Whether thumb-sucking, lying, swearing, and dirty words go beyond the limits depends on circumstances. At any rate, one can be sure that the boy was not harmed by this procedure; but neither was he helped to understand his behavior and change his motivation. Failure to do so is the prevalent deficiency of our counseling services.

MARSANNE C. EYRE

I have two contradictory feelings about this incident. First, a positive one. Here was a boy addicted to a habit that could cause him a great deal of trouble and which, apparently, persisted despite ordinary attempts to stop it. It may be that the use of so-called filthy language was only a symptom of deeper problems, such as the need to be important, or of severe hostility. Some symptoms are more acceptable than others; some will get one into mental hospitals or prisons. Our society is not, and perhaps may never be, totally permissive.

Teachers, school psychologists, and counselors have great demands placed on them and are unable to spend time treating a child in depth. It follows, therefore, that immediate, forceful, contrasuggestive intervention can be dramatic in its impact, even though it may not solve the total problem. For these reasons, I feel positive about this approach.

My negative feeling is that this is an example of over-manipulative behavior modification which disregards the individual and treats him as a thing which needs to be modified. Kenneth may have learned two lessons. The first is that other people, whom he probably regarded as his adult models, are dishonest and untrustworthy manipulators filled with power. The second and perhaps more advantageous lesson is that if you misbehave, you will get the consequences of your actions one way or the other. The consequences for Kenneth were embarrassment and humiliation when he became the target of his own use of language. The counselor and administrators used the same form of punishment against Kenneth as he used against the world. This probably will encourage him to avoid similar embarrassments in the future.

Although others may differ in their attitudes, I myself find "descriptive" language neither good nor bad but only inappropriate. The most common reason for its use is that of anger or hostility, combined with lack of control. In Kenneth's case it hardly seemed spontaneous and its use in a school situation was highly inappropriate. Then, of course, adult interventions of this kind are likely to have scandalous repercussions. Suppose the child had reported the incident and some righteous parent or crusading newspaper decided to make an issue of it. Imagine those involved trying to justify their behavior before a hearing board: "Well, I called Kenneth a black mother———because . . ." It's extremely dubious that any school board or commission would find such behavior acceptable.

Weighing my own positive and negative reactions, I believe the adults involved in the incident felt secure in their knowledge of the dynamics of Kenneth's behavior. I also expect that he understood, either immediately or eventually, that professional people really wanted to help him and were only "reflecting" his own behavior. I am still aware of the pressing reality of the situation that led to the use of this effective technique and feel those involved were clever and courageous. I'm still left with the gnawing feeling, however, that their behavior was unnecessarily heroic. In this case, it was a calculated risk that paid off handsomely, but certainly it is not a procedure one should use indiscriminately.

DANIEL W. FULLMER

If only results are important, then means are secondary. This can not be true for any profession that concerns itself with ethics and values. In this case the means employed did attain the desired end, but the question of the appropriateness of the means is the issue. Personally, in this situation I would have opted for a less risk-prone strategy.

Legal and ethical considerations should be a constant concern of the school counselor. At the present time counselors simply do not have unlimited freedom of action, at least not to the degree that older, more established professions do. Consequently, at the present time the propriety of a school counselor's behavior must remain an individual matter—a value judgment. The curious dilemma of particular interest in this case, is that the counselor violated social norms herself to correct the violation of social norms employed by the child. Since this strategy worked, the issue seems moot relative to propriety. The counselor, in a sense, gambled —and won.

However, a counselor risks being discredited by unacceptable behavior. Guidelines for proper behavior must go beyond the situation, must not depend on expediency; otherwise the eager counselor, anxious to attain results, may violate common sense and harm himself, his school, and his profession.

I don't know whether Kenneth was harmed. We have no information as to why he used such language, and we can only make inferences. We don't know whether the cessation of this symptom may have helped or harmed him. We just don't have enough data. I would guess that stopping bad behavior is generally helpful rather than harmful in the long run.

This incident is an example of paradoxical intent, in which the counselor tries to get a person to improve by doing more of what is wrong. Alternatives to this strategy might have been the following:

1. Have the counselor meet with Kenneth to explore the reasons for the behavior;

2. Arrange a "family" consultation with the counselor, the teachers, the principal, and other significant and concerned people to plan how to handle the matter;

3. Take no action that involves Kenneth directly but instruct and mobilize all adults to stop reinforcing his behavior by reacting to it;

4. Tape record Kenneth's language and replay it for him, then give him practice in using socially acceptable language on the tape replay sequence.

I would not attempt behavior modification techniques with him. Judging from the immediacy of his response to the paradoxical-intention technique, Kenneth seems to be a bright boy. He was intelligent enough to realize that they were using it. Behavior modification would be more appropriate for someone less bright than he.

In general, I can say that the counselor and psychologist took a chance and won, but that the risks involved in using such a dramatic procedure are too great for use with this problem in other cases.

GERALD J. PINE

Several aspects of this critical incident bother me. I am particularly concerned that Kenneth was called in by the counselor—he did not volunteer for counseling and he was not referred by a teacher. The counselor assumed that Kenneth had a problem because he used filthy language. In essence, the counselor made a value judgment regarding Kenneth's moral behavior and decided that Kenneth needed help. Did Kenneth need help? Who decidès whether a client has a problem? Behavioral counselors (à la Krumboltz) would suggest that the client and the counselor should mutually agree on what the client's problem is and work together in a participatory relationship to establish mutually acceptable goals. Counselors with an existential orientation might say that client initiation of counseling is an essential ingredient for a meaningful helping relationship and that any counseling situation structured toward the counselor's decisions infringes upon the freedom and dignity of the client. The latter point of view represents my own bias and influences my evaluation, comments, and conjectures regarding this incident.

Let's look at the counselor's behavior. *He* called Kenneth in; *he* initiated the session by focusing on Kenneth's language; *he* made it quite clear that *he* did not think Kenneth's language represented acceptable behavior; and *he* viewed Kenneth's behavior as useless. What it all adds up to is the counselor perceived Kenneth from the counselor's frame of reference and conducted an interview which could be best described as "counselor-centered." Responsibility, initiative, decision-making, and the course of the session emanated from the counselor who responded to Kenneth solely from his (the counselor's) own hierarchy of moral values. The counselor acted as a moralist and a judge and conducted a session which did not allow Kenneth, the client, to formulate what he perceived was *his* problem if, indeed, he saw that he had any problems. There was a marked paucity of acceptance, understanding, sensitive listening, empathy, and facilitative genuineness in the relationship.

Who is to say the client's behavior is useless—the counselor or the client? (It makes some sense to me to view all behavior as functional and purposeful *for the child*.) It's not difficult to understand why Kenneth "showed resignation as though saying, 'Oh, this again . . .'" The counseling he experienced appeared to be more an instrument for shaping him to the counselor's value system rather than an opportunity to think through concerns of importance to him. In summary, the relationship revolved almost completely around the counselor and his needs rather than Kenneth.

Let's go on. Several weeks later the counselor, the school psychologist, and vice-principal, deciding that Kenneth had a problem, agreed on an extraordinary approach which dramatically stopped Kenneth's "misbehavior" immediately and completely. This shock tactic is interesting, for the adults seemed to prostitute themselves and to violate their honesty and integrity as persons by playing "foul-mouthed roles." (I am assuming that this was not their ordinary style of behavior.) The reader may respond by saying, "So what? It helped the kid, didn't it? He stopped swearing." I submit that it is questionable whether Kenneth was helped to become a more fully functioning person even though he apparently stopped swearing. The chickens will come home to roost and it won't require much introspection on Kenneth's part to learn that he was manipulated by the phony behavior of three adults. Instead of helping Kenneth, I think their behavior will only serve to alienate him a little further from adults and to impress him with their hypocrisy and deviousness. Maybe he was "techniqued out of his shoes" at the time but he won't be fooled for long (if he ever was). Such behavior on the part of adults goes a long way in promoting kids' distrust of the adult world.

What could the counselor do? I think the following:

1. He could have developed a continuous, imaginative, and varied orientation program to motivate pupils to seek out counseling of their own volition. Well designed orientation procedures delineating the role of the counselor, the purposes of counseling, and the counseling atmosphere are necessary for developing a positive image of the counselor and the counseling relationship. Of course, the most valuable way of helping kids to freely choose counseling for themselves is through qualitative counseling relationships. The counselor who demonstrates a significant helping relationship to the pupils with whom he works can expect that they will initiate counseling and return for further counseling assistance. For pupils to relate comfortably to a counselor, they must perceive him as a person with whom they can be involved actively and freely.

2. He could have focused on Kenneth's needs, problems, and feelings. Existentially speaking, this would mean communicating to Kenneth that it is *his* needs and *his* concerns which are important, that *his* feelings and *his* experiences are of value and relevance. It would mean giving to Kenneth the feeling that he can trust in his own being and draw from the depth of his being to discover new meanings and to guide his behavior. Focusing on the client and his frame of reference enables the client to become more aware of his internal resources and facilitates in the client an understanding of the reality of his being in the school, in the home, in the world.

3. He could have accepted Kenneth. Accepting a person means allowing him to *be* so that he may *become*. For the self to be freed for growth it must be accepted as it presently exists. Acceptance of the client means an acceptance of his values and standards as an integral part of him. The counselor does not have to accept the client's values and standards as the counselor's own, but he must be willing for the client to hold his own values—for an individual is only free to change his values when he is free to hold them. He is not forced to defend his

values when he is free to hold them; and when he feels his values are not condemned, judged, or labeled as "bad," he can then allow them to be explored by himself and by others. Change emerges from such an exploration and new values are developed, based upon new ways of perceiving. It is only in this free atmosphere that perceptions and behavior patterns change. The freedom to have ideas, values, and beliefs—the permission to be oneself—exists in a counseling climate that is marked by a deep respect for the individuality and uniqueness of the client. The discovery of self, the unlocking of one's inner core, is a deeply personal matter. In the final analysis, each individual must discover his own unique being in his own idiosyncratic and highly personal way. Only in an atmosphere where uniqueness is fostered and difference is valued, can the full discovery of oneself as a unique individual of dignity and worth be found.

The counselor who has faith in kids and who can offer a relationship characterized by acceptance, empathic understanding, facilitative genuineness, respect, and confidentiality will attract the Kenneths of this world whenever they experience issues of real concern to them.

T. ANTOINETTE RYAN

The techniques employed by the counselor and other members of the guidance team should stand up against the tests of legal, ethical, and professional considerations. Any counseling or therapeutic techniques that might be considered damaging to a client's reputation or standing could be looked upon as suspect on legal grounds, as a charge of libel or defamation of character and the counselor could be taken to court. If the parents have been privy to the decision to use some particular therapeutic techniques and if the counselor administering the treatment possesses the qualifications and competence to practice the accepted therapy, the question of legality probably would not become an important issue. The ethics by which counselors and therapists are bound clearly stipulate limits within which therapeutic practices can be employed. Under no circumstances should a counselor engage in administering therapy unless he is qualified to do so. The misuse of shock therapy could have devastating long-term effects, and this kind of specialized treatment should not be attempted by the uninitiated.

The school counselor has professional responsibilities that set limits on the kinds of behaviors that can be included in his repertoire. He has a primary obligation to help each pupil in the school grow into a healthy, adjusted, fully functioning person. The extent to which he will be able to establish and maintain effective relationships with the total student population is determined, in large measure, by his image from the student's point of view. The counseling relationship should rest on a foundation of mutual trust and respect. To the extent that the counselor's behavior raises questions in the minds of the clients and decreases the esteem in which he is held by them, limits are placed on the potential for his effectiveness. It behooves the counselor to implement behaviors which will permit him to be respected by all the pupils in the school.

The counselor's concern over a child's continuing use of filthy language with the other pupils is justifiable, not only because of the responsibility to help the particular child cope with a problem which might be impeding his educational development, but also for helping to create a healthy learning environment for all students in the school. The question that seems critical in this case is not what the counselor was concerned about but, rather, how he set about to cope with the problem. There is nothing to indicate that the counselor and the boy had reached the point of agreeing that there was a problem or that there were goals to be accomplished to alleviate a problem. The case appears to be one in which counselor intervention was imposed from without, with the client in the role of object of the intervention. Something was to be done *to* him rather than having the child involved in the process. The counselor assumed that "all the usual methods of dealing with the problem were likely to fail." It is hard to know what the counselor meant by "usual methods." There is no indication of the reasoning behind the conclusion that failure was imminent. The technique employed seems highly questionable. On the face of it, it appears that a behavioral approach would have been more suitable both from the standpoint of competencies involved and the counseling setting. The research evidence available supports the hypothesis that planned use of counselor cues and reinforcement would increase "good" language verbalizations and at the same time extinguish the filthy language verbalizations.

The counselor raises three questions that bear directly on the issue of ethical and legal responsibility of professional personnel in school settings. The question of whether it is justifiable to use "wrong means" to get good results can only be answered in the negative. The counselor has a moral obligation as well as a professional responsibility to select from among possible available means those that not only appear to offer greatest probability of success in achieving the counseling goals, but also can be justified to the client, his family, and the community on legal and ethical grounds. Therapeutic communication used by a professionally competent specialist, implementing tested therapy techniques in a clinical setting, is not necessarily appropriate for an educational setting.

The question of whether the boy was harmed in any way or not is difficult to answer in view of the paucity of information given. The evidence on effect of shock therapy seems to suggest quite strongly the importance of using supportive techniques in conjunction with the shock treatment, if long-term ill effects are to be minimized.

E. G. WILLIAMSON

What a honey of a suggestion the psychologist made! How risky in that it might very well have traumatized Kenneth in a way that could have been damaging. Although it seems a desirable technique, one must be very careful in using it. The shock of hearing his own language in the mouths of those he has put up on Mount Olympus or consigned to the other side of the River Styx must indeed have been a dramatic shock to Kenneth. In my opinion, the technique was not wrong at all. It worked. It produced the kind of results that may have shocked Kenneth into maturity and into a more realistic perception of his own behavior, which he either lacked or at least didn't seem to be affected by.

I think it would have been preferable for the counselor to follow up on this matter by arranging a conference with the mother and father, being very careful about what was said, certainly not reporting on the youngster's traumatic experience. I suppose that some parents might prefer charges against the school personnel because they used unacceptable language, but I think the conference team could have justified the technique and gently have brought the parents around to see that the intention of the procedure was good and that the results were desirable. Possibly Kenneth was imitating his parents—at least I would explore that possibility.

I don't know about the counselor who pulled out his penis. Maybe his judgment told him that it was a congruent part of the situation, but I suspect that the preparation for such a traumatic experience was not as carefully made as in the case of Kenneth and therefore was rather crude and clumsy. I would not have dismissed him immediately, however; rather, I would have put him in therapy.

I don't think that Kenneth was harmed. I think he was helped. However, the people in the incident had to run the chance that word would get around to the other students and that they might misinterpret what happened. They were lucky to get away with it. Counselors once in a while have to take chances. Their bosses should be tolerant. Professional people frequently are unable to inform their superiors about the strategies they employ ahead of time, because of the desperation of the moment and the availability of limited alternatives. Such shock techniques can be devastating, but they can also startle people into becoming alive. Kenneth is a case in point.

The Counselor

and the Family

The family sends its children to school. The state demands that a family sends its children to school. A child is in school. He interacts with a counselor. Whatever occurs between the child and the counselor can have repercussions between the child and his family, the family and the counselor, the counselor, and the school administration. Such is the nature of our complicated world. And, perhaps for these reasons, counselors often tend to become timid and self-limiting in their behavior.

In Part II we deal with a number of incidents which involve the family more or less directly. It is important that the precise and exact relationships between counselors and family be established. Is the counselor free to be himself, or must he or she be an agent of the family? Is the counselor an independent professional person or is he but a representative of the child's parents, saying exactly what they say?

In Incident 10, the "Antipathetic Boy," we have a very complex situation, perhaps deserving of much more time and space than we have been able to give to it, with a most disasterous conclusion. We have the classic ingredients of a tragedy: an ambitious father and a discouraged child. Add to that a counselor who operated implusively and irrationally because he probably wanted to serve the parents rather than the child. This incident very clearly illustrates the absolute importance of having counselors who can deal with children fairly and who can be on their side.

In "Kinde, Kirche, Küche" we run a common problem relating to the differing attitudes of the counselor and the family. In several of the incidents in this part, what the parents want, what the child wants, and what the counselor thinks is right differ, relative to the child's academic future. But the real incident is not in what was done but how it was done. And this is often the central issue in professional work. No book, lecture, or demonstration can ever completely illustrate or affect the style of the counselor and how he comes across to his clients. In any event, faced with a tough situation, the counselor operated in an admirable manner and saved a bad situation from deteriorating into a disastrous situation for the child.

Suppose that parents are obviously harming their child—and insist on doing it—suppose that they refuse to see the truth, suppose that the reality of the situation is evident to all except the parents—this is the theme of "The Counselor Succumbs." What should he do faced with irrationality? Should he go along or should he stick to his guns? Mother in this incident wanted Yetta to be promoted at any cost. She finally frightened the counselor into acquiescence. While her dramatic means probably are highly unusual, any counselor who has faced pressure from parents will appreciate this counselor's predicament.

The school counselor often becomes a close observer of family relationships, and often he has to decide whether or not to intervene. In "The Incorrigible Parents" we have an aggressively hostile child whose behavior apparently was a direct cause of the parents' treatment and who continued his delinquent ways as a result of the failure of the parents to change. The issue here seems to be the counselor's understanding of the real problem but doing nothing about it, a very common situation. What is our responsibility when we see a child mistreated psychologically?

What is college for? Who should go to college? Who decides whether or not a specific child should go on to further education? What is the counselor's responsibility in the decision-making process? In "The Counselor Cops Out" we have a relatively clear-cut situation, contrasting with that of Incident 11, in which the perceptions and conclusions of the counselor and that of the parents are diametrically opposed. The counselor has one clear-cut idea: college is for the elite. The parents have an equally clear cut idea: they want their son to go to college. At issue is the counselor's perogative to speak as he wishes. He felt that what he was asked to do was against his ideas, his philosophy, and his understanding, and he felt also that what he was asked to do was wrong and harmful to the child in the incident. But he went along with the family in what he knew would be a mistake. This incident, it seems to us, is truly critical in the development of a proper concept of the position of the school counselor.

In "Cry Rape" we had an example of a child attempting to make trouble for a teacher. In that incident, the teacher stuck his neck out and apparently deserved what he almost got. However, in the case of

"The Pernicious Lie," the counselor seems to have been the victim of malicious intent without justification, and the title could have been, "Caught in the Middle." How to deal with the issue of unjustified accusations that come to a professional person is the essence of this incident.

The attitudes of some parents relative to their children's schooling may approach the pathological. Some parents who attempt to relive their lives through their children become quite disappointed if the child's behavior does not meet their expectations. Incident 16, "Degree or Trade," is a case of two boys, both of whom were indifferent students. One went to college, the other did not. The situation with parents and the students was handled well. The issue is what happened to the youths. Apparently, the one who did not go to college found more meaning in life than the one who did. While this incident is not particularly dramatic, as the contributor himself says, it does illustrate how this problem of further education can be handled, and what some of the consequences of either decision can be.

10

The Antipathetic Boy

CRITICAL INCIDENT

Background

My high school is located in an upper middle-class neighborhood in a suburb close to a very large city. The children who attend this school have parents who, to put it mildly, are highly competitive in every respect: socially, financially, athletically, and academically. It is not unusual for me to have at least one parent ask me daily why John or Seymour "isn't doing better?" or "Do you think Sandra will make it at Smith?" "What does a SCAT score of 98 mean," and so on. I spend a lot of my time trying to reassure parents, telling them that getting into Harvard is not the only important thing in the world and trying to explain to them that if their kids take a speed reading test this will not automatically raise their IQ. In this school, everyone aspires to become a doctor or a lawyer—provided they have rejected the idea of becoming bankers or investment advisers. I hope I have given the reader a sense of the kind of school it is.

When Mr. Meyer came in to see me and when he began his story about his lazy son, it seemed to me that I had heard this story over and over again. I looked over Philip's chart and it was quite evident that the boy was average for the population he was in, but by no means the genius that his father wanted him to be. The father had one theme: his son didn't do what he was capable of, and I had to motivate him, and to motivate the boy I had to call him in and tell him he was breaking his mother's heart, hurting his father's reputation in the community, affecting the school image, disappointing his relatives, and irretrievably harming himself by not studying harder and getting better grades.

As I usually do in these cases, I reviewed all the objective evidence with him carefully: grades achieved in elementary school, grades in high school, and psychological tests. But Mr. Meyer dismissed the importance of this data, telling me about his life, how he had pushed ahead, how he had conquered obstacles, how easy young kids have it these days, and how Philip would someday be appreciative of his father's efforts. Mr. Meyer, who had started his own business, was a man of extraordinary vitality and conviction and, under his sway, I began to wonder whether it were not possible that he might be right. In any event, I promised to see Philip and to have another meeting with the father.

Incident

There was a suicide attempt in this case, and I feel it was the consequence of the incident. I feel sure about that. And I think that my betrayal of Philip was the last straw. But let me try to explain my part in this tragedy and where it became a critical incident for me.

I called in Philip and I was first struck by the fact that he was singularly unattractive. He had buck teeth, protruding lips, sallow skin, an unpleasant voice. He had the look of a hounded boy. He was definitely quite fearful and his language was replete with "I don't know..." and other noncommittal statements. He was obviously uncomfortable and wanted no part of me. I found myself behaving differently with him than I do with other children. I disliked him instantly, and I could empathize with the father who had to put up with this reluctant, defiant, negative youth of fifteen. I tried to control myself and behave in accordance with the dictates of a professional relationship, but I was keenly aware of my feelings toward this boy whose behavior and appearance repulsed me. I could understand very well how he could drive his father to distraction. Nevertheless, for some time I tried to make contact, to be reasonable and friendly, even though I was constantly aware that I was not being genuine with him but playing a role. I wanted to say something like: "I can see why your father hates you; you are so ugly both in your appearance and your behavior. I want to be of some help but your manner is so damn antagonistic and even insulting that I too feel hate toward you." When I became aware of this feeling of antagonism, we were looking at each other, and I think we knew just how I felt and what I was thinking. I got up and went to my files, pretending to look up something, I was angry with myself for this almost uncontrollable feeling. When I felt calmer, I went back and made my speech.

> Look, Philip, you just seem to have a lousy attitude and I think your fairly poor academic performance is due to that as much as anything. I have just been with you for five minutes and you have already antagonized me. I have the feeling that you are operating on the revenge motive and have it in for everybody. I suppose that you don't study just to get your father mad. Well, my friend, you are going to be unhappy in life unless you learn to cooperate.

As I spoke I felt my anger toward him increasing and realized that I had gone too far. I had no right to talk to this boy in this manner especially since I hardly knew him. His eyes got small, his lips pursed to a point, and he just seemed to be glaring at me. I lost my temper.

> I think you are just ungrateful. I don't blame your father for being so damn disappointed in you. Here I want to help you and you just do nothing: stare and glare at me as though I were your enemy. Get out! Come back to see me when you have a better attitude.

I pointed to the door and he got up sullenly and left the room.

Discussion

Several days later I heard that Philip had attempted suicide. His mother heard a crash in his room, and running in, discovered him with a noose around his neck in his closet. Apparently, he had tied the other end of the rope to a hook in the wall of the closet, had jumped off a chair, and the hook had not held. He had not left any suicide note.

By the time that Philip had left me, I realized that I had made a very serious mistake in venting my own hostile feelings toward this unattractive, shy, and awkward boy, and that I had become the father's ally without any information at all, without really knowing Philip. I don't know if the suicide attempt was genuine or whether it was a sham to punish the father and perhaps me. I wonder if it was another aspect of his hostility toward the world, or whether it was a manifestation of his desperation. He did not return to school. I subsequently learned he had been put into a private mental hospital for a while and later transferred to a residential school elsewhere. I never saw the father again, and I have no idea whether the father knew of my encounter with Philip. I just know that years after this event I still feel badly about my own behavior.

Questions

1.   I showed my real feelings, but I think I should not have. This boy struck me the wrong way at the wrong time, and I empathized with the father and blasted the son. Do you ever have irrationally strong attitudes toward counselees? Positive or negative feelings? What do you do about them? Every once in a while I go overboard one way or another, positively or negatively, towards students.

2.   Do you think my behavior might have contributed to the suicide attempt?

3.   How the hell does one deal with these sullen, negative, "I dunno nothing" types? You want to help them, but all they want to do is get your goat?

4.   Sometimes I think that misfits like Philip are better off dead anyway, and that treating them kindly no matter how they treat others, is a mistake. I know I sound hostile, but there is a lot of hostility in the world and some of it is very blatant and open in this school. Are we always to nurture the sick egos of repulsive students?

COMMENTS ON THE INCIDENT

THE EDITORS

One of the functions of a profession is to nurture stylized behavior among its members. Thus, the minister, the doctor, and the lawyer behave in ways which characterize their professional identity. The counselor too learns certain "habits" which help identify him in the work setting. For example, we learn to become interested in people, we learn to keep our temper, we learn to listen, we learn not only to listen but to think while listening, rather than planning a rebuttal. One of the most important things we learn is to like people. If we understand a person, we like him.

However, counselors are human and counselors can succumb if they are not aware of such common human foibles as reaction to praise, bribery for acceptance, kowtowing to authority, anger to slights, and unwarranted antipathy to ill-mannered people. The statement: "I understand you, but I still don't like you" does not fit the counselor's role. Rather his habituated response eventuates in his concluding: "I don't like you because I don't understand you, but in the meantime I'm not going to let you know."

In this incident, a too-human counselor reacted strongly to an unpleasant child and the results were tragic. Some of our consultants take the counselor to task and advise him to get out of counseling. Does the reader agree?

THOMAS W. ALLEN

Working with students who are apparently dedicated to revenging themselves on a world which they see (perhaps rightly, perhaps wrongly) as having treated them shabbily, whose aim in life is to be the object of others' hostility, makes considerable demands on the counselor both as a practitioner and a person.

An "inside-view" of the client is essential to the counselor. He assumes such a perspective by utilizing his knowledge of psychodynamics to grasp the nature of the client's experience of the world. A person's feelings and behavior are perfectly "logical," if not in terms of common sense, in terms of his own special way of making sense of life. Understanding this "private logic" (Adler) puts the client's actions in a new light. In this light, they may well evoke less rejection in the counselor. While the client may not become lovable through this recasting, he almost certainly becomes more tolerable—and workable.

In this case, the counselor was indignant. His "reasonableness" and "friendliness" were not returned: "Here I graciously extended my hand in friendship and helpfulness and it was churlishly bitten. How vicious can a kid get?" However, this response arises largely because the counselor attends only to the meaning which Philip's behavior has within his (the counselor's) own frame of reference. It seems probable that if he construed the same events in terms of Philip's "private logic," the counselor would have felt and acted differently.

For instance, since the counselor felt attacked by Philip, his conclusion that revenge is a central objective for Philip is probably correct. Now the question becomes: From what sort of experience of the world does revenge arise? Revenge arises most frequently from pain, particularly from pain generated by a significant loss perceived to have been caused more or less maliciously by another person. Therefore, the counselor's feeling of being injured by Philip might have been modified by the thought that he was dealing with a boy who had suffered a good deal. Since Philip's desire for revenge seemed so pervasive and poignant, the counselor might have supposed that Philip felt cheated and abused by life. Further, Philip's fearfulness might have suggested to the counselor that he fully expects further injury will befall him, that he is likely to be beset from any quarter at any time.

The counselor might then have begun to seek evidence bearing on these hypotheses. He might, for example, have asked himself whether the behavior which he observed as part of Philip's general posture toward the world was prompted by some characteristic of the counselor. That is, was the counselor treated as an "enemy" because of some special qualification for that role?

After all, is it not the counselor's first task to understand the person he is trying to assist? His task is not deciding how worthy his client is of his approbation. At the same time, it must be recognized that feelings which a client evokes in him are important clues to divine the purposes served by problem behavior. In grasping these purposes the counselor gains a sense for the manner in which the client experiences the world, the basic assumptions upon which he operates.

Understanding is a necessary condition for counseling. In the present incident, we lack certain bits of data in developing a concrete understanding of Philip. Nevertheless, there is sufficient information to enable us to make some progress. The emerging picture of Philip is of an extremely discouraged young man. He has profound doubts concerning his ability to achieve much of a place for himself in the world by "patient striving" as Alfred Adler would have it. His efforts have been diverted into guerilla warfare against his father, the school, and its minions, among others.

To begin with, the father's demands are of such a magnitude that Philip must have despaired of fulfilling them long ago. In so doing, he most likely gave up on himself, particularly since he was unable to evaluate the validity of his father's admonitions. Of course, father was abetted by the prevailing atmosphere of the competitive community in which the family lived. Thus, Philip may have learned that nothing was to be gained by applying himself. Whatever was accomplished would inevitably be found wanting, i.e., not up to father's standards.

On the other hand, a good deal was to be achieved by *not* exerting himself. Father seems to be dedicated to what might be called "the myth of the exceedingly able but immorally recalcitrant mind." He maintains that Philip is, in reality, virtually a genius (after all, Philip is *his* son) and could move mountains if he but had the decency to hearken to his (father's) wishes. Thus, even in the midst of his rages against Philip, he attributes considerable worth to him implicitly. Father's sternest accusations seem to contain the message that father values Philip for what he "really is" beneath the dross of present appearances. This backhanded evaluation would be quickly rejected by persons with other varieties of support at their disposal. But for he who has nothing else, this meager offering is worth defending. Consequently, any wholehearted attempt to meet his father's expectations was out of the question. To fail after having tried was clearly much worse than to have failed without trying. In the former case, he risks his last tenuous claim to parental esteem and affection since in such a situation he might well be unmasked as merely a person of average ability rather than a slumbering but nonetheless awesome genius.

It is probable that Philip has time and again felt humiliated by father. Not the least of these humiliations may have arisen from father's implicit declaration to the effect that Philip's life belongs, in an important sense, to his father. Put the other way around, Philip is not even allowed discretionary prerogatives in regard to his own destiny. Thus,

Philip's behavior may well be, at least in part, the assertion of some of his fundamental human rights, a defense of his identity against the insistence that he is an object to be used at another's pleasure.

Two crucial considerations follow from this observation. One is a concrete strategy for dealing with Philip. The other has to do with the philosophical implications of this counselor's general position. Let us deal with the latter first.

The counselor seems to assume that his responsibility is to "motivate" Philip, i.e., to get him to behave in such a way that father's desires for prestige are fulfilled. But is this the counselor's proper calling? Is he in the business of supplying parents with more and better pawns to serve whatever personal objectives they may have? Are father's "reputation in the community," "the school's image," "the disappointment of relatives," or of a status-conscious mother his rightful concerns? I think not. The counselor's overriding allegiance is to the task of helping Philip find satisfactory ways of meeting what Adler terms the three great challenges of life, viz., human relations, vocation, and love. A dedication to one's priority in respect to his fellows, to surpassing others and impressing them with one's superiority (goals which Philip's father may well cherish) does not serve to meet these challenges. The clinical investigation of several generations of psychotherapists and a growing body of systematic research provides rich support for this thesis. Among his other difficulties, the disciple of the goal of personal superiority must constantly be vigilant lest someone usurp his place. Philip's father appears as an excellent case in point.

The second matter of interest here is a technical one. Had the counselor understood Philip in the foregoing manner his work with him might have begun on a different note. The counselor could, for example, have expressed some honest admiration for his doggedness and strength. After all, Philip has held out against a very powerful man for years. Indeed, there is plenty of evidence to suggest that Philip has been successful in resisting what had been for others virtually an irresistable force. Now that is strength! After all, the counselor knows from firsthand experience how powerful Philip is. In but a few minutes he succeeded in driving the counselor out of a stance which he had carefully cultivated over the years.

Suppose, then, that the counselor had used his own feelings, in this fashion, as a source of understanding. Suppose further that he had communicated both his concrete comprehension of the nature of Philip's world (e.g., "It must seem like you're getting hit from all sides. When your dad decides that he wants something, he really goes after it. It must seem like what you want just doesn't count.") and his respect for Philip's ability to stand his ground against formidable odds (e.g., "I don't know how you do it. Your father hits you with everything he's got and that's a lot! But still he can't move you. You're too strong for even a powerful guy like him.").

In such a way the counselor might well have established a climate wherein Philip could have been effectively introduced to other, less costly, ways of dealing with life. He might have been taught, on one hand, to avoid the pyrrhic victories with which he was satisfying himself and, on the other hand, to preserve his sense of self. He might have been gradually plugged back into the useful side of social life through those things in which he could find some success and recognition. He might have been shown how to establish himself in the world in such a way as to achieve a meaningful independence from father.

The suicide attempt? Certainly the present incident did nothing to improve the situation. Indeed, Philip probably utilized the counselor's response to him as another bit of justification for taking what might be considered to be his ultimate revenge on his tormentors.

The tone of questions three and four is distressing. Such an attitude, though understandable, is unquestionably the source of much destructiveness and has no place in education. In this case, it apparently arises from a failure to apprehend some of the important facts of human life (e.g., that such behavior as Philip's is generated by a profound sense of discouragement). This lack of understanding is aggravated by the counselor's personal discouragement. Both of these things are, of course, remediable, but it is essential that something be done. That is, the counselor must divest himself of this attitude by means of therapy and further training, or find another profession.

MARY A. BARBER

This case presents another common problem for high school counselors. Where there are such divergent and conflicting attitudes between parent and child, disappointment and disillusionment on the parents' part and rebellion or hostility in the student, with which side should the counselor align himself? Theoretically and ideally, the counselor should not take sides but should be an objective analytical observer, attempting to empathize with both participants and to facilitate compromise or convergence of attitudes. This is, of course, much easier to state philosophically than to achieve in practice.

In response to question one, every normal person occasionally has seemingly irrational reactions to other persons, *seemingly* irrational because they can usually be rationalized by analysis. Is it wrong to show your own real feelings? I would say it is not categorically wrong, but in a counseling relationship it is the counselor's responsibility not only to be real and sincere, but to use care and tact in the way he reveals his feelings, keeping the counselee's welfare uppermost in his mind. Perhaps the counselor could have let the student know how he felt but at the same time admit that he thought his (counselor's) feelings were somewhat biased. He might have said something like, "I can't help but feel angry when a student acts the way you do, but I'm more angry with myself for giving way to this feeling than I am with you." In truthfully confessing that he too had problems, he might have succeeded in establishing some rapport with the student. He might have tried to make the student understand that even though they had different standards of what was proper appearance or attitude, as long as this was known to both of them, as long as their biases were out in the open, they might still be able to communicate enough to work together. In another approach the counselor might indicate that he thought some of the parents' expectations were quite unreasonable and that it would be understandable if this made the student feel frustrated and miserable. If all such attempts to reach the student seemed to fail, or if it were just impossible for the counselor to conquer his own feelings of revulsion enough to keep trying, then it would seem that referral would be indicated. Rather than reject the student completely the counselor could have suggested that although the two of them didn't seem to be getting along very well, he thought someone else might be able to help. In other words, he would have held out some hope rather than give the student the impression that he was a hopeless case.

In response to question three, previous suggestions have been offered posing possible alternatives. I dislike the counselor's apparent assumption that this type of student is deliberately out to get his goat. Although it may seem that way in a temporary reaction to an unpleasant encounter, this could be a correct interpretation only insofar as the counselor represents the entire adult world or school faculty or whatever the student's hostility is directed to, but should not be taken so personally.

I confess that I am somewhat affronted by the statements in connection with question four and consider them antithetical to recognized tenets of counselor training and philosophy. As to nurturing sick egos of repulsive students, presenting a helping attitude and trying to bring the sick ego back to a more healthy state should not be considered as nurturing an illness. I would suggest that this final statement and question are perhaps unwisely worded as a result of a sincere counselor's frustration with a self-recognized area of inadequacy.

EDWARD S. BORDIN

Too much of the literature on counseling and psychotherapy conveys the impression that all people are likable. Sometimes, the emphasis on acceptance has carried that implication. It is certainly true that the role of counselor or psychotherapist is epitomized by a dedication to helping persons overcome personal obstacles toward fuller development and toward living productive and satisfying lives. The persons who seek out such professional responsibilities should and usually do have an interest in other people which transcends class, status, and personal appearance. Yet clients, as do all persons, differ in physical attractiveness, the richness of their personal resources, the prickliness of their reactions to others, and generally in the attractiveness of their personalities. If we assume, as many do, that a client's problems inevitably reflect interpersonal difficulties, some degree of strain in counselor-client relationships are the expected norm.

The successful counselor-client relationships are those in which, despite strains and momentary frustrations, there are basic gratifications to be obtained by both parties. Initially it involves their interest in each other. On the client's side, he initially experiences the counselor's understanding and commitment to be helpful and later the gratification of seeing desired changes occurring. On the counselor's side there is the pride in doing one's job well, the satisfying of curiosity, the desire for a limited kind of intimacy, and interest in influencing significantly the development of another.

The counselor's account suggests that there was virtually no basis for mutual satisfaction in this relationship. The counselor initiated the contact and did not seek to establish a positive motivation for counseling. In the counselor's words, "He was . . . uncomfortable with me and wanted no part of me." The counselor even before meeting Philip seemed more committed to his father's views than Philip's. Thus, we must ask how this counselor sees his task. Does he see himself as an agent of parents and school in exerting a socializing influence upon his clients? Or does he see himself as a special agent delegated to aid his clients in their struggle to attain self-integrity and integration despite external pressures? If he chooses the latter orientation, which is the representative one, then he must establish a base for operation in the client's desire for his help. He needs to learn how his client is willing and able to use his help. Such efforts often carry a counselor beyond initial feelings of dislike or aversion. The experience of intimate collaboration tends to increase our responsiveness to positive characteristics in the other and to decrease our sensitivity to less attractive characteristics, especially those of a surface variety. Nothing could be more destructive of a relationship than feelings of irritation and dislike, masked by a thin veneer of acceptance and benevolence. A genuine dedication to helping another coupled with basic interest can make honest expressions of momentary feelings of anger or dislike tolerable, even constructive. In this instance, the counselor gave honest expression to his adverse feelings toward the client, but without having established any commitment to the client.

The counselor seems so estranged from his clientele that one wonders why he stays in the school. Clearly, he sees both the parents and students served by this school as spoiled privileged persons undeserving of his efforts. Perhaps he could better tolerate the neurotic foibles of an underprivileged person. But one wonders whether he has made a proper choice of vocation. Counselors and psychotherapists must be able to respond to the underlying plight of persons which, because of their need for a corrective relationship, drives them into excesses destructive of the very relationships they seek. If the counselor is to interrupt that destructive cycle, his sense of the underlying confusion and pain must be strong enough to enable him to endure an uncomfortable period so that he can respond appropriately.

Philip, whose father appeared to have no interest in his son, except as his own status was enhanced or undermined, must have been an extremely unhappy boy. His apparent defense against becoming a despised pawn was stubborn inaction coupled with an effort to exaggerate the appearance and manner which others found painfully repulsive. He would express his anger at this rejection by using these qualities as weapons. The counselor was surely another in a line of such relationships. We are not told enough to be able to decide whether it was a genuine try at suicide and whether the encounter with the counselor was a decisive factor, but clearly this boy needed to give expression to his anger and despair. Most importantly he needed the experience of another's understanding interest to be able to search for the useful parts of himself.

JAMES DONOVAN

My first reaction to the counselor in this case is one of ambivalence. Although I find that he is quite honest in accepting his share of the blame in losing this youngster, I am disturbed with the evidence that indicates he has chosen the wrong field for his life's work. It is quite possible that his own frustration with the father triggered this bizarre reaction but I sense that a more general intolerance toward youths that choose not to play the academic game is really at the root of his incompetence.

This counselor must understand, if he hopes to be effective in any way, that he must function not as an agent of the father or school but rather in a much more general helping sense. The key problem here was a forced help which, in my opinion, can never produce results. I strongly believe that voluntary counseling with the counselee seeking contact is the only effective change agent. The counselor, however, cannot lock himself in the office and wait for someone to knock at the door. He must put himself in situations where contact can be encouraged on an informal basis at first and be ready to respond to indirect counseling requests. This may sound idealistic and, to some, downright impossible, but the counselor's attitude simply reflects that he is an untrained counselor lost in a jungle of unfulfilled needs—those of the students and his own.

This counselor may be a fine disseminator of information or a college placement officer; but some kids need to be helped in the deepest sense and here the counselor failed woefully. There is a need in the schools for both information-giving and counseling, but until we realize and acknowledge that the latter role demands intensive training the kids will continue to be the real losers.

The counselor in this case unfortunately represents the norm of today's counselors. We are doing everybody a disservice by asking the untrained, poorly-suited counselor to help the discouraged and confused among our youth. Some forward-looking school districts are meeting this problem by establishing human relations centers in high school staffed by qualified counselors and psychologists, leaving the information-giving and other functionary aspects of our work to our more academically-oriented guidance personnel.

MARSANNE C. EYRE

It is hard to believe that a counselor could be so tragically incompetent. I guess this is due to the notion that because a man has been exposed to theory and been given qualified training, we assume he is mature enough to cope responsibly with his own behavior. This also is a classic example of how partial understanding (or mere intellectualization on a verbal level) of concepts such as genuineness and empathy served only to act as a justification or camouflage for the acting out of what I consider irresponsible and unethical behavior on the part of the counselor.

Let's start by dealing with the serious dilemma of the counselor who feels he cannot maintain openness and rational behavior toward a student. Is he aware of his own inner conflict regarding whatever problem the student has shown? Perhaps there is something he cannot recognize or tolerate in himself that he has seen in the boy. If it causes him to become punitive or demeaning toward his client, the counselor *must* divest himself of this child and refer him elsewhere. Or, if no other counselor or competent person is available, he would do better to say "I'm sorry, but I don't believe it would be fair to you to try to counsel you because I am afraid my personal bias might be harmful."

The counselor's minor negative feelings toward a client should certainly be recognized and expressed, but not in such a directly hostile way (e.g., "Philip, I get the feeling that you are uncomfortable or angry about being here and I'm beginning to feel the same way myself. Do you think if we both tried to relax a little it might make things better?") In other words, offer some kind of "sharing" alternative to the direct and potentially destructive expression of negative feelings.

The counselor's defensiveness and hostility almost become paranoid as he wonders about the boy's right to live. If the boy were the least bit sensitive and fearful, there is a good chance that he understood the counselor's feelings, along with the obvious rejection. It could well have been the last straw. I would tend to take the suicide as bona fide due to the very fact that a note was *not* written. His depression may have been so intense and consuming that he no longer cared to try to make *any* contact with the world around him.

My concern is for the countless students who follow Philip into this counselor's office: "You want to help them out; all they want to do is get your goat . . ." How can communication on any positive level occur when in essence there is no recognition of the student's basic human value? This counselor must be helped to resolve his incongruency and provided with the experience of seeing "sullen, negative students" respond to real trust and caring. Perhaps this approach will result in the cessation of his destructive devaluation of troubled clients, replacing scorn with compassion.

ALLEN E. IVEY

This case represents an almost classic example of what the New Left might call the failure of the establishment. We see a "hounded" boy abandoned by a counselor in a moment of need. We see the father who sees the son as object rather than person. We see a guidance counselor hounded by an achievement-oriented society and school to the extent that he is not sure of his own self. And, finally, all too common, we see a school whose prime aim is to train students to fit into a tight mold, a school that is responding to a society that demands excellence at the price of personal and human development.

Who is the villain? The son repressed by his father? The father repressed by his job and society? The counselor repressed by the school? The school administrators who must meet the demands of the college and the upper middle-class neighborhood?

There is no villain. This situation, while dramatic, is not unusual. There are very few counselors who do not have a case in their files where they have failed a person in need. Too many parents see their children as extensions of themselves rather than as independent entities. Too many schools are more concerned about college admission over personal growth.

What can be done by a counselor to prevent such instances from reoccurring not only in this setting, but in others as well? Counselors must have, in addition to counseling skills and knowledge, a deep understanding of their own needs and feelings. Therapy and personal growth training for counselors is becoming more available as part of the standard counselor education program. Until counselors can understand themselves and have a sense of personal freedom, their chances of significantly aiding students in need is greatly reduced.

The role of the counselor in relation to the school must be considered. No matter how personally integrated a counselor is, if the school within which he works has inadequate objectives and methods, he cannot be fully effective. Individual or group counseling even at the highest professional levels in a school such as that described here will, at best, be remedial. Counselors must take an active part in humanizing their school settings. It has been a habit of the counseling profession to complain about the settings in which they work, but to do nothing about it. Models of developmental psychology, community mental health, and educational innovation all point to the need of a new counselor role, that of community consultant to the student developmental process in the schools. While counseling is a useful technique, it can no longer be considered the only behavior-change method of the school counselor. Counselors have a responsibility to work to make their schools more fully human through helping teachers with their classroom instructional procedures, administrators to sometimes sacrifice humanity for expedience, and parents to learn new ways of helping their children grow. The counselor can no longer accept a role as passive facilitator to the goals of society. Black and student militants have aptly pointed out that counselors have been a major force in maintaining "the system."

Instead of merely parroting a school's rules and goals, counselors must step out and take an active role in helping a school examine its purposes, relations with students, and serve as an active force for positive change.

The school needs to examine its role in relationship to its middle-class neighborhood. The academically striving school discussed here has been fostered by a community and society concerned with objective material gain at the expense of subjective human values. By responding to this press with emphasis on academic, as opposed to personal, excellence, the school has done the community a major disservice. Recent school upheavals at all levels clearly illustrate the need for the school to reexamine its values and relationship to the community. Are schools to lead society or follow?

Speaking more directly to the questions of the counselor, all counselors experience irrational feelings toward their counselees. Therapy and counseling are often recommended for those who are to become counselors so that they will understand their biases and work with them more effectively. If a counselor cannot live with his feelings constructively when he feels negatively toward a student, this student must be referred elsewhere.

The counselor's values and opinions are clear. He apparently sees such students as anxious to get *his* goat rather than as frightened individuals needing help. The statement, "how does one *deal* (italics mine) with these..." reveals the counselor's tendency to objectify his students. The counselor admits this, yet he still goes "overboard" with students. A counselor with attitudes such as this should honestly admit them and resign his position. As an alternative, intensive therapy seems necessary if the counselor is to remain in his position.

Yet, it is not wise to completely discount the counselor in this case. He has openly and honestly discussed a deep, personal concern. He seems angry and frustrated, but he seems also to be honestly asking for help. Let us not prejudge him, but encourage him toward future growth. With the statement of this case, he has made an important beginning.

To the question of how does one "deal" with sullen, negative students, the answer is simple. One does not prejudge, but waits to see the beauty emerging from within the beast. And, unless one has patience and trust in human nature, they will never see the true nature of the beast. And one who does not see potential beauty in even the most ugly is perhaps the one most in need of aid.

BARBARA A. KIRK

This counselor was scarcely engaging in that activity which we call counseling. Counseling starts with the counselee, starts with the commitment to understand the problems, needs, feelings, values, attitudes, and orientation of the individual with whom one is working. This is the starting point of counseling. After the feelings, needs, and situation of the person are expressed and evaluated, help comes in changing those aspects of the situation or person which require alteration or adaptation so that the counselee may enjoy an improved human experience. The counselor did not approach this student in a counseling fashion; rather, he was biased against him and adopted a punitive attitude toward him even before he began to work with him.

The original difficulty arose in the counselor's accepting the parent's attitudes without question. He should have seen the parent from the standpoint of the counselee. He should have recognized the extent of the father's fanatic attitude toward the son's achievements and goals and how crippling these demands must be. He should have tried to help the parent to see not whether what he wanted of the boy was right or wrong but, more importantly, the effect on the boy of the demands placed upon him, particularly in view of Philip's limited ability to deal with the requirements of this parent.

The counselor raises the question of dealing with his own feelings. The amount of punitive anger he displayed toward Philip and the intensity of his own feelings indicates that perhaps he would be better adapted to a profession other than counseling. If these destructive feelings are so easily and intensely activated, they may be too much for him to cope with in continuous counseling relationships.

On those occasions, however, when negative feelings arise, they must be dealt with in some way. If feelings are recognized in advance, particularly if they are strong, one can stay in command of the situation by carefully thinking through the ways in which one can control these feelings and can deal appropriately and helpfully with the client. If the feelings become uncontrollable, one can terminate the interview by explaining one's own dilemma to the counselee in as objective a way as possible so the counselee can get appropriate perspective on the problem as not being entirely of his own making and thus not assume blame for it. If the counselor is uncertain about his ability to manage his hostility, he may excuse himself from the case, asking a colleague or someone else to see a student he fears he may damage.

To respond to the second question—did he contribute to the suicide attempt?—one regretfully would need to say "probably, yes." This boy possesses few methods of coping with the constant pressure that a dominating father places on him. He, therefore, would be likely to look to anyone for help with a problem too great for him to deal with. He comes to see the counselor hoping he will find someone who will give him attention, interest, understanding, and concern. Possibly this is a first opportunity for him; possibly it is a last one.

He was met, however, with behavior which entrenched the father's viewpoint and made the boy feel conclusively that he is hopeless, unlovable, has no possibility of gaining approval or support anywhere, and that there is very little left for him to do. This may affect the possibility of future psychotherapy for this boy, since he is likely to equate any therapist with the counselor model.

One can empathize, to some extent at least, with this counselor's question about dealing with sullen, negative, resistive types. This counselor has difficulty in seeing beneath the surface of the fears, hurts, and frustrations that cause this sort of behavior. If one recognizes that extreme resistiveness and lack of communicativeness and responsiveness is an emotional illness, an ineffectual way of dealing with a problem too big to handle, a method which is self-destructive, one gains thereby the patience and concern to deal with it. There is no gainsaying that youngsters who have been badly bruised by their own family interactions may be particularly difficult for adults to deal with for they invariably transfer the same defiant-resistive attitude toward all authority.

Such problems are challenges for the counselor and they require time, patience, interest, and the highest level of skills to establish a relationship and the kind of rapport to make it possible for the youngster to trust and communicate with adults again.

In the case of Philip, if the counselor had empathy and compassion, he could have realized how desperate the boy was and transferred him to a competent therapist before Philip lost the vestiges of his hold on reality and became completely psychotic.

This counselor's attitude toward "misfits," as exemplified in his last question, indicates a lack of professional and technical knowledge about the possibilities of remediation. Apparently he is also unaware of the implications of the father's responsibility for the condition of the son. If there is detection and referral early enough, much subsequent misery for the individual and society can be averted and prevented.

JOHN D. MULLEN

The counselor who tries to force counselees to accept his advice is looking for trouble and, in my estimation, is violating the most important and fundamental principles in a counselor-counselee relationship—equality and independence. This is what happened here, and the consequences are evident. Counseling of this nature, filled with dislike and loaded with demands, is dangerous to the counselee—and the counselor.

The person counseling from a position of "I am better than thou" or "I know better than thee" will be unhappy and threatened because he will often be rebuffed or challenged. The advice he so earnestly and strongly imparts will be simply rejected. A counselee only accepts what is *his* thinking, and not the ideas a counselor promulgates. For a counselee to accept any advice as if from an infallible source is dangerous. Dependency is not what a counselor should strive for. Not only may the advice be wrong, but any counselee who accepts advice, and follows through without understanding or assessing it, is losing his individuality, spontaneity, and self-esteem.

Every counselee must accept responsibility for his own life. Only when it derives from his own judgments will his behavior really be mature human behavior and satisfying to him. Whether it is wrong or right in any one else's judgment is another issue.

The counselor in this incident typifies how a good counselor should not act: impulsive, hostile, judgmental, and deferring to a powerful father. Many troubled students, faced with a hostile world, need a person and a place where they can "cool it." Philip obviously needed such a refuge: a nonthreatening environment where he could think reflectively with the counselor's encouragement. This is what the counselor should have provided. Surely, dispensing information and giving orders to Philip might be in order at some point in his life but certainly not at this time.

Many counselors attempt to solve such problems in a "one shot" session. They feel that they can handle the problem nicely with promptness and dispatch, once they have said the proper things. Unfortunately, just saying the right things is appropriate only sometimes; some problems —and the one cited here is a good example—cannot be treated lightly or abruptly. There is no substitute for love and common sense in counseling. I don't think this counselor displayed either of these indispensable qualities.

HERMAN PETERS

This is a case of complex, interactive thoughts and feelings—mostly negative. The buildup for possible suicide was a processing of accumulated experiences. The confrontations in the incident are the conclusions of additive clashes. What was needed was immediate referral, not so much because of a possibility of greater competency by the referral agent as it was a need to break the chain reaction of negativism toward Philip. The counselor was pulled into the vortex of the storm before he knew it. This is always a real danger for a school counselor because he is physically located in the midst of the action. He does not have recourse to psychological distance as a counselor in a clinic would have.

The school counselor should have had another interview to share his own upset with the counselee. The humanness inherent in the disclosure of such feelings may have provided a basis for expressed mutuality in both working together. It may have cleared the air.

The counselor's behavior probably triggered irresponsible behavior; however, at this point any negative confrontation would have severely hurt Philip.

One must keep in mind that the "I dunno nothing" types are not developed by one failure. It is a process of failing or not living up to the expectations of others. Once the failures become numerous, the individual's self-esteem deteriorates rapidly. To reverse this is a long-term process. Some would even suggest that the harm is irreparable.

One does not nurture a sick ego. One tries to halt its cancerous growth, to nurture positive cells of development, few as they may be, in an effort to overcome, arrest, or control the realities of deficiencies which cannot be removed.

In question four, it is true that there is hostility in the world. It will not be lessened by current approaches to school counseling. The school counselor must be an active participant, not a clinician, in counseling. This is asking a lot when there is minimal social sanction for school counseling.

MANFORD A. SONSTEGARD

In this situation, the counselor clearly manifests his inability to deal with his clients, both parents and youngsters. For instance, in his session with Philip's father, "going over all the evidence on paper carefully, grades achieved in elementary school, grades achieved in high school, psychological tests, and the like" is a scandalous procedure! It is small wonder that the father "tossed all these aside." It is also interesting to note, in a society fraught with pressure in which youngsters are pushed and urged to be superior, that the one individual—the counselor—who could have been instrumental in helping parents and youngsters understand the crippling effects of pressure, failed to do so. The striving to be superior and yet feeling unable to attain parental standards led to the critical incident in this situation. Mental institutions, skid rows, and penal institutions are filled with people who are unable to fulfill expectations imposed upon them.

It is unfortunate that the counselor provides so little evidence that would pertain to the dynamics of Philip's behavior. One does not know if there are other siblings, and if so, what Philip's place in the family constellation is; one does not know the relationship between Philip and his father; between Philip and his mother; and between Philip and his siblings (if there are any). It is only possible to surmise that the youngster had been held up to standards to which he felt he could never live up. The pressures to which he had been subjected were manifested not only in his behavior, but in his physiological appearance. He resorted to defenses such as noncommittal answers and a defiant front to keep his sanity. The counselor's attempt to destroy Philip's limited defenses probably contributed to Philip's attempt at suicide. No one could blame Philip for turning on the people who tormented him; even tormented animals turn and fight.

Lack of space prohibits a treatise on how to counsel youngsters who are the "sullen, negative, 'I dunno nothing' type." Briefly, however, the first step is to establish a counseling relationship which enlists the client's cooperation. This in itself is therapeutic even if the counselor does not understand the purpose for his client's behavior. In this case, the counselor did not know how to establish rapport so he became angry and took his frustration out on a youngster who was unable to cope with the problems of everyday living. An unimpeachable rule of thumb in a situation like this would be: "If you don't know what to do, don't do anything." By adhering to this rule, at least harmful effects would be avoided.

The counselor's good intentions are not enough—the road to hell is paved with good intentions. Unless the counselor understands the dynamics of the behavior of his client, he can be of no help. It makes little difference if the counselor shows his "real feelings." The client immediately detects the true feelings of the counselor regardless of attempts to conceal them. Every individual has a right to be respected as a human being, and a counselor cannot expect to be respected unless he respects himself.

The counselor did not understand his own fictitious goals. A counselor who "wants to help them," "harbors irrationally strong attitudes toward counselees," thinks that "misfits like Philip are better off dead anyway," and questions, "Are we always to nurture the sick egos of repulsive students?" should seek professional help. It is difficult to envision a professional person, a counselor in particular, who reflects such attitudes. Knowledgeable laymen are apt to be more astute. However, one would probably be correct in guessing that attempts at affecting an attitude change in this particular counselor would be like the labors of Sisyphus. A person who states, "Years after this event I still feel bad about my own behavior," is not likely to do anything about it. Feeling guilty is an excuse for not dealing with the situation responsible for our feelings.

CHARLES B. TRUAX

The counselor in this situation "vented his feelings" rather than showing warmth and understanding. I cannot accept that these were genuine feelings on the part of the counselor. I think that if he had explored his own feelings he would have discovered his own prejudices and irrational attitudes. Antagonistic attitudes, such as those of Philip, are especially common in delinquent children or behavior-problem children. It is their symptom and, therefore, is the very thing that the counselor is committed to changing. I think that when we do go overboard one way or the other, we should stop seeing the client at that moment and consult with a colleague—that is, try some counseling for ourselves to work through our problems and discover why we are rejecting, hostile, or overidentifying and possessive. I think it quite likely that the counselor in this case did contribute to the suicide attempt. If a helping person is destructive, then to whom can the client turn for help?

In my own experience, the sullen and negative type of client is the easiest to deal with if you are truly empathic and reflect his feelings of hostility, anger, and hopelessness. It takes more than an attitude of wanting to help. It takes the actual work of being empathic to move the client from a sullen and negative stance to an open one. I guess I could feel more comfortable if the questions raised were not asked by the counselor. The very kinds of questions that are asked lead me to believe that the counselor should leave counselling alone and find some other field of endeavor. Moreover, I think that he would do well to consult with a therapist himself, so that he might work out his own problems.

Philip, no doubt, is a misfit, but he is a misfit because people made him that way rather than because he was born that way. It is difficult for us to imagine what it would be like to have buckteeth, be ugly, and have a father and mother who were trying to push and prod us into being a winner whether we were or not. It is an act of empathy that would have prevented the suicide attempt and saved the boy from a mental hospital. In retrospect, if if was a good mental hospital (which isn't very likely), this might have been the best solution since at least it got him away from his parents who were so destructive. It also got him away from a very destructive counselor.

11

Kinde, Kirche, Küche

CRITICAL INCIDENT

Background

I have been a high school English teacher for seven years. Although I have not been named to a counseling position yet, I have had the opportunity to help students with their personal problems on several occasions. I am sure that most teachers have had many occasions to do personal counseling during the course of their work.

In my fifth year of teaching I noticed in one of my college prep groups a girl who suddenly seemed to throw in the towel as far as her school work was concerned, even though she had been an honor student throughout the elementary grades. For the first few weeks, I simply commented that her work was certainly below her capacity, and I mentioned to her that she should begin working harder. She finished the first marking period with a *C*-minus which should actually have been a *D*. On her report card she also had two other *C*s and a *D*. Not expecting any real information, I asked her to remain after school one afternoon. I wanted to find out what was wrong, and I thought I would send a note home to her parents.

When I asked her what was wrong, she told me. She was the second oldest in a family of five children, and her family was quite poor. She had one older brother who had quit school in the eighth grade, gone to work, and then had been drafted. Her younger brothers and a sister didn't like school and were doing poorly.

During the summer her parents had told her that when she turned sixteen, in another year and a half, she would have to quit school and get a job. She told me that although she had put up a bit of a fuss, she believed she could never make them change their minds.

Upon hearing the story I blurted out my opinion that they had no right to make this decision for her; it was unfair to deprive her of an education for the sake of some extra income that probably wasn't absolutely necessary. I said a few other things to her and left her with the idea that she should plead her case once more with her parents. She left me with the understanding that she would try, but that it wouldn't do much good. She said unless they would let her stay in school she saw very little reason for trying to get better grades.

She went home that evening and brought up the matter with her parents. In doing so she apparently stated that her teacher had told her that "they didn't have the right to tell her what to do." She said something to the effect that they had no right to force her to go to work just so they could bring home a few more groceries and an extra case of beer. The very next day her father reported this to the office and my principal decided to let him settle the matter with me.

Incident

Her father, apparently feeling hurt and insulted, really lashed out at me. He told me I had no right to interfere that I didn't really know what life was like and he concluded by telling me that I should have minded my own damned business. He insisted that I should tell his daughter that I was sorry for what I had told her, and that she should listen to her parents. The critical incident, as I see it now, took place in those few precious seconds before I replied to him. I could have refused to do so and faced possible disciplinary action on the part of the principal, although I doubt this would have happened. I could have answered the father angrily and probably insulted him more by telling him exactly what I thought of him. And, lastly, I could have said nothing to him and walked out of the room, which is almost what I did.

Instead, I told him that I was sorry that I had apparently tried to overrule him in the eyes of his daughter. I said I would speak to his daughter again if he would just tell me why he and his wife had come to their decision. He told me that school was not really important for girls. Girls were supposed to get married and have children. Their place was in the home. I agreed that this was largely the case when he was growing up, but that today girls were thinking more and more of careers which they could pursue while raising a family and be able to maintain throughout life.

I asked him if his wife worked, and he replied that she worked in a local mill. I asked him to think of how great it would be if his wife could be working instead as a nurse, teacher, or secretary, or in a bank. I told him that this was what his daughter had probably thought about many times. I hoped he saw my point. He didn't reply to this, he merely nodded in the affirmative. I was polite to him and asked him to reconsider for himself and his daughter, and to speak with her when he got home. The next day, first thing in the morning, the girl told me her parents had told her she could stay in school. She went on that year maintaining an honor roll average, and she is planning to enter nursing school upon graduation.

Discussion

I don't think that my words influenced the father as much as my attitude did. My initial apology removed a great amount of his antagonism toward me and left him receptive to what I had to say. Had I gotten into an argument with him, I don't think I would have achieved the same results.

This incident taught me that in dealing with parents I had to first respect their rights as parents; and by doing so, I also learned the value of the expression, "You can catch more flies with honey than you can with vinegar."

Questions

1. Do parents really have the right to determine their children's futures relative to their education?

2. Should a school counselor speak his mind, contradicting what parents say, when he does not agree with them?

3. Should a school conselor, upon finding out that he and the parents do not agree, try to call in the parents and deal with them directly when he believes that the parents are harming the child?

4. Could I have handled the whole issue better? I feel I mishandled it in the beginning, but was able to extricate myself from a bad situation which I shouldn't have gotten into in the first place.

COMMENTS ON THE INCIDENT

THE EDITORS

What are the elements that enter into the delicate equation of a school counselor's behavior? He thinks, of course, of his client, of himself, of the school's and society's expectations; but there is another important element which can sometimes pull against all other forces—the wishes and determination of the parents. It often happens that parents have strange ideas of what their children can accomplish. The issue in this incident centers on the counselor's ultimate loyalty. Is he a surrogate for the parents? Does he represent the state? Is he the advocate of the child? What does he do when various factors pull him in different directions? What are his sources of strength and decisiveness? How does he know what to do? Whom should he serve?

This incident illustrates the value of a soft voice, a gentle approach, and understanding of others' views of what is best for the counselee and those who are involved with him. While the events in this incident are rather commonplace, they serve to illustrate the recurring problem of how to assuage parental wrath. They also teach what not to do.

The issues of self-sufficiency of a counselee, rights of parents, parent-teacher relations, authenticity in guidance, and too personal involvement in students' problems are discussed by the consultants in response to the counselor's questions regarding his handling of the case.

ANGELO V. BOY

Intervention in the life of a student is a time-honored tradition among teachers. Such intervention is often defended on the grounds that the teacher is justified in taking action because such action is, after all, for the welfare of the student. Teachers glibly talk about the necessity of students becoming responsible for their own lives, but contradict this dictum by engaging in certain acts of intervention.

It is tempting to intervene. When we see a person confronted with a difficult decision or situation, it is a natural inclination to want to help by doing something concrete. I often wonder whether intervention is actually helpful to the student or whether it is designed to appease our own consciences. I wonder whether we are really helping the student to be responsible for himself when we intervene, or whether we are making him more dependent upon the need for intervention by others in similar situations throughout his life.

If the teacher in this case had been a professional counselor, he might have established a counseling relationship in which the girl was able to discuss the various aspects of her relationship with her parents, to begin to sense how she could proceed to deal with her parents directly without anyone's intervention. That is, if the girl could begin to understand how *she* should deal with her parents, then this insight would enable her to communicate more effectively with them at other important decision points in her life. If she didn't learn to do this now, then she would always need someone to intervene. She would always need an uncle, an aunt, a teacher, or a social worker to be the intermediary between herself and her parents or her environment.

Counseling should enable a client to generate the courage to do something directly about circumstances in his life. If the counselor does that something to and for the client, then how does the client ever learn to take responsibility for managing his own life? When does he learn to confront and find solutions to his problems *on his own,* if he becomes conditioned to the crutch furnished by an intervening person?

In the beginning of my own counseling experience, intervention was part of my modus operandi until I began to realize that my interventions were fulfilling my own psychological needs rather than being truly helpful to my clients. At the end of each day I could close my office door with the comfortable feeling that I had *done* something. But what had I really done? In my evolution as a counselor I came to the clinical realization that behavior modification, if it were going to be internalized, operational, and long lasting for a client, had to be produced by the client. I became aware that counseling was viable and effective only when I was able to create a relationship in which the client could reach a point where *he* could make personally relevant decisions about his life.

The fact that this girl stayed in school and planned to enter a school of nursing is, indeed, noble. It fits our American concept of a success story. The English teacher can take satisfaction in the fact that he did the right thing in the incident depicted. He earned his keep. But I wonder if today this girl is a freely functioning person who is able to manage her own life? Or does she scurry to find someone to intervene whenever she is faced with a difficult situation?

DON C. DINKMEYER

This incident shows a way of developing more effective relationships. It relates closely to the democratic approach to solving problems that Dreikurs has developed.[1] The counselor basically refused to have a poor relationship with the father. He did not fight him, nor did he give in. Instead he listened and established mutual respect by showing his willingness to consider all opinions. Then he suggested that they attempt to solve the problem together. This is an example of the fact that we can only change ourselves, not others. It seems that as soon as the counselor demonstrated willingness to reconsider his position, the father felt free to participate in a reconsideration of his own position. It is true that an

---

[1] Rudolf Dreikurs, *The Challenge of Parenthood,* rev. ed. (New York: Duell, Sloan & Pearce, 1958).

argument would not have accomplished much. However, I think that the counselor feels that he was using a ploy by "catching more flies with honey than vinegar," and perhaps does not realize that he was simply utilizing a democratic approach to problem solving.

Certainly, parents don't have the right to determine the children's future relative to their education. On the other hand, if parents are to be financially responsible for that education, their attitudes and wishes certainly must be taken into consideration. I believe the school counselor should be prepared to offer a child other alternatives in such a situation, especially when the child desires to go on academically and is at a loss to find ways to finance his education. It would probably have been better if the counselor had first listened to what the child had to say and then dealt directly with the parents to determine how they felt about the educational future of their child. It is true that the matter was mishandled in the beginning and that this could have been avoided by a well-structured parent interview.

C. GRATTON KEMP

This incident focuses on two issues in interpersonal relationships: (1) shall I be genuine? and (2) what shall I do about conflict—shall I avoid it, ignore it, substitute pleasantries, or accept it and confront it? And if I confront it, how shall I handle it creatively? The English teacher in this situation was genuine in his discussion with the student and handled the conflict creatively in his interview with her father.

Genuineness is considered a basic necessity of meaningful interpersonal relationships. It also tends to be notoriously lacking in our communication with others. This lack stems from the fear of consequences to oneself, the inability to trust another sufficiently, and the pervasive feeling that genuineness may lead to conflict and that this should be avoided.

The result of these attitudes is that differences in values and methods are distorted, ignored, or glossed over in the discussion of critical incidents. And as a result neither party becomes sufficiently involved to undertake any significant action. Sometimes one party refrains because of fear or mistrust combined with doubts concerning the correctness of his ideas. Or he may not care enough to desire to do anything. The whole situation may be one from which he wishes to remove himself. His small world may not accommodate any lasting concern for others. Apparently in this situation the teacher was not inhibited by either fear of consequences or doubt of the correctness of his ideas. His caring for the student and interest in helping her led to his forthright statement of his perceptions of the situation. Whether or not he should assume that the parents alone must decide on the daughter's future remains a controversial issue. However, the involvement of the parents was necessary to initiate a reexamination of the issue. The genuine action of the teacher prompted genuine action on the part of the parents. Both parties were sincerely concerned and in this fact lay the hope for a better solution.

The teacher and parents possessed basic qualities which substantially affected the outcome. They cared for the girl. Their disciplined caring led to the direction of their imagination along constructive lines. They were genuine and their expressions were honest ones. Neither had any "hidden agenda" or an undue amount of self-concern which might have prevented him from looking at the situation logically and realistically. Thus the stage was set for a constructive resolution of conflict. Given these conditions the outcome was largely the result of the focus and method of the discussion between the teacher and the girl's father.

The teacher did the following.

1. Instead of responding to the father's words of hate and anger, he accepted the situation as it was. He did not assume an air of superiority, nor did he defend himself by fight or flight. He did not pretend that the difficulty was unimportant or nonexistent. He offered to make amends and did so without loss of dignity.

2. He kept his emotional standing place and did not allow his vision to become constricted. He offered amends on the condition that the discussion be carried on in a broader context, i.e., one which included the reasons for the parents' decision. This was a crucial step. It focused on a consideration of underlying reasons and motives.

3. He might have perceived the father as an unreasonable, unintelligent, and abusive parent. Instead he accepted his explanation and used it to help him view the daughter's future from a different perspective. The father gained insight when the teacher asked if his wife worked; and when the father replied that she worked in a local mill, the teacher suggested that he consider "how great it would be if his wife could be working instead as a nurse, teacher, secretary, or in a bank."

4. The new insight regarding employment was then focused on a consideration of the daughter's future and the possibility that she herself may have entertained these same thoughts. Thus the discussion was focused on the future and within a new and broadened framework. Where doubt, wonder, and indecision are honest they have a peculiar power to induce an experience of oneness. For however different we may be in our backgrounds we are mystically one in the experience of living in an imponderable universe. There is a creative power inherent in a shared bafflement.

5. The ending was left open; each could proceed as he saw fit without loss of dignity. Together they had kept alive in each other the broader sense of reality that conflict induces.

If the counselor is really going to be useful in difficult situations he must be able to let himself be known. The counselor who feels that his life is an open book is able more easily to view situations from the perspective of those he would like to help. Whether or not a counselor should speak his mind depends upon his motives. If he really cares about the person and his caring is disciplined, his ideas will be useful and generally well received.

Procedural questions become less difficult and troublesome when the counselor in loving concern reviews the possible means of taking action.

Generally he can trust his decisions regarding what to do if his motives are pure and known to himself.

To assume there is one way which is superior in any and all situations ignores the many variables both known and unknown which differ from one situation to the next. To place complete confidence in one plan is to forget that one is dealing with persons who are dynamic and possess the ability to do the unexpected.

The person who handles conflict creatively is relatively at peace within himself. He is able to keep his sense of possibilities alive. He recognizes the inadequacy of things as they are and expects that something can be done about them. He is able to consider a situation before making a response. He can wait.

JOHN D. MULLEN

One of the reasons for having counselors in the school system is to have individuals available with information regarding the many programs for, and means of, obtaining an education. The counselor has different possibilities to offer to such students as the one in this case. The circumstances that have to be taken into consideration when talking with a student differ with individual students and their families.

I think the teacher was observant and concerned and should be commended. Such fine observations can be the beginning of effective teacher-counselor cooperation. In this incident if the teacher, after discussing the problem, had put the girl in contact with the counselor (assuming the school had one), much unnecessary static and worry could have been avoided. This is not to say that all students with problems should be sent to the counselor by the teacher, but in this case the counselor should have been contacted. The point at which to send a student to a counselor is an area which needs much clarification among counselors and teachers in promoting an effective school system.

This girl probably should enter a work-study program. At least the availability of such programs should be explained to her and her parents. Often students can help themselves and their families financially—and let us not be so naive as to think that the wages earned by some of these students are not financially necessary to their families. Maybe by the girl's staying in school the full day and not working, one of her brothers or sisters will be forced to drop out. It would be better to have both children at work and in school than one out of school completely and the other in school full time. What about the advisability of the mother working in the mill weighed against this girl going to school full time or part time on a work-study program? Again this is the family's decision and not the counselor's; the counselor's role is to give the members of the family information and possibilities; they have a right to expect this from the counselor and this necessitates the counselor's keeping well-informed.

Common sense dictates that parents do not have the absolute right to determine the child's future relative to his education. Circumstances of the family and the ability and interests of the student form the foundation for family communication concerning the student's future vocation, the student necessarily making the ultimate decision. To contradict parents directly is surely not good for a counselor in matters involving differing opinions. To correct wrong information is a part of the counselor's continuing responsibility, including misinformation given by parents. The manner in which this is accomplished is important in maintaining the counselee's continued respect for the parents. This teacher showed good ability in extricating himself from a difficult situation.

MITCHELL SALIM

The title of this incident indicates a need for the counselor to understand and work with the several significant parental attitudes which influence the child.

During the counseling process the counselor attempts to listen, understand, and respond to the client. The counselor's frame of reference continually shifts from the subjective to the objective. He tries to construct a totality of what the client is expressing. The counselor recognizes that the client is both an active and reactive person. He affects and is affected by members of various institutions.

The teacher involved in this situation lost his objectivity momentarily. Possibly this occurred because of similarity of experiences. The pupil struck a responsive chord in the teacher. Overidentification of the helper with the client and his problem is one of the counselor's potential pitfalls, and it results typically in the counselor's loss of objectivity. In essence, the counselor then becomes part of the problem.

The teacher recognized the problem which he precipitated and moved magnificently not only to rectify the problem but to clarify a wider range of educational and occupational choices for the pupil. The method through which the teacher dealt with the problem was sound. He recognized that parents have rights concerning the direction of their children's development. He also was cognizant of parental needs. These two realizations seemed to develop through the experience of the incident. The critical strategy was to meet the needs of the pupil by understanding, accepting, and working through the status needs of the parents. Parents' anxiety tends to diminish if parents feel that the counselor or teacher understands and accepts them. This feeling can be developed through any mutual interaction and by any medium of communication.

Through his verbalized attitude, the teacher met the challenge of parental anxiety and continued on to facilitate parental insight and acceptance of the child. The interview with the father progressed to the point where the energies of the teacher and father became directed toward the daughter and her needs. The teacher earned her success through painful personal growth and a realization that the needs of the child cannot be automatically divorced from the self-image and self-interests of parents.

12

The Counselor Succumbs

CRITICAL INCIDENT

Background

Among my various responsibilities in the Valley Elementary School, I have the burden of deciding whether children should be promoted. I look over the child's records, and then after interviewing the teacher and the child, make a decision. I try to keep everything in balance—the child's aptitude for learning, his social level, his physical status, test results, grades, and so forth.

In reviewing the records of fourth-grade pupils, I found one girl, Yetta, who was a prime candidate for retention. First, her teacher stated that Yetta tried hard but did grossly inferior work and was not learning. Second, Yetta had been tested for intelligence many times. Her most recent appraisal had been conducted a few months previously by a psychologist who stated in his report: "Yetta is too bright to go to an institution for the retarded, too dull to profit from the usual school." Third, Yetta was very small for her age, and it was noted that she tended to play with children several years younger than she. Finally, when I talked with Yetta, she indicated that she would prefer to repeat the fourth grade because the work had been "too hard."

Before writing my recommendation, I talked to the principal, who told me that Yetta's older brother had graduated several years before with the highest grades. I told him my decision about Yetta. The principal agreed that her interests would be best served by having her repeat the year, although he had some reservations about how her parents would take it. How right he was!

Following the protocol in such matters, before making the final decision I sent a letter to Yetta's parents summarizing the facts, stating that both Yetta's teacher and principal had agreed with me, and outlining how the parents should inform Yetta and the other children about our decision to retain her. I ended the letter with the routine "If you have any questions or concerns please call me or come to see me."

Incident

Two days later, while peacefully working on a report, I heard a scream from the outer office and the sounds of a scuffle. I dashed to the door and saw Millie, my secretary, struggling with a woman who held a small brown bottle in her raised hand. Not knowing what it was all about, but thinking that perhaps the bottle contained acid which the woman intended to throw at Millie, I got into the act, grabbed the woman's hand and removed the bottle, whereupon the woman collapsed. Millie and I looked at each other and then at the bottle I found myself holding. I examined the bottle and noted a skull and crossbones on the label and the word *iodine* below it.

"She said she was going to drink the iodine if you didn't promote her daughter."

"Who's her daughter?"

"Yetta."

The end of this little dramatic scene was as follows. Mother was revived and came into my office. Emotionally she informed me she would kill herself if Yetta was not promoted. In a reasonable manner I went over the facts and pointed out that Yetta herself wanted to be left back, and that retaining her would be better for Yetta. Mother was adamant and insisted that she would kill herself if Yetta was not promoted. When I asked what the reason for all this was, the mother stated that for poor Jews the ultimate pleasure was to have bright children, the ultimate disgrace was to have stupid children. She informed me that her husband was a business failure and the one bright light in her life was her son who had done so well in school. Were Yetta to be left back, it would be a serious disgrace, and she would lose her status in her little community. The mother agreed that Yetta was not bright, that she had difficulty learning, loathed school and everything about it.

"Besides," she told me, "what difference does it make if a girl can read or write? It is enough she can cook and sew and make beds." Whenever I would try to explain the various reasons for the importance of keeping Yetta in the fourth grade, the mother became emotional. Finally, I reversed my decision and mother sailed out gaily, thanking me profusely.

Discussion

I'm still uncertain whether I did the right thing or not. I suppose that the mother would not really have tried to commit suicide. However, this incident made it painfully clear to me that for some families school failure is a family disgrace. I suppose that Yetta would not have learned much more by being left back in the fourth grade. In the fifth grade the same pattern of nonattendance and nonachievement occurred. In our school we have no special provisions for dull children, even though teachers make allowances for individual differences.

Questions

1.   I have never been able to understand why school success, whether real or apparent, is so important for some parents. I would like to have some explanations for mother's behavior, especially since she knew that Yetta wasn't getting anything out of school.

2.   Did I do the right or wrong thing in promoting Yetta? At the time I simply wanted to get rid of her. I didn't think things out. Was I fair to the fifth-grade teacher in giving her a child who had difficulty doing third-grade work?

3.   Was I fair to Yetta, pushing her ahead because of her mother's demands when she herself preferred to remain in a lower grade?

4.   How on earth can one make parents act reasonably in such matters? Every year I run into a handful of parents who think the world is coming to an end if their child doesn't get good grades or get promoted. I try to explain to them the dangers of pushing a child beyond his capabilities, but this makes little impression on them.

COMMENTS ON THE INCIDENT

THE EDITORS

It goes without saying that no amount of training, including intern-ships, will completely prepare anyone for all the contingencies found in professional practice. Also, no matter how well one knows one's subject, no matter how closely one operates according to protocol, the very fact that we deal with people means that events can occur that are not pre-dictable but which call for a quick and appropriate response on the part of the counselor. The very fact that a counselor has power means that others will try to get the counselor to use it to their advantage. Those who try to influence the counselor may use flattery, threats, bribes and various combinations of these means.

In the present case we have a clear-cut example of a counselor who made a rational decision, taking into consideration almost all factors—except a mother! And when faced with her fury, he backed down and reversed himself.

This issue of the child, the school, and the administration, as well as the family and its needs in our complicated and competitive society, is one that raises and will raise many questions. Our various consultants view the dilemma of Yetta and her mother as illustrative of many similar situa-tions which confront and confound practitioners in the field.

THOMAS W. ALLEN

Inspection of the background of this case raises a number of crucial issues. For instance, the counselor here seems to suffer from a disease which is apparently a side effect of the contribution which so-called dynamic psychotherapy has made to all professional helping relation-ships—tunnel vision. He tries to understand the child by using a wide range of resources "to get to the bottom of the matter." In so doing, how-ever, he manages to overlook some important issues. No child is a monad, who can be understood as a composite of innate dispositions and traits. He can only be understood within the social context of which he is a part. Consequently, before making a decision concerning a child, the structure and dynamics of his family unit must be assessed.

Such an assessment would include the position of the child in the family. Different problems are faced by children who occupy different positions within the family. Further, the counselor would want to ascer-tain the nature of the interpretation placed on various types of behavior in the family as well as the family's central values and cherished aspira-tions. A study of the family constellation provides one with a basis for understanding a child superior to that provided by an "in-depth" investigation. This results from the fact that even such characteristics as "intelligence" and "academic aptitude" do not have an independent existence. They are rather social functions, conglomerations of ways of relating to the world. A child may, for example, conclude that the most promising strategy to gain him a secure place in his world is to be thought incompetent. He may thus succeed in avoiding many of the obligations of life with which others must contend. With any luck, he may succeed in getting others to serve him.

Alfred Adler stated:

> The greatest difficulty in education is provided not by the limitations of the child, but by what he thinks are his limitations. If a child knows that his Intelligence Quotient is low, he may become hopeless and believe that success is beyond him.[1]

It is not simply a matter of the counselor failing to take the nature of Yetta's psychological environment into account as fully as was necessary, but rather that his emphasis in this case was misplaced. The counselor's job is *to defeat* such predictions, not to make them. The possibility emerges that Yetta was a discouraged child. As becomes clear from the encounter with mother, Yetta came from a family in which the burden for maintaining family self-esteem fell heavily upon the children. Yetta found herself confronted with an unattainable precedent. How could she possibly do anything which would even approach the accomplishments of her brother? He must have seemed so much more competent. Yetta's situation was further complicated by the conflicting messages she got. On one hand, she was told in many ways that she must not jeopardize the family's precarious position; on the other hand, she was apprised of the lack of esteem in which both her ability and potential achievement were held.

It would not be surprising, then, if Yetta had concluded that she had little chance of securing a place for herself in her world by straightforward methods. Whatever she, a clearly second-rate citizen, could achieve would obviously fall short of adequacy. Hence, Yetta may have withdrawn into incompetence. As time wore on, her failures and the attitudes of others toward her would tend to deepen her discouragement and to validate the wisdom of adhering to her "inadequacy" strategy.

How then might Yetta have been *encouraged*? How could she have been persuaded to experiment with more constructive approaches to life? Unhappily this question is not easy to answer, neither for parents nor for educators or psychologists. We are by and large masters of *discouragement*. Is it not true that our principal means of influencing others have a negative cast, for instance, threats, admonitions, sarcasm, invidious comparisons, punishment? Encouragement comes to us a good deal less easily.

One form of encouragement is understanding. In the present case encouragement might sound something like this: "Could it be that you want others to believe that you cannot do anything so that they'll get off

[1] Alfred Adler, *What Life Should Mean to You* (New York: Capricorn, 1958), p. 164.

your back and not make you do a lot of the things the other kids in school have to do?"

Another kind of encouragement is the recognition of heretofore overlooked strengths, perhaps employed in the pursuit of dubious goals. For instance, Yetta's success in frustrating the attempts of numerous adults to induce her to behave as they wished her to might be noted with admiration.

A third species of encouragement is systematic cultivation of assets. It is here that the so-called behavior modifiers have made a major contribution. The frequency of such desired behavior is increased by making rewards contingent upon its emission.

The main task in much counseling and teaching is to combat *discouragement*. Doing so involves understanding what the child is trying to accomplish by his misbehavior, e.g., respite from demands he feels he cannot meet, specialness, attention, or service, and providing socially useful alternatives. The child must believe, of course, that the alternatives are viable for *him*.

It seems infinitely better to encourage than to classify. The decision with which the counselor in this incident was faced initially should have been made on these grounds. That is, the central question to which all of his considerations should have been subordinated is: what can be done to encourage Yetta? Is it, for example, reasonable to confirm her view of herself as someone who is not up to par, who is best advised not to try? The answer seems unproblematic. It is likely that, given encouragement, Yetta's behavior and achievement in class on tests could be quite radically changed. But without encouragement she may well spend her life living up to the pessimistic views of her "labelers" (or perhaps it should be "libelers"!).

Finally, the counselor's lack of understanding of parental overconcern for grades seems anomalous for two reasons. First, having met this problem on many occasions, it would seem that a concerned professional would have gained more insight into it. At the very least, it would seem that he might have formulated some reasonable hypotheses. After all, Yetta's mother gave him a more than plausible account of the dynamics of her feelings. Second, one wonders how a person could have been involved in education to any extent without becoming aware of the strength and pervasiveness of the forces both within the educational establishment and in society at large which promote such feelings in children and their parents by inducing them to equate human worth with the prestige derived from surpassing others.

MARY A. BARBER

From the background given I would assume this to be a situation where the counselor's position is at least quasi-administrative, in which he has too large a caseload to do much personal counseling with individuals and performs as a consultant to a number of teachers. Assuming these con-

ditions and assuming that there were no provisions for borderline mental
retardation cases within the school, the original disposition of the case
sounds like a considered, logical resolution. In the critical incident with
the hysterical mother the counselor's actions possibly were the only way of
solving the immediate problem. However, giving in to the mother's selfish
wishes represented a disservice to the child in the long run, for it meant
condemning her to conditions which would probably prolong her failure
pattern. If Yetta had only minimal learning ability but was pushed into
situations where she would undoubtedly continue to fail and fall farther
and farther behind, the prediction is that she would drop out of school as
soon as she was old enough or resort to various kinds of acting out in
response to her unhappiness.

This sounds like a case in which family counseling should have been
instituted if such services were available. Obviously the child was being
used as a pawn in the game of upward social mobility which the mother
was rather unsuccessfully trying to play. Even following the suicide
attempt (which was probably not real, since it was melodramatically performed in front of an audience), the mother might have been calmed
down by a promise to delay the decision and review the case rather than
completely reversing it. If the counselor had made a play for more time,
a more constructive resolution might have been possible. There might
have been a chance to instigate counseling with the whole family, and the
mother might have been lead eventually to a more realistic attitude.

Parents who measure their social status in terms of the achievements
of their children are demonstrating the level of their own emotional
immaturity. In this day and age children will eventually rebel in one form
or another against the kind of extreme domination exhibited by such
parents. Trying to make such parents see the almost inevitable outcome
of their actions is not an easy task and it is a function of the social services
available and the parents' willingness to use them. Lacking adequate
referral sources or the time to work with individual cases, the disposal of
this case may have been the only one feasible.

Whether the decision to promote Yetta was fair or unfair to the fifth
grade·teacher would depend on whether or not she had the ability, willingness, and time to give Yetta the special attentions she undoubtedly
needed.

How to make parents reasonable in such matters poses a very general question and there can be no satisfying universal answer. Each case,
each family, represents a unique combination of personalities and interactions, and where there seems to be a serious degree of unhappiness or
instability, counseling with the whole family would be desirable. In this
particular case, where the mother seems so completely self-centered, re-
gards her husband as a complete failure, and perceives her family's suc-
cesses or failures as reflections of her personal worth, there would seem to
be a definite need for protracted counseling. There is not much information about the father, except for the mother's reference to him as a failure
and a disappointment to her, but it could be surmised that he has many
problems too. Ideally, through a continuous program of adequate coun-

seling, they both might be brought to a more accepting attitude toward their own and Yetta's limitations and encouraged to appreciate whatever positive resources they have.

EDWARD S. BORDIN

The incident and the counselor's questions illustrate a complex set of conflicting responsibilities. First, there is the responsibility to Yetta, which in my view should be paramount. Then there is the responsibility to the school, its efforts to maintain standards and to educate. Finally, there is the responsibility to parents or other persons with whom the student is connected. If his role is to have any special value, the counselor more than any other school staff member must not compromise his commitment to his client, the student. Even acknowledging the cogent reasons favoring assigning the responsibility for the promotion decision to the counselor, one must question its wisdom. Would it not be better to leave that responsibility with the teacher where it belongs? The counselor is still available as a consultant to the teacher and, when confidentiality does not interfere, as a source of additional information.

The counselor is amazed and frustrated by the single-mindedness with which parents push for their children's success in school and the despair with which they face failure. An examination of the forces operating both from within and without, some rational, some irrational, makes this more comprehensible. What is more natural than for parents to want "the best" for children? Our highly technological society enshrines formal schooling as the sure road to its treasures. Though this concept is currently challenged, most still see becoming an educated person as the key not only to attaining material goals but to living a deeply rewarding life. "Striving for excellence" virtually became a national slogan of the post-Sputnik era. The nation was pushing parents, who passed this pressure on to their children. Especially among certain ethnic groups, such as Jews, where schooling is held in special reverence, this "striving for excellence" creates a social climate in which the search for higher social status is tied to schooling, and shame for failure is accentuated. Increase the vulnerability of the parent even slightly and you have the conditions necessary for unrealistic tenaciousness and despair.

Yetta's mother appears unusually vulnerable. She seems extremely dissatisfied with herself and her husband. With so little information we can only guess, but one senses that instead of confronting herself she seeks to live her life through her children. She appears to have adopted a shallow and manipulative stance, vulnerable to the attitudes of others and seeking to influence by primitive methods. All suicide threats or attempts are serious messages. I can understand the counselor's feelings of distress and helplessness when confronted with such behavior. The possibility of anyone's death, not just our own, touches deeply laid emotions. Our own lust for life and fear of death impel us to fight to preserve another's life. But, if the counselor's assessment of Yetta is accurate, failure is inevitable.

Sooner or later Yetta's mother must come to grips with the question of whether living and Yetta's success are synonymous. Perhaps the counselor could have helped the mother to make a start at coming to grips with herself by responding to the reality of her distress rather than to the unreality of externalizing it in Yetta. I must confess that I am not at all sanguine about the success of such a maneuver.

Finally, I must register some disquiet about the assessment of Yetta. I do not speak of the question of whether she should be promoted. I am concerned about the estimate of her intellectual potential. Yetta's older brother is reported by mother (not a reliable source) to have been a successful student. Yetta's reported level of intellectual performance does not preclude the possibility that she has been cast into this role by her mother's distorted needs. I would be interested in obtaining a second, perhaps more searchingly clinical, assessment. The qualifications of the psychologist are not described. The second clinical study should be done by a psychologist of the level certified by the American Board of Examiners in Professional Psychology.

NATHAN T. CHERNOV

In Jewish culture an extremely high value is placed on education, and one's worth is often measured by it. Because of this, Yetta's mother had difficulty accepting her daughter's failure in school. She might view the failure in the following manner: if my daughter has to repeat, then she is worthless; if she is worthless then I who brought her up am a failure and lack worth; I am therefore a bad mother.

The question of whether the counselor was right or wrong in promoting Yetta remains open. There might not be a truly right answer. The counselor was faced with a suicide threat, and that form of blackmail is most difficult to resist because such threats can be carried out. On the other hand, the parent's infantile tantrumlike behavior was reinforced.

The teacher should have been informed as to the achievement level of the child as well as assisted in identifying methods that might best encourage her. In this way the teacher might have been prepared to handle Yetta in her class.

There are many factors that one will have to consider before passing judgment as to whether or not the counselor was fair to Yetta. The present writer would question the validity of Yetta's IQ test. When one considers that Yetta's brother graduated with high grades, one can see how a younger child might give up rather than compete with a brother who is bound to win. Since brother uses his brightness as a means of gaining attention in school and in the home, it might be that Yetta has opted for being dull as her way of finding a place in life. If that is the case, keeping Yetta back would increase her discouragement and reinforce the likelihood of her assumed disability in learning. Moreover, children who repeat beyond grade three seldom show as much growth during the repeating years as they do if they are promoted.

Parents who allow themselves to become overly involved in the accomplishments of their children at school are often most easily and bitterly hurt. Children frequently fail to learn in order to gain their parent's attention and thus defeat parents and themselves in the process. Parents should remain uninvolved in such cases.

By initiating parental group counseling, the counselor can meet the ever-recurring problem of parents who are upset and unreasonable when children fail in school. This counseling might be instituted as part of an ongoing program where parents would be made aware of how they might best encourage their child in school while gaining insight into handling other problems at home.

MARSANNE C. EYRE

The inevitable repercussions of not promoting a child might have been handled more deftly had the counselor been resourceful and responsive. At no point was contact made with Yetta's parents *before* the decision was reached. The school took a remote position of dominant control. The counselor passed on to the family the nasty job of notifying the child, which further emphasized the negative aspects of the retaining procedure. The counselor highlighted the impersonality of the episode by using a letter (instead of personal contact) containing the routine conclusion "if you have any questions or concerns," etc., inferring that this was merely a polite but meaningless closing of the issue.

Surveying this series of depersonalizing "put-downs" to the family, let us consider what the counselor's first step should be in establishing *real* contact with the family. First, she should contact the parents in person or on the phone, asking them to share in the counselor's concern about their daughter. Let them see that the school is working to help Yetta and not to fight them or humiliate them.

Protocol maintains distance. Open and trusting personal contact reduces it. We often use the excuse of not having enough time to see people because we lack the courage to risk dealing with situations we are not wholly sure of. By running away from problems on one level, we end up multiplying our problems on another.

Let us consider the counselor's desire to understand Yetta's mother's behavior. From what we have seen, we are confronted with a very powerful figure—a woman who will go to the greatest extremes to get her way. The child almost seems insignificant in the ensuing battle. When sensing her child's rejection by the school, the mother defiantly cries, in effect, "My blood will be on *your* hands" and grabs for the iodine bottle. The counselor's alternative might have been to be sympathetic to the mother's needs, but to show strength by making it clear that she would not reach a decision after such an emotionally-charged scene. One might request,

"Would you please come back and see me and perhaps bring your husband when you feel we can discuss things calmly?" If the mother were willing to agree to this, a definite appointment should be made.

If a stronger alternative was called for due to further resistance, the counselor could ask the mother, "What good will your suicide do Yetta?" Stress the idea that Yetta needs her mother's understanding. If the counselor doesn't feel secure enough to deal with the problems of this family, she should refer them elsewhere.

The counselor is rightly concerned with Yetta's getting a fair deal since the child herself wished to be left back and seemed to understand the benefits of such a judgment. Again, the need for personal courage on the part of the counselor is paramount.

If we wish to change the attitudes of overambitious parents we can begin by showing the value of less competitive forms of behavior. Many schools are adopting nongraded systems on the elementary level. The counselor is often in the position to enlighten the administration and point out the possible gain in adopting such a scheme. There are apparent changes in Yetta's school that need to be undertaken.

All in all, the main emphasis should be placed on creating a closer rapport between counselor and parents and effecting a mutual clarification of the school's and the parents' responsibility.

E. LAKIN PHILLIPS

It is important to realize that school success *is* very important to some (or perhaps many) parents. This motivation may be abnormally high —as perhaps it was in the case of Yetta's mother—but it is also abnormally *low* for some families. It would appear that the counselor has to take this fact at face value.

Whether promoting Yetta was right or wrong hinges, I think, on other considerations: spending more time with the mother regarding Yetta and her achievement problems; finding other, possibly nonacademic, solutions for Yetta and "trying these out" on the mother.

The feeling that you have to "get rid of" a client is natural and occurs to all of us at times, but to act on it without seeing the possible consequences can often be disastrous. The general family situation should have been given a greater consideration in the counselor's dealing with Yetta and her mother. This is easy to say after the fact, but when there is a parent who is really adamant about an important matter of concern to the child's welfare, it is a time when the counselor or therapist can suspect trouble.

Pushing Yetta ahead need not be a clear-cut decision, even if she is promoted to another grade or class. There are always such possibilities as an ungraded class—or an ungraded assignment to a given class—and setting up work at the child's level, perhaps under the supervision of a responsible and sympathetic teacher who can cover a lot of ground for the counselor and can help the child and the family at the same time.

Perhaps a teacher, sensitive to unrealistic expectations on the part of parents (and we all know numbers of these exist!), can set up some group conferences, or can hold group discussions on grades and achievement problems, or the like. The counselor or teacher, in taking the first step in such a matter, can often dilute the severity of the problem of achievement and grades, and help toward educating parents at the same time. All teachers and counselors have to face such problems from time to time, and it is well for schools and their faculty to meet the issues of educating parents. If we wait and work with parents only when critical issues occur, we can often be catapulted into undue risks in policies or untimely efforts.

E. G. WILLIAMSON

Yetta and her mother's behavior are rather typical in every school, and such incidents are common in the life of every school counselor. Progress for a child in his education has become such a status symbol, particularly for the upward-bound middle class and selected members of the lower class, that it is understandable that Yetta's mother would be upset by her being held back. A more achievable realistic attitude in the modern school system would be not to care whether she was making progress so long as she was making an effort to learn and getting satisfaction out of the school-going experience, and as long as she was gradually maturing so that she would become a more serious student. That would be the end goal that I would hope would emerge.

The counselor asks whether he was right in promoting Yetta. I think one could argue that the counselor was both right and wrong in this action. I would say to him: "Under the circumstances you were not unfair to the fifth grade teacher in promoting into her class a girl with third grade mentality. But you did have an obligation to explain to the fifth grade teacher why you were doing this and to give her a chance to express her point of view and her willingness or unwillingness to have Yetta in her class. No, I don't think you were fair to Yetta in pushing her ahead because of her mother, but I don't see what else you could have done under the circumstances, given the necessity for an immediate decision. Sometimes we have to take the least desirable of the possible alternatives when action is required immediately."

We may look at this problem in another way. To let Yetta remain in a lower grade too long could produce a whole symptomatic pattern that in itself would be very difficult to deal with. The counselor is between the Devil and the deep blue sea; one has to go one way or another, and one has to make the best decision one can, as is true of every situation that calls for judgement on the part of the counselor. There is no way I know of that we can make all parents reasonable in such matters, because school success for their children is a precious status symbol, and they have less than full appreciation for the most part (particularly parents from lower economic levels) of the intellectual demands involved in the mastery of the subjects, especially at the upper levels of education.

And so again I would say to the counselor: "Please be sympathetic with the parents if they use their children's progress as a means to satisfy their own need for status. This is perfectly normal. Every counselor will recognize this if he has children of his own."

Counselors should understand that in some problem situations, such as the one in this incident, there is no clear right or wrong thing to do. We just have to muddle through and pick up the pieces when the world comes apart. We can't expect people to use logic or rationality in the face of such strong irrationalities as the upward-bound motivations of some parents relative to their children. It sometimes takes years to get parents to see the facts of life. We must keep trying, and unless we have this kind of eternal optimism, we had better get out of the counseling field.

13

The Incorrigible Parents

Background

I was in my fifth year as guidance counselor in a junior high school. During the five years of my tenure, we have had many disciplinary cases similar to the one I'm about to describe. What distinguished this case from the others was the extreme manifestation of a student's behavior which was so obviously indicative. The fact that his actions were so aggressive and his attitude so contemptuous should have alerted us to the likelihood of worse things to come. The problem in this case should have been easily identified before it neared the critical stage.

Ken, a ninth-grade student, had been in our school since the middle of his seventh grade. He had come from a parochial school. He had a twin sister and two older brothers in high school. Both Ken and his twin sister were above average in academic ability and performance. The sister was an aggressive and disruptive child in the seventh grade. In the eighth grade she calmed down. Ken's behavior suddenly changed at the beginning of the ninth grade. His grades dropped off sharply. He created incidents in the classroom that brought the teachers down on him. On occasion he struck other students for no apparent reason. In one such incident, he struck a seventh-grade student causing the boy to spend five weeks in a hospital with a badly-broken jaw. School personnel were fearful that a similar incident would occur again. The parents were talking of having Ken committed to the state youth correctional institution. He had been suspended on three occasions and was currently on probation. Ken seemed outwardly defiant toward guidance personnel. If I would even approach him, he seemed to get upset. Through the whole of three months of such periodic troublemaking, he still impressed me as being a likeable and capable boy.

Just prior to the incident, Ken left home and had, as a consequence, been suspended from school again. He kept in touch with his twin sister who kept us informed of his whereabouts and activities. He relied on her to get clothes to him from home and to report conditions at home and at school. The father was out of town working. The mother refused to concern herself with him and his disappearance. She simply listed him with the police as a runaway.

Incident

On the third day of his disappearance, I was on my way home from school when I passed Ken riding on a bicycle with a friend. I felt sure that Ken would run and hide before I could stop him, so I drove on home and exchanged my car for one he'd never seen before. I drove back to the vicinity of his appearance. As I drove around the block I saw Ken walking, alone, in an alley. I stopped near the exit to the alley and waited. I noted that he had no shoes on. I jumped out of the car as he came out of the alley, and approached him saying that I wanted to talk to him. His first impulse seemed to want to run. Surprisingly he decided to stay and listen; perhaps it was simply because he didn't have his shoes on and couldn't have run very effectively.

I asked Ken to get into my car and he complied. I explained his status as far as the authorities were concerned. If caught while a runaway he would probably be charged as such and be committed to a juvenile detention home. If he returned voluntarily he might avoid the charge and the commitment to a juvenile home. We talked for about an hour. During this talk, Ken opened up and told me about his problems and the reasons for changes in his behavior at school. He was fighting the attitude of his parents who were constantly downgrading him by comparing him to his older brothers. He was convinced that he could not compete with his brothers in athletics. He noted that his teachers were always comparing him with his brothers. He was completely fed up with it all.

I didn't offer to take Ken home, or to the police station. I wanted him to know that the decision of what to do would have to be his own. However, I hoped our talk would influence his decision. He said he had to do some more thinking first. I dropped him off where I'd picked him up as he requested and went home.

That evening I got a phone call from Ken. He said, "I am home now and I want to thank you for taking the time to talk to me. No one has ever done that before."

I said, "Fine, Ken, I'm glad that you decided to go home. I would like to have you and your mother come to my office in the morning and we'll discuss how to get you back into school."

Discussion

Ken and his mother came in the next morning. They had discussed his problems at great length the night before. There was a different attitude on both sides and there seemed to be more understanding in the family. We arranged with the court to have Ken's custody handled through the guidance office during school hours. Ken's grades improved; he had no more clashes with his teachers and he was a much improved student during the remainder of the year.

Ken and his family moved to Tacoma as soon as school was out that spring. I was in Tacoma during the latter part of the same summer and called Ken to see how he was getting along. His father answered the phone. I explained to him who I was and that I was curious as to how Ken was behaving. His father said, "Let's not talk about him; did you hear that our oldest son is at a baseball summer camp now? He's trying out for the ———— team," and so on. He never again mentioned Ken during the conversation.

Things didn't work out well for Ken; I received a request for his school records from a state and county detention and correction home for boys a short time later.

Questions

1. Frequently we cannot understand unusual behavior on the part of children. Do such behavior changes often have to do with home conditions?

2. I got the impression that Ken was actually rejected by his parents, and that he behaved as he did out of desperation. I have always thought parents would protect a child who was handicapped or not as able as others. Is the behavior of the parents unusual?

3. When I related the incident to several others, they felt that I had made a mistake in not taking Ken home or driving him to the deten-

tion home. The idea did not even occur to me. Does anyone think I should have done other than what I did in this case?

4.   We certainly didn't do much real or lasting good for Ken in view of his father's unchanging attitude and Ken's later trouble. I wonder in retrospect what I could have done that would have been more helpful. Any ideas?

COMMENTS ON THE INCIDENT

THE EDITORS

There are two contrasting approaches to social misbehavior. One approach is impartial punishment, without concern for "reasons." The punitive agent says, in effect, "I don't want to know why you did it; you did it, that's enough." The other approach emphasizes understanding. In this approach, when someone deviates we want to know why, and we want to help the person rather than to punish him.

Thus, in some wars, those who deserted under enemy fire were shot as "cowards." In later wars such people might be labeled "shell shocked" or "battle fatigued," given treatment and possibly even pensions.

When a child misbehaves in school, the school authorities usually assume that the reasons for the behavior reach back into the home where they, the educators, have little or no influence or control. To what degree can teachers and other individuals employed in the school intervene on behalf of students as far as the family is concerned? In this incident, we have a common problem relating to the probable causes of misbehavior, and the problem of the limits of intervention.

Such complex cases make counselors "throw up their hands in despair" because they just can't go where logic dictates. It is still a free country and parents still spoil and harm their children. Maybe in the long run, it is best this way. And then, maybe not.

RUDOLF DREIKURS

This example is significant, because it shows how far a "good" counselor can succeed and where he will fail if he is not sufficiently trained to understand faulty behavior and motivation and how to correct them. The counselor described the aggressive and disturbing behavior of Ken well. Her lack of psychological training made her assume that he hit other students "for no explainable reason." There is always a "reason" for whatever a child does, but there is no indication of her trying to understand and help him.

In a direct confrontation she acted well. She did not criticize, condemn or preach but helped the boy to decide to do what would be best in the situation. She listened to his complaints, although she did not understand their meaning. She did not understand his own overambition when he could not live up to the demands of his parents and teachers who compared him with his apparently successful older brothers. The fact that she listened to him seemed to be the turning point, and the boy improved.

Now comes the crucial question: What has been achieved by the guidance office? The student obviously received much help since he improved for a whole year. But why did he relapse after he moved away? One can only guess that the counselor was encouraging and appreciative. This accounts for the improvement. But did she change the basic pattern on which the boy operated? Apparently not. This can be seen by the counselor's reaction to the boy's father. She sided with the boy and felt sorry for him to the extent that she spoke about "incorrigible parents."

There is a basic fallacy. The less mother knows what to do with a child, the better she knows what father should do; and the less the teacher or counselor knows what to do, the better they know what the parents do wrong. The father's remarks indicate the tremendous overambition which probably characterized all members of this family. Ken was just like the others, and the counselor probably never recognized to what degree she played into his hands by treating him as something special during the year he worked with her. He switched from a good to a horrible and then back to a good boy which reveals his overambition. If he can't be the best, he becomes the worst. Had the counselor understood these dynamics, she could have helped him change his pattern. As it was, in a less favorable and supportive environment, Ken reverted to a "bad boy" role.

1. Unusual behavior must and can be understood by a trained counselor. The personality of the child is greatly influenced by home situations, but the trained teacher and counselor can undo the harm which family and environment have done in the past.

2. There are definite reasons for a child to change his behavior, from good or bad, and they may or may not have any connection with domestic problems. The improvement in the sister's behavior may have been a factor, since the competition between brothers and sisters usually leads each in the opposite direction. All this does not explain why Ken suddenly became so violent and aggressive. A counselor should have investigated the situation and recognized the factors instead of blaming the parents for having rejected him. In many instances, the "rejecting" or critical attitude of the parents is provoked by a child who gets his status and significance through disturbance and defiance.

3. It was the sensitive and sensible reaction of the counselor to a boy in trouble which brought about the improvement. It is interesting to note that other professionals expressed their doubt, when actually the counselor's behavior was correct.

4. Here is the crucial point: One must agree that the counselor "did not do much real or lasting good for Ken." But, instead of realizing where she failed, she blamed "father's unchanging attitude" for Ken's later trouble.

HAROLD KOZUMA

I want to discuss this problem from both a philosophical and theoretical perspective. This case is beautiful in its ugliness, and seems to point out some extremely important issues. As I read it, a child became a delinquent (effect) because he was rejected by his parents (cause). The issue in such cases is "Who is responsible?" There seems to be no question that there was a clear-cut cause-and-effect relationship, and that Ken reacted as he did to his total life situation because of conditions in the home. His parents rejected him. They labeled him inferior. They expected little good from him. And he reacted exactly as they expected him to react: by becoming a delinquent. From one point of view, therefore, Ken was only the pawn in a chess game his parents were playing.

Now, the real issue is this: when a school counselor sees a situation as clearly as this, what should be done? You, as a school counselor, will see from time to time many children heading directly into trouble for one reason or another that has something to do with the behavior of the parents, whether it be rejection, brutality, unfavorable comparisons, or too high standards. Should the counselor just stand by and watch a child being pushed into delinquent behavior or does he have an obligation to speak out or do something? This is a matter of responsibility, and I think that in such clear-cut cases we, as school counselors, cannot just say that it is a matter between every counselor and his conscience. It seems to me that we should take a stronger stand in such matters. Where is our loyalty in such cases?

One possible procedure is to wash our hands and proclaim our innocence by saying that we are only parental surrogates and, hence, should mind our own business. This occurs all too frequently, I am afraid and, possibly, not getting involved is the worst way to handle the situation. A second possible procedure is for a counselor to take an aggressive stance and intrude into the family situation, as gently as he can, and affirm how he sees things. I believe that almost all parents have enough concern for their children, even those not too highly valued, to be able to understand and to change their ways. Of course, it depends on how the counselor handles the matter.

The counselor asks what he should have done when he found Ken. If he sees himself as a policeman, as the old-time truant officers did, he would put "handcuffs" on Ken and take him either to his home or to a detention home. Or, he could have handled the problem as he did, leaving it up to Ken to do what he wanted. I think that he handled the situation quite properly, but I feel this was a tough decision to make. We cannot overvalue the importance of showing respect to a child.

It seems to me that the counselor possibly didn't do as much as he could have in two ways: First, as already indicated, he should have called in the parents to share his feelings with them; secondly, he should have written or called the counselor at the new school, apprising him of his understanding and feelings. Sometimes an extra bit of concern and interest can pay off enormously in helping children. I sometimes wonder why more children don't become psychotic or delinquent considering what they have to put up with. And sometimes one kind word can undo a great deal of unkindness.

T. ANTOINETTE RYAN

Counseling should be directed toward helping individuals develop behavior repertoires and implement decisions to insure their playing productive roles in the social environment. The counselor's task is to provide services needed to help pupils acquire a total education, that is, to become fully functioning members of society. In accomplishing this goal the counselor directs his resources and efforts to help each pupil meet the developmental tasks of his age successfully and realistically. The problem of identity is a central one during the adolescent years. Coming to grips with oneself is one of the primary tasks to be achieved by youths like Ken in the early high school grades. By performing in a supportive role, and providing carefully selected cues to guide cognitive and affective behaviors of the boy, the counselor in this instance was able to help Ken develop a more realistic understanding of himself. The counselor provided information relevant to the decision at hand, and reinforced the boy's decision-making capacities. The outcomes to be expected from this approach to counseling can be seen in the behavior changes which took place in Ken during the remainder of the school year.

The importance of looking at any problem situation in the context of its environment cannot be overemphasized. What this means to the counselor is that efforts to understand or modify a client's behavior should take into account factors in the environment which may impinge upon the person. It may be that the desired change in a client's behavior could only be achieved through changing the reward system of the person's environment. In this case there apparently was little, if any, reinforcement being provided from the home to encourage the kind of school-oriented, adjustive behavior which would characterize a fully functioning adolescent. The counselor's decision to have Ken and his mother come to the office to discuss the problem is an implicit recognition on the part of the counselor of the need to consider home environment. Since the father, as well as the mother, functioned as a critical variable in the boy's environment, it seems most unfortunate that the counselor confined his efforts to working with the boy and his mother. The apparent lack of long-term success in achieving counseling goals in this case may have been related more to what was not accomplished, rather than what was done.

Whether or not the counselor should have taken Ken to the detention home could be answered only by looking at the counselor's goal in relation to Ken and the ethical considerations involved in the case. In this instance, it appears that the counselor was concerned mainly with helping Ken to develop a better understanding of himself and to make the decision himself. As long as the counselor could satisfy himself that he was not ethically bound to perform in the capacity of truant officer, then he need have no compunctions about not turning the boy in to the authorities.

The counselor raises the question about the apparent lack of long-term effects in this case and points to the father's unchanging attitude to the boy. This suggests that perhaps what was missing was the commitment of the father to the plan which was worked out by the counselor, Ken, and the mother. The father apparently was a key factor in the situation from the start, and to avoid involving him in the plan for helping the boy probably was a serious error of omission. The opportunity for success in helping Ken realize his full potential was indicated by the short-term changes in the boy's behavior. Perhaps, more in the way of long-term effects might have been attained had a plan of family counseling been instituted at the time of Ken's return to school.

MITCHELL SALIM

Contemporary research is reinforcing the philosophical statements of the earlier part of our century regarding the "whole child." We know that a variety of genetic, psychological and social variables can effect academic achievement. The existence of pupil services in the schools rests on this concept.

While we are intellectually aware of the mutual interaction between home and school, we find it most difficult to implement an adequate program of pupil diagnosis and intervention. In this incident, the counselor was expressing a feeling of frustration concerning the inability of the school to offset home influences which impede the educational development of the pupil. The counselor was limited in his understanding of the dynamics of Ken's family. Perhaps an awareness of the patterns of social interaction would have prompted the counselor to consider the parents' methods of need satisfaction and the influence of this life style on Ken's development. Another point that should have been explored was the effect of Ken's life style on his parents.

The counselor behaved as a prudent person by not forcefully taking Ken home or to school. If for no other reason, the counselor was acting as a friend and not as an institutional representative.

The limited success experienced by this counselor reflects the limitations of pupil services in general. We must develop the kinds of skills, understandings, and programs needed to stabilize or reduce nonfacilitating home influences.

PAUL W. SCHMIDCHEN

As to the first question, the answer may well be, to paraphrase an old song, "More than you know!" It is amazing, to me at least, how well we manage in school, day after day, despite conditions in a home far from conducive to any constructive growth. Adolescents react compulsively, usually emotionally, precipitately, and completely. Add to this a sad dereliction on the part of some of our teachers who apparently feel and/or expect that all youngsters, all the time, come to them "as blank sheets of paper." The fact that there is not more uproar is, indeed, very surprising!

I give credit for whatever stability Ken possessed not to the adults involved, but rather to the inimitable buoyancy of the young. Both the parent, so totally unconscious or absolutely unconcerned about early training and habit-formation, and the teacher, not wishing to be personally involved while processing his particular subject matter, contributed to Ken's despair.

At the risk of offending our very righteous and subjecting oneself to the presumed hazard of being overly permissive, I find the guidance counselor's handling apt despite his chagrin over the eventual outcome of this case. Yes, the parents may have been idiosyncratic and censorious but not really any different from so many others in the sometimes callous insensitivity they show. The school becomes, I'm afraid, a court of last resort (too often, literally, just another court!). If we do not possess appreciative adults at this level, we are in a bad way, and society will experience a generation gap of rising proportions.

By all means, it was well to be receptive to Ken's problems. We can't do much to change parental viewpoints, even if we were so enjoined, but student dilemmas are specifically within our province. If we don't talk and listen to a youngster's evinced perplexity, no one else will, as note Ken's thoughtful aside. Consequently, it is nice to assume that a mother or father is the first port of call for a bedeviled adolescent, but don't count on it. And if such guidance is lacking or bankrupt, the school has the responsibility to supply it.

14

The Counselor Cops Out

CRITICAL INCIDENT

Background

My own background includes going to college rather late in life due to economic reasons. During the Second World War I worked in the shipyards to earn enough money to go to college, and then my college work was interrupted several times due to financial demands made by my own family. However, I finally got a B.A., taught for several years while attending graduate school at night and received the M.A. after six years of struggle. At long last, I was appointed a school counselor. I mention these items to indicate that I personally worked hard to get a professional education, and to show that I believe that one should try hard to get ahead. Also, I have very often argued and pleaded with bright students who do not plan to go to college (I am a high school counselor) to do so, and have helped several to find ways and means to get further education.

I believe that colleges should be training grounds for the intellectual elite, and not for everyone. Since half the population has less than average academic aptitude, I believe that at least half the population should not go to college. They will not get much out of it; they will only retard others; college degrees won't mean much; and on top of it, going to college for such kids is likely to be a disastrous experience. To put it simply, I think some kids should go to college whether or not they are interested or can afford it and some kids should not go to college. I believe that one of my functions—perhaps my main function—is to advise high school seniors and their parents about the wisdom of any kid going to any college.

One of my counselees was Peter who was below average in everything. We had rather complete records on him going back to kindergarten. He had taken about a dozen IQ tests or general academic aptitude tests over the years, as well as tests of achievement, and not a single one of them showed that he was above average. His grades were above average, however, which I assumed to be a function of his docility. He was a good kid who did what he was told and never got into any trouble—a spiritless, mild, meek, inadequate boy, with very little spunk, drive, or will. He always complied and tried his best, but his best was below average in every objective measurable respect. He had few friends and, to put it simply, he just existed. I had seen Peter several times on routine matters and found him to be more or less a lump. Whatever I would recommend, he would accept. He had no ideas of his own. His modal response to almost every question was: "Hudunno" (translated: "I don't know"). He was a scared rabbit of a boy.

The specific background relating to the incident has to do with a counseling session I had with him which centered on what he should do when he graduated from high school. I asked him what he intended to do and I got one of his "Hudunno" sounds. I asked him what his parents wanted him to do and was told "college." Peter had a habit, incidentally, of answering questions with one key word. When I heard that he was being encouraged to go on to college, I was shaken. I knew that, given his level of knowledge, he did not even deserve a high school diploma. I was certain that any college would soon throw him out, and that this would be a traumatic experience. I was certain that his parents would be quite upset were he to go to college and not succeed. I felt that it might also be quite a financial as well as emotional burden for all concerned.

I then told Peter that he should carefully think over whether he really wanted to go beyond high school and to talk things over with his parents. I also told him to tell them I would be happy to talk with them about the matter. He seemed to understand. The next day his mother called and asked for an appointment. I set it for the first time I had available.

Incident

Both of Peter's parents came in, and the session started cordially enough. I told them I was interested in Peter and that I felt that the three of us should discuss what would be best for their son. I carefully went over Peter's tests and objective grades with them and interpreted his school grades. I then tried to explain to both of them what college was like. (Neither of the parents had gone to college, and there was none in this town.) I told them that in my judgment Peter had almost no chance to succeed in college and that going there would most likely be burdensome on them as well as possibly traumatic for Peter.

The father nodded from time to time in agreement with me, but the mother just glared at me and I began to realize that she was upset. I continued, trying to be as neutral and yet as persuasive as I could, giving them all the information I had, and trying to let them understand the whole matter from my point of view. I reminded them that this was "my opinion" and that the decision was "theirs" and that what was important was "Peter's welfare and happiness." But I felt that I was not getting through to the mother. Finally I finished and awaited their reaction.

The mother began to accuse me of not wanting Peter to go to college. She told me that he had always wanted to go, and that when he had come home several nights before he was all shook up and disturbed about what I had told him. She said I had had no right to say what I did. It was none of my business. My business was only to help him select the best college for him, and not influence his decision to attend college. This was the family's decision and not mine. He was now refusing to study or do his homework. He would do poorly on the finals due to my discussion with him. I had not encouraged him. Where there is a will there is a way. If he had had good grades in high school he would also have good grades in college. What did I know about tests anyway? Which were better indicators of college grades: tests or high school grades? Did only people with high IQs have a right to go to college? Wasn't college supposed to help someone use his talents as best he could? What should Peter do now? Become a linoleum layer like his father?

To the last question I answered, "What is wrong with being a linoleum layer?"

Her answer shocked me: "Better he should be dead."

I realized at this point that I was not dealing with a rational woman, but what made this a critical incident for me was her next statement and request. She had thought it all out clearly.

"Peter has a right to go to college and try. My husband and I have worked hard and saved money for this. We want him to enjoy himself at college, and get a chance to learn something which may help him in life. You have now discouraged him. I want you to call him in and undo the harm you have done. Tell him you were joking, tell him you were mistaken. Tell him anything, but get him motivated to pass his examinations as well as possible."

Shaken by this scene which had gone so differently from how I expected, I looked at the father, who shrugged helplessly. "I think maybe you ought to do what she says. After all, she is the mother. Peter is our only son. We want what is best. Both of them think he should go. Maybe you ought to go along with her. I see your point. Maybe you are right. But he should get his chance. Otherwise she will always hate you."

The incident occurred for me right then and there. I closed my eyes and thought carefully. I knew I was right and I was positive the mother was wrong. I knew that Peter should not go to college. I could see the whole thing. My problem was what to do: stick to my guns, tell them this was how I saw things, and that right or wrong I would do what I thought was right, that I was a professional person, hired by the city to give my judgment on academic-vocational matters. Or, should I do what I thought was unwise, go along with the ambitious but unrealistic mother and thereby harm the child? I knew that I really didn't know what the right thing to do was, that the matter might be seen differently by different counselors. But I could not pass the buck to anyone else.

My decision was to go along with the mother. I agreed, called in Peter the next day, and more or less said to him what the mother wanted.

Discussion

Peter did get into college, and at the end of the first semester returned home, and entered his father's business. I called a faculty member at the college with whom I had considerable contact in placing students and asked for information about Peter. I was told that he had not adjusted well, that his grades had been very poor, that he had been on academic probation, that my judgment had been faulty in recommending him to them. In the future, he indicated, he would be much more skeptical about my recommendations.

I explained the situation, and the faculty member stated he understood my problem and that this was a fairly common problem for high school counselors. Probably about all that could be done, he felt, was to go along with parents.

Questions

1. Should a counselor operate only as a technician, doing what the "clients," (i.e., students or parents) want, rather than as a professional, doing what he thinks is right?

2. In this instance what would you have done that I didn't do? Try to get another professional opinion; try to argue and convince the mother and refuse to change my opinion?

3. How should one handle such problems? Should one just refuse to get involved? Would this not be malfeasance?

COMMENTS ON THE INCIDENT

THE EDITORS

There are two quite different concepts of a counselor. One is that he is a facilitator, a catalyst. He helps others to grow by questioning, probing, listening and accepting. The other concept is that he is an authority, a source of knowledge and wisdom. He helps others to avoid mistakes by giving advice, information, admonishing, setting limits, and initiating action. While in theory, many counselors subscribe to an essentially client-centered model of counseling, in fact, and probably as a function of the urgency to make quick decisions ("I have to know by this afternoon") or the pressure from others ("Please tell this boy that . . .") as well as other contingencies, school counselors are probably more controlling and authoritative than they themselves would prefer to be.

In this incident, a counselor who apparently feels deeply about himself and his role in the school, did what he thought was best, and encountered considerable emotionalism and opposition. The views of the child's parents clashed with his own convictions and the issue centered on whether he would stick to his views or shift to those of the parents when neither point of view was necessarily a tenable one. A conflict of philosophies, attitudes, values, and expectations ensued.

Our consultants are more or less united in their attitudes concerning the posture a counselor must take on such life issues as going on to higher education when the prospects for success do not appear promising. In this incident, there is a general compatibility of views among our consultants.

ANGELO V. BOY

This counselor states that, "I believe one of my functions—and perhaps my main function—is to advise high school seniors and their parents about the wisdom of their child going to any college." He also indicates that he has *pleaded* with bright students to go to college, considers college to be a training ground for the intellectual elite, and that only half of the students in high school should go to college. The counselor goes on to indicate that he was quite accurate when he advised Peter and his parents that he should not go to college. He was ultimately vindicated because, although Peter did attend college, he returned home at the end of the first semester. On the basis of the evidence of Peter's failure, the counselor can churn on, playing the role of the oracle in deciding who is fit for college and who is not.

Once again, we see this counselor defining his role as one of essentially assessment and advisement. He gathers the facts and evidence about a student, evaluates that information, and makes his judgment. His bias shows through because no matter what intellectual distribution exists in his student population, only half should be permitted to go to college.

The counselor in this case is the epitome of Big Brother in an autocratically controlled society. He is denying his students the right to choose freely. He is infringing upon Peter's personal liberty by attempting to discourage him from making what the counselor considers to be an unwise choice. Perhaps Peter terminated his college experience because he was uncertain of himself and insecure in his ability to succeed. And perhaps the seed for his lack of confidence was planted by the counselor who told him that he would never make it through college.

I'm not suggesting that the counselor should have given Peter false hope by telling him some sugarcoated story—a story in which a student overcomes all odds and ends up being a success simply because he tried! I am suggesting that the counselor should have created a counseling relationship which is quite different in terms of quality, scope, and depth than the advisory association he had with Peter. In such a counseling relationship the counselor would put aside the standardized test results and engage Peter in a dialogue in which Peter could explore himself as a person; his aspirations, his strengths, his weaknesses, his hopes, his fears, his innermost feelings about himself, life, and his relationships with people. Such a counseling relationship would be part of a process of self-exploration for Peter that would demand that the counselor provide him with at least an hour a week over a period of many weeks. In fact, Peter should have had access to this kind of counseling long before his senior year in high school.

If Peter had the opportunity to sift, weigh, and unravel the many facets of his self-structure and his existence, he could have reached the point where he could make a personally meaningful judgment regarding whether or not he should go to college. He could have looked at the evidence without being threatened by it. He could have made his own decision regarding college because he would have known himself more deeply and what he could and could not accomplish. He might have become sensitive to the existence of junior colleges, technical institutes, and community colleges. He might have become interested in not going to college. He might have become interested in going to a four year college, but he would have entered with an entirely different set of attitudes which might have enabled him to graduate. Peter could have developed this personally sustaining attitude if he had had access to a series of personally inclined counseling relationships with a counselor who was professionally skilled in an evocative approach to counseling.

The counselor in this case is attempting to preserve Peter from the perils of failure and so he advises him not to go to college. At first glance, it appears noble to intervene and protect a person from failure. But failure is a curious term which, when defined, is colored by the idiosyncratic bias of the person rendering the definition. The counselor was attempting to protect Peter from the trauma of failure. But would flunking out of college really have been so traumatic for Peter if he were a psychologically well integrated person who was able to make a nondefensive appraisal of his intellectual limitations and decide that he would fare better in the business world? If Peter became more of a whole person as a result of his experience in a series of qualitative counseling relationships, then he could easily accept the termination of his college experience as a fact of life without any traumatic or psychologically damaging undertones.

Sometimes in our zeal to protect others from the pitfalls of life we indicate our own insecurities. We indicate a distrust of the other person's ability to make accurate decisions about circumstances in his life and we tamper with the decision that the person wants to make. If man is allowed to explore the facets of himself and the dimensions of the decision that is to be made, then he can make personally relevant decisions about himself. What is considered to be a self-determined and realistic decision by a client might not be judged to be realistic by a counselor. But what is reality? Is it the client's or is it the counselor's concept?

If graduate programs in counselor education continue to perpetuate the type of counselor depicted in this case, then why have such programs? A qualitative counselor education program should produce professionals who possess the skill and sophistication to help clients to become more sensitive to the rationale for their behavior, more psychologically mature, better able to make personally relevant decisions, and more competent in their ability to manage their own lives.

RUDOLF DREIKURS

One can understand the difficulties of the counselor in this particular situation when one considers his background. He was very correct in providing it; it explains his utter blindness in regard to the damage he did, as a consequence of the high standards he had set for himself. Because he worked very hard to get his M.A., he became an intellectual snob, looking down on those who did not come up to his standards.

Tied to this general attitude is his exaggerated opinion about the significance of a college degree. He really believes that college is for the intellectual elite, from which the rest should be excluded. First of all, there is often no correlation between a college degree and competence in the field. The degree is reserved for those who have the ability to pass examinations. And we are becoming aware that many students who do not qualify for college are much more successful, even intellectually, than those who are admitted on the strength of test scores. When less intelligent students are denied admission to college, it deprives them of the opportunity to obtain better jobs; many students want to go to college only because their financial prospects will be significantly improved.

But all this is, of course, beyond the grasp of the counselor who is fascinated by the importance of intellectual superiority. And the student had to suffer for it.

The fact that his grades were "above average" did not impress the counselor; he took the achievement test average as a basis for his assumption that this student was "below average." It is obvious that the counselor did not like the student by the way he described him. It never occurred to him to understand Peter's handicap, his discouragement, particularly in dealing with a demanding "superior" which he, the counselor, was. For him, Peter's peculiar behavior was apparently a sign of intellectual inferiority. His anticipation of Peter's inevitable failure was a critical variable and was much more harmful to Peter than the consequences of a certain college failure. It is obvious that Peter felt inadequate to meet demands; that may well explain his low performance on tests. Discouraged as the boy obviously was, the counselor did his best to discourage him further.

The interview which the counselor had with the parents is a masterpiece of self-deception. He was furious about what the parents, especially the mother said, and apparently was utterly unaware of what he himself did. It starts off with the statement that he tried to be as neutral as he could, while every act and sentence revealed his own prejudice against the boy and his reluctance to understand what the mother had to say. He stated that "the mother began to accuse me of not wanting Peter to go to college." For heaven's sake, wasn't that exactly what he tried to do? Then the mother described the boy's reaction after the counselor had told him he should not go to college, that "he was all shook up and disturbed." The counselor certainly was not disturbed by that, nor did he recognize the harm he had done to the boy who now refused to study and to do his homework. He could not see how correct mother was in blaming him for the probability that the boy would do poorly in his finals due to the counselor's attack. She was justified in assuming that if the boy had good grades in high school, he may also have good grades in college. But the counselor believed more in tests than in the actual performance of the boy. Her evaluation of a college education was much more accurate than the distorted view of the counselor, when she said, "wasn't college to help anyone to use his talents as best he could?" And then the counselor even exceeded himself in his utter blindness to the situation. He was enraged that mother did not want the son to become a linoleum layer like father. Why was the counselor not satisfied with working in the shipyards and instead worked so hard to get a college education? Wasn't it the same desire for higher status that motivated mother? But this the counselor could not see.

In other words, it was not the mother who was irrational. She was correct in condemning the action of the counselor. The function for a counselor is to understand and to help, not to sit in judgment and to condemn. A boy who can make above average grades in high school is entitled to get a college education. It would be up to the counselor to help him find a college with lower standards if he thinks that the boy may have difficulties. Instead he discouraged him, not only in regard to a possible college education, but in his functioning at the moment. The mother was justified in demanding that he undo the harm he did, and to "get him motivated to pass his examinations as high as possible."

Where did the counselor go wrong? All his professional training did not provide him with the ability to size up the situation. We have seen many cases where, on the basis of tests alone, faulty evaluations were made, people were discouraged to go to college who, when they ignored the advice, went and succeeded, sometimes even with top grades; and conversely, students who seem to be eminently qualified for higher education failed miserably.

In this sense, the counselor was a victim of a system which will be increasingly recognized as faulty and inadequate. He compounded his mistaken evaluation of the situation with his personal concern with the elite, with intellectual righteousness. For him the question was whether he was "right" or not, regardless of what happened to the student. His description of his interview with the mother showed his blindness in regard to the role he played in the boy's life.

To answer his questions: The counselor is not obligated to do what clients, students, or parents want; but he should use better judgment in dealing with a touchy situation. It is not enough that the counselor does what he thinks is right; it is more important that he has a better idea of *what* is right. And his performance, beginning with his critical and contemptuous attitude toward Peter, was not professional but highly subjective and personal.

What could the counselor have done? First, he would have to deal with the boy's attitudes: his overambition on the one hand, and his self-doubt expressed by his inadequate social adjustment on the other. After reconsidering these factors, he may have been better able to call Peter's attention to the risks of academic failure, unless Peter learned to function more adequately in general. The counselor overlooked the specific problems of this student entirely and merely acted on the basis of his psychometric findings.

As long as our system produces counselors whose sole technique is to give and evaluate tests, such examples of an utterly inhuman approach to student counseling will continue to plague us.

ALLEN E. IVEY

The basic problem in this case lies not in the questions raised by the counselor at the close of the case, but in the third paragraph where his very explicit statement of his own values makes clear his expectations of less-than-average students. We see here an intellectual elitism, a complete acceptance of the validity of tests and grades as the prime indicators of who should go to college (despite considerable evidence to the contrary), and a godlike attitude ("my main function [is] to advise high school seniors and their parents about the wisdom of any kid going to college.").

Until this counselor examines his own personal values and realizes the potential destruction that lies within them ("Peter . . . (was) . . . more or less a lump."), he will be of only minimal value to the students he serves. He will probably continue as the college "traffic cop" helping only the apparently bright and gifted individual to higher possibilities. And could it be conceivable that some of these individuals might be more effective salesmen than professionals?

A more open and encouraging posture to all students seems required of the counselor. This does not mean that the counselor should encourage Peter to go to college. Rather it means that the counselor should explore with Peter how he really feels about his future. Accepting the one word answer "college" after "Hudunno" does not impress one as exploration, counseling, or perhaps even conversation.

In this case, it must be granted that the student perhaps has only minimal chance for success in college. A series of interviews might explore Peter's interest and future plans in some depth. It seems strange that no one ever really asked Peter what he wanted to do. The counselor should not neglect his values and opinions in this case, but there is no need to impose them on the student. The counselor might point out the problems inherent in college attendance, but could also indicate that individual differences and personal motivation determines eventual success. Peter then could take this data and use the information in his own decision-making process.

Peter and his counselor could explore alternatives to college, and whether or not college was the decision, the counselor could go to the meeting with the parents with an informed sense of Peter's position. Some additional preparatory work with the parents might be useful before a final decision session. What are the parents' goals and aspirations? Have they fully considered alternatives? If college is the eventual decision, a variety of alternative institutions can be considered where Peter's chances for success are maximized. By careful choice of college and an honest, truthful admission recommendation, the counselor's problem with the college admissions office could have been avoided.

In short, if the counselor had known Peter as a person before the session with the parents, the confrontation with the mother might have been avoided and a more compatible decision for Peter, the family, and even the counselor might have resulted. Unfortunately, the counselor remained a prisoner of his own values and was unable to listen to or see the situation he encountered. This case illustrates a problem all too common in counseling. The focus here is not on the child, but on the wishes of the parents and the counselor.

ORVAL G. JOHNSON

This incident, in innumerable variations, is repeated thousands of times every year, usually with the same results. It reveals the irrationality of many parents insofar as their children are concerned. I have counseled parents of a mentally retarded child whose plans for their child, when they entered the counseling sessions, were that he go to college and major in medicine. Counselors must be prepared for lofty parental ambitions for mediocre students. When the mediocre student is an only child, the emotional investment is that much greater.

How do you prepare against this kind of incident? First, by establishing a relationship with either the child or the parents or both *before* a crucial conference of this kind. The counselor tried to do more than was possible in a conference—establish a relationship, develop trust, give technical information, make suggestions, and bring the parents to accept *his* decision. Most counselors are assigned so many counselees that they cannot effectively carry out the counseling process. In this case, it appears that the counselor revealed his feelings about Peter in the interview with him, and the relationship went downhill from that point. The first interview might better have been devoted to drawing out the counselee, encouraging him to talk about his plans, his feelings about his parents' plans for him, his feelings about school and studying, or anything that he felt like discussing. If Peter had felt that the counselor was really interested and concerned about him, he would have interpreted the advice about college differently. As it was, Peter now had a basis for rationalizing: "He doesn't like me, so he doesn't want me to go to college."

Secondly, the counselor can avoid this kind of incident by refraining from direct advice or decision-making for the client. Many factors go into making a successful college experience, and they are difficult to ascertain with any precision beforehand. One of my counselees, a girl with just average scores on intelligence tests, a modest high school record, and an ambitious mother (a pattern well suited to failure in college), went to a highly respected state university and graduated with a *B* average. I doubt that any counselor would have predicted such success. Suppose she had not had the opportunity to go—would she have fulfilled her potential in some other setting? The counselor may give all the information he feels the student and parents can assimilate to help *them* make the decision about college. If he detects that they are determined that the child go to college, he can discuss the advantages of different kinds of institutions, such as, in this case, a junior college if one is available. It should be one of the functions of every college, however, to serve as a trial-ground for marginal students, some of whom *will* make the grade.

Question 1: The answer is obvious. Counselors must be more than technicians, and they must do what they feel is professionally "right." Making decisions for others is seldom "right," however, because it deprives the client of an opportunity to grow and learn through taking responsibility for his own decisions. Furthermore, it absolves the client of responsibility for any undesirable consequences of the decision. The counselor in this case had an opinion which he attempted to impose on the boy and his parents. His opinion of the boy's chances in college was accurate, judged by later events, but he misjudged the emotional commitment of the parents (mother primarily) to their boy's higher education.

Question 2: It is always easy to second-guess someone else's actions, but there are two points that should be emphasized. First, having the title "counselor" does not confer credibility upon anybody. I have heard high school students say that the *last* person they would seek out for personal advice is the school counselor—they would even talk to their parents before the counselor! Therefore, the counselor must establish his credibility as a counselor, and this must be done *before* a crucial interview like this. Second, while supporting the parents' wish for furthering their son's education, and praising their interest and willingness to make the financial outlay, the counselor can prepare them for possible disappointment by pointing out the study and self-discipline necessary for academic success. He could then work with them to find the college best suited to their son's limited academic aptitude.

Question 3: The counselor must always be involved with all students—he cannot cop out. One can, however, become much too concerned over a marginal student's failure in college. Failure to make it can contribute to one's personal growth and self-understanding, if it is properly handled and interpreted by others. Is it worse to have the opportunity and fail to make it, or never to have had the opportunity to try? A person may learn little academically, but much about himself in the process of "failure."

C.H. PATTERSON

In addition to the specific nature of this incident, it raises a more general question which I have found is not recognized by counselors with whom I have talked until it is pointed out to them. I would like to discuss this general question first.

It appears that counselors have taken on the assignment of recommending students for admission to colleges with no protest and no recognition of its inconsistency with their counseling obligations. College admissions officers have wooed them with praise for the significance of their recommendations, telling them that these recommendations are as useful as grades and tests. The colleges have stopped just short of rewarding high school counselors with money. Yet, the point may be made that if counselors are in effect selecting students for the colleges, the colleges should be paying them for this. If counselors are recruiters and selectors for colleges, they should be employed by the colleges, and students should know that they are serving the colleges and not the students.

There is a basic inconsistency in presenting oneself as a counselor to students, to help them with all their problems, personal as well as educational, presumably on a confidential basis, and then to write recommendations regarding college admission. Yet counselors with whom I have talked do not recognize this until it is brought to their attention. So strong is human vanity—or so weak is professionalism among counselors. Perceptive students, as well as others with whom counselors are involved, recognize this inconsistency. It is not surprising that students seldom seek out counselors for help with personal problems. As a result, in most schools there is no source of help for students with personal problems even though a number of counselors are employed. This basic issue has gone virtually unrecognized.

The counselor in this incident is an extreme example of the extent to which a counselor can cease to be a representative, or "agent" of the student and become the agent of an institution, in this case the colleges. His biases on the subject of college education are clear and need no elaboration or comment here. Fortunately, there are probably very few counselors who would take such a position.

The counselor's personal bias against Peter is also evident. It was so strong that it led him to make a serious error in evaluating Peter. Peter was not "below average in everything . . . in every objective, measurable respect." His grades were above average. It is well known that high school grades are in general better predictors of performance in college than test scores. Peter's mother knew more about this than the counselor did. It is entirely possible that, with good—or real—counseling both before and after admission to college, Peter might have been successful. The counselor, even though capitulating to the mother, did nothing to help Peter, and his handling of the whole incident—with his obvious judgment that Peter would fail—must have hindered him and may have been a major factor in his failure.

The counselor's lack of counseling ability is obvious in his report of the interview with the parents. To paraphrase: Hell hath no fury like a mother whose plans for her child are foiled. Even the father understood this fact.

The counselor's main concern about the incident is not Peter, but his reputation with the college. The questions which he raises about the incident are irrelevant. I am almost tempted to believe that this incident is a "put on," manufactured to stimulate reactions. If it is not, I was about to say that it is fortunate that there are few counselors of this kind. But after reading a number of other incidents included in this book I am not so sure. I have been jarred into the suspicion that the state of counseling in our schools—and the preparation of such counselors—is much worse than I could have imagined.

T. ANTOINETTE RYAN

A primary function of the high school counselor is to provide academic and vocational guidance services. This involves disseminating information on post-high school occupational opportunities and educational options, and helping students develop decision-making behaviors so they can make realistic vocational choices and decide on educational and training plans. The counselor's responsibility is not to make the decisions and plans for the students, but rather to help them develop information-seeking behaviors and skills of decision-making so they can make considered choices by selecting from among possible alternative courses of action those most likely to offer success and satisfaction. The counselor needs to determine what information is relevant to the educational and vocational decisions of high school students, to see that this information is made accessible to the students in organized, meaningful form, and to help students learn how to use the information for effective, efficient decision-making.

In order for a student to make effective decisions about his post-high school plans, he needs to know what options are likely to be open to him and the probable consequences associated with each alternative. A multiple regression analysis can be made to determine which factors are most critical for predicting success in post-high school programs, and experience tables summarizing relationships between these factors and grades on other performance criteria in various post-secondary institutions can be developed. There seems to be little, if any, occasion for a counselor to "advise high school seniors and their parents about the wisdom of any kid going to any college," unless such advice were to take the form of describing post-high school options and presenting information on success probabilities associated with each for students of differing backgrounds.

In this case the counselor's suggestion to the boy to think about his post-high school plans and to talk the matter over with his parents could hardly be questioned, as this places decision-making responsibility squarely on the shoulders of the boy. A question might be raised about the counselor's failure to direct the boy to information relevant to the decision at hand. The boy might have used to advantage information on the probabilities for success in various post-high school options for students like himself, with similar grades and test scores. He could have been shown what had happened to previous high school seniors who had enrolled in junior college, Ivy League college, state college, vocational-technical school, or specialized skill training programs. In consulting with the mother, the counselor might have avoided the ultimate encounter with the mother had he talked in terms of expectancies based on what had happened to a significant proportion of other students after enrollment in various kinds of programs in different post-high school institutions. As it was, he had only his opinion to offer, and little in the way of solid evidence to back up his feelings. No wonder the session turned into a debacle. It was a case of two conflicting opinions, with the mother's position being fraught with all the emotional charge one could expect to find in a mother-son relationship. In the final analysis the counselor's prime responsibility was to the client. It is difficult to justify how any counselor could be condoned for advising a client to behave in a manner which the counselor believed would prove harmful. The counselor asks whether he should function as a technician or as a professional person. The idea of counselor certification presumes a difference between the professionally trained counselor and the paraprofessional technician. The program of studies for counselor preparation is designed to provide instruction and supervised counseling experience to equip a person for making sound counseling decisions. If the counselor finds himself in a situation where he feels incompetent to function, it would behoove him to seek assistance from a supervisor or colleague rather than resign himself to the position of letting the client tell him what to do.

There are several options the counselor might have taken in this case other than the one he followed. In the first place, he could have talked to the parents in normative rather than idiosyncratic terms; that is, giving them information about probabilities of success in different programs for students like Peter, leaving the decision making to the boy, and avoiding the editorializing about "college for whom." The role of the counselor is not implemented in arguing, so little would seem to be gained by trying to convince the mother of the "rightness" of the counselor's opinion. He could, however, have made very clear to the parents the evidence on which his opinion was based. Unless evidence to the contrary were at hand, he would hardly seem to be justified in "changing" his opinion.

MITCHELL SALIM

Counseling may be seen as an individualized service directed toward facilitating the growth and development of the client. Through the counseling process, the client may develop an increasing awareness of self and the many aspects of his dynamic environment. Hopefully, any decisions reached by the client, as a product of the counseling process, were made with personal clarity.

Human beings typically attempt to influence each other as they strive toward adequacy. Manipulation is everpresent, whereas opportunities for personal decision-making without external manipulatory pressures seem rare.

The counselor must possess the necessary skills and qualities for building and maintaining the special kind of relationship needed to facilitate the counseling process. If he doesn't possess these professional qualities, the counselor cannot expect his client to develop this self- and environmental-understanding.

The counselor must be perceived by the client as one who understands, cares, and accepts without any strings. These conditions cannot obtain if the counselor is preoccupied with his own needs. Peter's counselor was acting like "people in general" rather than as a counselor. Throughout the incident it appeared that he was more concerned with his status needs than with genuinely helping Peter. The counselor's anxiety to prove his point, be an informational expert, and have the key to what was right for Peter was manifest.

The counselor's questions were presented to screen him from his own uncertainties. It is evident that the counselor must, with assistance, explore his personal-professional attitude in the light of our democratic educational philosophy. Questions such as: "Why do I find myself in this position?" "What am I really trying to do?" "Am I genuinely helping my clients?" and "Do I really make a difference in how my clients live their lives?" should be of paramount concern to the counselor.

The counselor could have been more effective if he had helped Peter and his family examine their goals and possible conflict areas, examine entrance information to colleges and relate them to his school achievement. Discussion in terms of probabilities rather than categorical statements would have been desirable. The decision and responsibility for the decision was a family matter.

In summary, if the counselor had acted like a counselor ought to act, he would have been helpful.

15

The Pernicious Lie

CRITICAL INCIDENT

Background

I had been teaching for about five years in a high school in our town, which has a population of about 10,000, when I was asked by our superintendent if I would like to be a counselor. He said he had observed that I often talked in the halls with the pupils and seemed to enjoy it, and he felt that I would make a good counselor. I felt complimented, was intrigued by the idea, and decided to start at once getting the necessary credentials. It involved traveling to a university about fifty miles away one long evening each week for the whole year and attending both summer sessions the following summer. I completed the work and was given a contract to work half-time in the counseling office the following year.

In the meantime both the superintendent who had hired me and the principal of the high school were replaced. The new principal, Mr. J., was particularly interested in the problem of unexcused absences, or "ditching," as it is called here. He asked me to spend some of my time each day checking on absences and contacting the parents of offenders. Each day I went to homes to check on pupils who were absent, and whose parents had not called the school, as the school handbook requested.

This was about ten years ago. At that time our school was comparatively free from the problem of numerous pupil pregnancies and marriages and the apparent complacency concerning sexual situations that seems prevalent today.

Incident

One day Mr. J. asked me to go to the home of one of our tenth-grade girls, Annette, who had been absent during the afternoon classes the previous day but had been seen shortly after school getting out of the car of her boyfriend, Jack, a senior. She was seen entering the bus for her ride home later. The principal told me he felt that the parents should know that Annette, who was supposed to be on campus, had instead been off campus with a boy.

As it happened, two of Annette's older sisters were in my classes and I had enjoyed knowing them. They were intelligent, cooperative, and of good character. When I went to the house, I was, therefore, able to favorably introduce myself to the mother by making pleasant remarks about the older girls. Then I told her that the principal had asked me to report that Annette had been seen with her boyfriend the previous afternoon at a time when she was supposed to be in school. I took pains to make no comments about it, avoided discussing it in any way, and recall that my facial expression should have indicated that I sincerely felt it was simply a plain case of "ditching." As a matter of fact, no other thought had even occurred to me. Annette's mother thanked me, and told me that Annette had matured early, had too great an interest in boys, and that she had been very worried about her. I listened to the mother but made no comments.

That evening, I was working in the yard at home when a car pulled in with two young men in it, one of them being Annette's friend Jack. I went to the car and greeted them. Jack said, "I understand you have been saying foul things about Annette." Shocked at this, I asked him exactly what I was supposed to have said. He then told me that Annette's mother had said to him that I thought Annette was pregnant. I told him it was not true that I had said that, and urged him to bring Annette's mother to school for a three-way discussion. I could not believe that she would lie to both of us about it. He then told me he didn't really believe that I had said that and his folks, who knew me, had told him it could not be true. We parted with his feeling better about it, I am sure.

As soon as I arrived at school the next morning I told the principal exactly what had happened. He went with me to see Jack who was on detention for "ditching," and told him he had made a serious charge saying that "it could affect Mrs. K's whole career." I asked the principal to go with me to see Annette's mother, who lived about ten miles away and did not have transportation to school. He agreed, and we left right away for Annette's home. The mother came to the door, and I introduced the principal and said that I wanted her to tell him exactly what had happened when I called on her the previous day. She told him what had happened, just as I had told him. So Mr. J. thanked her, and we turned to leave. Just then Annette, who was at home that day, came to the door and said, "Mother, you know you told me Mrs. K. said that about me." The mother in obvious embarrassment said good-bye to us and propelled her daughter into the house.

Mr. J. commented that it was obvious the mother had tried to frighten her daughter and that is how the misunderstanding occurred. He assured me that he believed me and told Jack how he felt when we returned to school. Again Jack remarked that he hadn't believed it anyway.

I thought the incident was over and assumed the mother would straighten out the matter after our visit. But the next day a teacher told me she had heard some of the girls talking, and they said that I had told her mother that I thought Annette was pregnant. Naturally this distressed me very much, but I felt that confronting the girls and denying it would only prolong the issue.

When Annette returned to school, I made a point of seeing her and asked her if she was now sure of my innocence in making such a remark about her. I will never forget her reply; "No, my mother said that she didn't want to let Mr. J. know that you said that because she was afraid you'd be fired."

It later developed that the girl who spread this gossip at school was pregnant at the time and, no doubt, felt that stories about someone else would somehow minimize her problems.

Discussion

This could have been a shattering experience for a beginning counselor. Since Mr. J. was a new principal in our school, he could hardly be certain of my innocence. I had a horrible fear that Annette's mother would not tell the truth, and it would be a question of her word against mine. When Mr. J. told Jack my whole career could be affected by this matter, he probably meant to convey to Jack that it could be dangerous to make such statements about me. But at that time I felt he was considering having me dismissed in disgrace.

Today, I would feel quite different from the way I felt ten years ago. After several years of happy work with young people, I know I enjoy the respect of most of them, as well as that of the administration.

I always regretted having to leave Annette believing I made that statement about her, but felt it was better for her to resent me than her
mother.

It may be a comfort to some beginning counselor reading this book
to know that these things probably happen most often when you are
starting out and seldom afterwards. As you earnestly try to help young
people find themselves and solve their problems, the unpleasant incidents
decrease as the pleasant ones increase so that almost every day brings
a glow of pride that you have contributed in some small way to the
happiness and satisfaction of the young people in your school.

Questions

1. Assuming that students and their parents will sometimes lie
about a counselor, what can counselors do, to avoid being lied about,
misinterpreted, and so on?

2. What is the most proper course of action when an absolutely
untrue statement is attributed to you?

3. Was it a mistake for me to go with the principal to confront
Annette's mother? Was it a mistake for me to defend myself to Jack? If
so, how can one reply to a report of a false accusation?

4. Perhaps the more important issue can be found in another question: Should I have followed the principal's suggestion to tell the mother
about Annette's being seen with Jack? Was it my business to do this?
Should school personnel feel they are obliged to tell parents about their
children's behavior? (Sometimes I feel even report cards are unwarranted
information). What, if anything, should school personnel report to parents
about their children, and what should not be reported to them?

COMMENTS ON THE INCIDENT

THE EDITORS

By the very nature of his profession, a counselor is likely to encounter a small but noxious population of clients—parents and students,
mainly—who not only have problems, but who are problems. For example, counselors can be criticized unjustly, accused without foundation, lied
about and otherwise treated poorly by the very people they are trying to
help. It is no use complaining; this is the nature of our work.

The issue in this case seems to have been a deliberate, fantastic lie which others involved in the issue accepted as fact. When one is unjustly judged because of false testimony and when one is innocent, but there is no way to prove it, the consequences can be both dramatic and unnerving.

Possibly the only defense against untrue allegations is stout, dignified denial. Some of our consultants who think that prevention is better than cure, make general suggestions to enable counselors to avoid getting themselves into such untenable situations in the first place.

GEORGE J. BREEN

The central issue of the incident is probably contained in the last question. My initial reaction was to the role that Mrs. K. accepted unquestioningly from the principal, Mr. J. Although the problem of unexcused absences or "ditching" is important, it is not my opinion that the role of policewoman, which Mrs. K. accepted, was appropriate to a guidance counselor. Frequently, much of the confusion that exists in the minds of guidance personnel today, insofar as their functions are concerned, has its origin in their uncritical acceptance of tasks which are inappropriate to them. A functions precedent is then unfortunately established for future counselors in that system to inherit.

Therefore, Mrs. K. left herself open for the difficulty she encountered primarily because of the very nature of the role that the principal assigned to her. One can safely assume that serious distortions, if not outright lies, can often develop from the type of potentially threatening messages that Mrs. K. delivered in her assignment. In short, she should have either turned the assignment down or dealt differently with the problem of unexcused absences. For example, Mrs. K. could have confronted the student initially, rather than the parent, as far as the self-defeating behavior or "ditching" was concerned. This would avoid the indirect or "three-party line" type of communication so conducive to ineffective problem-solving. The consequences of the student's actions could then be explained to her, rather than the parent. Not only could this serve as an incentive to the student to become more responsible for her actions, but it would also be done in a true counseling setting.

Only if the student persisted in her self-defeating behavior should the parents have been notified. Furthermore, this notification need not have been effected by a personal visit from the counselor. A simple, straightforward written message from the principal of the school would have left little or no room open for misinterpretation. If anything, the role of Mrs. K. would have been to counsel the student and parents together in order to deal with the problem. In other words, school personnel, namely administration, should only report to parents when the behavior of the student clearly indicates he is not interested in, or capable of being, responsible for himself.

If Mrs. K. had suggested the aforementioned procedure, she would have minimized the possibility of being lied about or misinterpreted. Annette and her mother would have only been present in the counseling office if the unexcused absences went unchecked and the parent sought counseling assistance. This type of self-referral is generally more conducive to effective counseling. Admittedly, this procedure would not preclude the possibility of lying or misinterpretation. Therefore, the counselor who feels compelled to make third party interventions with the parent and the child in matters of discipline would be wise to tape-record all such sessions. Unfortunately, the other great advantage of taping sessions via self-supervision is all too often overlooked, particularly by school counselors.

Mrs. K.'s second and third questions can be answered together in that one can best reply to a false accusation or to a statement that is absolutely untrue by vigorously and straightforwardly denying it. It certainly was not a mistake for the counselor to defend herself to Jack or to go to the mother's home with the principal, although her judgement, when similarly confronted by Annette, was quite irrational. The resentment that Annette felt for Mrs. K. was a good example of the kind of self-sacrifice that serves no useful purpose. Annette's mother could only be encouraged or reinforced to behave similarly in a parallel situation as a result of the counselor's illogical decision. If a duty of a counselor is to teach students effective means of coping with reality, as I believe it is, would Mrs. K. be really helping Annette toward this goal by protecting or encouraging her mother's disturbed behavior?

JAMES DONOVAN

Sometimes I wonder at the many ways there are to keep a counselor from functioning in a professional manner. No doubt this case illustrates one of the common traps employed by school officials—combining discipline and counseling. Young and naive counselors jump in only to find that they have lost the opportunity to contribute uniquely to the school. It is important to realize that schools must have some form of discipline and we need fair and competent people—maybe even someone with a counseling background to perform the service. But schools defeat the purpose of counseling services by involving them in such truant-officer activities and policelike visits to the home. Unfortunately the opposition perceives this stand as the counselor wanting to keep his hands clean and remain the good guy. But if we carefully examine the roles of school personnel we recognize the need for confidential and nonthreatening parent contact so that such troublesome subjects might be freely and helpfully discussed. The school that confuses the counselor's roles with other school personnel does all concerned a disservice. A successful school works as a team, all members of which strive for the same ultimate goal of helping the youngster experience life satisfactorily and find meaning in his existence.

A counselor must move cautiously when it appears that someone is distorting the truth or actually lying. Overreacting on the counselor's part usually gets in the way of his being helpful and perceiving the dynamics of the problem clearly. I have found, when confronted by situations like this one, that simply stating my position and making clear my desire to continue the relationship, allows the original incident—be it a lie or misinterpretation—to find its proper low level of importance.

ORVAL G. JOHNSON

This incident started out as one of many everyday occurrences in the life of a counselor, and then ballooned into a more-or-less major affair because of a chance combination of circumstances: a worried and rather unscrupulous mother who was already concerned about her daughter's morals; a girl not connected with the incident who evidently felt that her own troubles would be lessened by focusing attention on someone else's difficulties, real or unreal; a concerned boy friend; and an inexperienced counselor. The incident shows clearly how a relatively unimportant event took on significance because of the emotional needs of the persons who eventually became involved in it.

The conflicting roles assigned to the counselor are probably more responsible for this incident than any other single factor. This issue has been debated for years, and out of the mass of opinion and (little) research we can only glean the suggestion that few counselors can successfully manage the roles of disciplinarian and counselor. Sometimes the counselor is responsible for all disciplinary cases. In this situation, the counselor was also the attendance officer, and that role is likely to handicap any counseling relationship. Even parents, with their small "case load," find the two roles difficult to reconcile, and because of their responsibility for the personal safety and well-being of their children they often find it necessary to emphasize the role of disciplinarian.

The problem of how much to tell parents of what we see and hear at school is a knotty one. It is difficult to evaluate how much information a parent can effectively handle. In this case, the obligation of the counselor functioning as attendance officer was merely to inform the parents of the unexcused absence. In a real sense, where she had been, or whose car the girl emerged from, was not at that point a legitimate concern of the school. The counselor was on firm ground in informing the parent of the girl's absence from school, based on compulsory attendance laws. Beyond that, it is the parents' responsibility to evaluate the reasons for and conditions surrounding the absence from school. In most schools, hopefully, counselors are not required to engage in law enforcement, except incidentally in their roles as citizens.

Another point exemplified by this incident is that if the counselor has established a positive relationship with the young people in his school, unfounded negative rumors about him do not thrive. The counselor's reputation with students comes from his individual contacts plus the kind of talk that goes on among students. His reputation is crucial. It is "in" for students to go to some counselors and "out" to talk with others.

As in some other critical incidents, the emotional context of a message overwhelms the objective content of the message. We frequently think we have communicated so clearly that no one could misinterpret us, and yet we do not recognize statements attributed to us when they come back to our ears. It is futile to try to establish what one may have said, because it is usually at variance with what someone has heard. The counselor can more profitably deal with the question of why his message was distorted.

MANFORD A. SONSTEGARD

There are many interesting aspects to this case; for instance, the method of choosing a counselor is interesting. Also interesting is the role the counselor came to play as an administrator's cat's-paw, checking absenteeism rather than counseling. The counselor's role had no similarity to the role set forth by the American School Counselor Association's "Statement of Policy for Secondary School Counselors and Guidelines for Implementation." Surely an office clerk with a telephone could have performed the functions the counselor assumed. And, if a parent is to be merely informed of his child's conduct, then the principal is in the best position to do this. The principal, apparently, had an intriguing way of avoiding administrative duties.

The function of the counselor is to discover the reasons for the youngster's behavior. In this case, why did she leave school? What purpose did her actions serve? Merely informing a parent what is happening is not providing professional counseling service.

Annette's situation is understandable; she had two older sisters who were "intelligent, cooperative, and of good character," with whom the counselor as a teacher had "enjoyed good relations." It is probable that they were good students and Annette, by all indications, was not. The "goodness" of the older sisters had, in all likelihood, been held up to Annette many times. Convinced she could not attain the status of her older sisters, she became discouraged and turned to useless behavior. Perhaps she could gain a place by being popular with the boys. When they sought her out, she felt important. The mother's lack of understanding of Annette's behavior led her to try desperately to control her daughter.

It is unfortunate that the counselor was of no help to either Annette or her mother. This approach, stemming from an inadequate preparation for the job, discredited the counselor and led to a frustrating situation. A counselor should have adequate training and experience to deal with such situations. Talking to pupils in the halls and seeming to enjoy it is not a valid basis for selection for positions as complicated as counseling. Experience and training are vital elements in enabling the counselor to render professional service in the school setting.

If the counselor had discovered the purpose for Annette's behavior, he would have known what steps to take to redirect her mistaken goals.

This would have involved counseling sessions with both teachers and parents, as well as Annette. These sessions should take place in the counselor's office, where the businesslike atmosphere and equipment would be more conducive to developing a professional counseling service. The counselee's home and backyard is not an appropriate setting for counseling.

16

Degree or Trade?

CRITICAL INCIDENT

Background

When I first began my work in education I was a high school science teacher. I went on to get a master's in administration, and wrote a thesis on counseling. My principal gradually transferred me to counseling, and at the present time I am a full-time counselor. One of my concerns over the years has been with a fairly common problem-type of students and it seems to me that any book of cases should consider these individuals. They have good academic potential (as evidenced by their performance on intelligence tests) and ambitious and affluent parents, but they have neither the interest nor the basic preparation for academic work.

In my first semester of full-time counseling I worked with two seniors in the high school, both of whom fell into this category. Larry was eighteen, a star baseball player with high academic potential, low grades, and limited interest in academic work. His parents were quite well-off since his father ran a trucking company. Harry, also a senior, was on the football team, and not quite as bright as Larry, but had enough ability to succeed in a college with average academic standards. His grades were very low and his family was well-to-do, since his father was one of the major contractors in the area. After discussing their problems with them, I found myself saying more or less the same thing to both of them as follows:

"You want to please your parents by going to school, but you have shown very little interest in academic work, getting very poor grades. On the other hand, your grades and your attitudes do not really indicate that you can profit from college unless you change your habits and really work at school. No one is "sentenced" to go to college, and while it is good to try to please your parents, it is also important to consider your own future, your motivation, your interests, and your ambitions."

My contentions led to several discussions with the students who began to discuss such matters as working, marriage, military service, and future careers. In each case the parents were called in and a four-way discussion ensued in which I tried to support the boy's right to determine his own future. Both sets of parents said more or less the same thing: the decision was up to their son. They hoped he would go to college; if he didn't that would be all right; if he wanted to enter father's business that was acceptable, too. I felt both sets of parents were able to change their thinking about the importance and necessity of college, even though both were disappointed with their children's limited academic commitment. I tried to soften the information I gave them by deemphasizing the importance of college.

Incident

The incident was not especially dramatic. The decisions of the boys and subsequent events proved interesting, however. Larry opted for college, Harry did not. I talked with both of them, and each felt he had made his decision freely. I kept my opinions to myself—(secretly I felt that neither should have gone to college)—and I decided to follow them up.

Discussion

The incidents occurred just eight years ago. Larry finished with a bachelor's in business administration, getting very poor grades. I use to call him every summer when he came home from school. He is now working for a local company as a sales clerk and office worker. He was employed for a while by his father but apparently there was some disagreement between them. Harry is working for his father's company as a skilled laborer and is happy and well adjusted.

I understand that when Larry returned from college, he did not want to become a truck driver but wanted to start in a management capacity. Apparently, he and his father disagreed and Larry went on his own. Harry, on the other hand, started as an apprentice and now, as a skilled laborer, is earning a much higher salary than Larry. Incidentally, a laborer in our town earns more than a high school counselor. (There may be a moral in this too!)

It seems to me that going to college can sometimes be a mistake, and over the years I have seen many cases of the Larry-Harry variety. If parents and the school conspire against high school pupils to force them into almost certain failure in college and career, I don't think we are doing anyone a favor. I wonder what someone else thinks about this common situation. As for myself, I feel proud of having encouraged Harry to consider alternatives to attending college, and somewhat responsible for his eventual pursuit of a satisfying and successful life.

Questions

1. Why do so many parents want their children to go to college when there is every evidence that their children do not like to study and are having difficulty in school?

2. How can one reeducate parents to the likelihood that some children would be much better off going into the trades, or into business?

3. Where do parents get the idea that employment agencies, personnel men, and so on, will not even interview young men unless they have a college education?

4. Why is there so much propaganda for college? It seems as though every high school student thinks of nothing else.

COMMENTS ON THE INCIDENT

THE EDITORS

What role should a counselor play: is he mostly an information giver, or is he an advisor? To what extent should he officially stick his neck out? Suppose a child wants to do something that in the counselor's judgment is absolutely wrong, should he just smile and nod and let him do what he wants, or does he have an obligation to speak out and advise? And if people disregard his advice, does he then insist they follow his advice or does he merely keep quiet?

This problem is one of the most troublesome that counselors have, for they often can see clearly that students and parents are heading for disaster, or at least a rude awakening. But often people don't want to know the truth, don't want to be warned, and resent any advice giving. Should one tell parents of a child who clearly is academically retarded and clearly is unable to learn simple mathematics, that the child is highly unlikely to become an engineer or an accountant? Parents are usually not responsive to probability statements. They have no liking for nomothetic prediction data. They want to know only yes or no and about their particular child. And so, the issue is raised of what a counselor should do relative to advising children and parents when he knows his advice contradicts what his clients want to hear.

Another issue raised by this incident and by the consultants' commentaries points to the uniqueness of a counselor's advice. Assume that counselor X believes that only a favored minority, the intellectual elite, should go to college and assume that his opinions contradict those of the principal, all the teachers and the counselors in the school, and the child's parents. Should the counselor be censored? Should he have the right to speak out? After all, just because he is in the minority, does not mean he is wrong. His aberrant opinions may at times prove correct.

But to what degree should a counselor's unique views be tolerated when they are clearly prejudicial and controvertible? Suppose he uses his position to express his biases? At what point should his views and influence be countermanded? While this is not an explicit issue in this incident, it is certainly worth considering, especially in school counseling where the student is rarely accorded any freedom in the selection or changing of counselors. Ordinarily, a student is assigned to a counselor and that is it.

BENJAMIN C. BELDEN

I feel that college should be dispensed with in favor of quality secondary education. These are the formative years and the proper time for major education. A college degree should not be essential for membership in the human race. Unfortunately too many secondary schools are detention camps for students on their way to the real world or college. I believe that there must be some better way of keeping young people out of the labor market or out of their parents' hair.

Parents want their children to go to college not because they are particularly concerned about what their children want but rather because of what they want for their children. As long as parents feel that college is going to make their children better than their parents were, they will want children to go to college. It is part of the American dream—or fantasy—that each generation be better than the last. Thus college becomes especially important for parents who feel that they aren't all that good themselves.

This counselor also calls our attention to the fact that a laborer in his town earns more than a high school counselor, and that he himself was actually trained as an administrator. I wonder how *he* feels about his job? It is apparent that he has some misgivings about his profession and its status in the community. This counselor may have a vested interest in discouraging students from attaining superior roles and vocations. After all, the higher they go the lower he falls by comparison. How does a school counselor deal with this issue?

Actually, there isn't really so much propaganda for college. It is an assumed positive norm of our culture, like becoming a "real" man. But as long as colleges need students, professors, buildings, and national guardsmen there will always be some "propaganda."

Things might be changing, though. I understand that Ph.D's are in oversupply in some academic marketplaces and that they are not commanding significantly more money than those with lesser degrees. I have also heard that industrial organizations are looking less for college graduates and more for people who can do the job irrespective of their educational background. Perhaps the college-or-all-is-lost syndrome will give way someday to a realistic appraisal of people on their own merits.

ANGELO V. BOY

In this incident, the counselor seems to be saying, "I was right about Larry and Harry. Neither one of them should have gone to college. Larry went to college and is now working as a salesclerk and office worker, the poor soul. Harry didn't go to college and look at him now—he's happy and well adjusted as a laborer and even makes more money than Larry the college graduate, and myself!"

I was impressed that the counselor bigheartedly allowed both Larry and Harry to make their own decisions. I'm disappointed not only because the counselor secretly felt that "neither should have gone to college" but that he even possessed these feelings. From my viewpoint, the professional counselor should not possess such a covert value judgment. If he truly believes in the right of the client to make his own decision about his life, then all of his psychic energy goes into helping the client to make that decision and he doesn't need to viscerally place his stamp of approval or disapproval upon the decision that is made. If he deeply and honestly believes in the right of each client to make his own decision, then he doesn't need to tell us, eight years later, that Larry's decision was wrong, while Harry's decision was right. Let Larry and Harry live with their decisions, since they were freely made, without judging the merit of these decisions. The counselor seems to be saying, "The right decision is the one with which I concur."

What about Larry and Harry? How do they feel about their decisions eight years later? Is Larry regretting the fact that he went to college and is, as the counselor implies, *only* a salesclerk and office worker? Is Harry, the laborer who didn't go to college, as happy and well adjusted as the counselor indicates? What is the behavioral evidence which indicates that Harry is happy and well adjusted? Might it be that the counselor is seeing Harry as being more successful than Larry because he wants to? Because the counselor wants us to know that he was right about Larry and Harry from the very beginning?

The counselor, at the point when Larry and Harry were making their decisions about their post-high school plans, didn't interfere with those decisions and this, in a sense, is commendable. But he did possess a covert opinion that neither Larry nor Harry belonged in college, that both would be better off not continuing their formal education. If the counselor had some reliable evidence to go on, other than his opinion, then he would have been far more honest in his relationships with Larry and Harry if he had said, "According to the following information, it appears that college might be more than you can handle." In an open and honest counseling relationship he could then wait for his client to react, and then begin to respond to the feelings undergirding the client's verbal reaction. By responding to these feelings and engaging the client in a *series of counseling sessions*, the counselor would enable the client to unscramble some of the attitudinal components which would affect his decision about college.

If Larry, the college graduate, is indeed unhappy today as a sales-clerk, then the counselor did Larry a disservice eight years ago, not by allowing him to decide to go to college, but by not furnishing him with a series of qualitative and evocative counseling sessions in which Larry could uncover *why* he wanted to go to college. If Larry had discovered eight years ago that he was inclined to college because of external pressures, (his father, prestige, the sociology of the community) and attending college wasn't really *his* idea, then he might have made a different decision regarding his post-high school plans.

When counselors function merely as gatekeepers to the hallowed halls of higher education, when they mechanically attempt to match each student's ability with post-high school opportunities, then why call school counseling a profession? If it is to be a profession, then counselor education programs must begin to produce counselors who can deal with students with a deeper level of professional sophistication than the counselor depicted in this case. One of this counselor's problems might be that he earned his master's degree in administration rather than in counseling. I acknowledge that he did his master's thesis in counseling, but his behavior in this case may be more of a reflection of his administrative training than his thesis.

DON C. DINKMEYER

This is an interesting case because it presents a common problem for counselors in those school districts which encourage students to go on to college whether or not the students are interested or have aptitude for higher learning. If we should ask the question "Why do parents want their children to go to college at all costs?" we find the answer not only in the natural desire of parents to obtain the best advantages for their young, but also from the continuous propaganda that the school emits.

Almost from the day their formal education begins, children are told that they are learning in order to be better prepared for work in the upper grades of elementary school, high school, and college. We are always preparing them for an academic future. Our goal often seems to be unconnected to reality and only to academic matters. Teachers invariably hold college admission as the final goal to which pupils at all grade levels must aspire. No wonder there is such a demand to go to college.

If one were to talk with members of a school board and question the necessity for a dubious course offering, the reply typically is, "This is required for college admission." The buck is always passed on to the next higher level. It isn't that we require it, but, rather, that someone else wants it.

It seems to me that the counselor in this incident operated sensibly in counteracting the propaganda of the universal value of a college education. He helped the students know that college was not a "sentence" and that it was important for these young adults to consider their own interests and ambitions as well as considering the demands of their parents and of the cultural milieu.

Parents have a strong desire for their children to go to college because of the considerable pressure placed upon them from the propaganda put out by educators in the elementary and secondary schools. The remedy to this misconception may include indoctrination in the opposite direction at PTA meetings which would expound the theme that there are many ways to be successful in life; that college education is not necessarily the best thing for all students; and that not all children, even if academically capable, should attend college. This counterpropaganda will not be well received when the general mores and traditions of the community preclude the possibility of success in life without college. Another simple suggestion is to invite personnel men into the school to propagate the idea that college is not necessary for many jobs, and demonstrate that many good jobs can be obtained without a college education.

If high school students are thinking of going to college despite their lack of academic ability, lack of academic interest, and lack of intention of using the knowledge acquired in college in their work, certainly the schools should take their full share of the blame for propagating this meaningless obsession. It appears that we in academia have oversold ourselves indeed!

ORVAL G. JOHNSON

This incident represents a persistent and thorny problem for counselors. On the one hand, one of the fundamental tenets of their profession is to make it possible for students to go as far academically as their talents will allow. On the other hand, most colleges and universities are overcrowded, and the counselor has the obligation to recommend students who can benefit from advanced education. Some counselors feel that if they recommend students who are not successful in college, they will lose the confidence of the admissions officers and their recommendations will be considered meaningless. How can we know whether or not a particular student can benefit from higher education? We cannot, consequently we must avoid doing anything that will deny the student an opportunity which might be potentially beneficial to him.

The counselor in this case used one of the most effective techniques in guidance, namely, helping the client to perceive viable alternatives to a doubtful course of action. For many high school graduates, there is no honorable alternative to college, because of family aspirations and the precedents which older children and friends and neighbors have set. They need special help in coping with the pressures exerted by others, in realistically assessing life goals that someone else has set for them. The counselor can help the client develop a broader approach to decisions regarding his future, so that he has alternatives and understands the rationale underlying each alternative.

When the counselor is considering college as an alternative for a counselee, it is natural to think of his own college as the standard by which to judge the student's chances of success. In this instance, the counselor could break down the college alternative, so that if the student chose that course of action, he would have several kinds of colleges from which to choose. These should include some colleges which are oriented to the marginal student, providing special help with study skills, tutoring, and intensive guidance and counseling services.

The counselor asks why parents want their children to go to college when they have shown little academic aptitude previously. Whether the parents see college graduation as vocational preparation, as preparation for a fuller life, or as a prestige symbol, it is valued highly enough so that their feelings interfere with objective thinking. Thus, they can easily explain away poor high school grades. Furthermore, there are always handy examples of other students who, despite low grades in high school, blossomed in college.

The counselor's second question is concerned with how one communicates to parents that some children would be better off elsewhere than in college. Although parents do believe that some children don't belong in college, they seldom believe that about their own children. Having lived with their children, they see characteristics that are not always brought out by the school environment, characteristics which strengthen their chances for succeeding in college. Whether or not they are right, they have invested enormous amounts of hope in their child's future, and it takes extended counseling to modify that hope.

The counselor then asks why parents feel that employers will not interview young men without college degrees. There are many positions for which employers require college degrees, especially those involving professional training which can only be acquired in a college or university. Employers do interview high school graduates, but not ordinarily for the kinds of positions that will satisfy the aspirations of most parents.

The counselor's final question, "Why is there so much propaganda for college?" can be answered based on our changing attitudes toward education. In the past college was for the rich or the exceptionally talented, while today it is accessible for almost everyone. The average graduating high school senior now feels an explanation is necessary if he is *not* planning to attend college. Furthermore, the American faith in education persists. It is the surest path in our society to upward mobility for lower- and middle-class youth.

BARBARA A. KIRK

It seems that society, as represented particularly by the school and the parents, conspires to encourage, urge, press and, in many ways, force most young people into a college education. There is such social pressure towards education in an academic setting that there is all too little general knowledge and appreciation of the equally extensive and frequently intensive trade and vocational type educational programs.

This counselor has been doing a yeoman job in attempting to support and assist the boys with whom he works to make their own decisions in relation to their own gearing, interests, aptitudes, abilities, orientations, values, goals. He is thus doing the very kind of thing best calculated to counteract the social pressures on any individual, by giving him support in finding his own unique way and encouraging his parents to be supportive of him in finding it and pursuing it when he finds it.

Specific information on the varieties and levels of technical, trade, and vocational training opportunities is a must, as well as specific occupational information on outlets, including numbers in the labor force, salaries, and opportunities for the future. A collection of these kinds of data can be helpful both to students and their parents. An additional counteractive measure is to encourage the community to develop the kinds of courses that involve employers and unions, courses at secondary or post-secondary level which lead directly into employment. School systems can contribute markedly in developing higher-level, better-regarded, and more educationally-effective training programs in other than academic subjects.

This counselor points to one of the major problems of our times for a substantial proportion, probably more than fifty percent, of our total student population.

There is, however, just a word to be said on the other side. There are still many parents who do not believe in college, especially for their own children, even if those children have very strong desires to go to college coupled with the aptitudes and the talents needed for success in college. Essentially, then, the major problem is individualization, with the counselor directing his efforts to assisting the student to think through his own situation, helping him determine the most advisable goal, and then encouraging the parent to understand and support it, whatever it may be.

JAMES N. PEPPER

There is a possibility we have oversold the log-cabin-to-president concept that education is the key that can unlock the door to success, happiness, and self-satisfaction. This concept, based on our pioneer thinking or our immigrant inheritance, is passed from parents to children. Every parent wants his children to be more successful in life than he has been and so, for this reason, if not for the more selfish reason that his children's achievements affect his social standing, parents push education and educators push parents. If the father is an enlisted man in the armed forces, he wants his child to be an officer. If he is a blue-collar worker he envisions a white collar for his offspring. If the father is not educated, he usually feels that this lack has been his handicap and education for his child becomes the important goal. I sometimes think that all parents educate their children to become eligible to be trainees at IBM.

It is the responsibility of the school counselor to explore with the student and the parents all avenues of vocational choice open to the student, but the ulimate decision must rest with the individual whose life is being discussed. Counselors, like parents, should not be tempted to play God with peoples' lives. Since education usually allows a person to begin higher on the ladder of opportunity, parents are tempted to urge their children to begin their vocational life with as much advantage as possible. The bottom rung for an educated person could possibly be the top rung for an uneducated person who starts at the bottom rung.

The counselor in this case could have had a personal hangup about education. Why did he get a master's degree in administration and then transfer to counseling? Why were the two students he cited both athletes? Does the implied unhappiness of the Larry-Harry variety reflect a failure on their part or should part of the failure lie with the counselor? Is it possible the counselor is overstating the basic problem? Has he given enough evidence for the thesis he makes? Aristotle in the *Nicomachean Ethics* wrote: "One swallow does not make spring, nor does one fine day." I feel here that the counselor has some unexpressed thesis or attitude which he substantiates by "evidence." After all, counselors are human too, and they have all kinds of problems and hangups. Luckily, counselees and parents have their own wisdom and they don't buy everything that everyone has for sale.

PAUL W. SCHMIDCHEN

We in the academic world have sold a bill of goods to the country at large as well as to ourselves! In essence, many people have accepted education as a panacea. They believe that there is hardly a problem, social or otherwise, that can not be solved by education, whether or not youngsters are interested. And this point of view will increase before it is tempered by reality.

With the increase of affluence in our society, the baby-sitting function of our schools will increase. A place must be found to sequester youth and to keep them out of trouble. The answer, of course, is more formal education. That the premise is false needs no more verification than the headlines reporting student unrest in many of our best colleges. We are witnessing today the logical consequence of unresolved inequities and dissatisfactions, which could not be solved by merely adding to the number of years spent in school. This belief that education will solve everything has proven fraudulent and bankrupt.

The entire rationale of higher education should be reexamined; but the impression of its urgency and value has been made and will not be reduced overnight. There are too many basic fallacies involved in the myth of going to college. It is just as wrong to assume that an IQ of 120 or more is a prerequisite for college entrance as it is to assume that without much potential, perseverance is enough to ensure success.

In estimating the chances of academic success, the judgment of experts has proven suspect in the past. We need think only of a respected teacher of musical composition who said of one of his pupils, "Beethoven never has learned anything and never will learn anything—as a composer he is hopeless." We can call on Edison, Einstein, and Churchill as further exhibits to show how wrong teachers can be in assessing children's success or failure—whether it be from experience or test scores.

A major error in educational philosophy seems to be our noble fixation of insisting that one can teach another something just because one wants to do so. All we have to do is show him, and he will learn! This is such a basic error that it seems incredible that it continues. Learning comes not only from exposure, but from the combination of exposure, motivation, and ability.

The essence of this incident might be best characterized by the old adage, "The young know everything and the middle-aged suspect everything," with the added refinement, "The old believe everything." It is my observation that the older generation believes that a college education is essential for success in life. I say to that, "It ain't necessarily so."

part III

The Counselor

and His Colleagues

Perhaps the greatest difficulty that school counselors face is in relations with their own professional peers and supervisors. Any new profession encounters all sorts of roadblocks and problems. There are people who are jealous of the privileges and prerogatives of people in the new profession. There are those who feel threatened and want to keep things under control. There are often instances of deliberate sabotage. It is not unknown, as one of our incidents indicates, for a supervisor to flagrantly violate the spirit of the counseling position. We must realize that these various annoyances have occurred in one way or another with all nascent professions and must expect that they will continue. It does not make the burden that counselors face any easier. However, the counselor who at the present time is suffering with various injustices, mistreatments, and so on, may get some wry comfort from knowing about others and how they handled their difficulties, and also some consolation from the advice our consultants give.

In "A Matter of Principle," a new counselor unwittingly got himself into a most complex situation, involving a wife who did not understand why he took a particular stance, a dean who assumed that he would provide her with confidential information and a pusillanimous member of the psychology department. The issue had to do with money: if the counselor accepted the job he would be paid travel expenses; if he turned it down, he would have to pay his own expenses. The issue of relationship between the client and a supervisor is dramatically recounted.

In "What to Tell Whom" the issue of confidentiality arises again. While almost every counselor knows that the essence of effective counseling lies in discretion, nevertheless it must appear that there are some things that a counselor can discuss with concerned parties, especially favorable items. For example, in private practice, if a physician refers a patient to another doctor, the referring physician may be informed by the consultant about the patient's condition. Now, suppose a teacher refers a child to a counselor, should the counselor report back to the teacher anything about the child? In this incident, the counselor told and the client took the telling amiss.

The situation in "The Counselor is Devious" is a common one. A new employee threatens an older one, who begins to make life uncomfortable for the new man. The situation also involves a discrepancy between official policy, as stated by the principal, and how things work out. In this incident a new counselor decides to fight back in a devious manner, and gets what she wanted. The consultants, however, take a very dim view of such Machiavellian behavior.

When one takes a new position usually one has some indication of how things are, what the official policy is to be, ones rights, obligations, and duties. But what is one to do when how things are said to be and how they actually turn out are considerably different? In "Deserting a Stinking Ship" the counselor comes to a simple and logical decision. Did he do the right thing? Our consultants indicate a variety of opinions of what one should do in such an uncomfortable situation.

Perhaps our most unusual incident is "Give Him a Break." Written by one of our contributors, the child in the incident is himself! And the person who served as a counselor is some unknown teacher. What happened in the space of a few minutes seems to have changed the course of the writer's life, and so it was a critical and a crucial incident for the writer. We would have liked to have had more first person accounts in which the client was the writer, but we are fortunate that we did get this one by the recipient of mercy and understanding who now is himself a school counselor.

"The Counselor Acquiesces" is a rather complex account with some rather unusual aspects. The counselor is put on a spot and he gives in, doing what he thinks was wrong, as a result of "political" pressure. It turns out that he did the right thing in the long run, which is a commentary about the state of our art.

We suggest a very careful study of "The Case of the Phony Genius." It is a fine incident for reading and class discussion, relative to whether the counselor did or did not handle the situation properly. Even the editors disagreed on the handling, showing that many of these problems are not cut and dried, but do present real and difficult issues. In any event, this somewhat unusual incident should afford an opportunity for considerable discussion and consideration.

In "Hip or Sick" we have another complicated problem: what should a counselor do if his colleagues, his supervisors—everybody—has one opinion and he sees things quite differently? A considerable amount of discussion can be generated about this counselor's problem, which can be expected by any person who enters a school in which there is a particular cultural bias. Thus, a very conservative counselor entering a liberal school may find that others have a common attitude about certain issues with which he does not agree and he may find himself considered peculiar. However, it is much more likely for the counselor to be considered too liberal or too advanced. The issue in this incident lies in the aggressive attitude of the counselor. Instead of handling the situation diplomatically, he used cutting language to express his opinion. Apparently, his expression of opinion led to various other consequences. Another aspect of this incident, well worth detailed consideration, has to do with matters of religion, custom, and tradition, which are not elements in the curriculum. How much tolerance should a school system have for unusual ideas and behaviors?

In general, these eight incidents pose problems relating to the very crucial issue of where the school counselor fits into the school vis à vis the teachers and the administrators. We suspect that the structure and the dynamics of school counseling must separate the counselor from others who have to meet immediate problems, and have no time for contemplation of the individual and his particular problem. This means that eventually counselors will tend to move closer to students and further away from teachers and administrators. This trend is likely to be self-defeating in the long run. New concepts and practices must be developed which serve to utilize the counselor's relationships with members of his staff to produce better schools and better services.

17

A Matter of Principle

Background

When I was about to receive my Ph.D. in psychology from a major university, I answered an advertisement for a college counselor in a fairly prominent southern university. Some time after I applied for the position, I was informed that I was a candidate and that I could travel to the interview and have my expenses paid provided they accepted me and I accepted the job, or if they rejected me. But if they accepted me and I rejected the job, then I would pay my own expenses. I had very little money at the time and since the trip, even by the cheapest means, was quite expensive, I was rather sure that if accepted, I would take the job. Arriving at the city, I was met by a member of the psychology department who informed me that virtually the whole department had resigned at the end of last semester because of their dislike of the dean of the division, a power-hungry woman. In view of the school's rather desperate plight, it was highly likely that I would be offered the position even though I might feel that my qualifications were minimal. Somewhat shamefacedly, he told me that there were overriding reasons why he remained, although some of them, such as quick promotion and much more money than he could get elsewhere, were admittedly not very commendable.

At the university I met Miss Dee, dean of the division, a high-pitched and powerful woman who told me without much preliminary sparring that the world was composed of two kinds of people: those who were responsible, God-fearing, and clean and those who were lazy, godless, and dirty. She told me that this institution was dedicated to taking good people and educating them, and that it would be one of my prime functions to determine which students were in the second category and to let her know who they were. "In your counseling you will learn about the use of drugs such as marijuana, about sexual escapades, alcoholic binges, and other highly undesirable behavior. I want to know the names of the students involved, and then I shall take steps to insure their failure and they will leave our school without their knowing how or why."

Incident

She seemed to assume that I accepted her terms, and she began to talk about salary and other matters, when I interrupted her. "I am very sorry, but if I counsel students I shall keep in confidence what they tell me."

"You don't have to worry," she replied. "All information you give me will be kept in that locked file"—she pointed to a filing cabinet—"and only I and my secretary have the key."

"You don't understand," I told her. "It has nothing to do with your security. I just wouldn't give you any detrimental information about a student who confided in me."

She smiled prettily and began to talk confidentially. "You don't understand. First, I have a doctor's degree in education. Second, I am your supervisor and so I am legally and ethically entitled to all information that you, my subordinate, will have. Third, all the information that I would want deals with illegalities in this state, and you do not have either a legal or an ethical right to withhold such information from your direct superior. Fourth, you have a duty to the good students, a duty to the institution that pays you, and a duty to all decent honest people in this state."

"You may be right, but I simply will not promise to give you any information about my counselees. Any information I obtain I shall consider confidential and I will not reveal any information unless I—and only I—consider it in the best interests of the individual involved, or of others, to do so. That is, I don't obdurately refuse ever to reveal any information but rather I refuse to make a commitment to reveal any kind of information at all times."

She nodded reasonably. "Now, tell me this. In this state only a medical doctor, a minister, and a lawyer have the legal right to retain information that comes to them from their patient, parishioner, or client. Since you are none of these, you don't have immunity."

"I don't care about that. I'll be a good counselor, but I just will not be a stool pigeon or spy."

"In which case," my interviewer told me, "I am offering you the job, and if you refuse it, you'll have to pay your own expenses."

The financial facts of my life were horrible. I was married, we had bills to pay, and this was the best job available. Since the climate and locale appealed to both of us, my wife was praying that I would get the job. I knew she wouldn't understand my moral plight. If I didn't take this job, I didn't know what I could get. It was so easy to say yes and have mental reservations. Perhaps after I had the job, I could better refuse to go along with her. However, I said "Go ahead. I'll never work under you or under the conditions you've described here."

"Suit yourself," she told me. "You can go now." And go I did!

Discussion

After I left the interview I met the member of the psychology department who was waiting for me and he asked me what had happened. He was waiting to take me to the airport. I didn't want to talk about the matter but finally I exploded in a rage. "You wrote to me and should have told me. I turned down the damn job. I think you are unethical yourself in offering people a job when you know that others have left for these reasons. Had you told me that you wanted me to be a spy I wouldn't have come to this school in the first place."

I was very angry. He drove rapidly without saying anything. When we got to the airport, he left me and drove away. I got my tickets and waited for my plane, angrily thinking of the scene I would have with my wife when I told her I was offered a very well paying job and that I had turned it down for reasons I felt she would not understand. I heard my name called and this faculty member came over to me. I had expected that he would be back at the school by now. He was puffing. "I parked my car and called my wife and told her what you had said. She told me to quit. So, I just called the dean and told her to stick her job up her ass and I quit too. So, now we are both looking for jobs!" We went and had a drink, and I flew back home in a glow.

Questions

1.   This incident occurred about fifteen years ago, and I look back at it with great satisfaction. I wonder if the consultants who will com-

ment on this incident, can guess or understand my satisfactions? (My wife didn't understand then and still doesn't. She will be reading this incident, if it is selected, and I would so much like to have some outside verification for my actions.)

2. Was my behavior immature, as my wife said, and was there a better way to handle the situation?

3. Did I mistreat and mislead my colleague? How can his behavior be understood?

4. How about the dean? Was her position tenable? She felt she was doing the right thing. Was she? From her point of view, perhaps, we were all out of line.

5. Where can one go for a decision in such matters? Who is the last court of appeal?

COMMENTS ON THE INCIDENT

THE EDITORS

One of the major functions of professional organizations, formally and informally, is to establish normative patterns of behavior for its members. This, in turn, creates a set of expectations among nonmembers, as to what members can and cannot do. Thus ministers, doctors, and lawyers have developed well-understood canons of membership behavior and the public has, more or less, acquired expectancies which are consonant with them. Since school counseling is a relatively new profession, the "rules" of the profession have yet to be firmly established in the minds of our various publics. As a consequence, discrepancies can occur between expectations and outcomes. School counselors are still searching for an identity. Not surprisingly, normative behavior and a clearly defined professional image are lacking.

In this incident, a newly graduated Ph.D. in psychology interviewed for a position as college counselor, meets a faculty member in the department of psychology and then a woman dean who is to be his supervisor in the counseling department. The attitudes and the behavior of both these individuals disappoint this new graduate and he finds himself in a position quite distressful to him because of his understanding of his professional relationships and his code of ethics. There is also an economic problem.

The issue at hand deals essentially with what a counselor might do when he finds himself in a situation in which the behavior of his colleagues and supervisors are disappointing to him and when their expectations are unacceptable to him.

DONALD H. BLOCHER

This incident represents a situation in which a counselor is confronted directly with a challenge to his own ethical principles. No reputable professional could have accepted a position under the circumstances described. It seems clear too that the psychology department member who helped to recruit under these circumstances was not discharging his professional obligations adequately.

Unfortunately, neither the narrator of the incident nor the colleague mentioned considered the alternative of an active fight to secure the defeat of an administrator engaging in behavior designed to bring the profession of psychology into disrepute. One wonders what would have been her reaction if the response to her offer of a position had been: "Yes, I will accept the position offered, and will view as my first duty working to change the policies which have been established and if necessary obtaining your dismissal as an unethical and immoral person. I will begin by calling your behavior to the attention of the ethics committees of my professional associations and will not hesitate to take this matter to all of the groups in the university involved, including the students themselves."

The kind of behavior implied in the above statement is behavior from which most professionals would shrink because it involves tension, risk, conflict, and all kinds of unpleasant interactions. Perhaps much of the present conflict on college campuses comes from competent and ethical people leaving the students in the tender care of bigoted and immoral administrators as described in this incident.

In regard to the questions posed it seems easy to understand the feeling of satisfaction that the counselor experienced in refusing to become a part of the spy network that masqueraded as a counseling service in this particular university. The counselor's behavior certainly seemed natural and ethical in so far as his refusal to accept the position under the conditions outlined.

It seems clear that the colleague in psychology was remiss in assisting in recruitment under these conditions. His obligation to oppose actively such policies should certainly have been stronger than that of a new applicant. This incident represents a situation in which professionals need to call upon their professional associations for help and support in upholding ethical practices essential to the welfare of the profession.

In so far as the dean in this case is concerned, the fact that she may have believed that she was right seems no reason at all to condone her behavior. The incident makes clear that she was attempting to coerce counselors into clearly unethical behavior and that she subsequently engaged in conspiracies to remove students from the university that may in themselves have been illegal in depriving students of their rights.

Very clearly her claims to have a legal right to confidential information is nonsense. Privileged immunity refers only to immunity before a duly constituted legal body. No such question is at issue here. It is doubtful if any question of legal responsibility to report criminal behavior revealed by a client would even be involved, but if such a question were raised the legal obligation would not involve revealing the information to a university administrator.

When seeking advice on an ethical decision, counselors should be aware of, and ready to use, the ethics committees of professional associations such as APA and APGA for consultation and support. It seems clear that this situation should have been reported to the APA and that the offending institution could at least have been prevented from recruiting through professional organizations.

GEORGE J. BREEN

The satisfaction that this Ph.D. in psychology gained is easily understood and his stand can readily be defended. His basic strength, in my opinion, lay in his insistence on upholding the confidentiality of the counselor-client relationship. Essentially, the main issue to be considered here is whether or not the welfare of the client or the institution takes priority. There are two basic sources that a professional engaged in counseling can go to in such matters.

One source is the ethical standards section of the professional association of which the individual is a member. Since the incident occurred about fifteen years ago, such standards may not have been as carefully defined as they are today; yet, they probably would have offered some specific guidelines for the decision in question. For example, under "Section A: General" of the *Ethical Standards of the American Personnel and Guidance Association* it states:

> The member has a responsibility to the institution within which he serves. His acceptance of employment by the institution implies that he is in substantial agreement with the general policies and principles of the institution. Therefore, his professional activities are also in accord with the objectives of the institution. Within the member's own work setting, if, despite his efforts, he cannot reach agreement as to acceptable ethical standards of conduct with his superiors, he should end his affiliation with them.

Since the writer of the incident obviously was in substantial disagreement with the policies and procedures of the institution as represented by Miss Dee, it was quite logical not to even begin an affiliation that was likely to end quickly.

Furthermore, the specific issue of confidentiality is dealt with explicitly in the *Ethical Standards of Psychologists of the American Psychological Association*. In "Principle 6: Confidentiality" it states:

> Safeguarding information about an individual that has been obtained by the psychologist in the course of his teaching, practice, or investigation is a primary obligation of the psychologist. Such information is not communicated to others unless certain important conditions are met.

At this point, it may be helpful to examine critically certain of Miss Dee's statements to see if these conditions would have been met.

She states initially: "In your counseling you will learn about the use of drugs such as marijuana, about sexual escapades, about alcoholic binges, and other highly undesirable behavior." When these specific actions are weighed against the first condition, it is quite doubtful that Miss Dee's judgment is valid. This condition states:

> Information received in confidence is revealed only after most careful deliberation and when there is clear and imminent danger to an individual or to society, and then only to appropriate professional workers or public authorities.

Although we could possibly apply some of the specific examples Miss Dee speaks of to this condition in some exceptional cases, I doubt that a case for a "clear and imminent danger to an individual or to society" could be made for the usual range of sexual escapades or alcoholic binges that college students typically engage in. Admittedly, the use of drugs, particularly if it becomes habitual, could be a serious problem to the individual. However, given Miss Dee's fascistic dogmatism and unscientific code of values, it would be questionable in my opinion to consider her as "an appropriate professional worker."

The second source where an individual can and usually has to go for direction in such matters is basically himself. Even if there are carefully spelled out ground rules or codes of ethics, one still has the basic responsibility of answering to oneself. Although the writer of the incident did not unfortunately, receive support from his wife, the time and energy that he would have been forced to dissipate by working in such a hostile environment, would far outweigh any social or material advantages. Married or single, a man still lives essentially with his integrity. My opinion regarding the second question, is that if there were more critical inquiry on the part of the writer in this case, he could have possibly avoided the incident in the first place. When I first read the conditions attached to the position, I sensed what seemed to be gimmickry concerning the three alternatives for travel reimbursement. In view of the financial problems of the applicant, he could have telephoned or written to Miss Dee personally and confronted her with specific questions that may have given him the insight he needed to reject the position without incurring the actual travel expenses. I suspect that Miss Dee would have given out some hints concerning her counseling philosophy—particularly if she had been tactfully asked. Although this strategy may not have worked, the only loss would have been the cost of a telephone call or postage stamp! At any rate, this is speculation on my part and the best alternative may have only been the one that was chosen.

The faculty member in the incident certainly was not misled. He seems to have been a passive individual who probably needed the shock or motivation that the writer of the incident provided. In the face of the rapid turnover that had taken place at the university, the incident could perhaps be best viewed as the straw that broke the camel's (colleague's) back. The new man provided him with a behavioral role model of resistance to the "power-hungry" dean.

Miss Dee's position, in the last analysis, may have been tenable if the legal and political code of the state is taken as the prime criterion. Yet, compulsive and inflexible adherence to the established code has all too often been an excuse for lack of change or improvement. Miss Dee, from this point of view, was mistaken. Some of the present enlightened activities of students, faculty, and administration clearly demonstrate that the established code can and should be challenged.

RUDOLF DREIKURS

This incident presents a most unusual situation. It would not be worth special discussion unless one could identify a fundamental principle violated by the counselor. It is his inability to cope with a tyrant, to solve conflicts without fighting or giving in. And since the counselor was not sure of his ability to cope with the situation, he did what most people do under such circumstances—he blamed the other faculty member for his predicament, by calling him "unethical" and "irresponsible." He had even less right to this criticism since he was informed, immediately after his arrival, about the predicament of the department caused by the dean, "a power hungry woman." Informed about this, the counselor should have been prepared to cope with her, particularly under the conditions stipulated for remuneration of the expenses.

The description of the incident shows clearly that he was no match for a scheming female. He simply did not know how to respond to a tyrant: one has to do the opposite of what most people are inclined to do. They first argue, and then give in, which is the opposite of what one should do. The dean had a right to her opinion—but so has the counselor. And there was no need to argue. The dean told him what she expected him to do, and all he needed to do was to tell her what *he* would do, i.e. not to give her the required information—and leave it at that. This would have put the dean in the position to decide, rather than leaving the decision to the counselor. He was willing to be a good counselor, but not a stool pigeon or spy. Despite that, the dean offered him the job. All he had to do was to sign a contract. The dean had no power to force him to reveal confidential information. If she wanted to fire him, that would have been a different matter. It is doubtful that she would allow herself to be dragged into a public scandal.

To answer the five questions:

1. One can well understand the counselor's satisfaction of having made a great sacrifice for a "good cause." But was it worth it? No. Actually, he gave in to her demands when there was no need for it. If he had accepted and maintained his standards of counseling, he could have perhaps influenced the whole institution. The hitch was that none of the faculty members was a match for the dean. She overpowered them all, either forcing them to submit or firing them.

2.   I would not call the behavior of the counselor "immature" as his wife did, but there certainly was a better way to handle the situation as outlined above.

3.   There was no need to attack the colleague. He did his best. He informed the counselor immediately of the situation. How could he have known that the counselor was a weakling, who retreated instead of facing it?

4.   The dean took a very definite position in line with what she thought was right. She had the right to attempt to persuade the members of the faculty. But it was not their obligation to succumb to these demands.

5.   It is not a question of morality, as the counselor put it, but of different concepts of what is morally right or wrong. The dean was as much concerned with the problem of proper morals as was the counselor. Only their concepts and their methods differed. He had no right to tell her how wrong she was, nor the obligation to accept her standards. That is part of the democratic form of conflict-solving which we all have to learn.

GERALD J. PINE

The APA code of ethics states that "individuals and agencies in psychological practice are obligated to define for themselves the nature and the directions of their loyalties and responsibilities in any particular undertaking and to inform all concerned of these commitments." It seems to me that this is an important ethical principle which should be thoughtfully considered by anyone who is exploring and negotiating a professional position in counseling. It is unfortunate that a number of people are willing to accept a counseling position under conditions which attenuate their effectiveness and compromise their personal and professional integrity.

In the type of situation described in this incident it would seem that an individual would have three alternatives:

1.   Accept the position under the conditions set down by the dean.

2.   Accept the position under clearly stated conditions. Negotiate by defining and reflecting the ethical principles contained in the APA [American Psychological Association] and APGA [American Personnel & Guidance Association] codes of ethics.

3.   Decline the position.

Let's examine the possibilities for each of the alternatives.

To take the position under the conditions formulated by the dean to me would represent a violation of the principles of both the APA and APGA Code of Ethics. But more important it would place the applicant in an untenable personal situation in which he would continually find his loyalties to his clients being compromised by his loyalty to the dean. The issue of confidentiality is crucial in the practice of counseling. Maintaining and respecting the confidences of the client is essential in effective counseling. If a client cannot feel secure in revealing himself and his attitudes about institutions and persons to the counselor, it is highly doubtful that counseling will be helpful and facilitating. Self-revelation and explorations take place only in an atmosphere of trust. The issue of confidentiality is often expressed in the question, "To whom does the counselor owe his first allegiance: society or the individual?" I feel that the counselor's primary obligation is to the individual, but this does not mean a negation of obligation to society. It is not an either-or proposition. The counselor can serve the school and society most effectively by not revealing confidences, but by developing a facilitative relationship characterized by trust, a relationship in which the individual can realize and actualize himself as a responsible and socially competent person.

To accept a position in which one would find himself in conflict with his personal and professional standards may for some be expedient but in the final analysis it is professionally debilitating to the counselor and unfair to his clients. There are persons who would assume a position under unfavorable conditions with the idea of changing the system. But how many people do we know who have walked into a position with their eyes wide open and with the convenient rationalization that they'll change the attitudes of the institution only to find themselves several months later cursing their lot and placing responsibility for their fate on the unprofessional and excessive demands of their employer. In too many cases the person who is in an unethical and unprofessional situation is there because he chooses to be. Ethically it would seem unjustifiable to accept a position under one set of conditions with the purpose in mind of altering the conditions later on through "professional guerrilla warfare." The applicant who plays games with his potential employer by verbally agreeing and accepting the philosophy and the outlook of the employer while at the same time overtly disagreeing and not accepting the conditions of employment is dishonest (see Section A.1., APGA Code of Ethics).

To negotiate, define, and accept a professional position under clearly stated conditions reflecting acceptable ethical standards is an alternative which is recommended by the APA and APGA codes of ethics. The candidate who directly, openly and honestly articulates his role as a professional counselor and who takes a position in which he can function effectively and ethically will render a more significant service to the employing institution, to clients, and to the profession. A well delineated role is a necessary beginning point in the development of sound counseling services and can prevent the emergence of relationship and communication problems with administrators, colleagues, and clients. The applicant who does not define his role in the process of negotiating employment becomes the victim of the whims and fancies of the employing institution and should be prepared to sleep in the bed he has made for himself. Often complaints by counselors about the unreasonable conditions under which they work usually serve to cloak the fact that they never assumed responsibility for defining their roles and establishing the conditions of employment.

A person owes it to himself, to his clients, and to his profession not to accept employment in an institution in which he knows he cannot function according to acceptable ethical standards of conduct. To accept an appointment under the conditions described here would require that the individual violate his moral integrity and the standards of his profession.

However no personal standard regarding ethical behavior can be determined and established by any one organization. Unless a counselor has internalized the reasons for ethical conduct there is little likelihood that codes of ethics will have any meaning or impact. Each professional must determine his own standard within the confines of his conscience. The secure counselor, who has been able to translate the philosophical foundations of his viewpoint into the practicality of his daily work, is aware not only of the depth of his obligation to the client in matters of confidence and ethics, but of the many uncomfortable moments he will have in holding to his moral position. Keeping confidences and behaving ethically is often a burdensome and uneasy task for the counselor, but one that the counselor can manage in proportion to the depth of his commitment to his client, himself, and his profession. Every man must live with himself, and a man who cannot be true to himself will be ineffective as a counselor and a person.

PAUL W. SCHMIDCHEN

This case essentially concerns itself with professional autonomy and respect. In essence, this counselor, like most professional people, strives for independence in the practice of his competence and skill in the work setting. To be asked to be a "stool pigeon" or a spy cannot be taken lightly. For him, a request to operate in what he clearly regarded as an unethical way caused such a strong reaction that he could not put it aside. And having a "power-hungry" woman as the supervisor could only aggravate the situation more. So long as these unethical expectations persisted, our correspondent could hardly be expected to do his best professionally.

If we apply the golden rule to the situation we find an interesting problem. Apparently the supervisor expected him to give her confidential information. Would she have wanted him to do the same with her: give information to the students about her? Would she want a one-way system of information from the students through the counselor to her; but not from her through the counselor to the students? I refer, of course, to any sensitive and confidential matters that might originate from her office.

It seems to me that we should take not only a short-range but also a long-range point of view. Miss Dee undoubtedly had the best interests of the school at heart. She might not simply have been power-hungry and may have thought that she was operating in the best interests of all, including the innocent students who might have been corrupted by those who "drank" and used drugs. Probably many parents and legislators would have agreed with her, and even possibly her own supervisor, the president of the university. Hence, rightly or wrongly, in addition to the important issues of academic freedom and professional ethics, there are ramifications here which reach beyond the bounds of professional self-interest. Medicine, law, and theology have learned that what is told in confidence to members of these professions is to be held sacred for very good reasons and not just to maintain the exclusivity of its members. It is not easy for a new profession to gain the stature of these older professions, and we may as well face up to it. That is, if we are ever to assume any legitimacy as upholders of confidentiality, we must give evidence that we do it for the common good as well as for the benefit of the individual concerned.

In such matters, when there is no legal support, and when diverse opinions exist, what is the court of last resort? I find no problem here. A man must live with his conscience. It is easy to do the easy thing: what is popular, what others want, what others do. However, the true professional tackles the nitty-gritty, the unpalatable part of a job in a responsible manner, being his own measure of morality and ethics. This is the sign of the truly mature professional. And, as far as I am concerned, this is just what the proponent in this incident did, and I for one applaud him for his honesty and his courage even though I can appreciate his inner sufferings.

BRUCE SHERTZER

The contributor of the incident asked whether the commentators could "guess or understand" his satisfaction. The obvious answer is that the individual's sense of satisfaction stemmed from demonstrating that he was, in fact, a professional who had assimilated a code of ethics to guide his behavior. Further, that his ethical behavior (concern for the client's privacy) could be maintained even under personally difficult (somewhat trying financial) conditions. Without question, the individual, the institution which prepared him, and the profession should be justly proud of and pleased with his behavior.

Further explanation of the contributor's satisfaction may lie in less obvious, more submerged reasons. Based upon his frequent references about his concern over his wife's reactions, it could be speculated that she was the audience whom the "play" was designed to impress. The individual "knew" that his wife would not understand (last paragraph, incident), and he thought of the scene in which he would tell her that he had turned down the job "for reasons ... she would not understand" (second paragraph in discussion). Presumably, the incident enabled the contributor to demonstrate to her his power, autonomy, and maturity and this therefore, was highly satisfying to him.

The question of whether the author's behavior was immature fails to specify whether he had in mind his interaction with the dean or the colleague. His description of his interview with the dean certainly reflected mature behavior. Indeed, the author can be commended for retaining emotional control when confronted with her unreasonable and highly unethical demands. Whether his behavior with the colleague was mature or immature seems somewhat academic. Undoubtedly, his angry outburst triggered that which had been in the colleague's mind for some time: to leave a compromising position. While the same result might have been produced by a less emotional response, the context and circumstances virtually dictated an angry, basically human reaction.

Nothing in the critical incident would seem to justify the conclusion that the author misled his colleague. Without doubt, his angry remarks, direct and to the point, communicated his frustration and disappointment. Whether he "mistreated" him is more difficult to ascertain. In the first paragraph the author states that he answered an advertisement, completed an application form and was notified that he was a candidate for the position. His remarks to his colleague were that the colleague wrote him and further, offered the job without explanation of the conditions associated with it. These two fragmentary accounts leave many unanswered questions about the extent of the colleague's personal involvement in the recruitment and employment procedures. But whether the colleague's personal involvement was direct or not, his continued association with a university faculty that permitted such a practice to exist was compromising and apparently became personally and professionally unbearable. His failure to notify the candidate about the deplorable conditions associated with the counseling position could be understood from the standpoint that he acted out of some loyalty to the institution which employed him and further, that the students' need for a counselor was to be met in some way. His decision to quit could be understood in that the author's reactions to the situation was but one of several similar responses (other staff members had left) and provided the individual with the courage to act upon his convictions.

The dean's position of expecting a counselor to disclose information received in counseling was ethically untenable. Those who seek counseling usually reveal highly intimate, personal details and experiences which they do not wish disclosed to another. Confidentiality encourages full disclosure which enables the counselor to better help the client. The professional counselor is obligated to protect the best interests of his client by maintaining confidentiality.

The dean's statement that psychologists in her state did not enjoy privileged communication (could not be subjected to arrest or prosecution for withholding information about a client needed by a court in its determination of truth) was undoubtedly legally correct since it characterizes the condition that exists in most states. But to use the legal realities as justification for flagrant unethical practices seems the height of absurdity.

The questions of where individuals go for a decision in specific matters and who constitutes the court of last appeal are somewhat ambiguous. For the individual who applies for a counseling position in which unethical behavior is demanded the decision itself is inevitably his to make. However it should be noted that the ethical codes of the American Psychological Association and the American Personnel and Guidance Association are abundantly clear in their statements about extending confidentiality to clients.

The individual staff member who knows that unethical behavior is being practiced in his institution is professionally obligated to seek to correct it. A possible sequence of procedures he might follow can be briefly outlined. He would first go to the person who engages in the unethical conduct and attempt to modify the situation. If that failed, his next step would be to seek change through the supervisor or administrator of the program in which the unethical behavior was being practiced. If that failed, he would then be obligated to report the practice to the professional organization's ethics committee (some APGA state branches have such committees) whose members would investigate and decide upon remedies they deemed appropriate.

Determining the position one will take when confronted with behavior that is contrary to established ethical practice is not done easily or without emotional cost. The counselor who ignores that which is ethically wrong does a disservice to himself and to the profession he represents. In reality, he has no choice but to actively intervene to correct the situation despite the personal drain in emotional stress and time. Certainly, such factors as personal gain, status, threat of financial loss, should never be used to rationalize away the failure to discharge an ethical obligation.

18

What to Tell Whom?

CRITICAL INCIDENT

Background

During my first year as a high school guidance counselor, Danny was assigned to me as one of three hundred freshmen. I had spotted him as needing more than routine counseling during the fall semester, and in spite of some resistance on his part, had gradually built up what I felt was a fairly good relationship. Danny had moved to our suburban area from a more congested urban situation where he had had a number of minor conflicts with authority and had once been on probation from juvenile court. According to his story, the probation had been caused by his refusal to squeal on a friend. His test scores indicated above average potential but his academic marks consistently hovered near failing. For the most part, his relationships with adults were characterized by suspicion and resentment. He was a poor reader and seemed to have trouble in his English class. The English teacher was often exasperated by Danny's lack of motivation and poor progress, and had, several times, been quite critical of him. Danny reacted to this attitude with poorly concealed defiance or apathy.

In an interview, I gave the teacher some information about Danny, hoping to promote deeper understanding and a more sympathetic view of the boy. Danny had told me that an employee of his stepfather, a man in his late twenties, had become his friend. Danny thought his friend, Joe, was being held back from promotion to assistant manager because of his poor reading ability, so Danny was trying to help and encourage Joe by reading newspapers and magazines with him at work. This information which I passed on to the teacher led to the following incident.

Incident

As the year progressed, Danny seemed to be less reluctant to come in for counseling; our meetings were usually instigated by me. Therefore, it was with some surprise and much satisfaction that I received a request from Danny for an interview. When he entered my office he closed the door but refused to sit down. Finally after several minutes of discomfort and obvious tension, he blurted out, "You lied to me. You said you wouldn't tell anything I told you and then you went and told Mr. T. about my helping Joe read. He [the teacher] made a fool of me in front of the whole class." I was just shocked by the information and Danny's reaction. It took quite a bit of persuasion to keep Danny from leaving immediately, but since he had to wait for me to sign his pass, I was able to keep him for a few minutes. I stalled as long as I could, trying to explain and get him to see that I had considered some of the things he told me as not highly confidential and that my motive in telling about Joe had been to try to get the teacher to understand and appreciate Danny more. I apologized for my apparent lack of judgment. Both my explanation and my apology fell on deaf ears and Danny left saying he wanted to have no more to do with me.

Discussion

This was the lowest point in my counseling career. I began to question whether I had the insight and perception necessary for helping others. As it happened, the incident did not cause irreparable damage, but it did cause a definite setback in my counseling relationship with this boy. I did not contact him for several weeks. I knew that I had made a grave error in judgment and hoped eventually to reestablish rapport with Danny. Finally, some routine matter having to do with scheduling gave me a reason to call him in several times. Each time I had an opportunity, I restated my reasons for doing what I had done and tendered my apology, and finally we began to get back to a more trusting relationship, although I never felt that Danny completely trusted me again.

This incident was critical for me in several ways. In my own development as a counselor it brought home to me the realization that I needed to get to know people better before assuming that they assessed a situation the same way I did. My first reaction had been anger because the teacher had misused the information I had given him, but later I realized that the confidential aspects of this same bit of information had been viewed from three different perspectives: highly confidential by Danny because of his emotional and personal involvement (which I had not perceived); not at all confidential by the teacher who tried to make use of this information as a learning aid (an example of inconsistent behavior which he cited to his students); and as somewhat confidential by me (to be prudently shared). If I had taken the time to know the teacher better, I might not have given the information to him, or I might have given it in such a way that it could only have been used for the ultimate benefit of the student.

This was critical to the student-counselor relationship because it almost destroyed it completely. The experience was good, if painful, in that it taught me a valuable lesson about myself. It contributed to my growth as a counselor by dramatizing an area of inadequacy which I have since consciously tried to repair.

Questions

1.   Should one keep everything confidential that one learns in counseling interviews as a matter of course? If not, what guidelines exist with reference to disclosing data compiled during an interview to parents, teachers, administrators, other students, or other counselors? Would such guidelines be useful in helping us achieve the status of a profession?

2.   How can we put across to teachers the inviolability of information we give them? How can we convey the sense of professionalism inherent in the safeguarding of information?

3.   Should one make promises to students about confidentiality? Personally, when a student says to me, "I'll tell you something about — but you have to keep it in confidence," I reply, "I promise you nothing. You have to trust my judgment." What do you think about this attitude?

COMMENTS ON THE INCIDENT

THE EDITORS

One of the most common problems in school counseling has to do with communication: what to tell whom. Certainly, we all know that some things must be kept confidential, otherwise we lose respect and we lessen our reputation; we all know also that some things need not be kept confidential. A subtle problem, but a fairly frequent one, has to do with passing along some "innocuous" bit of information for the "good" of the client. However, every one of us has probably found that conveying some seemingly innocuous information to another person has eventuated in a good deal of unpleasantness. Some days it seems best never to say anything about anyone.

This incident is a classic case of the above: a student gave some information to a counselor. The information, in the counselor's mind, showed the student in a favorable light. The counselor, in turn, passed this information on to the teacher, who also thought it favorable, and so he innocently passed it on to the student. The student reacted negatively to this "betrayal of trust."

Our consultants consider the complexities of this delicate issue and attempt to tease out the etiology of the student's reaction and present some guidelines for assisting the counselor who becomes party to information garnered during the counseling interview to decide when, what and how much to share.

THOMAS W. ALLEN

Confidentiality is simultaneously one of the counselor's foremost privileges and one of his heaviest burdens. It is frequently his passport into the sanctity of another person's inner life. At the same time, however, this commitment may be a source of friction between him and his noncounseling colleagues. For instance, many teachers resent what they consider to be the one-way street that the counselor maintains. He always seems to be taking information from them but is loathe to offer much from his rich storehouse in return. Some teachers feel their professional standing or personal integrity to be impugned by this one-way behavior. Some feel that the counselor is thereby aligned with students rather than with them. Even many of those who recognize the practical and moral necessity for respecting a student's confidence are displeased when they themselves are not granted special dispensations, when they are not allowed at least limited access to such material. Well-meaning administrators can be especially difficult in this respect. (After all, they merely want to use their power in a way which will promote the student's growth.) Parents pose a similar problem. They are eager to learn what to do in regard to their offspring and who, they argue, has more right to know what their child is up to?

Ironically, many breaches of confidentiality seem to rise from the counselor's intense desire to be of service to his client. Frustrated in his attempts to help in a direct way, the counselor may divulge privileged information in the hope of obtaining assistance from others or, at very least, of diffusing his personal responsibility for the student's destiny. Less commendably, the counselor may inform others in order to justify his failure to produce the changes in the student which those who referred him to the counselor expected.

When these pressures are added to the numerous other social, professional, political, and legal assaults on the counselor's pledge to keep his work with students confidential, the considerable weight of this responsibility becomes more obvious. In virtually every instance, however, confidentiality is an essential part of the implied contract between the client and counselor, a contract not subject to unilateral abrogation on the part of the counselor—even in what seems to the counselor to be the client's interest. For example, a counselor may be aware of extenuating circumstances which if brought to the attention of others in the school would substantially mitigate the severity of the administration's response to a client for, say, academic failure or breach of school rules. The counselor's obligation here, as in virtually every other instance (save those where serious harm to someone is involved), is in obtaining the student's permission to release information concerning him, but then to abide by his decision in any event.

Unhappily, a benign paternalism has all too frequently carried the day with untoward long-term effects. Indeed, part of the perplexing general uprising of young people is aimed not at their elders' maliciousness but at such "benevolence." The admonition not to trust anyone over thirty is designed, in part, to keep the young from succumbing to the blandishments of those adults who would kill something valuable in them with "kindness." It is one thing to challenge a person's course of action, to try to persuade him to pursue a different one, leaving the ultimate decision and responsibility on his shoulders, and quite another, to deprive him of choice, either by imposing one's will or acting behind his back for "his own good." The difference is a crucial one. It is disregarded only at considerable risk.

From a purely pragmatic point of view (eschewing the relevant ethical considerations) the counselor in the present case would have been especially well-advised to have honored his commitment to keep his client's communications strictly confidential. It is clear at the outset that "trust" is the central issue in Danny's life. Much of his difficulty appears to arise from his assumption that adults are untrustworthy and from its corollary, that he is entitled to do unto others before they do it unto him. Of course, behavior premised on this corollary tends to be self-validating. Danny "does unto others" provoking them to "do unto him" which, of course, confirms his dim view of society's hospitality. Accordingly, the counselor's most important task might well be to interfere with this vicious cycle of distrust. He was called upon to perform what Alfred Adler referred to as "the maternal function" of the counselor. In Adler's view, a person's first interest beyond himself is generally his mother. If the mothering which he receives is adequate, this interest is transferred to increasingly larger sections of society. But the process is by no means foolproof and difficulties in adjustment result from its failures. Danny's disturbing behavior may then be taken as an indication of such a malfunction.

Here, then, the counselor's first and most important task is the winning of his client's trust. For to help Danny he must poke at least a little hole in the dike separating him from society. He must by personal example demonstrate the invalidity of Danny's conviction that no one, particularly no one in the Establishment, is to be trusted. However, he need not expect this to be a simple undertaking. After all, Danny has built his life upon the belief that all others are untrustworthy and he is not likely to surrender that belief without a struggle. Thus, the counselor might anticipate having his behavior subjected to close scrutiny by Danny; he might anticipate attempts to trick or provoke him into some indiscretion which Danny could use to support his jaundiced view of others. Like Caesar's wife, the counselor must remain above reproach in his relationship to Danny if he is to become the vehicle for establishing a more viable connection between Danny and society.

EDWARD S. BORDIN

The answers to the counselor's questions are to be found in an examination of the purposes and nature of the confidential relationship in counseling.

Trustworthiness. Any student, especially one as defiant and suspicious as Danny, must develop a sense of trust to make full use of a counselor. This feeling of the steadiness of the counseling relationship does not require absolute confidentiality, but it does require that the student know its limits. In my own counseling relationships, I make clear that my commitment does not extend to situations where serious harm to my client or to others is involved. Other counselors because of the way their roles are structured or because of theoretical orientations may want to define the limits of confidentiality differently. No matter where they place the limit, the requirements of an effective relationship demand adherence to this contract.

It is not, of course, the verbally stated contract which ultimately develops trust in a counselor. It is the gradual accumulation of a sense that he is dedicated to your welfare, that he is not seeking to judge you by some impersonal standards. If, however, the verbal agreement does not promise some critical degree of confidentiality, only those students in dire need may ever get close enough to the counselor to be able to test his helping qualities.

Role relevance. Questions about confidentiality, such as those surrounding this incident, most frequently arise out of conflicts in two possible roles of the counselor, one as agent in his client's direct struggle with inner conflicts, the other as intermediary in the client's efforts to cope with and use the persons and conditions of his life. There are impressive arguments supporting the usefulness of each of these two roles. Inner conflicts can stand in the way of a person profiting from the most favorable circumstances of life. Yet even well-integrated persons may experience less than optimal development because of the influence of well meaning but insensitive persons or adverse physical circumstances. But the counselor who seeks to serve both roles with the same client may find that the second interferes with the first.

One difficulty is that we are all so constituted that it is easier to focus on external obstacles than inner ones. To the degree that the counselor turns his attention to the influences outside his client and bends his energies toward altering them, he stimulates his client to turn his attention away from the inner obstacles. In Danny's case, we may conjecture that his teacher's unsympathetic attitude may have been a minor obstacle compared to his own anxieties which stimulate him to provoke these unsympathetic reactions, which perhaps in turn, justify his own defiant and apathetic response. All of this in the service of a self-defeating pattern of seeking anxiety reduction.

A second difficulty is that the mediating action will often undermine a client's confidence in his capacity to cope. The counselor will be seen as lacking confidence in the client's ability to cope with life. Adolescents, who are normally still struggling with the question of whether parents or other adults accept their approaching adulthood (of course, they are themselves uncertain about their adult status), are prone to great sensitivity on this score.

A final difficulty arises only when the counselor is pursuing more ambitious therapeutic aims of aiding his client to become aware of projections of past infantile relations into his current relationships. The technical conditions that make such progress possible require that the counselor keep free of entanglement in his client's current real life relationships. In this way, he creates the conditions which will bring into sharper relief the unreality of his client's infantile-determined projections on to him.

I will close with some remarks on the strategy which dictated the breech of confidentiality. The counselor clearly counted on his disclosure changing the teacher's attitude. He treats the teacher's response as though it were a misinterpretation of the level of confidence that the disclosure represented. I suggest that the teacher's act was a hostile one. The problem, then, is to be able to relate to the teacher so that he treats his difficulty with Danny as a problem of his attitude toward him. Naturally lacking more specific knowledge, I cannot suggest how the counselor might act on that problem, but I do suggest that understanding the problem in these terms will point to the way to go about solving it.

RUDOLF DREIKURS

This incident is an excellent example of a situation in which a "good" counselor finds himself, if the training to which he was exposed did not provide him with an understanding of motivation. The counselor completely misunderstood what happened in his transaction with Danny. He sincerely tried to have a good relationship, to be fair and openminded —in short, he had all the qualities which one can expect from a good and sincere counselor. And yet, his lack of understanding of the motivation of the student made him an utter failure as far as helping and working with him is concerned.

The counselor gives all the information which permits a fairly reliable guess about Danny's personality. But he did not grasp the significance of minor conflicts with authorities. He accepted the student's evaluation of his joust with the juvenile court, attributing it to "his refusal to squeal on a friend." Such a statement is sufficient to guess the student's motivation, if one is trained to understand goals. Otherwise one is the victim of *factophilia*: waiting for more "facts" often prevents the perception of the whole personality.

If one encounters such a report, then one can immediately guess the student's main efforts, that is, to appear as an innocent victim of some mean and unfair authority. This is, of course, only a first guess in a stochastic process, where one can dare to make assumptions which then are either supported or modified by the next bit of information. Support of our guess is provided a few sentences later when the counselor realized that the student's relationship with adults was characterized by suspicion and resentment. Now we can be sure that the student succeeds in looking down on unfair and unreasonable adults, assuming a moral superiority which characterizes the attitude of many juvenile delinquents. He obviously is in a power conflict with adults, either defeating them openly or through passive resistance. As can be expected, his teacher has no more understanding of Danny than the counselor, falling for the student's provocations and permitting himself to be drawn into a struggle for power with him.

A crucial point is the deficiency of counselors who try to make the teacher "understand" the student while they themselves do not understand him. How could the counselor "promote deeper understanding and a more sympathetic view of the boy?" How could the teacher be "sympathetic" when he is constantly provoked and defeated by the student?

Like so many of his kind, Danny is overambitious. He probably will look for various situations where he can be successful and can demonstrate his abilities. Danny's willingness to help a friend who was a poor reader is a clear indication of the condition under which Danny can best function i.e., when he is superior. Instead of helping the teacher to understand Danny's motivation, the counselor only informed him of Danny's effort to increase his friend's reading ability.

Had the counselor perceived Danny's tendency to look down on adults in order to feel superior to them, he would have immediately understood why Danny "accused" him of a breach of confidence. Instead of the repeated apologies, which only reinforced Danny's assumption of moral superiority, the counselor could have immediately called the boy's attention to what he was doing. Naturally, this should have been done in previous discussions of the way in which Danny treated adults. At any rate, there was no reason to fall for Danny's efforts to prove again how unfair people are. After all, what the counselor did was not degrading or humiliating in any way. Why then did Danny react so violently? Is it true that the teacher made a fool of him as he asserted? Did the teacher really "misuse" the information by pointing to something good which Danny did? Of course not! The incident merely provided Danny with a wonderful opportunity to verify the unfairness of the counselor and of the teacher, when in reality no such unfairness existed. There was neither a violation of confidence nor any lack of judgment on the part of the counselor. He was merely the victim of the boy's scheme of provoking and condemning adults. This is the reason why explanations and apologies "fell on deaf ears." The servile attitude of the counselor only reinforced the contempt of the boy. In this way the counselor just played into his hands.

It is now clear why the questions which the counselor formulated are completely out of focus. He had not learned anything from the lesson which he considered "valuable." The incident did not contribute to his "growth"; what he considered as "an area of inadequacy" was not his real inadequacy; it was rather his inability to understand the student.

Now let us consider the questions. The counselor wants guidelines for communicating information obtained during the interview. Naturally, confidential material should not be divulged to others. Obviously, any material which is humiliating, degrading, or harmful should be kept confidential. But the fact that Danny helped a friend obviously did not fall into this category. Therefore, we are not dealing here with the problem of violating a confidence at all.

If some information could be of value to others in understanding and helping the student, then the counselor is justified in giving it. As it happened in this case, the counselor did not feel that talking about Danny's friend was confidential and there is no evidence that Danny really believed the counselor had violated a "promise." Danny merely used the opportunity to get another adult scalp added to his collection. This was the issue which the counselor should have discussed with Danny instead of attempting futilely to win him back with weak apologies and "explanations."

Two facts stand out in this incident. One is the counselor's lack of understanding of Danny's motivation and the second is his tendency to cater and to coddle him. Here we see the two exponents of the contemporary adult attitude for defiant youth: the teacher who tries to fight and subdue, and thereby creates more rebellion; and the ill-advised "sympathetic" counselor who pities, "understands," and condones transgression and rebellion, losing respect and influence in the process.

BARBARA A. KIRK

This is an excellent critical incident, highlighting the entire issue of confidentiality. In the case of Danny, confidentiality is an especially sensitive area in that the counselor already knew that his relationships with adults were characterized by suspicion and resentment. In such a case one needs to be especially alert to being in the position of contributing to the client's already existing distrust and, at the same time, earning real trust.

I would agree that anything and everything that one learns in a counseling interview should be kept confidential as a matter of course. There is the expectation and belief on the part of students that anything said to a counselor is sacred, and will not be communicated to anyone else. If a counselor does communicate without the student's knowledge or consent, he is essentially betraying what may not have been explicit and overt, but what is expectation, belief, and confidence on the part of the student. There is the danger that if such betrayal occurs, a counselor or therapist of any kind will never be trusted and that the pupil will never again communicate anything which is private or secret to any adult in such a position.

The issue of confidentiality relates to the kind of structuring or understanding which exists in the counseling interview. If the content of the interview is not to be entirely confidential, then the client should be made completely aware of this condition. That is, if a counselor feels that there will be the need of communicating what the student has said to anyone, such a statement should be made prior to the interview itself. A counselor must indicate in advance that what the student says will be utilized by the counselor and in what ways and with whom in order that the student may have the free choice of withholding communication.

The third question regarding promises of confidentiality speaks to this point. The counselor's tactics of promising nothing is satisfactory only if the student is absolutely free to withhold this communication. He must really understand that it will not be held confidential, or under what circumstances it will be utilized, for example, only if there is significant danger to the student himself or to others.

Communicating with parents, teachers, administrators, other students, or other counselors, should also be a point that is clearly structured and conveyed to the student. Such communication should be made only with the student's consent and foreknowledge. Furthermore, in order to eliminate misunderstanding and distortions, the counselor's projected use of interview material should be carefully rehearsed with the student so that he knows exactly what will be said about him and what is transmitted of his own communication. In this way, there can be no misunderstanding, concern, or suspicion about betrayal.

One more point needs discussion. A counselor may never assume that anyone else, neither teacher, counselor, nor administrator, will see things exactly as he does, understand the principles and ideologies of confidentiality, or know how to utilize information in a wise and effective manner. This involves the need for careful consultation with and education of those with whom the counselor works. Rather than making any assumptions of others' perceptions or behavior, the counselor needs to act as a consultant in aiding educators find ways in which the student can be most helped. An experienced counselor will learn that it is really never necessary to betray confidences in order to assist a teacher, administrator, or parent to be constructively helpful to the student. Rather, the counselor speaks of the goals and needs of the student, the ways in which he can be approached or helped. This can be done in a very constructive and fruitful way without divulging the specific client data on which the counselor's recommendations are based.

Maintaining confidentiality is a fundamental aspect of effective counseling. Unless the counselor is able to retain confidences, no matter how inconsequential they may seem to him, he will be ineffective with, or ignored by, his sensitive and discerning clientele.

E. LAKIN PHILLIPS

This is a ticklish but common situation that therapists and school counselors often meet. It is usually a matter of judgment, rather than simple straightforward ethics, as to what information is to be given to another professional person. Sometimes matters backfire, as they did here.

As a general rule, some data can be discussed with faculty, but not personal matters or any data that links a given client or patient to another person. Early in faculty meetings, the counselor might take advantage of an opportunity to discuss matters related to counseling in regard to communications: items such as data that can easily be transmitted, other data that are matters of propriety, and finally information that is "top secret." A few examples can usually suffice to acquaint faculty with ethical and discrete considerations.

Case examples, such as the one cited here, can be of inestimable value in highlighting problems in counseling, and more particularly problems involving professional peers. Teachers have to be taught how to use information, and how to motivate students without embarrassing them in the manner suggested in this vignette.

Usually a counseling or therapy interview is posited on trust and propriety, if not secrecy for items considered inviolate by the client. To say to the client that nothing is promised him in the way of discretion is to fly into the face of ethical practices that seem to be well established. A better tact might be to say that matters are confidential, but when issues involving an institution which is the employer of the counselor (school, clinic, hospital) are at stake, there might be matters of propriety and common interest that would allow the counselor to use some information to the benefit of all concerned. Usually though, I believe that avoiding discussions of parallel ethical problems is desirable, for one cannot display the whole range of ethical considerations to a client in discussing with him your ethics and a concern for his welfare.

T. ANTOINETTE RYAN

One of the professional responsibilities of the school counselor, as defined in the *American School Counselor Association Statement of Policy for Secondary School Counselors* is to "assist all members of the school staff to understand the importance of the individual pupil and to provide information, material, and consultative assistance aimed at supporting their efforts to understand pupils." This statement of professional ethics quite clearly relates to the counselor's responsibility for providing consulting services to teachers, administrators and parents, so environments can be created to facilitate realization of the school's educational goals. This involves sharing with the teaching staff information about individual students, so teachers can select instructional materials and devise teaching strategies appropriate to the needs of their learners. At the same time, the counselor is ethically bound to respect the privacy of his clients.

The concept of counseling is predicated on a basic assumption that there will be a relationship of mutual trust and confidence between counselor and client. This means the client must have faith in the counselor, just as the counselor must respect the client. Ideally a counseling relationship should involve a contractual agreement between counselor and client. The counseling goals should be clearly understood by counselor and client, and the responsibilities of both in working toward these goals should be spelled out.

The case of Danny illustrates a fallacy about counseling. This is the mistaken notion that the counseling process can be implemented without the active involvement of the client. This view is reflected in the situation wherein the counselor decides what is "best" for the client, and then sets about to see that this goal is realized. The goal, known to the counselor but not the client, cannot give orienting or purposive structure to the counseling relationship. In such a situation it is not unusual for the client to be concerned about what the counselor does and why he does it. If Danny and the counselor together had seen one of the counseling goals as Danny's improved performance in English class, then it would not have been so difficult for Danny to accept the counselor's sharing relevant information about Danny with the English teacher.

The question of "what to keep confidential" does not lend itself to a simple, unequivocal answer. The issue must be decided for each counseling situation in terms of the problem at hand, the needs and characteristics of the client, and the counseling goals. A counselor who promises not to tell anything that a client tells him is bound to observe the promise until he is released by the client.

There are both official and unofficial ethical standards to which counselors can refer for guidance. There are professional resources which a counselor might tap for support in situations like the one described. Consultation and discussion with colleagues and participation in local, state, and national meetings of professional organizations can be helpful to the new counselor who is apt to face problems for which he has not been adequately prepared through education and training.

The code of ethics approved for its members by The American Personnel and Guidance Association in 1961 stipulates the counselor's responsibility to protect the rights of the client. A counselor is ethically bound not to reveal, nor to volunteer to reveal, information received in confidence about a counselee.

There is no way to avoid the issue of the counselor's responsibility whenever information about a student is shared with others. A number of decisions must be reached before the sharing of information can take place. The counselor must decide *what* information can be shared. This involves consideration of confidentiality, privacy, and purpose. The question of *who* is to receive the information needs to be resolved. This means looking again at purpose, and also thinking about who has the right to know about the client. After the *who* and *what* questions have been answered to the satisfaction of the counselor, then the major issue is *how* to share the information. At the crux of this question is the basic principle that the sharing of information about a client with another concerned individual must be purposive and planned. In no sense of the word should this kind of information-sharing be in the same category as indiscriminate, spontaneous "did you know..." kind of conversation that often occurs in faculty rooms or social gatherings. The counselor must decide what the information means, and how the teacher might use the information effectively in relation to achievement of the counseling goal. In sharing information with a teacher, or for that matter, with a parent, administrator, or other concerned person, the counselor is morally obligated to interpret the information in terms of the counseling goal, and to suggest to the listener ways in which the information might be used to further the achievement of the goal.

In considering whether or not to make promises to students about confidentiality, the issue again seems to be directed to the concept of counseling as a process in which the counselor employs his background of knowledge and specialized skills to help the client achieve goals on which they have agreed. This subsumes a prior condition of mutual respect, and the willingness of the client to accept the counselor's decisions which are assumed to implement the best interests of the client. At the outset the client should be made aware of the counselor's ethical responsibilities for sharing information about clients, and the ground rules for the counseling relationship should be clearly defined. Under these conditions, the question of promises rarely becomes a major issue.

CHARLES B. TRUAX

It should be considered highly unethical to disclose any information obtained from a counseling interview. I think it is possible to communicate with parents, teachers, administrators, other students, and other counselors in broad general ways without disclosing specific information. It is definitely nonprofessional to communicate to anyone, information obtained during a counseling relationship if the individual who originally gave the information or the people about whom information was given, can be identified. I think it can be easily explained to teachers and administrators that counseling involves privileged information which we are not allowed to divulge to anyone for any purpose. If you promise nothing, you may get nothing. I would certainly consider the client foolish to share very deeply with someone who might disclose the information to third parties who might or might not act responsibly with it.

19

The Counselor is Devious

CRITICAL INCIDENT

Background

After being a teacher for several years, I became eligible to be a school counselor, as a result of graduate courses and passing an examination, and was sent to the XYZ school. The principal of this school, on meeting me, was quite cordial, and among the various things he told me was that I was to be directly responsible to him and to him alone, and that I was to do my work as I saw fit. His clerk showed me to my office and I noted that there was a hole in the wall near my desk, and on a platform in the hole was a telephone. I looked through the hole and saw another office. I asked the clerk about it, and she told me that the office next door was occupied by Mr. John Doe, and that we were to share the telephone. Although I did not like the lack of privacy implied by the hole, and sharing a telephone, I decided to do nothing about it. I wondered about my colleague who, the clerk told me, was also a counselor.

I sat at my desk, examined the various desk drawers, and set my things right, when the door was opened and a man entered who, by his manner, soon made it apparent that I was his assistant.

"Now, Miss Roe, this is how I want things . . . this is how things are to be done ... And when you ..." his one-way conversation went along in this manner.

He seemed to be a nervous little man, emphasizing his words as though he were talking to a fifth-grader, and seemed high-strung and almost fearful that I might contradict or fight him. I thought I saw through him immediately. As an unknown, I represented a threat, and he wanted to make sure that I knew my place right from the start. As he talked to me, he did not look at me directly, and I had a most uncomfortable feeling that I had unwittingly stepped into a potentially nasty situation. However, I played the role of a newcomer, listening without saying much, being careful not to contradict him or set him straight. I determined to keep my mouth shut, do my job, try to be friendly and hoped that eventually our relationship would improve. But such was not to be the case.

Mr. Doe began a campaign of intimidation and harrassment. For example, instead of returning the phone to its pedestal, he would leave it on his desk, so that if it rang, and if he were not in his room, I would have to kneel on my desk and reach in through the hole in the wall to get the phone. This was quite embarrassing, especially if I had a counselee with me! I got the distinct impression he would be eavesdropping when I was interviewing a student. Sometimes he would yell at me, giving me some order or other. He sent me a lot of memos, indicating that I was no longer to use a particular test or that I should no longer see a particular student since he was taking him over. He maintained a constant flow of messages. When I met him he was officious, and openly hostile. As a matter of fact some of my counselees mentioned his attitude, but I carefully abstained from making any comments about him to students or staff.

From time to time I would see the principal who would ask me how things were going and I invariably said "fine." He and Mr. Doe seemed quite friendly. I kept getting madder and madder about our relationship and kept wondering what I should do. How could I get Mr. Doe off my back without complaining about him and making an enemy in the process? Apparently my attitude and my behavior were not working.

Incident

What finally settled this problem was simple: I had told a counselee to do something, and he came back several days later telling me that Mr. Doe had found out what I had asked him to do, and Mr. Doe had contradicted me and had ordered this boy to ignore my instruction. He informed the boy that I was being supervised by him, that I was only a student trainee, and that he couldn't do anything until Mr. Doe gave his permission.

I assessed my situation carefully before committing myself to a course of action. While the principal had told me that I could run my work as I saw fit, and while it was evident that Doe was a bully, I felt quite certain that if I confronted Doe and the principal that the principal would back up Mr. Doe. In effect, I was convinced that as a result of my complaining, I would be told that Doe *was* my supervisor and things would be much worse for me. I saw my alternatives as (a) going along with Doe, (b) fighting him, or (c) trying to get away from the situation. I assumed that he was shrewd enough to know that his bullying was annoying me and that he was just waiting for me to make a complaint to the principal. I decided to try to be a bit smarter than he, and embarked on a plan of action.

I began to keep a diary and would indicate when I tried to get in touch with him and he was not there. I began to send him notes asking for his help with various situations, noting carefully the day and the hour, and whether or not he did help me. I began to ask him for an opportunity to talk with him about problems—and he usually had no time for me. Finally, I wrote a long and detailed complaint to the principal about the lack of supervision I was getting, giving days and hours and details in a formal manner with copies of pertinent memorandums. I requested an investigation of my complaint and suggested that if I didn't get a satisfactory answer I would bring the issue to the central office. As a result I was called to the principal's office and Mr. Doe was there.

The meeting was short and sweet. The angry principal reminded me that he had told me I was to do my own work without bothering Mr. Doe. He made it very plain and very clear that we were working along parallel lines and that no one was anyone's supervisor. Furthermore, if I couldn't do my work without bothering Mr. Doe and tying up his time, then, he continued, I would be asked to leave the school. I was to refrain from asking Mr. Doe to do anything for me and he was not to ask me to do anything for him, and that both of us reported only to him.

The whole point of the meeting was a bawling out for me for being so dependent—but in reality it was just what I wanted because the principal made it very clear to Mr. Doe that he was to leave me alone too. Doe was put in a very awkward spot: here I was asking him for more time and more help when he expected me to complain that I was being bothered by him. And here he was being told by the principal to leave me alone, which was just what I had hoped for.

Discussion

The problem of a colleague who overreaches himself, acts like a bully, and who takes advantage of another can sometimes be handled, as

I did in this case, by apparently going along with the bully and moving in his direction rather than moving against him. This is a principle of judo where one uses an opponent's strength to defeat him. Had I complained about the behavior of Mr. Doe, he would have been defensive, and so would have been the principal; but by asking for even more "help," Doe was thrown off and the principal made it clear he was not to help me or supervise me or, in effect, annoy me. Since school counselors' roles are not clear in the minds of a great many people, including other school counselors, it would seem to me that general rules of behavior and relationships should be developed for this emerging profession.

Questions

1. Was my behavior ethical? After all, it was devious, and I did plan it, and it did work out just as I expected that it would. However, neither the principal nor Mr. Doe (at that time anyway) knew what I was doing and they took me at face value. But I sometimes wonder if I shouldn't have done things differently.

2. What other ways are there of handling a situation of this sort where someone is a bully and the one who supervises you is a friend of the bully? I can't think of any other method besides the one I used that was sure to work.

3. I guess the more important question for me is the following: suppose I was sure that the method I used would work and free me from the unwanted domination of others and that a more honest method such as fighting it out with the bully face to face would not work, which should one use: the honest but ineffective one or the dishonest or effective one? After all, there are students, other faculty members, society, and so on to consider.

COMMENTS ON THE INCIDENT

THE EDITORS

In any organization, the issue of proper relationships between a supervisor and employees can arise. The wise supervisor promulgates common sense rules in accordance with proper principles of management and makes certain that everyone knows what they are. He attempts to anticipate difficulties in line and staff relationships by making clear who is who, what is what, what is permitted, who reports to whom, who gives orders to whom, and so forth. Very often, such relationships are spelled out in manuals, memos, and the like.

Problems can arise in any organization when a new member arrives. Sometimes, as in this incident, problems are caused by the apprehension of an older employee towards the threat posed by a younger one. Sometimes they are caused, as may have happened in this case, by an honest misunderstanding, e.g., when employee A hears that employee B is arriving and assumes that B will be his subordinate.

Regardless of the cause of the problem, the question is how does one proceed to resolve it? The author of this incident explains her unique way of dealing with a relationship problem. In general, our consultants have strong feelings, pro and con, about the wisdom of her solution, which while ingenious, poses a number of interesting questions.

MARY A. BARBER

One of any counselor's primary responsibilities is to establish good working relationships with colleagues. If any considerable amount of time is wasted in petty squabbling, the effect can only diminish the counselor's effectiveness in working with students. I really don't see how the counselor in this case found much time for her clients since she seemed so preoccupied in feuding with her co-worker and resenting the deficiencies in the physical arrangements. This preoccupation with somewhat minor annoyances and her inability to establish a harmonious working arrangement with the other counselor make me wonder if her personality was suited or her training adequate to her position. There is a possibility that her impressions of Mr. Doe and his deficiencies were to some extent the result of the projection of her own feelings of insecurity.

The shared telephone and the hole in the wall were certainly undesirable conditions but could have been easily alleviated. The first and simplest suggestion that came to my mind was to put a poster or picture over the hole in the wall when privacy was desired during conferences with students. In addition, the counselor should never have subjected herself to the indignity of crawling through the hole in the wall to answer the telephone. Some kind of shared time arrangement except for emergency calls, surely could have been arranged. Perhaps having a secretary or clerk take messages and defer all but emergency calls, would have supplied a suitable compromise where an ideal situation was impossible. Collaborating on these minor physical adjustments would require a smooth and positive working arrangement with one's colleague and developing this kind of a relationship should have taken precedence over the underhanded tactics employed here.

The counselor's delay in taking action to clarify her position was most unfortunate since the longer she tolerated the situation, the worse it got. As a new employee, she undoubtedly felt insecure and reluctant about forcing issues, hoping that through conciliatory and compromising attitudes on her part the situation would improve. However, as soon as she was convinced that this would not happen, she should have brought the problem out into the open by confronting the bully in a firm but reasonable manner or by insisting on a three way conference with the principal as she did later. As I see it, there was no real solution to the problem because there was no movement toward real understanding among the persons involved. It merely resulted in the counselor's jostling for position and her slight gain in status but at the price of a reprimand and a probable devaluing of her worth in the mind of the principal.

Was the counselor's behavior ethical? While I suppose it was not actually dishonest to document all the slights and discourtesies which she felt had been directed toward her, the cloak-and-dagger aspects of her actions seem immature, unnecessary, and inappropriate to a situation where professional relationships should exist. There are some unethical aspects to her pretending to ask Mr. Doe for advice and direction and playing the role of the overly dependent novice in order to collect evidence to use in undermining his position. Obviously I think that she might have had more satisfactory results if she had acted differently.

What other ways are there of handling this type of situation? This counselor probably could not think of other more reasonable ways because of her preoccupation with her own precarious position and her resentment toward the perceived insults being heaped on her. Admittedly other courses of action might have taken some courage, but if Miss Roe's evaluation of Mr. Doe's character was accurate, he may have been almost as insecure in his position as she was in hers. If she had had the courage to confront him early in their acquaintance and honestly explain her own interpretation of her role as described by the principal or projected from her training, or if she had requested the air-clearing conference with the principal earlier, the devious documentation and the culminating explosive encounter might have been avoided.

BENJAMIN C. BELDEN

Frankness in a climate of low trust accomplishes nothing. In adverse settings such as this one, members of the organization see their professional progress as a function of keeping others down. This is especially true if the others happen to be young and bright, as was Miss Roe. Administrators and teachers are too busy protecting themselves to be prepared for straightforward leveling. Fine chance here for "openness and honesty"! One is content with survival. Furthermore, ethical behavior and sheer openness are not synonomous. People are masters at self-deception. How easily we fool ourselves and justify our most perverse actions! We are open and honest to the extent that it is safe to be so. In this climate it was not safe.

Miss Roe was able to survive by employing deception and intrigue. Her *reductio ad absurdum* proved effective. She was aware of her low status and that her options were limited. She chose to grab the organization in a vulnerable place and twist it to serve her own ends.

She had yet another organizational skill. She knew how to keep her mouth shut, a skill rivaling virtuoso violin-playing or intricate eye surgery when applied in organizations. Miss Roe needs only ten or twenty years of maturity to give her the necessary cynicism requisite to becoming general superintendent of schools for a major school district.

GEORGE J. BREEN

As the counselor suggests in her third question, the prime issue is really one of effective versus ineffective counselor behavior. However, before dealing with this issue, it would be helpful to examine some of the general aspects of the case.

In the first place, the counselor made the initial mistake of "deciding to do nothing" about what obviously was a poor counseling environment. The fact that there was a hole in the wall near the desk of the counselor implied considerably more than a mere physical inconvenience. This lack of privacy raises the important question of client-counselor confidentiality as well as the matter of the nuisance of telephone calls (to either counselor) which could interrupt counseling sessions in progress. More important, however, was the counselor's knowledge that Mr. Doe's "attitude" was questioned by some of the counselees. How much effective counseling could take place in an office where students would be subjected to the "eavesdropping" and "yelling" by Mr. Doe to Miss Roe during a session? Unfortunately, this environment, or something closely akin to it, is not too unusual in some school guidance offices.

Furthermore, the counselor continued to make the mistake of "playing the role of a newcomer . . . determined to keep my mouth shut" which could only serve to reinforce Mr. Doe's nastiness and hostility. Even as the situation worsened, Miss Roe, when questioned as to "how things were going" by the principal, would reply "Fine." How far from the truth!

Therefore, we return to the essential issue of effective versus ineffective counselor behavior, which encompasses the three questions raised by the counselor. This problem might best be solved by critically, yet briefly, analyzing the harassed counselor's strategy with Mr. Doe and the principal. First, there was really no good evidence that the principal, in spite of his friendship with Doe, would have made him Miss Roe's supervisor. Upon closer inspection, the evidence suggests the contrary. During the first meeting between Miss Roe and the principal, she states that he was "quite cordial" and more importantly that she was to be directly responsible to him and him alone and that she was to do her work as she saw fit.

Perhaps the counselor may have had some feelings of insecurity in view of her exposure to a new school position, yet her initial encounter with Doe, could have eventuated in her avoiding all the difficulties that followed. Instead of passively accepting Doe's initial rude and threatening behavior, Miss Roe could have confronted him directly, honestly, and straightforwardly. By immediately refusing to concede to Doe's arbitrary and dogmatic demands, Miss Roe could have set the relationship straight once and for all. Otherwise, she only gave reinforcement to Doe's negative behavior and entered into a "neurotic agreement" through her passivity.

On the other hand, this strategy may have led to a much earlier meeting between the two counselors and the principal. In view of the very short period that would have elapsed between Miss Roe's hiring and the suggested confrontation, I doubt that the principal would have fired her. In short, the timing was most important since the principal's statement of Miss Roe's responsibilities and relationships would have been quite fresh in both parties' minds. Thus in spite of the "friendship" that existed between Doe and the principal, Miss Roe would have been able to remind the principal much more readily of his recently stated policy to her.

The question of ethics raised in the first question needs to be rephrased, particularly if the principal were to take sides with Doe. The real issue would then be one of bowing to the principles of Mr. Doe and/or the principal which would only lead to an ineffective counseling role for Miss Roe in my judgment. In other words, the issue of ethics would involve the more important choice of either responsibility to self and students first or responsibility to others (authority). Too often, the latter choice is made by school counselors. Can there be little wonder why so many counselors experience disenchantment in this emerging profession?

Finally, the strategy that Miss Roe used leaves many doubts in my mind as to its long-range effectiveness. My belief is that the time used in this roundabout approach was quite inefficient. Instead of keeping a diary, sending notes to Doe, taking careful account of his behavior in the situation, and finally "writing a long and detailed complaint" to the principal, Miss Roe could have used this time more constructively by counseling students. If she had confronted Doe successfully from the very beginning, the harassment and frustration she received would have ended or, at least, been significantly minimized. Otherwise, she could have requested a transfer to another school where she might have been able to function in a more appropriate fashion. Often, counselors compromise their integrity by worrying that they could be fired or severely punished if they stand by their principles (and not necessarily their principals). Since Miss Roe had been a teacher for several years, I doubt that she could have been released as easily as she speculated. Furthermore, could not Doe have continued his harassment of Miss Roe in a more subtle and less direct way even after the meeting between the three participants? I can still envision Doe fiendishly leaving the telephone on his desk instead of the stand, making unnecessary noise during Miss Roe's counseling sessions and generally continuing his nastiness in a quietly ruthless way.

Therefore, in my opinion, Miss Roe's most effective long-range strategy in this incident, would have been immediate, direct, and honest confrontation with her antagonist, Mr. Doe.

DWAYNE COLLINS

The writer of this incident, even though she is anonymous, should be congratulated for exposing a common, although seamy, aspect of schools. These struggles, infighting, backbiting, and maneuverings are frequently found in all schools, though most often in schools with poor administrators, principals who turn their backs to such matters, denying their existence. When such conditions arise, weakening the faculty morale, the effects trickle down to the students and the school is operating badly, even though the problems may not be evident to parents and occasional visitors.

It is easy to be retrospective and omniscient about the things that could have been done in this case, but it seems to me that Miss Roe made her first error in accepting at face value the principal's statement that she was to be directly responsible to him alone and she was to do her work as she saw fit. A principal who describes the work of a new counselor as simply as this needs help in getting the best help from his counselor. Further evidence of his need for her help came when he had a clerk show her to her office. We note that he failed to introduce her to Mr. Doe and that much later he called the meeting for a confrontation without giving her information of the purpose of the meeting. He didn't tell her that Mr. Doe would be present.

If Miss Roe had been alert to the principal's deficiencies she would have requested a more extended orientation, or if there were no time, would have followed up by asking for another, extended interview. Such statements as, "I am interested in the counseling program as you envisage it—your hopes, your goals, the facilities, the faculty, establishing working relations, etc." would have been appropriate. I feel rather certain that this principal would not have been too happy with this much attention.

Had Miss Roe said, "Our national association has suggested effective ways of helping principals get the most from counselors' skills. I have here (and now she could give him brochures and other printed information)—would you like to look these over and give me your reaction to them?"

Had she caught on to the principal's lack of interest or his discomfort with her, she might have asked him to show her about, and to discuss the various people she would work with. Undoubtedly this would have led to Mr. Doe. In this manner he would be showing her his plant and he would feel more comfortable. Had they gone to her office and had she then seen the telephone she could have mentioned to him that privacy is necessary in counseling and might have been able to get him to install two telephones.

Mr. Doe, too, needed help in working out ways to maximize counseling services. The first step to help him feel less threatened would be for Miss Roe to find simple ways of serving him with occasional kindness. A good way to deal with an enemy is to do him favors and thus make him into a friend. But had the hostility continued, a direct confrontation with Doe in the following manner should have proven fruitful. "I have a problem and I need your help. I feel that you and I are not getting along well, and I feel guilty and frustrated with it. Can we talk about it?"

Should this not be a fruitful approach Miss Roe should have suggested they both go to the principal for help. If Mr. Doe refused, Miss Roe should inform him that she felt the need to inform the principal. She would state that she would go alone if he would not come along with her.

Miss Roe had been dishonest with the principal when she told him that things were just fine. She should have said, "Most things are going well, but I seem to be unable to work things out comfortably with Mr. Doe. We want to try to resolve our differences but if we don't make any progress we will want to come to you for some suggestions."

In other words, to be blunt about it, I find that Miss Roe did not act in an honest or honorable way, and she met trickiness with trickiness. Would she have advised her students to meet a similar situation as she did?

But what to me is overriding in importance has to do with her future relations with Mr. Doe. I assume that he needed help, that his officious ways were really indications of his insecurity. Now, she is one up on him. How does he feel? How can he function? What will now be their relationship? How will their relationship affect students? How will she feel about the school, about the principal and about Mr. Doe and what she did to him? Good old-fashioned honesty and courage, kindliness and love are required in such situations. I see three pretty unhappy and discouraged people: principal, Mr. Doe, and Miss Roe to start off with. After Miss Roe's Machiavellian behavior, things were worse, not better. I think that I would have suggested to Miss Roe that she enter politics or go into business and get out of school counseling had I known all the facts about her behavior. Her rationalizations and her maneuverings seem to me somewhat paranoid—she seems to see a world of people who are indifferent to her and who are hostile to her.

Of course, I must be charitable enough to say that sometimes things are just as she said they were, but even then the means do not justify the ends—not if we want to counsel students to be better people rather than only to find better solutions to problems.

E. LAKIN PHILLIPS

This is a very clever report on how the counselor beat a bully at his own game, but in an ethical way. I think the counselor's behavior was ethical, inasmuch as this solution was a preferred one, and one needed for the fulfillment of the counselor's or therapist's role vis à vis the student and his needs.

One question raised by the reporter is whether there are other ways of handling a situation of this type. Perhaps informal talks with both persons—the "bully" and the supervisor—over coffee or at lunch would be effective. Since quick and easy solutions are usually not forthcoming, a more painstaking and indirect approach is likely to provide better results.

A confrontation is not, in itself, ethically superior to the way the counselor proceded, as far as I understand the ethics of the situation. Rather, I see either approach as different tactics intended to reach a reasonable goal (freeing oneself for effective action and self-determination), and the differences between them are not a matter of ethics as much as they are merely different tactics attended by different consequences.

What many people have done when involved in a situation like this one is simply to resign. The more skillful handling and the apparently more constructive outcome in this case are assets to be admired.

GERALD PINE

It seems to me that this particular incident clearly demonstrates how counselors often create their own problems. As I read the description of the incident and the counselor's relationships with her colleague and school principal, I couldn't help but think, "Isn't it rather ironic that the counselor who is expected to be professionally competent in human relations and communications would significantly contribute to developing a problem situation which reflected a lack of communication, authenticity, sensitivity, and ethical behavior?" The counselor's problem began before she assumed her counseling position in XYZ school. In my opinion, the counselor could have prevented this situation from occurring if she had:

1. achieved a sense of personal identity
2. developed a rationale for counseling
3. translated her identity and rationale into a viable role description
4. presented the role description to her principal and colleague so it could be discussed and negotiated by all concerned, directly, openly, and honestly
5. oriented pupils, teachers, and parents to the role of the professional counselor
6. behaved in an authentic and congruent manner with her counseling colleague and the school principal
7. implemented her role and rationale through her daily interpersonal contacts with pupils, faculty, principal, and colleague.

I wonder whether Miss Roe has a professional identity. Has she thought about what counseling is and is not? Does she have an explicitly stated rationale and role description to use as a beginning point in developing a counseling program? Is she familiar with the APGA code of ethics and the ASCA policy statement for secondary schools? I believe every counselor must resolve certain basic questions regarding the nature of man and the world in which he lives before he can communicate effectively with clients and school staff. Has Miss Roe resolved these questions? The point is that Miss Roe will get nowhere if she doesn't know where she is going and has nothing to communicate.

Notice, too, how phony she is in her contacts with Mr. Doe and the principal. She does not like the lack of privacy but says nothing about it;

she admits to playing a role—that of "newcomer." When the principal asks how things are going she tells him everything is fine when she knows that they are not. She experiences anger and embarrassment as a result of Mr. Doe's intimidation but refuses to express what she experiences. She is reluctant to be genuine and to confront Mr. Doe with her feelings. She deviously manipulates Mr. Doe into an awkward situation so that he will be told by the principal to leave her alone. In essence Miss Roe presents us with a role model of the incongruent, unauthentic, and unethical counselor.

I am concerned about Miss Roe's personal style of behavior. A counselor is a person whose human qualities express themselves in his relations with pupils, teachers, principal, and colleagues. It is difficult for me to see how Miss Roe can behave in unauthentic ways with her colleagues and at the same time be authentic in her relations with counselees. If she behaves one way in the counseling relationship and in other antithetical ways outside the relationship, her incongruence will give pupils, teachers, and colleagues little to respond to in a positive way. The barriers that inhibit congruence and genuineness in her communications and interpersonal relations reside in Miss Roe. Again this seems to reflect a level of behavior which probably emanates from a lack of personal and professional integration. A counselor cannot do away with his personal style of existence—it comes through. Being a counselor requires an existential honesty with oneself and with others. It calls for courage to look at oneself honestly, to remove the cloak that conceals the real being. Such a look, I think, is necessary for Miss Roe to be congruent and real.

There can be no justification for a counselor to be unprofessional because those with whom and under whom he works are unprofessional. Professionalism is more than a synthesis of education and competence. It is ethical behavior; it is an attitude which can be perceived quickly by one's colleagues. By projecting an attitude reflecting personal security and identity, professional competence and awareness, and by acting consistently in accordance with her philosophy of counseling, Miss Roe can do more than perhaps she realizes in gaining acceptance and support. By developing a basic positive and humanistic attitude toward people she will be able to function with greater ease and congruence. This will obviate the need to continually grope for questionable methods for facing new situations; her basic attitude, once developed, will enable her to react and respond with sensitivity and honesty and to obtain a harmonious approach to people and life.

20

Deserting a Stinking Ship

CRITICAL INCIDENT

Background

After receiving my degree in counseling, I accepted a position in a rural consolidated high school. During the hiring interview, I found that I was to be the school's first trained counselor. Therefore, I carefully explained my philosophy and techniques to the principal, who was nearing retirement age and, as I later discovered, was very authoritarian. He seemed to understand my suggestions for explaining my role to the students, parents, and community.

Before school began, I ran a series of articles in the county newspaper explaining the role of a school counselor. As a result of my efforts, I received calls and visits from parents and their children. I established good rapport with most of the students whom I saw. One possible reason was that I was one of the youngest members of the faculty. Most of the faculty members were in their fifties and sixties.

When school began, the math teacher became ill and was unable to continue his duties. Since I minored in math I was appointed substitute math teacher for three periods. The remaining three periods were to be counseling periods. This situation was to last only until the second semester when a new math teacher was to be hired.

At first, I thought I would have more trouble being accepted by the other teachers. However, this proved to be no problem. The principal was a different matter.

He did not like my using part of my class time to explain math-related careers. His comment was, "When a teacher is in class he is to teach his subject not guide or counsel." I tried to explain the guidance responsibilities of a teacher. His reasoning was that a teacher could not cover the text if time was spent on other functions.

Once during the PSAT test he ignored the *Do Not Enter—Testing* signs, entered the room and gave a when-I-was-your-age speech to the students. When the STEP-SCAT tests were administered, the principal would not allow me to help. According to him, the superintendent and aides had always done the testing and would continue doing so. During the test I glanced in one of the testing rooms. The proctor was not there. I need not tell you what the students were doing. I found the proctor in the lounge. When I questioned her, she replied that she had started the students on the test, but had left the room for a smoke. I reported this incident to the principal, mainly because he used these test results to place sudents. His reply was, "Oh, that won't hurt the students or distort the test results."

He wanted me to be his messenger service. I refused because he had an office staff for that purpose and they were not busy during the times he made his requests. If his office staff had been busy and I had not been involved in actual counseling during his requests, I wouldn't have minded helping him. However, I did not like having my counseling sessions interrupted.

As hard as I tried, I could not get the principal to agree about my duties, although I thought I had explained them thoroughly before being hired. Since most of the students and I got along well, I looked forward to the full-time counseling schedule during the second semester. This schedule failed to materialize when the prospective math teacher decided not to accept the position.

Incident

Near the end of the school year, the teachers were called into the principal's office for a discussion of plans for the next year. I had not made my decision. I felt that I should find another position; yet I liked these students and the community. The students had been asking me to stay. I thought I might remain in the school system if I were offered a full-time counseling position.

I reported for my appointment. The principal said that he was satisfied with my work and asked me to return. I replied, "I would like to return because I like the students and community. However, I will return only if I am given a full-time counseling position, and if we both try to understand each other better. The students have sensed the friction between us this year."

The principal then pushed back into his chair, took off his glasses and wiped them. Replacing his glasses, he replied "For your information, the only reason I want a counselor on the staff is so that this school can meet North Central's requirements. Counseling is one of those expensive frills—a fad. We didn't have counselors when I went to school and kids didn't get into trouble as this generation does. Why pay money for a counselor when that same money could be used for a regular teacher? When you have been in the business as long as I have, you will become sensitive to the demands of the community. We are trying to get a pay raise now. I can hear those people saying 'Need money? Why? They are paying a teacher just to sit over there and not teach.' If you want to return as a teacher it will be fine. I will try to arrange it so that you can have a couple of periods for counseling. In that way, I can report to North Central that we meet their requirements and we will remain accredited."

I waited a short period before replying, mainly to cool down. I knew he had little regard for counseling, and I had hoped to change his ideas. However, I didn't know he held my skills and services in such low esteem. I had that "used" feeling, and here he was again offering to "use" me again next year. That really "tore it," as the students say.

I finally replied, "Now I know I sensed your feelings correctly. I cannot work where a Berlin Wall has been erected and where compromises are not beneficial to the students or myself. The rapport I have with the pupils would soon be completely destroyed. I cannot do my job well if I am unhappy. Therefore, I am going to seek a position in a school whose philosophy agrees with mine."

The principal stood up. "Very well, if that is what you think best, although I wish you would return, for we will be short on teachers next year because of the salary dispute."

I left the office feeling better than I had felt in a long time. The tension and uncertainty were gone.

Discussion

I think I should have investigated the school system more thoroughly before I accepted the position. I was full of youthful idealism, therefore, since the principal at that time seemed agreeable and open to new ideas, I accepted the position. Later I found the principal was so eager to get teachers that he would promise them anything in an interview, so long as it would get them to sign on the dotted line.

As the year passed I think I became too forceful. The more I tried, the more resentful the principal became. He disliked aggressive people. I had never considered myself aggressive, but the situation brought out the aggressiveness in me. Perhaps I tried too hard because I was eager to make guidance accepted and did not want my beliefs to be compromised. Perhaps it was youthful idealism that the principal resented. Most of the young teachers were having difficulties applying what they had learned in "methods" courses. The principal saw these methods as too extreme. The morale of the entire staff was poor. As a result there was a great loss of teachers that year among the young and those older teachers who had not established roots in the community.

Early in the next school year the school system came under investigation by the Professional Rights and Responsibilities Committee for alleged violation of teachers' rights.

Now, I'm very happy as a full-time counselor in a new school that shares my philosophy. The faculty morale is good and there is mutual confidence among the community, school board and faculty. If my former principal had not said what he did, I might have still been stuck in the old school system which was rapidly going downhill. I'm glad I'm not going down with it.

Questions

1. Is it right to just get out of a bad situation such as the one I was in and find a better situation, or should one stay and fight?

2. Would it have been best for the community as a whole for me to have remained in the situation, gently trying to make changes over the years, trying for evolution rather than revolution?

3. If one suspects that there is a discrepancy between what a hiring authority says and means, is it worthwhile trying to get witnesses, or trying to have the agreement spelled out by means of a contract, memorandum, etc?

4. Should a counselor just refuse to do what he believes is not part of his job, such as serving as a messenger, or should he go along with such requests?

5. Is the counselor essentially a teacher assigned to counseling duties or is he a counselor who may fill in for a teacher? If either, what percentage of his time should be devoted maximally to noncounseling duties, assuming as is the usual case, that giving one hundred percent of his time to counseling is not enough to meet the needs of the school population?

COMMENTS ON THE INCIDENT

THE EDITORS

Every school counselor must be a teacher in an unintended sense. He has to explain himself and his profession to other teachers, students, parents, and principals. However, in many cases, those who are to be taught do not want to learn. One should not mistakenly assume that only children are teacher resistant and have a will to fail. Principals can also fail. The problem often is, that these "students" don't know that they have failed, and they often have the power to hurt the teacher. All this may seem a bit vague, but the real problem that a school counselor may encounter is the discrepancy between his supervisor's and his own expectation of what his job should be; and when two expectations clash, one can anticipate trouble.

This incident presents a classic illustration of opposing expectations. A young, dedicated, idealistic counselor comes into conflict with an old, embittered, hardened, cynical principal. The inevitable occurs. What should one do when the enemy has all the cards? Our counselor chose the path that many others would take—escape from an apparently impossible situation. Our consultants take a variety of positions on this issue which apparently occurs all too frequently for school counselors.

DONALD BLOCHER

In this incident we have an example of a basic role conflict arising from a set of role expectations on the part of a school principal which are totally incompatible with the role conception of the professional counselor. The difference in perceptions between counselor and principal are absolutely basic. The principal does not see the counseling function as a worthwhile professional activity in any sense. It would seem unlikely that a counselor could change these perceptions radically enough for him to operate in a climate of full professional respect and cooperation.

The question posed then is whether the counselor should leave to seek a school in which his professional function is sufficiently accepted to allow him to operate effectively, or whether he should stay and attempt to build a base of support in the school and community that will make him relatively independent of the school principal. The latter decision would require a number of years of very frustrating effort, and could probably not result in any very satisfactory situation until the retirement of the principal.

The answer to such a question is primarily a personal career decision rather than a general professional one. If we assume, however, that the energies of a professional counselor do indeed represent a valuable social resource, it seems questionable that such resources should be spent in the kind of uphill fight that would be represented in a decision to stay in a school headed by a man totally unprepared to give even minimal support or cooperation. It seems that a sensible and reasonable decision is simply to leave and find a school in which one can work best with one's professional abilities.

JOHN D. MULLEN

In this incident, the problem seems to have several dimensions or layers. In retrospect, the counselor might be inclined to think that he had originally made a mistake in letting himself get into an untenable situation—one in which his and his supervisor's perceptions of the position differed so greatly—and he may have come out of the school system determined not to make a similar error in the future. This kind of learning from experience is useful for anyone, and presenting such a case in this book is useful for people who might get into a similar fix if they didn't watch out.

The first level of this problem might simply be a kind of diagnostic test of a school system to make certain that there will be a compatible atmosphere. However, the question then arises, Did the counselor do the right thing in just pulling out and finding another school system in which he felt accepted? Naturally, he must have thought so, and so might most of us who are unwilling to try to change things. Doesn't a professional person have some obligation to the children and to the community to do the job he was hired to do? I wonder what the counselor might have experienced if he had simply rejected the principal's request that he teach math or if he had refused to go along with the principal's cynical point of view. Wouldn't the principal have been surprised to find that the counselor really believed in what he had been spouting and that he was ready to stand up for his ideals?

Wouldn't it be possible that the principal give up his point of view and respect the counselor more for his refusal to give in? Sometimes standing up to tyranny leads to victory. Running away, although understandable, is often the wrong thing to do.

But something else about this whole case concerns me. What about the obligation of the counselor to his successor? Is it right for this counselor simply to pull out of a bad situation, find a better one for himself, and then leave the situation intact for the next counselor? It would seem to me that he might have publicized his situation more by informing teachers, the county superintendent or the Board of Education, the local newspaper, the accrediting board, and so on. I don't suggest that he should do this. I do suggest that he consider whether he has an obligation to alert others as to what is going on, especially other counselors.

All of this might be automatically handled if some accrediting organization such as the American Personnel and Guidance Association kept a file on all schools, and if all school counselors could send ratings and reports on the school. Then, whenever a school counselor was interested in a position, he might simply ask for an evaluation of that school. In this particular school, if the outgoing counselor had made a report, a new applicant might be presented with the following assessment:

> The outgoing counselor reports that the principal does not believe in counseling and sees it as a frill. He will try to get the counselor to teach. He does not believe in any discussion of occupationally related issues in class, but rather in adhering rigidly to the curriculum. It is also reported that he does not follow the common courtesy of keeping out of a classroom while standardized tests are being administered. In addition, these tests are administered in such a manner that cheating can take place, and the principal accepts this as commonplace. The counselor is used as a messenger. We recommend that any counselor who is aspiring to a new position check very carefully with the principal in view of this report.

We might expect that this kind of report would make it very difficult for the principal to fill the position and, if the accrediting agency were to send this report to the principal, it might change matters radically. Now, this suggestion is not a novel one. Hospitals are visited regularly by accrediting teams and if standards are not met, accreditation is forfeited. Perhaps the same sort of thing might work with schools. I can just imagine how the superintendent of schools might react were he to receive such a report—and I can imagine how the principal might be tempted to consider early retirement.

Tyranny, ignorance, malice, and cynicism have to be fought constantly and at all levels. It seems to me that school counselors as a group should find ways to protect themselves along the lines described here.

MITCHELL SALIM

This incident reflects the acute need for counselor education programs to help their students understand schools as dynamic social organizations and devise strategies for implementing their roles within the school. Essentially, it presents a need for the counselor to understand and consciously use his counseling theory in role development.

The counselor in this incident was trapped by his emphatic attempt to explain his philosophy, role, and functions to the principal. The principal was not encouraged nor forced to reveal himself. The counselor's perception of reality, limits, and expectations might have been different if he had "sounded out" the principal. Questions such as "In what ways do you think I might help your pupils?" "Do you feel that the community is ready for a program of guidance services?" "How might I be involved in administrative or teaching areas?" could have resulted in a more realistic appraisal of the situation. However, this does not mean that the X-ray would ever be complete or that situations remain static. Again, understanding and developing successful strategies for working in new situations form much of the input for subsequent job satisfaction.

From the presentation of the course of events it appears that the counselor followed a path which began with his preliminary perception of the school environment. Frustration occurred due to the role conflict between the principal and counselor. The counselor attempted to discharge his frustration in a defensive manner by seeking pupil support which increased the conflict. The counselor felt guilty because of being disloyal to the principal. Eventually, the counselor began to develop insight regarding the conflict, his contributory behavior, and the need to discover, weigh, and make choices. The decision that the counselor made was good for him as he freed himself from a frustrating, inhibiting situation which affected his personal-professional development and limited his contribution to pupils. Counselors, like all others, have a right to decide how they will develop their potential.

The problem of noncounseling or clerical duties seems to approximate the distribution on a bell-shaped curve. A small group of counselors may spend one hundred percent of their time working in a wholly counseling or conferring manner. A few individuals may be vastly engrossed in clerical kinds of duties. The majority of workers find that two-thirds of their time is devoted to professional-level functions, while the remainder is not compatible with their professional capabilities. Use of support personnel in guidance, and applications of new technology should increase the professional contributions of the counselor.

In conclusion, counselors function as members of a social organization. Typically, the counselor will encounter frustration due to conflict between his professional expectations, and the expectations others have for him. The counselor must ask himself: "Does the total composite of this setting meet my personal-professional needs?" It is unusual to find a school counselor who has the opportunity to maintain a continuously perfect correlation between his desired professional role and functions, and the demands of reality.

Perhaps the most exciting facet of the school counselor's role is the challenge of "reality," i.e., the perceptions and needs of significant people and their effect on the lives of our pupils. Cannot this "reality" be developed as a positive pupil resource?

BRUCE SHERTZER

Whether it's right to leave a bad situation is a value decision that can only be resolved by the individual concerned. Asking it is like asking whether the end justifies the means or whether the purchase is worth the price. Obviously, this depends upon what is purchased, what is paid, and what the consequences will be of the purchase and the payment. Some things, though desirable, may not be worth buying at any price. For some things it may be worth paying any price.

Given the situation as described, I believe that I would have made the same choice as the contributor. I would have left that school for another because the principal's actions and attitudes do not enable one to have any hope that change could be made in that situation in the fore-seeable future. This choice also assumes that the principal's decisions on the use of the counselor's time had been approved by the superintendent or executive officer of the school district and that the higher administra-tion generally shared the principal's attitudes toward counselors. To stay and fight is a noble idea but as Santayana said some time ago:

> That life which once seemed to spread out infinitely before us is narrowed to one mortal career. We learn that in mortals the infinite is a chimera, and that in accomplishing anything definite a man renounces everything else. He sails hence forth for one point of the compass.[1]

One can speculate in many ways about whether the community would have benefited if the counselor had remained in the school and tried to bring about changes gradually or "gently." If he could have remained and sought change without becoming personally embittered, hostile or cynical, then undoubtedly the community would have been bet-ter because he was there. On the other hand, it is true that the individual who is continually frustrated in achieving his goals, sometimes becomes a barrier and an impediment himself, because nothing is ever good enough. Thus, if he remains in the community, the stress upon the counselor's per-sonal and/or professional effectiveness cannot be ignored.

The question was asked as to whether one should get witnesses or some type of written agreement if one suspects there is a discrepancy between what an employing authority says and means to do. In my judg-ment, a counselor ought not to accept the offer of employment if he has any doubt about that which the employing authority promises and the realities of the employment situation. It would seem that if the doubt were over an issue vital to his functioning in the position, that in itself should be sufficient for the individual to withdraw from negotiations. A memorandum stating what one believes has been agreed upon is often useful in clarifying at the outset the differences and commonalities that exist between two people engaged in a negotiation. That would seem to be the major contribution of such an endeavor. Whether such a statement (agreed to and signed by both parties) attached to standard teacher con-tracts, which are usually used in education, would have any legal utility or not, could, of course, only be determined by court action. It is doubt-ful that many school executives or school boards would be very enthusi-astic about attaching a memorandum of agreement to standard contracts or writing such an agreement within a standard contract. And most adults know that, despite contracts and written agreements, subtle (and some not so subtle) ways of manipulation are available to those in authority who wish to use them.

This commentator has never met a professional who is compelled to do some things in his position that he believes he ought not be required to do. At every level of education—elementary, secondary, and university

---

[1] George Santayana. *Reason in Society*. New York: Charles Scribner, 1905, p. 35.

—and even outside education, most individuals engage in some weary, routine quasi-administrative or clerical tasks that plague and encumber them. But it's also true that counselors often seem to be encumbered by these assignments more so than others in the school. In part this may be because, first, their position is the most recently established in the school (positions established last in any institution are usually tagged with those responsibilities not wanted by others) and second, because the belief is very pervasive in education that one truly earns his keep only by teaching. Since he is not in front of a class, it's easy to think that the counselor has the time or the flexibility to perform unwanted chores. Third, many school counselors may engage in these quasi-administrative or clerical tasks because the results of such activities can be quantified and thereby used to justify one's existence to oneself and to others.

The question remains: "Should a counselor refuse to do that which he believes is not part of his job?" I believe that a counselor should refuse to perform such tasks if he is asked and if he has exhausted every opportunity to convince the principal that he should not do them. If I were "ordered" to do so, I would probably comply but would look for another position at the same time. One final reaction in response to the latter part of the question—Should the counselor go along with such requests?—is that this is exactly what far too many counselors do. Many have never discussed such matters with their principal either before or after employment. They have never presented their case as to why they should not do substitute teaching, lunchroom supervision, and the like. The principal assigns the activity and they go along. While they think they should not have to engage in the activity (and they tell their fellow counselors they should not), they never remonstrate or seek to clarify the matter with the principal. Somehow, he was or is supposed to know that it's wrong.

The last question pertains to whether the counselor is essentially a teacher assigned to counseling duties or whether he is a counselor who "may fill in for a teacher." This commentator does not like either alternative nor does he believe that either alternative accurately describes contemporary counselors. The school counselor is a professional in his own right. He has a professional identity not from being a teacher but, rather, from his art and skill in establishing and maintaining a helping relationship. Such a professional identity, of course, is what the American School Counselor Association and the Association for Counselor Education and Supervision have sought to develop and promote. However, it should be noted that, in a legal sense, this view has yet to be established. Recently an Ohio court held that a woman who had been employed full-time in school counseling for some years was under contract as a teacher, rather than as a school counselor. This individual sought legal redress because she had been removed from her full-time counseling position and had been assigned teaching responsibilities. The court held that her contract specified employment as a teacher and that there was no statutory definition for the position of school counselor in Ohio.

The final question asked what proportion of the school counselor's time should be devoted to noncounseling duties. What the author had in mind by "noncounseling duties" is unknown. However, I believe that, generally, a school counselor should spend seventy-five to eighty percent of his time in counseling and the remainder of his time should be devoted to activities (such as program planning, career information, or consultation with teachers and parents) which support and contribute to his primary responsibility of counseling.

E. G. WILLIAMSON

This fascinating story uncovers a widespread type of unhappy relationship between unreconstructed principals and modern, trained counselors. One can dismiss this man as an old fogey, but we don't get anywhere with such derogatory categorizations. All the instances in which he did the wrong things from the counselor's point of view can, unfortunately, be reproduced in many, many schools and these conditions and conflicts will continue to be perpetrated for decades. And now, I'd like to talk directly to the aggrieved counselor.

I don't know of any really effective ways of making it clear to a principal, ahead of time, the conditions which you believe must obtain in order for you to be most effective. A principal may listen to your requirements, but he has his own point of view, his own objectives, and his own picture of where you fit into the whole scheme of things. And, fortunately or unfortunately, he is the principal and has more power than you do in administrative matters.

In this unhappy case I think you would have been wise to have left the school earlier—in time to find another job during the school year—because I doubt that you or anyone else could have changed a principal who has reached this state of intellectual rigidity. I think you said and did the proper things, but they didn't work. I almost wish you would have precipitated a showdown earlier.

It is very rough to find out that there are persons with this bureaucratic rigidity in a school system, but you will find them in the home and in industry—everywhere—and there should be no guilt feelings on your part if you find yourself getting aggressive toward such a person. If you had not become aggressive and had been submissive, I would wonder about you as a counselor. I don't know how people get to be this way as they get older—maybe it is part of the aging process. One should keep in mind that it is often difficult to make a proper fitting between the management apparatus in a school and the counselor. The principal wants control and order and the counselor wants a certain amount of elbowroom. And when a new counselor comes into a well-established school with an entrenched principal the difficulty in managing a mutual fitting between counselor and principal, taking into account the rest of the school and the parents, represents a never-ending problem. You will find this wherever you go.

Yes, I think it is best to find a new situation when you reach the conclusion that you have exhausted your own ingenuity and usefulness.

You did right to fight as long as you did. But there seems to be nothing to be gained by remaining in the community. It becomes a power contest which the counselor cannot win. You can't win a revolution without a showdown.

There is no way I know of, speaking as an administrator, that you could produce an agreement so spelled out in detail which anticipates all future troubles and relationships. You may as well forget that. Just take what comes: see if your concept of what you are to do fits in with the rest of the school administration and personnel, especially the principal. But don't be surprised if creaks and squeals and cracks appear as new situations arise that no one could have anticipated.

To come to the issue of serving as a messenger, I have mixed feelings about this. I suppose all of us have to do a certain number of disagreeable chores, but I think we can be abused. When you reach the point you think this has occurred, the thing to do is to say this openly with the best counseling method of communication.

The counselor is both a teacher assigned to counseling and a counselor filling in as a teacher, at least that is the way it is in many instances. I don't know how one can say, except arbitrarily, how one's time should be distributed in performing various duties. In many schools, some teaching gives you better relations with pupils and teachers, as well as with the community and parents. In other situations, somebody who preceded you as a counselor may have established an ideal concept of counseling, so that you find it easy to slip into spending one hundred percent of your counseling time with students. You have to work out these things pragmatically. This has been my experience as an administrator.

21

Give Him a Break

CRITICAL INCIDENT

Background

This incident happened to me. That is, I was the student in this little drama, and it was an event that changed my life sharply. I graduated from elementary school in 1928 at the age of fourteen, and went to work rather than to high school. I had hated elementary school, had done very poorly, and when I went to work I thought I had put all academic work behind me. My mother wanted me to go on to school, not wanting me to become a laborer like my father, who had died several years before. But as the oldest son, I told her I thought I should start supporting the family, and besides I just hated school. And so I took a job as a delivery boy which paid low wages and had long hours. I worked from June, 1928 until December, 1929 when I was laid off because of the depression. I looked for work without success. My mother also lost her job, and our family had to go on relief. We were like most of our neighbors: down and out, broke, and on welfare. My mother kept insisting that I go to high school, giving me all kinds of arguments that I would do much better by preparing myself for a white collar job. I argued with her that school wasn't necessary. But the truth was that I had little confidence in myself since my elementary school grades were very poor. Besides, I had disliked the children who conformed and who received good grades for their compliance. I knew I was a rebel, and I disliked the forced conformity required in school.

Anyway, I went to see a counselor at the relief office and I had to take some tests. I was told I had to go back to school, and that I could do well since I had a lot of academic aptitude, something which puzzled me since I had earned poor grades.

When I mentioned this to the counselor, he assured me I had a high IQ and if I were interested and would work I could do very well. My mother was at the interview and she was all aglow and kept telling the counselor how smart I was, and how I had shown my intelligence in so many ways. She was sure I could become a lawyer. Although uncomfortable, I felt excited about going back to school and secretly decided to do well, even go to college and make my mother proud of me and help her.

Well, I registered for high school and on the first day we had a big assembly where the principal spoke. He was rather angry about one thing: punchboards. It seemed that there had been a lot of gambling the last semester with these punchboards and that he didn't want the situation repeated this year. He told all students that anyone caught in possession of one of these gambling devices would be immediately expelled. He pointed out the evils of gambling, how many kids had to do without lunches because they lost money, and how much he hated the little gangster who preyed on young children, and so forth.

I soon found myself with a tough crowd. During my year of working I developed friendships with older and tougher kids and I suppose I gravitated toward similar kids in the school. One day one of the fellows approached me and tried to sell me a punchboard. The punchboard was kept in one's pants under the shirt, and held up by the belt. Any kid could punch a hole, paying a nickel for the privilege. A little slip came out indicating whether or not he had won. There were one hundred punches which equaled five dollars, and one paid out two dollars in prizes, making a profit of three dollars. However, my gangster friend pointed out he had "fixed" the board, cutting it in half, taking out the dollar slip, and then regluing it, so that there would be a four-dollar profit from each board. The board cost twenty-five cents, and he told me that the suckers would use up my board in two or three days, and that if I kept my eyes open that I would not get caught. He claimed to have made over a hundred dollars last semester.

I bought the punchboard, and he was right, business was good. By three o'clock I had sold at least two dollars worth of punches and had paid out less than a half-dollar in prizes when—wham—there he was— a teacher who held me by the shoulder in his powerful hand and without a word began to walk me towards the office. I knew that my academic career was over, that I would not even finish my first week. I realized how my mother would react. As he walked me to the office, I twisted about and just looked at the teacher.

Incident

Our eyes met, and he stopped walking, relaxed his grip and then dropped his hand, watching me carefully—to see if I would run, I suppose.

"Give me a break," I pleaded.

He looked around, and then nodded in the direction of an empty classroom. I went into the room, and he followed me. He sat on one of the desks, faced me and said: "We were told if we caught anyone with a punchboard to bring him to the office. You know what that means."

"I'll be kicked out."

"We have to make an example. There is too much of this sort of thing."

"Give me a break. I'll throw away the board. I swear to you I'll never do it again." I felt so weak, so powerless, so helpless. My fate was in the hands of this stranger.

He looked at me and seemed to be making up his mind. "I am a substitute teacher. Maybe I'll never see you again in my whole life. I don't know if you mean it or not. I don't know if I am doing the right thing. Get rid of that board. I'll believe you."

Gratefully I left the room, and turned to him and said, "Thank you. I mean it."

Discussion

Needless to say I did get rid of the board, and I did stop this kind of activity, and I did finish high school and college. But I have never been able to forget this man. I feel as certain as I can be of anything that had he decided to take me to the office, I would have been expelled (as several others were) and that my whole life would have been very different. I would have hurt my mother badly. I might have gone along criminal ways.

I have often thought of this man, and wondered what his motives were in not turning me in. I think of all the incidents that have occurred in my life, none was as meaningful or significant in changing or affecting me as this one. If this man should ever read this book, I want to tell him that his faith in me was not misplaced. Even though it occurred forty years ago, I remember it as though it were yesterday. I do appreciate his instant kindness and faith in me. He believed in me.

Questions

1.   Under what circumstances does a teacher acting as a counselor have the right to make decisions that go against school policy?

2.   Does a principal have the right to make universal decisions about what teachers and counselors can do relative to behavior with students?

COMMENTS ON THE INCIDENT

THE EDITORS

What is the proper role of a school employee relative to orders of a principal? Should they be obeyed unquestioningly? Suppose your principal gives a peremptory order that seems unfair or harsh or unwise, and suppose that you are asked to enforce it despite your disagreement with it. The opportunity to express your own feelings may be denied, as happens when a principal announces a new policy at an assembly of teachers and students, and once the pronouncement is made, leaves abruptly without discourse or debate.

What are the consequences if a counselor deliberately disobeys such orders and uses his own judgment, feelings, or principles to act independently? What should the consequences be if such an individual stands up for himself and against the order?

This incident is unusual in that it is an account of an incident involving the counselor himself as a high school student some forty years earlier. He disobeyed a principal's order—and so did the teacher in the incident. Did two wrongs make a right? Or was there only one wrong?

These philosophical issues are considered by our consultants who wrestle with the age-old issue of means and ends.

THOMAS W. ALLEN

In the brochures with which we petition society for status and moral and financial support, we educators parade our concern for the growth and development of the individual child. We expatiate on the virtues of attending to the peculiar needs of each student. In practice, however, the "brochure values" give way too often to the dictates of convenience and our apprehensiveness of the young. "School policy" is usually the codification of these interests. It is Holy Writ that some teachers are elected for "salvation" (administrative posts) and others are damned (left in the classroom to face the "enemy"). It is not surprising then that many schoolmen are guilty of the baldest sort of idolatry in regard to "school policy." What is more, many school counselors adhere to this gospel with singular ardor. Their insecurity urges them to prove to one and all that they are not subversives, that they are not soft on the "enemy," that they are loyal to "school policy" before *all* else, especially before the students.

However, there seems to be much to recommend the belief that schools are for young people and not the reverse. Under this admittedly more arduous conception of the school, school policy returns to its proper station as the servant of the educational process. As such, it yields readily to the interests of the school's charges rather than dictating their fate like some benign but intractable Oriental despot. It is not enough to determine whether a given student has transgressed one or another commandment of the policy and therefore is subject to this or that penalty. The requirement should be rather that every effort be bent to understand the perspectives and purposes of the student, and to channel his strivings into useful and satisfying avenues.

On one occasion when I made this point, an experienced school counselor expressed his appreciation for these ideals but appended his serious reservations concerning their feasibility, the world being what it is. He noted that each day the vice-principal of his school faced a large number of discipline problems and he had no choice but to render "justice" in a rather impersonal but efficient manner. When I inquired whether the vice-principal dealt with different students every day, the counselor replied that there was a good deal of continuity in the daily groups of offenders. At this point it became clear that the routine administration of punishment actually saved the vice-principal no time in the long run though it might appear to do so in the short run.

It may be noted in passing that when an elementary school in the Midwest made adjustments of this sort in their practice, the number of broken windows in this school declined from 75 to 21 despite the general upsurge of vandalism against schools elsewhere.

The present case lends credence to my suspicion that many problems of school children are "pedagogagenic." That is, the school is frequently much more than a victim, more than heir to the sins of others. To wit: ". . . the truth was that I had little confidence in myself since my elementary school grades were very poor, and besides I had disliked children who had conformed and who had gotten good grades in that manner. I knew I was a rebel, and I disliked the forced conformity required in the school."

The hero of this incident may have resorted to undesirable behavior as a result of his being discouraged by the school atmosphere. Such attitudes are, unhappily, not unusual, as numerous observers of American education have testified. The educational system in the United States appears to be organized and administered in such a manner that kids are readily typed and locked into types by expectations for themselves which have been affected by a host of relatively trivial factors, such as teacher

judgments, grades and other marks on paper which masquerade as pene-
trating insights with monumental portent for the pupil.

The importance of the quality of a child's expectation of himself
has been underscored in a number of recent studies. That is, a student's
low opinion of his intellectual ability leads to inadequacy of performance.
Such "recognitions" are all too frequently generalized to the detriment of
further attempts to achieve mastery in that sphere or related ones. Myriad
observations suggest that the sequence—expectation-to-behavior—is often
the case of poor performance. The present incident is one such instance.
Two others are as follows:

> A visitor came into a classroom and saw the teacher atop a tall ladder
> decorating the ceiling. She was aghast to note that his precarious perch was
> supported by two of the most notorious boys in the school. When she
> expressed her dismay at the arrangement, the boys whose behavior had
> been impeccable began to rock the ladder.

> Malcolm, a black child, was acknowledged to be one of the most outstand-
> ing students in the school. Not only was he popular but his academic work
> consistently placed him near the top of his classes. But one day all that
> changed.

> Malcolm's English teacher had inquired as to Malcolm's vocational plans.
> He replied that he was considering the law. The teacher who had encour-
> aged much less competent white students in ventures more ambitious than
> this admonished Malcolm to pursue a more modest and more appropriate
> objective. At that point, Malcolm's despair of school and of the "straight
> life" crystallized. He could no longer expect that what *he* did would be
> good enough. He was patently beating a dead horse. Shortly thereafter he
> left school for a career of crime.[1]

But if discouragement is a corrosive, encouragement is a potent tonic, an
elixir.

> The teacher looked down at the visitor and calmly observed that he felt
> perfectly secure in the hands of the two boys who were tending his ladder.
> The rocking stopped.

> After years of variegated criminal activity and drug usage, Malcolm X
> became apprised of the teachings of Black Muslim leader, Elijah Muham-
> med, which he found persuasive. Thus, Malcolm suddenly found himself
> with a noble heritage, a heritage whence remarkable deeds might reason-
> ably be expected to emerge. The resulting transformation of an inarticulate
> third-rate hoodlum into an eloquent leader and master polemicist was an
> astonishing metamorphosis.[2]

The evidence is impressive: If we can avoid discouraging children,
if we can remove the discouragement of those already oppressed with
doubts about themselves, other factors, such as academic skills and social-

---

[1] This anecdote is based on an incident described in Malcolm X and Alex Haley's
Autobiography of Malcolm X (New York: Grove Press, 1966).
[2] Ibid.

ized behavior, tend to fall into place. The essential task of the counselor, of all educators, then, is the conversion of the school from a discourager of students, to an institution organized to encourage all of those who pass through its portals. The failure to join in this struggle represents the final disbursement of the educator's moral capital and his declension to a petty bureaucrat.

DON C. DINKMEYER

We adults sometimes forget that we can be important in the lives of children, and that as teachers and counselors our words can make a deep impression and our actions can have grave consequences. To know what is right, which way to go, when to say yes and when to say no is almost frightening.

This case seems to be an example of one-trial learning. Such periods do arrive in peoples' lives when they are so sensitive that a slight nudge one way or another, can affect them strongly. It may be a student hesitating between taking French or Spanish. It may be a decision to go to Columbia or Penn State. In any event, the student comes into contact with the teacher-counselor, and the counselor may make a decision crucial for that child.

In this case the teacher went against school policy. He was wrong as far as the school was concerned. However, the question is not what is right for the school (or more properly, the principal) but what is right for the student. It is fascinating that this incident is written not by the actor, the counselor, but rather by the re-actor, the counselee—many years later. It is evident that this isolated instance in which a teacher assumed responsibility for releasing a child caught in a delinquent act, changed the child's self-concept and his approach to the tasks of life. Using Adler's terminology, he changed for the better, from a useless frame of reference to a useful frame of reference. What might have happened had this teacher simply taken the student to the front office and handed him over triumphantly? Surely, expulsion. And what of the student then? He was quite likely to have continued in his useless pursuit of aggression against society. I believe that this teacher helped change this student from a criminal to a productive citizen. This is why some forty years later, the writer remembers the incident so vividly.

While no one can condone deliberate disobedience or defiance of legitimate orders, I believe we can make a case for the teacher's behavior, not only in terms of results, but also in terms of process. The school is not the principal; it is not his creation; he can not be a dictator; teachers and counselors have to operate in accordance with their own values. In this case, the teacher made a sound decision, one which told the child he was valued, accepted, understood—and trusted—and this built the child's self-concept and helped mold him into a useful citizen.

As I see it, this incident tells us again, if we need to be retold, how a momentary event can have enormous effects on others. As counselors, our behavior can have major effects on human attitudes, values and behavior.

MARSANNE C. EYRE

This episode is a crucial example of external support at the right moment. What is difficult for a counselor to know is when this turning point is reached. When establishment of new goals is followed by a drastic and positive change in behavior, growth is almost an accomplished fact. Let us review the precarious element of risk the counselor committed himself to and see if it was justifiable.

The crux of the experience, as I see it, revolves around the words of the teacher-counselor after the boy had been caught with the illicit board and promised never to use it again. "I don't know if you mean it or not. I don't know if I am doing the right thing. Get rid of the board. I'll believe you." Here is a man who has the power of academic survival or destruction over the boy. Rather than using this power in a punitive way, the teacher makes a personal decision with this unspoken answer: "I cannot sit in judgment of you, for I cannot know what is really going on inside you; I am also in conflict with myself regarding the 'rules' as to whether in the final analysis they are logical and helping. Change your behavior (i.e., get rid of the board) and I will take the risk of trusting you, for I sense a worthy person in you." In this manner a "contract" was established which seemed to be the catalyst needed by the boy. This was preceded by the teacher's awareness of the boy's sense of realization of the consequences of his errant behavior. The experience up to that point was traumatic enough to be a sufficient lesson.

We don't know what might have occurred if our boy wasn't "given a break." In spite of its frequent use, making an example of a "bad boy" rarely is much of a deterrent to the behavior of others. What is worse, it can drive the boy into a position of revenge.

In regard to a teacher's dilemma about going against school policy; it is best if the counselor assesses policy carefully as soon as it has been established, rather than waiting for the development of a crisis situation to precipitate some belated and hasty soul-searching. If he believes the policy is for the ultimate good of the students, he has an obligation to uphold it. There are times when it would not be doing a student a favor by "giving him a break" because it would be showing that natural and logical consequences can be avoided if the authority is lenient or inconsistent.

If, however, a teacher-counselor cannot support a policy because of conscientious beliefs, there are various steps he should take (some may even be considered heroic by our societal standards). He can inform his principal of his beliefs. If he is earnest enough, he might even be able to convert the administrator to his point of view. Failing that, he must pursue a course of action that is consonant with his own sense of justice. The consequences can be painful or, as in this case, immensely gratifying.

DANIEL W. FULLMER

The issue in this punchboard incident seems to be, Do two wrongs make a right? If the teacher had not done wrong, the child would have suffered the consequences of his behavior, and the incident would never have been reported. However, perhaps luckily, this did not happen. Some analysis of the situation is called for.

The formal policy of the school banned punchboards. The punishment for violation of this policy was expulsion. This meant denial of further education for the culprit. However, the unspoken informal culture that the teacher responded to had a different policy, and the unspoken priority value led to a second chance. By this I mean that the teacher himself committed a second wrong: he violated the formal school policy and made himself a judge of what to do. This is what is known in police circles as "nightstick law." Lawyers know that too harsh laws are not prosecuted and that juries will not convict. They modify judgment without common sense. Consequently, this incident is an accurate example of how the nonverbalized informal culture gets transmitted to the young from older authority figures during a direct behavior action.[1] Children learn their social behavior by observing and experiencing the actual choices made by adults around them. Values and ethics are more frequently *caught* rather than *taught*. Admonishment and precept are far less valuable than observing and experiencing. What one does, and not what one says, is what counts.

This incident is an example of how powerful one-trial learning can be. The lesson can literally last a lifetime. Good teachers and counselors can have a profound impression on the young by the way they behave towards others.

The questions posed have given professional counselors some disquieting moments. School policy exists for the education of children. Counselors and teachers perhaps have the duty to violate rules that violate this principle. The counselor is an advocate of the child, and may stand between the child and the principal and any rules that may harm the individual child. While ideally there should be no conflict between the counselor and the school policy, at times, as in this incident, there was. The teacher, acting as a counselor, felt that rigid adherence to the rule could have been harmful to the child. When this happens, in my judgment, the principal should lose and rules should be violated. Implacable obedience to rigid rules violates common sense. The principal of any school is not even a minor god, and he does not have the right to make unilateral decisions that are to affect a child's whole life. In any school, the counselor-administrator relationship should permit these adults to meet to discuss proper behavior in any violation of rules. I would want no absolute rule whether the violation be minor or major.

There is a possibility that the principal had become psychotic due

---

[1] E. T. Hall. *The Silent Language.* New York: Doubleday, 1959.

to extreme stress. Continued frustration can drive one to the brink of insanity. However, more frequently, unreasonable policies are the result of poor judgment.

This incident is a wonderful accident. What might have happened had a rigid revenge-seeking teacher collared this student? The one-trial learning he might then have experienced may have led him to frank delinquency. The writer of the incident is lucky to have been picked up by a teacher who acceded to the informal culture which permitted a second chance which is life-giving rather than to the formal culture which would be life-threatening.

GERALD J. PINE

The ASCA *Policy Statement for Secondary School Counselors* points out that "because the school is a democratic institution using group objectives and methods and because learning, maturing, self-realization are inevitably individual processes, a paradox or conflict for the student is implicit within our educational structure." This paradox often emerges in relation to questions of school policy. Rigid school policies which do not accommodate individual differences and needs activate more problems rather than prevent them. It seems to me that school policies should have sufficient latitude to provide elbowroom for the consideration of teachers and pupils as unique persons. Such policies, I believe, evolve in a democratic setting under the leadership of a secure and democratic administrator. The democratic administrator has a strong faith in the willingness, sincerity, maturity, and competency of his staff and student body to solve problems, make changes, and determine policies. He strives to bring out the potentialities of the members of the "community in the school" by creating an atmosphere conducive to their growth. He has respect for the integrity and worth of each individual. He is willing to recognize leadership in others and allows others to take over leadership functions. He is willing to wait patiently for the more fruitful results that come from democratic interaction; he does not seek the "expeditious" and "more efficient" results of authority. He is more concerned with the growth of individuals than with freedom from annoyances. Under his leadership common agreement is achieved through the interaction of different kinds of individuals and ideas.

In this kind of atmosphere a different school policy regarding student use of punchboards might have been developed. But the fact of the matter is that in the situation described a hard and fast policy was established by the principal and he expected it to be enforced. This brings us to an important question—what is the counselor's role in the implementation of school policy? I believe that the counselor's role is unique in that his focus is on the facilitation of individual human development in a nonauthoritative, nonjudgmental, and nonmoralistic atmosphere. His role is not that of an enforcer of rules but that of a facilitator of self-actuating behavior within the framework of the policies formulated for the operation of the school. He provides an opportunity for the pupil to perceive himself more accurately and to become sensitive to the causal anatomy of his behavior. He deals with discipline problems by giving pupils the chance to discuss and examine their behavior in a free and nonthreatening atmosphere. In this sense he does not make decisions which go against school policy.

He accepts pupils so they are not required to defend themselves. Accepting pupils means giving them the opportunity of holding and expressing their meanings without ridicule, attack, or moralization. In an atmosphere of psychological safety, pupils can explore all dimensions of the school and its policies and express their feelings openly. Negative and disruptive behavior is often caused by a lack of opportunities to express negative feelings. An emotional release of negative feelings many times will obviate the need for negative action on the part of the pupils.

There needs to be someone in the school who does not have a punitive responsibility. Rules and regulations control symptoms but very seldom do they mitigate causes. A blind adherence to policy and enforcement creates more problems than it solves. Repressive, picayune, meaningless, and absurd policies and rules do not facilitate learning, promote growth nor, in the long run, prevent discipline problems. The counselor in his relations with students and teachers can get a real feel for the attitudinal tone of the school. One of the most significant contributions he can make to the educational process is to provide school staff and administration with some feedback regarding the pupils' perceptions of the meaning and relevance of school policies and rules. This can be done in his consulting role without violating the confidentiality of the counseling relationship.

It seems to me that one of the ultimate goals of counseling is to enable the individual to discipline himself so that he can control and manage his own life without infringing on the rights of others. The counselor cannot help the pupil to move toward this goal by acting as a policeman. To the degree that the counselor can facilitate within the pupil fully functioning and mature behavior, to that degree does he enhance the operation of the school and the educational process which takes place therein. A democratic school and a democratic society depend upon self-actuating responsible populations for their existence. When the school or society can only be maintained by overt disciplinary measures then it no longer is a democracy.

22

The Counselor Acquiesces

CRITICAL INCIDENT

Background

My whole life has been spent in school: from age 6 through 22 taking courses; age 23 to 35 teaching; age 35 to 38 teaching and taking courses for a graduate degree; and age 38 to 43 counseling. Therefore, I am used to doing what I am told: attending meetings on time, submitting reports on time, and generally behaving as I am supposed to. I suppose that you can call me well-adjusted. I am married to a nice wife, have three nice kids, a nice home, and I'm well respected in the community and in the school.

The school with which I am associated includes grades seven to nine and is known as an intermediate school. This school is part of a very large system with eight other intermediate schools in the district. Ours is probably the best because it is in the best neighborhood. The superintendent is a very fine man, always worried about public relations, and quite strict about appearances. Our principal is a miniature version of the superintendent: a fussy little man, always worrying about minor details, such as rubbish on the front lawn of the school. He is highly detail-minded and gets furious at being crossed. On several occasions I have seen him go into a temper tantrum and it is a terrible sight to behold.

This incident concerns me, the principal, and a member of the school board. Personal contact with board members is almost nonexistent for people at my level. We get to see them at ceremonial dinners and during infrequent inspections of the school.

Through the grapevine, I heard reports that one of the board members had been putting pressure on the administrator of one of the senior high schools to raise his son's mark in chemistry. Allegedly, this was done against the teacher's will, and as a result the teacher resigned. In any event, it was an unconfirmed rumor, and there was a lot of discussion about the propriety of the request and the integrity of the principal for demanding that a teacher change his marks for political reasons. I remember saying something about academic freedom and how I thought such behavior was most unprofessional.

One of this particular board member's children came into our intermediate school at about the time I was to pick up the incoming seventh grade. I placed the child in the second ability group on the basis of his grades and objective tests. I remember giving his case special consideration because of the rumor, but there was no question that he belonged in the middle of the second group. Before school actually started, I received a call from his mother, asking me about the group in which her child had been placed. When I told her, she didn't seem too upset, but she did ask me some questions about how I had come to this decision. I requested that she come in and see how the grouping procedures were determined, but she didn't think she could make it. She did ask me a number of questions and expressed disappointment about her son's lack of application in school. She mentioned that he was the only one of her children who was not in the highly-prestigious honors group.

Towards the end of the year the father called me twice to discuss his son's progress in the seventh grade. At both times the father told me how interested his son was in math, and how the son had told him he would like to take math with the honors group in the eighth grade rather than with the regular eighth-grade group. I told him on these occasions that this would only be possible if the math teacher recommended him as honors material. When recommendations were finally made by the teacher, this board member's son was not on the list.

Incident

Following the end of the school year in June, I was making up the eighth-grade class lists when the principal came into my office.

"Where are you placing————?" he asked me, referring to this boy.

"In the regular eighth grade."

"His father wants him in the honors group."

"I know."

"Well, are you putting him in?"

"He wasn't recommended by his teacher."

"Is that so?"

"Yes, I checked. The father called me twice."

"He's a board member, you know."

"I know."

The principal looked at me. We understood each other perfectly. He didn't want to tell me to put the boy in the honors group and he wanted me to volunteer to do it.

"Put him in, won't you?"

"Yes, sir." And the principal was gone, and I was committed. I duly entered the boy's name on the honors list.

Discussion

This is how corruption begins. Take a decent fellow like myself, who only wants to do what is right: I was placed in a spot to make a decision, and did what was expected of me even when I knew it wasn't right. I was disillusioned with the principal for knuckling under pressure, and I was disappointed in him for putting pressure on me. As soon as I said "Yes, sir" I was angry with myself. At the same time I was happy that I could blame the principal for taking me off the "hot seat" and handling the matter.

Incidentally, the boy surprised me. He received a grade of 97 on the state end-of-the-year algebra examination, and a final average of 87 for the course. Right now he is successfully taking ninth-grade geometry, and I get good reports on him from his math teacher. Apparently getting into the honors group motivated him considerably because the quality of his work in math improved appreciably.

Questions

1. I suppose that political pressure of this kind more or less occurs subtly all the time. How is it usually handled?

2. Was there any point in my trying to stand up to the principal anyway? What would I have accomplished?

3. Could it be that the father knew that if the son was put in the honors group that he would do better?

4. What might explain the boy's very good showing, which really was not consistent with his prior pattern of accomplishment in math?

COMMENTS ON THE INCIDENT

THE EDITORS

Suppose we contrast the relationship between a hospital superinten- dent and a doctor with the relationship between the superintendent and a second clerk. On an organization chart, the superintendent is dominant to both the physician and the clerk. Yet, a lay superintendent would not dare to suggest methods of treatment to the doctor; but he would demand compliance on the part of his clerk.

One of the dilemmas in this case centers on the issue of who pos- sesses the ultimate authority when conflicts occur between a principal and a counselor. Who can tell whom what to do? Is the counselor an inde- pendent professional person who cannot be told what to do or how to do it by anyone, or is he an employee who must obey his supervisor? In this incident, the counselor was under some pressure to do something he did not think was right. He submitted against his better judgment. He feels that he compromised his integrity as a professional by complying to the demands of others.

This incident strikes at the core of the major issue of autonomy for counselors in the schools as they strive to practice their understanding of their professional role. Our consultants have a variety of opinions on this and other issues found in this deceptively simple incident.

ANGELO V. BOY

Some modern schools, at the time when pupils have to be grouped into subject matter areas for the following school year, have instituted self-selection procedures whereby the student can freely choose which learning level or group would be best for him in each subject. Such a self- selection is not only logical, but it places the burden of responsibility for making an accurate choice where it belongs—in the hands of the student. If, during the following school year, the student decides that he has chosen above or below his capacity in a particular subject or subjects, he is given the opportunity to change his learning level. Pupils engaged in such a self-selection system review their standardized test profiles, noting areas of strength and weakness, seek out the consultation of subject mat- ter teachers when necessary, and ultimately make their own decisions regarding which learning level is most appropriate for them in each sub- ject matter area.

Schools are theoretically the citadels of democracy, but in practice they often deny the student the right to choose freely in important areas of concern to the student. This case is a good example of how most school counselors function in the process of grouping students. They peruse the standardized test results of the student, gain the recommendations of the current group of subject matter teachers, and make a judgment regarding which is the most appropriate learning level for the student. But where is the student's involvement in this important decision? Nonexistent. Why? Because most schools have little or no faith in the pupil's ability to make this decision. But these very same schools expect the student to become a concerned adult who is involved in the affairs of a community. When the student becomes an adult and is apathetic, displaying the attitude that, "You can't fight City Hall," schools have made a large contribution to the development of such an attitude because they have conditioned students to accept quietly the decisions of a higher authority.

The counselor, in this case, has been conditioned throughout his own education to do what he is told. In his words, he says, "I am used to doing what I am told." He has learned to fear authority when he states that, ". . . the principal gets furious at being crossed," and "I have seen him on several occasions go into a temper tantrum and it is a terrible sight to behold." It is no wonder that when the principal approached the counselor about having the school board member's son placed in the honor's group in mathematics, the counselor had no recourse but to say, "Yes, sir."

Later on in the incident, the counselor says, "This is how corruption begins." He knows the questionable character of what he did, but yet he did it! He salves his conscience, however, by indicating that the school board member's son did do well in the honors group in mathematics. But what about the truck driver's son? The factory worker's son? The students whose parents have no political clout? Either they comply with the decisions of authority or they learn how to play the game of political advantage. They learn how to see somebody who knows somebody and to beat the system. But is this democracy in action when one has to gain political advantage in order to get something done?

What about the boy who got what he wanted through the political intervention of his father? Wouldn't he be less psychologically eroded if he had existed in a school which allowed him the right to choose freely his learning level in mathematics? Instead, he resorted to using the best weapon at his disposal—his father's political influence—and it worked. When the college student with long hair and granny glasses yells from the middle of a protesting mob, "The system is corrupt!" he may, indeed, know what's going on.

Although I am dismayed with the counselor's behavior in this case, I am more concerned with the sociological and political dimensions of the system which conditioned him to say, "Yes, sir." I could write an epistle regarding the existential concept of personal courage and integrity, but doing this would be like tossing a feather into a hurricane. Greater gains will result if we attempt to control the hurricane; and this will begin to occur only when there are existentially committed individuals who viscerally care about controlling the hurricane. Otherwise, it will eventually devastate this land of promise.

NATHAN T. CHERNOV

As I read it, there are two problems in this incident: (a) how can we stand up to pressure without hurting or being hurt; (b) why did this child succeed despite the counselor's predictions?

To stand up to and to contradict or defy authority is anger-producing, painful, and unpleasant on both sides; and may even lead to loss of position for either or both of the combatants. However, for a professional person to submit to an unethical request is destructive to one's integrity. It is for this reason, among others, that educational associations have initiated grievance procedures to handle such problems. In numbers there is strength, and if strength is known to exist, sometimes potential problems just do not appear.

However, in this case I don't think there was a justified grievance, and I don't think there was corruption. I believe that the principal may well have had not only legitimate power to make this suggestion to the counselor but possibly, also, good reasons for making the change. It appears to the present writer that the assigning of children to ability groups is often administrative rather than professional in nature. As a matter of fact, if grades and tests are the only criteria used for assigning pupils to groups, much of the work could be handled by clerks. Professional judgment no longer exists. But this is not the way things should be. Such factors as drive and ambition, the emotional well-being of the child, the feelings of parents, pupil-teacher relationships need to be considered. By overlooking these factors we become, in actuality, glorified clerks. For example, I wonder if it couldn't be said that the principal was the professional in this case, basing his assessment on a complex of criteria (after all, he was right in view of the boy's subsequent performance) and that the counselor was acting only as a clerk by mechanically and routinely deciding who goes where.

What has been entirely left out of the discussion of the case is the boy's attitude. Was he genuinely interested in mathematics or in being in the honors program? Was he being pressured at home in this respect? What was his drive to succeed academically? What we keep on learning, over and over again, is that if there is motivation and will to succeed, we can throw the score book out.

DON C. DINKMEYER

The author of the incident refers to political pressure and how it is usually handled. It is interesting to note that while the political pressure seems to have been applied by the parent, a member of the school board, the school at the same time, through its system, was applying pressure to the child. The school's pressure, of course, was more subtle because it related to the system which we have all come to accept. It is obviously all right to group children and put them under the pressure and discrimination that occurs in ability grouping. However, it is unethical pressure for others to attempt to fight the system. While this is not the basic issue, perhaps it is something counselors should look at.

The way in which political pressure is handled is perhaps to help the parent see what he is doing and the way in which he is disrupting the educational development of his child by interferring in school matters. It is quite unusual for a principal to be so accommodating to outside influences. Administrators are frequently quite inflexible about established rules. The problem the counselor should be most concerned with is his dealings with the principal. From the character description given in the background, the principal would be a difficult person to "stand up to."

I believe the basic function of the counselor in this situation is to become involved in a real investigation of the honors program and the effect that these programs have upon students, teachers, and parents.

When we try to explain the boy's very good showing in the honors group we are confronted with a new dilemma for the counselor. The boy did well in his course work and received an outstanding grade on the state examination. Obviously he had the ability to do high-level work. This is an example of a situation in which faith shown in an individual may produce much more than paper and pencil ability tests would indicate.

I believe the lesson to be learned involves the counselor's role in working with administration and curriculum people to provide each student with a chance to be as motivated as this boy seemed to be by his placement in the honors group. Whether it was superior teaching, association with more capable peers, or some other factor that explains his success remains undetermined. We need to provide highly motivating experiences for all students and we must question whether honors programs and multiple level systems aid or retard educational development.

JAMES DONOVAN

Whenever the system creates a hierarchy in school, parents will naturally attempt to have their youngsters ascend to the top and those with the most power will be the most successful in his endeavor. The political implications of the case, in my opinion, are irrelevant; at least, they don't interest me. If a parent and youngster insist on being in a certain top-level class, they should be accommodated but cautioned to examine their motives.

The significant aspects of the case rest in the results the boy had in the math class. How many others could achieve more if we didn't provide artificial boundaries for learning? Grouping is morally wrong, misleading, and often downright unsuccessful in operation. Sufficient research is available to justify discontinuing ability grouping. One of the factors responsible for retaining it is quality teaching. Homogeneous grouping puts less pressure on the teacher and over the years teachers have become conditioned to the extent that even minor misplacements in grouping bring strong protests from the teaching staff. With removal of grouping more creative and secure teachers will be needed.

It would appear that the counselor's relationship with the principal in this case leaves something to be desired. If counselors are to be viewed as experts in the area of communication and interperson relationships how can we rationalize such a "servant-master" relationship.

PAUL W. SCHMIDCHEN

This is indeed, how corruption begins—but much of it may be in the eye of the beholder—since real corruption is not what is outside, but rather what is inside. Running a public school today is no longer like conducting a brass band with only a few instruments, but rather like running a symphony orchestra. Nowadays, the complexities are much greater than in the "good old days." This means complications, and the professional and ethical considerations that must be kept in mind in dealing with school personnel would make many an old-time principal turn in his grave.

As an administrator I would not obdurately push my weight and use my authority to force a change against opposition to another person's reasoned and considered stance, but I would find nothing wrong with reasoning together even if it may seem to the other that I had more ammunition to reason with! After all, if the word *professional* means anything, it means that the child's welfare is primary, and it is here where our professional commitment lies. But we must consider that sometimes some professionals get their backs up because of their selfish vested interest, however decorously defined.

The fact that the boy's scholastic showing was very good despite the counselor's contrary expectations, should be sufficient evidence to indicate that counselors don't know everything. I would expect that in any case of discrepancy between the implications of test scores and the judgments of humans (including principals), man's ability to think and deliberate, must be accorded priority. After all, the human brain is still superior to the computer. This is how I feel, and I believe that is precisely how my professional peers (counselors), for whom I am organizationally responsible, would also feel.

Our purpose as educators is to give every child a chance to become better than he was. With it comes an opportunity for classroom success. If deprivation of any kind, such as retention or downgrading on a multiple track system, leads to any other outcome, then we should think things over again. In this case, to look at the boy's previous academic achievement as the sole determining measure for deciding where he should be placed would be as wrong as giving in to political pressure. I submit that the real incident in this case was not the counselor's acceding to the principal's suggestion, but rather his inability to see that his own placement was wrong in the first place, as evidenced by the results. Maybe the principal knew what he was suggesting! We have to consider many factors in making decisions about children—including the parents.

In answer to the contributor's last question, I would say that the past is not necessarily the best predictor of the future. If we don't know why the person did poorly (or well) in the past, we cannot really predict his performance in the future. As teachers we have built-in occupational hazards; acting as a triad of prosecutor, judge, and jury, we succumb to the evidence—prior grades and test scores. We should operate according to Goethe's dictum: if you want a person to be what you want him to be, treat him as though he were already that what you want him to be. Nowadays, this is known as a self-fulfilling prophecy. Recent research has shown the truth in this. Therefore, I suspect that when the boy, having enough potential, was put in the honors group, he simply responded appropriately and did well. Had he been put in the lowest group, he probably would have also responded appropriately—that is, poorly.

Thus the issue, to me, is not necessarily one of corruption. You can't corrupt anyone else. You can just corrupt yourself. The writer had his feelings hurt by the boy doing better than he had expected—and this, I suspect, is his real beef.

MANFORD A. SONSTEGARD

The background information indicates that the school system has no well-formulated educational program and policy. One might suspect that there has been neither faculty involvement nor community participation in the development of school policies. In such a tightly controlled, autocratic school, critical incidents, such as the one described, become prevalent. Political pressures become untenable whenever there are educational programs and policies that are not arrived at through democratic processes. The path of expedience, rather than well formulated educational objectives, usually leads to one critical incident, or crisis, after another. It can be surmised that the administration has not kept pace with social and cultural changes.

Ability grouping has been a popular educational expedient for several years. With the mechanical procedure, as in this particular case, and without any consideration of the individual, it becomes an impersonal placement in "terms of grades and objective tests." The use of grades and test results in this manner need not be belabored; the frequency of misuse speaks for itself.

It is not surprising that the mother declined an interview when all the counselor had to offer was to "come in and see how the grouping procedures were determined." How different it could have been if the counselor had been interested in people rather than in mechanical, impersonal grades, and test scores. There was no need for the counselor to attempt to confront the principal. He had marshalled no data or information of a significant nature upon which he could take a stand. An astute counselor would have had such information.

The statement made by the mother that "he was one of her children who was not in the highly prestigious honors group" indicates the pressure under which the youngster was forced to operate. One can readily envision a boy surpassed by his siblings to the point that he felt discouraged and inferior. He felt he could not do as well as they did and consequently he gave up too easily. The counselor, as an agent of the school, was about to reinforce the student's feeling of inadequacy by assigning him to a lower achievement group. Political pressures prevented this and, in this case, seem justified, regardless of the implications.

Placement in the honors group was encouraging and stimulating for the boy. Someone believed in him—his father. He felt worthy; he had a place after all. It can be surmised that he would have done as well in other honors groups. It is interesting to note that it was the father and not the counselor who realized what was needed—encouragement and the means by which it could be accomplished. One cannot help but wonder how many other discouraged pupils, who did not have the backing of an influential parent, were left to languish in low-ability groups although they had ability.

23

The Case of
the Phony Genius

CRITICAL INCIDENT

Background

I am a high school counselor. One day I received a term paper from a teacher with a note: "What do you make of this? Do you think the kid is crazy?"

The term paper, written for a class in high school physics, was entitled "New Directions in Electronics," and although written in fairly good English, it sounded like a mishmash of physics, psychology, and neurology. I quote one sentence which gives the flavor of the twelve-page essay: "Lasar-like emanations occurring from the distal end of the energy tube fluoresce against the rhodium shield and will generate nerve impulse speeds close to the speed of light." The general theme of the paper was that a race of supermen could be created by shooting rays, called "Z-rays," during what the writer called "the primal scene."

I went to see the teacher to get more information about the writer. I learned that Herman, the student, was a high-school sophomore, that he had gotten the highest grades in the two objective tests given so far in the class, but that he was, as the teacher put it, "a pain" during discussions. He dominated the class, and the flavor of his comments was, like the essay, a mixture of advanced knowledge and speculation, generally irrelevant to what was going on in the class. "We either have a genius or a nut, or maybe both," the teacher told me. "He sure is strange. He always has a tie, sits right up front, and is alert, always has his hand up, and I am growing to fear him and his remarks."

I looked up Herman's records and found that his grades for the first year followed the most unusual pattern. Of the twelve grades five were *A*s, five were *D*s—two were *F*s. On the various objective tests his uniform score was in the ninety-ninth percentile.

My next step was to call Herman in for an interview. He was a slight, pale, intense, neatly dressed, formal child. I soon learned that he had no friends, didn't play games ("they are for children"), that he wanted to become an atomic scientist, and wanted to solve the genetic secret of life, and that he read college physics for a hobby. He complained about the physics teacher who, he said, belonged in Newton's and not Fermi's era. He informed me that he didn't care for literature, history, art, music, or physical education but that he intended to become a scientist, and that was all that he lived for. I listened with an accepting attitude, and encouraged him to try to be well-rounded, pointing out that if he wanted to go to college he had to have good grades in all subjects. Herman informed me that he had no intention of going to college, and that he was only going to high school because of legal requirements. When he finished high school he was going to start a laboratory of his own and support himself by advanced inventions. When he left, I still didn't know precisely what the problem was, but I scheduled a home visit with his parents.

The family lived in a fairly prosperous part of town. The father was a successful businessman. The mother was a short, fat, nervous woman. With great pride they showed me Herman's laboratory, which looked like something out of a science fiction movie. In it, he had cages of rats, electronic gadgets, and miles of wires, rheostats, capacitors, and half-completed radios. In talking with them, I learned that the family had moved to our town from a large city in another state. And in this city, while Herman was in the sixth grade, a citywide intelligence test had been given to all students in the school system from the fourth grade up, and Herman had gotten the highest score. He had been referred to in the local paper as a "genius" and the newspaper clipping which the parents proudly showed me had the headline "One in a billion, psychologists say" with the story that out of 20,000 school children, Herman had been first by a wide margin on this college entrance intelligence test, his score being in the ninety-ninth percentile of college freshmen. It became clear that in the bosom of this family was another Einstein, and that both parents were dedicated to the nurturing of this genius. Apparently this was not a question of a *folie à trois* for I learned that the whole family—

grandparents, uncles, aunts, and cousins—were all convinced that their family had been marked by fate to bring forth a person of the most superior ability, who was destined to lead mankind to greater glories. That the parents didn't understand what their son was talking about or doing was evidence to them of his consummate superiority. I left the house a bit shaken, not quite knowing which end was up.

I went back to the physics teacher and asked him whether he could come to any conclusion about Herman's ability, and I again was told that he felt Herman was either a genius or a nut or, probably, both. He also informed me that unless Herman calmed down and went along with the rest of the class, he was inclined to flunk him. It appeared that Herman had flatly refused to do the standard experiments called for in this first semester high-school physics course, but that he wanted to bring in some of his own equipment and do some nuclear research. The teacher had informed him that he either would conform or flunk. "I have just about had it with him," the physics teacher told me with finality. I told him about my experience with his parents, and the teacher replied: "My God, they're all crazy." He agreed not to do anything until I did some more research.

I brought the whole problem to my supervisor, a clinical psychologist, who looked over all the evidence and suggested that I see a university physicist and show him Herman's paper. Right on the spot he called up Dr. X and made an appointment, after telling him briefly and in a neutral manner what the problem was. Within minutes I was on my way to the university, and within a half-hour, Dr. X had read the paper.

"Sheer nonsense," was his comment. "This is kid's stuff, putting together unrelated and half-digested concepts with big words. On top of it there is plagiarism." He looked through some journals on a bookshelf, leafed through one of them and finally said, "Read this paragraph." I read a technical paragraph which didn't make much sense, and then Dr. X showed me the same paragraph in Herman's article.

"What he apparently did", said Dr. X, "was to take a number of paragraphs from various sources and assemble them with some filler material. You can tell the kid is really bright, but this whole essay is just a confused mishmash. I wonder if it isn't the same kid I heard about recently who tried to break into a nuclear society meeting a couple of months ago? It seems they had a meeting recently and this kid—a little fellow, with glasses—got up and began talking about his theories of the origin of life or something. Sure sounds like him."

Back I went to my supervisor with this information, and I asked him what I should do. "It looks as though we sure have a hell of a sticky situation here which could develop into a real problem for this kid. From what I gather, this boy got a lot of recognition out of being a genius through getting a high score on an IQ test. All the members of the family

have equated a high IQ with his being a genius, and this poor kid is sad-
dled with an instant reputation which he is trying to live up to. If we try
to disabuse them, we are just jealous of him. Any teacher who fails him is
a damn fool. This kid thinks he is superior to all of us and is making his
own world. The situation has to be handled with great tact. I recommend
that we have a conference with the parents, inviting as many people as
possible, including the physics teacher and Professor X, and try to bring
them back to reality."

I made the arrangements. About a week later we had a conference
which included the parents, the principal, Dr. X, the college professor of
physics, the high school physics teacher, the school psychologist, and
myself.

Incident

I ran the meeting and said that this extraordinary conclave had been
established because we were all interested in Herman and wanted to be
of help. I went over what I had found: Herman's high score on a college
level intelligence test, his elementary and high-school grade pattern, the
opinion of his high-school physics teacher, the opinion of Dr. X, and the
general agreement of all of us that Herman who, we all agreed was very
bright, and could contribute considerably if well-handled, had been
apparently put on the spot by his parents and relatives by being considered a genius, which was leading him to a completely unrealistic conception of himself.

To my surprise, after making what I thought was a reasonably
moderated and accurate summary of the facts, the father accused us all of
being jealous of his son, and he informed us that he knew that we were
plotting against the boy and the family, that we were prejudiced against
genius, that we were intolerant of those who were superior to us. Both
parents were shaking with rage at this "assault" on Herman. The meeting
went on for an hour. Even when Dr. X read the two paragraphs, one
written by Herman about two weeks before and one published about a
year ago, this had no effect on the parents. In the middle of the session,
the father got up, followed by his wife, and left the room. The rest of us
were just speechless. We all realized that we had failed in our attempt to
clarify matters.

Discussion

After Herman's parents left, the principal got up and ran down the
hall to stop them. He came back a minute or so later and informed us

that they had refused to talk to him, had picked up their son, who had been waiting in the hall, and had driven off. He rejoined us, and we all tried to figure out what the situation was, what had happened, what could have happened, what we had done wrong, and all we could think of was that we had done everything right but that the whole family was crazy.

Later I found out that Herman's parents had sent him to relatives, and that he had enrolled at a school in another city. I have not followed the case and often wondered what happened to him.

Questions

1.   The main question is whether I did anything that might be viewed as inappropriate or unsound. What else could I have done?

2.   Is it possible, as the parents stated, that Herman was a genius, and that perhaps he had memorized a paragraph from a technical journal, and that we were jealous of him and unable to understand him?

3.   How can one handle unrealistic parents—people who just cannot be talked to? Was the conference too threatening?

COMMENTS ON THE INCIDENT

THE EDITORS

It is the hope of the editors of this book that the reader will learn from the mistakes of others and in this way become more resourceful in meeting new situations adequately. Some of the cases reported in this book are fairly simple and common; some are unusual and difficult. The incident in this case is of the latter variety.

How do we as counselors handle deviates from the norm? Are our schools geared only for the "typical" or "average" child? Can we be flexible and imaginative enough to handle unusual situations? How do we respond to problems when the whole system in which we operate is threatened?

In this case we have an unusual situation in that to "help" a high-school boy and his parents, the counselor involved a teacher, a college professor, a clinical psychologist, and the principal of the school. Presumably, every one of these individuals meant well and agreed to the plan of action described—and presumably they were all wrong!

Our consultants respond to this incident critically and definitively. We recommend, in this as well as in other cases presented, that the reader formulate his own conclusions prior to reading the opinions of others. What would you say to the writer of this incident had you been invited to serve as consultant?

RUDOLF DREIKURS

This example clearly shows the bankruptcy of our educational system. Instead of helping the student in trouble, we criticize and condemn him. It is tragic if the school ruins a student with unusual abilities; what is worse is that most teachers and counselors, confronted with such a situation, would act in the same manner, without any understanding of the problem. This is the consequence of the inadequate training teachers and counselors receive in most colleges and universities.

Here we have a boy who got the highest grades in tests given in the class, who, in the sixth grade, got the highest score in a citywide intelligence test, who had been first in the college entrance intelligence test, scoring (in the sophomore year) at the ninety-ninth percentile of college freshman, and who had to be taken out of the school because nobody knew what to do with him. Apparently, no adult dealing with him had the slightest understanding of the situation.

Let us see what happened. In physics he wrote an essay that perplexed the teacher because of its grandiose and unfathomable language. Was he "a genius or a nut?" Throughout this paper, this was the only question which seemed to bother everyone. One had to consult with a university physicist to find out that he was not only "putting together unrelated and half-digested concepts with big words," but also plagiarizing. Neither counselor nor supervisor knew what to do about it. They considered it to be "a hell of a sticky situation which could develop into a real problem for this kid." And sure enough, they endeavored to make it a real problem. They found out that the whole family treated him like a genius. And instead of helping him, they blamed the parents. Their inability to understand the boy's behavior prevented them, the educators, from coping with him. Let us see how he behaved.

He was a "pain" during discussion, dominated the class, always sat right up in front, and always had his hand up. The teacher grew "to fear him and his remarks." Here the trouble started. The teacher could not see how this overambitious youth always had to be first, on top, the center of attention. There is not the slightest indication in this report that the teachers tried to cope with this undue demand for attention and display of intellectual superiority.

There were many other indications that a trained teacher could have recognized as the boy's overambition. "Of the twelve grades, five were As, five were Ds, and two were Fs." Instead of recognizing that this is the typical pattern of overambitious students, that they either are the best or the worst, the teacher called it "the most unusual pattern." Since the boy refused to do the standard experiments, wanting, rather, to do nuclear research, the teacher threatened to flunk him if he would not conform. In other words, the teacher got himself solidly engaged in a power conflict, from which he could not extricate himself. But apparently it made no impression on the counselor when the teacher told him "with finality" that he "just about had it with him." Neither did he recognize the significance that the boy had no friends, did not play games ("they are for children"—and he was too superior for that), that he wanted to become an atomic scientist, to solve genetic secrets of life, and that he was much too advanced for college. After all this significant information the counselor states "I still did not know precisely what the problem was." So he contacted the parents, as if *they* could do anything about it.

Now the fun really started. The counselor brought the problem to the supervisor and to a clinical psychologist, who could do nothing except suggest that a university physicist be consulted. He, of course, verified that the essay was "just a confused mishmash."

Now they contemplated what to do. They realized that "this kid thinks he is superior to all of us and is making his own world." But what did they decide to do about it? They came to the conclusion "that we have a conference with the parents, inviting as many people as possible, including the physics teacher and Professor X and try to *bring them back to reality*." [Italics added] What was this reality? They all agreed that the boy was very bright and could contribute considerably if well handled. Amazing, how close they came to the real problem! But the "reality" of which the counselor spoke was different. The boy was "put on the spot, by his parents and relatives being considered a genius, which was leading him to a completely unrealistic conception of himself." And on top of it, the counselor expressed surprise that the parents did not take the blame graciously. They fought back, "shaking with rage at this 'assault' " on the boy. They argued for an hour, and the parents left when the physicist tried to prove to them that their son had plagiarized. Now "the rest of us were just speechless. We all realized that we had failed in our attempt to clarify matters." He continued that "we all tried to figure out what the situation was, what had happened, what could have happened, what we had done wrong, and all we could think of was that we had done everything right, but that *the whole family was crazy*." [Italics added] Even after their complete failure, none of them realized their own mistakes, and they blamed the trouble on the parents.

Now let us come to the questions:

1.   What could the counselor have done? He should have dealt with the real problem of the boy's overambition, his conviction that he had to be on top, even by deceitful means. Instead of that, the counselor was concerned with the insignificant question of whether the essay was real or fake. Instead of finding out what the boy *was*, he should have understood what he was *up to*, his direction, his movements. Providing the student with insight into his goals is still the best and most indispensable corrective approach. This can be done in individual consultations but, even better, through group discussions. Herman's problem was his relationship to others, to the world. This was the issue to be concerned with. And this the counselor, psychologist, teacher, and supervisor failed to do.

2. There is no question that Herman *was* a genius. Telling the parents that he was not was not only an insult but incorrect. They were right in their contention that all his educators were unable to understand their son. Instead of helping the parents to "understand the situation"— it is not quite clear what the parents could have learned to understand— the educators needed to understand the boy, and to know what could be done with him.

3. As long as one blames the parents, one cannot expect any cooperation from them. This is particularly true when one considers them unrealistic; but it was the educators who were unrealistic. The boy was a genius and the parents knew it; only the educators failed to see it. The use the boy made of his superior intelligence is a different matter. This was the problem to which the educators should have addressed themselves. Their failure to cope with it and change it led to the traumatic experience for the boy from which he may never—or at least not for a long time—recover. The school has missed its chance to save a child and thereby deprives society of the contribution of a genius who, instead, moved even further toward antisocial attitudes.

ALLEN E. IVEY

Confrontation may be defined as the meeting between people holding opposing viewpoints in a struggle for power. In a typical confrontation, no one listens to the other and only one point of view can prevail. This might be contrasted with *communication*, which is an exchange of views—often a friendly exchange—but with no effort at behavior change or accommodation. It is represented by what happens in the sensitivity training or "T" group. *Encounter* is confrontation with communication where both parties recognize the need for a decision, listen respectfully to one another, and then mutually arrive at a resolution.

Unfortunately, confrontation was the model chosen by the counselor in this case. One cannot question his observations and conclusions; he did a fine job identifying many facts about Herman and his parents. Few people, however, enjoy being labeled. The counselor and the many professionals he consulted had built a good case. Only one dimension was missing—an understanding of what Herman and his family were trying to accomplish. Were they listened to? What happened in other school settings? The counselor, his supervisor and fellow participants apparently never bothered to do the lengthy, time-consuming detail work of discovering the depth and nature of the family, what types of experiences they provided, or what type of learning they felt should be provided for their son. This is the type of work that should be done by the counselor over a period of time. It does little good to confront someone with true facts if satisfactory alternative routes are not presented carefully. The counselor in this case appeared to be concerned primarily with his objective data and seemed little concerned with Herman as a person.

One cannot help but wonder why the counselor did not talk with the high-school physics teacher who demanded that Herman "conform" even though he far outranked his classmates on all objective tests. The counselor, for example, could have visited the class and advised the teacher how to work more effectively with Herman. Possibly Herman should have been working as a teacher-aide instead of taking the course. It seems sad that some teachers have trouble accepting the fact that inevitably they will work with students brighter than themselves.

In this type of case, the teacher has an opportunity to show what true excellence in teaching is—helping the student reach beyond the teacher. A skilled counselor-consultant could have been of real value to the teacher and the student in this situation. The counselor may even use this situation to help the teacher grow and gain new skills in communicating with bright students.

In addition, the counselor should want to know why Herman received Ds and Fs. Were they for nonconformity or for lack of performance? One of the most dehumanizing aspects of the schools today is the time honored curriculum that demands conforming participation in a series of often irrelevant experiences and then fails to reward actual learning and performance. From this frame of reference, the school, as well as the parents; may be equally responsible for Herman's difficulties. This case clearly illustrates, again, the importance of the counselor working within the school system to change it and make it more responsive to human needs.

It is possible, of course, that Herman was a genius. But, more important, that he was a bright and promising human being. By placing undue emphasis on his intelligence and the possible incident of plagiarism, the counselor reinforced emphasis on Herman's intellectualism. If the counselor had dealt, instead, with Herman's humanity and his feelings of frustration with a school and family unable and unwilling to understand him, a common basis for encounter between Herman and the counselor might have occurred.

In summary, difficult situations such as this cannot be resolved through objective data and threatening parent-school conferences. Rather, a depth-encounter approach is called for which demands a real commitment of time and skill from the counselor. Some may object to the approach suggested here, saying that the counselor does not have enough time in his busy schedule to spend this amount of time with one individual. However, the time spent with the physics teacher may help that teacher assist future students more positively, thus preventing some future referrals to the counselor. Through working with the parents and helping them learn to work with the school, the counselor himself will learn new skills which will enable him to work more effectively with other parents, his colleagues, and the school. It is suggested that by applying himself more fully in this case, the counselor may, in the long run, be saving time for himself and for his students.

It is recognized that the encounter or "listening with action" approach suggested here may not be successful. No counselor ever can marshal enough subjective and objective information so that his decision is always right. The counselor in this case did, in fact, do many things well.

He is to be complimented for a sincere, but incomplete, effort. One must tune in to all aspects of a complex situation such as this, evaluate one's actions, and then move forward to use these data more effectively in encounter with new situations.

ORVAL G. JOHNSON

There is a pervasive and fallacious assumption underlying the strategy of the counselor in this incident: that the issue or question can be settled by establishing the "facts" of the case. The more firmly the counselor established the facts of plagiarism, scientific dilettantism, and superficial reasoning the greater would be the resistance of the parents under the conditions described in the conference. The conference could not succeed for a number of reasons.

First, the counselor's objective for the conference was to communicate information that the parents could not accept emotionally. The psychology of the family needed to perceive Herman as a genius, and anything interfering with that perception would be rejected. Furthermore, there was good evidence to indicate that their son was, in fact, brilliant, if somewhat misguided and perhaps a bit unscrupulous. Again, however, whether the boy is or is not a genius is not crucial at this point. He is a boy with great potential and many problems.

Second, the counselor invited too many threatening figures, especially the professor and the psychologist, to the conference. The deck was stacked against the parents by the makeup of the conferees. They must have felt tricked and plotted against. They came to school on the invitation of the counselor to talk about Herman. (Were they in any sense prepared for what was to transpire?) They were then told that he was a fraud and that they were largely to blame because they had "put him on the spot" by considering him a genius.

Third, the possibility of modifying long-standing perceptions and attitudes in one conference is very slight. Unfortunately, many counselors are burdened with clerical and administrative housekeeping details that prevent them from doing the extensive background work essential to preparing for a conference like this. Ameliorating the conditions described in this incident would ordinarily take many conferences, or much contact with Herman, the object of concern.

Fourth, because of his desire to settle the issue in one meeting, the counselor, apparently, did most of the talking. There is an implicit principle of counseling which is that if a counselor feels he has so much information to impart that he must do most of the talking, he is trying to get across more than the counselee(s) can assimilate. This case raises the issue of whether or not "telling" is effective counseling or, at least, it brings up the question: under what conditions one can communicate effectively?

We have here a brilliant, confused, maladjusted boy, perceived by his relatives as the vehicle on which they will ride to fame and fortune. The most promising approach to the whole situation is through Herman —to develop a relationship with him such that he can be helped through what must be a very difficult period of his life. He is in danger right now of developing a life style of aggressively defending his reputation as a genius, rather than using his high intellect in the pursuit of some socially productive and personally satisfying goal.

WALTER G. KLOPFER

This whole case is a saga of how adults have conspired to make life confusing and intolerable for an adolescent boy. The first person who should take the blame is the one who released confidential information about Herman's extraordinary intelligence test results to his parents and relatives and to the press. No psychologist in his right mind would do anything of this kind. It is well known that people with abnormal intelligence, at either extreme, have special problems in relating to their peers. Rather than emphasizing the ways in which Herman was similar to other boys and girls, everything was done to emphasize the ways in which he was different.

In this situation the ridiculous question of whether he was a genius, a nut, or both is repeated several times. In the language of counseling, there are no geniuses and no nuts; there are some students who learn more quickly than others, and some whose emotional disturbances are severe. But to try to dichotomize "genius" and "nut" and imagine that they are alternative labels flies in the face of reality.

In my opinion, the conference was a bust because the parents had the experience of having something taken away from them without anything being given back. What if they had accepted the fact that their son was not as unusual as they had thought? The one important thing in their life would have been taken away and nothing would have been suggested as a replacement. It would have been much better for the school authorities to devise an enriched program for Herman in which he received individualized instruction and had a chance to work with people who really admired his intellect and were interested in the things that interested him. All too often bright children incur the resentment and wrath of teachers and other adults because they just do not fit the mold, and there is nothing quite as ludicrous or tragic as failing a student who is achieving in the ninety-ninth percentile because he is not doing the little exercises that the teacher wants his students to do.

From this incident, I feel that no one really made any effort to understand Herman. What is important about him is that he is not only bright, but also severely maladjusted. Obviously, he is not like other students; he does not dress like them, or talk like them or, probably, feel very accepted by them. He tries to relate to adults, but his ways of doing it are so clumsy that they constantly result in rejection. At the time of the incident, Herman seems to be slipping into a world where fantasy, reality, knowledge, and ignorance are becoming indistinguishable to him. The question is not whether Herman is a genius or not, but how he can be helped to be happy and successful. The question of his adjustment is much more important than the question of his intellectual achievement, and much more attention should be paid to it.

E. G. WILLIAMSON

I am bothered by the use of the word "phony" although it may well be justified. Undoubtedly this boy has been overmotivated by his parents. I don't know what can be done to help him grow up and away from his parents and become a more serious, competent student, achieving his potential. He is a victim of the overzealous journalist who created the wrong impression about Herman's intellectual ability. And the ambitious and tragic parents fell for it.

The documentation of his incident is superior; the case is beautifully prepared. The counselor did everything that could be reasonably expected of him and so did the teacher. I think the teacher's exclamation "My God! They're all crazy!" is probably right in the sense that the parents are deluded into believing that this boy is a genius and therefore beyond good and evil (i.e., is justified in plagiarism). But with this kind of reinforcement from his family I don't see how the poor boy had a chance to break into anything like normalcy. I see nothing but trouble ahead for him regardless of what is done in the school by anyone, including the counselor.

Someday the boy may end up an Eric Hoffer, but it is more likely he will end up as a trashman with bitterness and delusions. This is a pessimistic point of view, but I think it is quite realistic. The reaction of the parents was quite in keeping with their delusions about the boy.

I don't think the counselor did anything out of the way. I don't think there was anything that could have been done more constructively because the case was decided long before the counselor appeared on the scene. The parents' overindulgence, high expectations, and misinterpretations of the exaggerated journalism had done their job and nothing could counter them.

Of course, the boy has a great deal of ability, but it probably will not be used until he grows up and by then it is too late. I know of no technique to handle such unrealistic parents. Of course, the conference was too threatening, but what else could have been done? One can only assemble the data and present them as fairly as possible, stating the facts as they are. I wouldn't count this incident as a miss in counseling but simply as an unfortunate misappraisal of the boy by others. The counselor never had a chance to make a normal level-headed appraisal of the boy or to get him started thinking reasonably and productively about his prospects.

24

Hip or Sick?

CRITICAL INCIDENT

Background

I was hired by a school system as a school counselor. My office was located in the district office. Students were referred to me by various vice-principals, usually by means of notes which went to a secretary who, in turn, made appointments for me at the rate of one per hour. I had a variety of problems assigned to me, but one of them became a critical incident. Before proceeding to the incident itself, let me say something about myself and my philosophy of life which is important in acquiring an understanding of the incident. I strongly believe in the freedom of people to do what they want as long as they do not harm others. I strongly believe in nonviolence. I believe in the primacy of conscience. I don't believe in conformity at all costs. I am inner- rather than other-directed.

After I had been on the job for about a month, John was sent to see me. He was tall, dark, slim, and had unusually long hair that rested on his shoulders. He sat down and I opened his folder, reading it while he sat next to me. His progress in school had been normal; his grades were distinctly above average; his behavior had been quite acceptable. And in the folder was a note from a vice-principal which asked me succinctly: "See if you can get him to cut his hair."

We had a very interesting and informative chat. It seemed that his whole family believed in spiritualism, ghosts, ESP, and other supernatural phenomena. The family held seances, studied astrology, and much of their life rotated about occult matters. They ate organic foods, practiced yoga, were pacifists, and belonged to an obscure Oriental religion which revolved about the revelations of what he called the "dancing goddess."

John felt that all of society was against him and his family and that they were being picked on. He stated that they made many concessions to society. For example, they believed in nudity, but they dressed even in the privacy of their home. They did not believe in wearing shoes, and went barefoot as much as possible. His father did not believe in shaving and wore a full beard.

School was a nightmare for John. Teachers were forever making fun of him, and trying to get him to do things unacceptable to his conscience. Recently, the vice-principal, who had been trying to get John to get a haircut, tried to strike a bargain with him: if John would just cut a bit of his hair off, even one-eighth of an inch, this would be acceptable to him. John had thought of clipping some hair from a friend's head and putting it in an envelope but he felt this would be dishonest, and had refused to even let a single hair be clipped. What had finally brought things to a head was a conflict with a woman teacher. While passing her in the hallway she said to him: "You are disgusting." He in turn replied to her: "You are disgusting to me. Your hair is bleached. Your eyebrows are shaved and on your forehead are painted eyebrows. You are just thick with paint and rouge. I am natural, the way God made me. So, you are disgusting to me." This teacher made a complaint about John which had gone to the vice-principal who, in desperation, had sent John to me to see if I could get John to conform in his grooming and dress.

I discussed the matter with John, and the more he talked, the more sympathetic I felt toward him. He was a harmless eccentric in a harmlessly eccentric family. While I did not believe in all the occult nonsense his family valued, still this was the family religion, and I felt that no one had any right to try to force John into conformity with reference to his appearance. In discussing the subject, John got quite emotional at one point and said that his family was thinking of moving to another country where they could be left in peace, and even stated that he was getting to hate the United States because they permitted such intrusions into family privacy. At one point I merely inquired whether one could not conform in appearance and grooming and yet be as individualistic as one wanted in one's beliefs. But John firmly squelched this notion, saying that not cutting one's hair or not putting on make-up was part of his family's way of life. I noted, incidentally, that he was sprouting patches of hair on his face, and when I inquired about it he told me that he didn't expect to shave either.

Incident

The incident lay in my official reply to the vice-principal. My note simply said: "It is my judgment that the person I should see would be whoever objects to John's appearance, and not John."

Discussion

I found out later that my short reply had considerable consequences. A faculty meeting was held about my reply, and rather violent discussions were the result. Because my immediate supervisor is a district superintendent, I serve as a consultant to the schools and am not under the direct control of the principal. The school administrative personnel polarized in terms of what to do about my reply. Some wanted my scalp, and insisted that I be either reproved or discharged. Others thought I was correct. Finally, the decision was made that I was right in my attitude, and that the vice-principal and several others who felt that proper grooming (i.e., what they felt was proper) was most important, changed their minds about students' appearance and agreed that long hair and beards were permissible.

An interesting corollary to this incident is that, subsequently, some amount of trouble between top faculty and students took place in other school districts about wearing hippie-type clothing, long hair, and beards, but that there were no problems at the school in which this incident occurred. I believe this was because the discussion about John more or less settled the school's philosophy about such matters.

But what made this incident important to me is that instead of my trying to follow orders—do what a vice-principal, who outranks me in terms of salary, asked me to do—I followed my own ideas and refused to go along with what I considered an unreasonable request.

Questions

1.   While freedom and opportunity for the expression of one's individuality are important precepts, restraints and rules are an inevitable aspect of any society. Perhaps this is a lesson John needs to learn. Did I fail him in the long run?

2.   The family's esoteric preoccupations suggest that they may be a "sick" family. Tolerating their eccentricities or, worse still, employing them as guidelines for school practice may mean the perpetuation and contagion of a pathological condition. How does one differentiate between

the wholesome expression of man's uniqueness and the neurotic display of his syndromes?

3. I believe that the school has no right to dictate anything to any student if the matter is strictly nonacademic and if the performance is legal. If it is legal for kids to go about in the streets in shorts and halters, if it's legal for them to have beards or to shave their heads, then it is absolutely none of the school's business how children dress. But if it is illegal for example, for a person to expose his genitals by going naked, then the school cannot permit it. Many of my colleagues disagree with me on this issue. What is the consensus?

4. School should not be a tool of some segments of society (such as the squares) in inculcating their philosophy. Hippie-type philosophy (to which I do not ascribe) has a perfect right to exist and be permitted if it does not contaminate the true purpose of schools—to teach academic matters. Do the consultants agree with me?

5. I believe that the teacher who told the student that he was "disgusting" should have been reprimanded for not minding her business. What do the consultants think of this?

COMMENTS ON THE INCIDENT

THE EDITORS

There are institutionalized ways of assessing behavior or evaluating events. Policemen, for example, tend to take a point of view about social behavior which differs substantively from that of social workers. These institutional codes are a function of the stresses and strains that people encounter in their interpersonal relation and of the convictions and opinions which characterize the members of various subcultures. For example, we can isolate five general "subcultures" in a school: the custodians, administrators, teachers, counselors, and students. Problems can arise relative to any issue or to any individual due largely to competing institutionalized ways of looking at people and events. Some behavior that may upset a teacher enormously may be viewed as a favorable sign by a counselor, and vice versa. A counselor may regard an introverted, timid, fearful, and silent child as a problem; a teacher may regard such a child as a blessing.

In this incident we have an example of a conflict between a teacher and an administrator, on the one side, and a counselor on the other. The counselor in this case took quite an aggressive stand, possibly because the administrator was not the counselor's supervisor! Eventually, it seems to us, as the role of the counselor becomes clarified and as counselors increase in number and their services improve in quality, there will be more open confrontation of issues and authority and greater need for constructive resolution of conflict between opposing sides.

EDWARD S. BORDIN

In recent years, many have pointed out that "adjustment" is a fictitious goal for counseling. Too many teachers and counselors have mistakenly, often unconsciously, assumed that students must be influenced to conform to both the formal and informal demands of society. Others, in revolt against this view, have been caught up in its negative expression of assuming that their task is to induce noncomformity. In my view, neither of these positions represents an appropriate statement of the task of the counselor. Regarding his direct service to the individual, the counselor seeks to set him free which means to help him assess accurately the environmental and inner realities of his life and to forge the life pattern and style that is the most creative and satisfying response. For a very few individuals massive conformity to external pressures might be a meaningful result, but most persons will find it necessary to act on some external factors while accepting others. Social change, so necessary in response to growing knowledge and technology and other changes of the times, grows out of such processes of individual growth.

This counselor's direct and courageous act illustrates a facet of the counselor's responsibilities which stretches beyond direct service to individual students. The counselor's training and his contact with students equips him to offer direct feedback to the school system on ways that it is organized, or responds unrealistically, regarding the welfare and development of students. Sometimes this feedback involves the welfare of a single student but, more often, as in this incident, the system is influenced to the advantage of all students. How far he goes in developing this role as change agent for the system will depend upon the kind of person the particular counselor is, his resources and satisfactions, as well as on how his job is formally structured. This particular counselor's placement in the district office once he has overcome the resistances thrown up to the "alien" outsider takes him outside the pressures and obstacles created for someone working inside the system of the specific school. Providing he has his superintendent's trust, he can raise uncomfortable, even painful, questions with personnel who outrank him in salary or other status symbols.

In raising questions about the soundness of the family, given the deviance of their beliefs and practices, the counselor confronts us with the difficulties of extricating our personality assessments from social biases. In some cases it is clear. Certainly the assessment contained in the diatribe of the woman teacher was bias rather than veridical evaluation. Yet, it is an established fact that severely disturbed families of the sort that produce psychotic or borderline-psychotic individuals are likely to be marked by similarly deviant beliefs and practices. The only answer is to use such observations only as a basis for raising the question but not to answer it. The answer must come, as it did in the case of John, from an assessment of the individual or the family's total pattern of action. How coherent is it? What are the underlying feelings toward self and others? For example, while John gives indications of strong feelings they seem modulated compared to the stress under which he and his family have been placed. Though he did not conform in many social beliefs and practices, John was able to behave in conformity with the major requirements of the school. He was making normal progress and could behave acceptably in class. However, it may take special knowledge of psychopathology and well-developed interviewing skills to uncover indications of thought disorders which must be separated from whether we agree or disagree with the conclusions an individual reaches.

The question of school rules and the methods of arriving at them needs and is being reexamined. The counselor implies that school rules should confine themselves to academic matters and that all else should be governed by formal law. I believe any social group, whether family, school or club, puts too great a strain on formal law or on itself when it seeks to rely solely on the laws of the larger society for its self-government. Each group needs some explicitly stated standards for behavior to give shape and coherence to its particular life. A difficulty in many schools and families is that there is an unrealistic division of responsibility in determining what rules are needed. Certain realms of behavior are dictated by law and, of course, cannot be contradicted by rules. Others represent matters of taste in which students should have as much to say as teachers. In matters of dress and grooming, teachers, students, and parents have, it seems to me, equal interest and, therefore, should be equally represented in decisions on such matters. Other rules bear on mechanical functions of the group, such as traffic patterns in halls, and are the business of teachers and students. Above all, teachers and counselors bear a heavy responsibility to offer their students the opportunity to learn to participate in group decision making which respects the rights of minorities and fosters a spirit of mutual respect.

GEORGE J. BREEN

The counselor's first question is probably the most important since the major concern should be one of helping the student with his problem. Although the counselor demonstrated some understanding and was sensitive to John's problem, he did not provide him with any real learning or insight into the long-range consequences of his behavior.

While the counselor states, in his first paragraph, that he does not believe in conformity at all costs, he overlooks the converse of his belief. Can nonconformity at all costs truly give an individual the maximum freedom of conscience and behavior that one would really want? This is the issue that the counselor has overlooked and that should have been dealt with in the incident.

John's attitude that "all of society was against him and his family and that they were being picked on by society" could only lead to continued self-defeating feelings of hostility, blame, and resentment. Therefore, the counselor missed a major opportunity to challenge the young man's negative or irrational ideas. For the real issue here that the counselor overlooks seems to be the *choice* that the young man is making in his life. If he was truly what I would consider to be a healthy nonconformist, his role would really have evolved by his own choice. His family seems to be rebelling for no good reason and the occult style of life they practice points to a strong compulsiveness. Therefore, John's nonconformity suggests that it was thrown upon him by his "sick" family. His self-image seems to be an ever-increasing mirror of how his family has conditioned him to react.

Furthermore, by the counselor's own admission, "school was a nightmare for John." If the student was, once again, a healthy nonconformist, what real difference would the teachers' making fun of him matter? A healthy nonconformist would believe, understand, and accept that what he was doing was correct. He would be guiltless about the choice that he has deliberately chosen for himself and would thoroughly accept himself in spite of adverse reaction. John certainly does not fit this model and here is where the counselor misses the opportunity to confront the young man with the realities of his ego development.

Although John's reply to the woman teacher who said to him that he was "disgusting" may have been correct and deserving, what good did it accomplish for John? No severe punishment was attached to his reaction in this incident, but one can well imagine the consequences that would probably follow if this chip-on-the-shoulder attitude persisted in the future.

The main point that I am making is that the counselor never carefully examined with John the probable consequences of his present behavior. Choices were never critically considered. For example, John's "threat" that his family was thinking of moving to another country to be left in peace was not even challenged by the counselor. This idea that the "freedom" to be gained in another culture usually overlooks the personal infringements that frequently may accompany this new "freedom."

While the official reply to the vice-principal was certainly to the point, it could have been more tactful and effective. Although the school's philosophy concerning the incident was ultimately resolved, much of the vice-principal's initial hostile reaction was probably due to what he considered to be a rather blunt and rude communiqué. The counselor may have been able to accomplish the same results by personally discussing the issue with the vice-principal, consequently avoiding the mayhem that followed the official reply. It is not suggested here that what the counselor did was mistaken but, instead, that the way he pursued his goal could have been more graceful.

The counselor's belief that "if it is legal it should be acceptable in school" is a false analogy. For example, although it is legal and appropriate for a girl to wear a bikini on most public beaches, it would probably be quite distracting to the academic learning of males in a class-room. If we followed this analogy to its logical conclusion, then racial segregation in the classroom prior to 1954 was justifiable since it had not yet been declared illegal.

Moreover, although I agree that schools should not be a "tool of some segment of society (such as the squares)," the counselor's statement that, "hippie-type philosophy has a perfect right to exist . . . if it does not contaminate the true purpose of schools—to teach academic matters" has dangerous overtones. We cannot simply accept a philosophy that veers so sharply from the societal norm without critical inquiry. Educators too often overlook the fact that a "subliminal curriculum" exists beneath the surface of most school programs. In order to be truly objective we should begin to apply the evergrowing storehouse of knowledge inherent in the behavioral sciences to all societal philosophies that influence the student's attitudes, values, and beliefs.

NATHAN T. CHERNOV

I feel in this incident that the counselor overidentified with his client who had been put into a compromising situation of either being true to his own values, and those of his family, or giving in to the demands of school authorities. The counselor also was put into a com-promising position, being asked to try to get this youth to behave in ways contrary to the boy's principles. A counselor who accedes to requests that are in conflict with his own philosophy feels corrupted and can become upset with himself if he gives in. Submission of one's integrity can change enthusiasm, liking of people, and concern for the school to discourage-ment, depression, ineptitude, and lack of interest.

What bothered me about this incident was the counselor's apparent peculiar mode of operating, giving on the one hand the impression of accepting the school authorities' values while actually rejecting them, resisting by means of a thinly-veiled insult.

It would seem to me that placed in this kind of situation, in which an angry teacher or administrator wants the counselor to be a hatchet man, the counselor should say, in effect, "I will be happy to take this child in counseling. However, I shall not try to make him conform by any kind of coercion."

Now, it could well be that the student needed counseling. It could be that he was "sick" and also his family. It could be that his hostile feelings to society were exaggerated, and that the family's behavior did provoke curiosity and amusement. If so, John needed someone who could be sympathetic and empathetic. Now the counselor could listen, could accept ideas and feelings, could clarify and do all the things a counselor should do with a child filled with anger and frustration, who feels the establishment is wrongfully encroaching on his liberty. It would seem to me that the issue of the length of his hair would soon be subordinated to the larger issue of his whole relation to society.

The note of the counselor was a challenge and, as I see it, perhaps unnecessary. It was a reproof. His comment, nonetheless, apparently brought the whole issue to a head. I note a bit of pride on the part of the counselor in the fact that he instigated official discussions on the matter of student dress and appearance.

Standing up boldly and demanding a confrontation is what this counselor seems to have done. Perhaps it was because of overidentification. Perhaps it was because of the counselor's own problems of hostility to authority. And, to be charitable, perhaps it was because of his ideas of freedom.

For counselors not so bold, perhaps a compromise, rather than a confrontation, might be better. For example, could not the counselor have (a) taken an honest stand and (b) have smoothed over the situation, thereby saving everyone's face by asking for an exception in the matter of hair length in deference to the boy's religious views? I believe a clever counselor would be able to make school administrators understand the necessity to protect the rights of minorities, and change their attitudes towards this boy.

BARBARA A. KIRK

This is a boy characterized as making normal progress in school, achieving distinctly above-average grades and behaving very acceptably. His only deviation was adherence to his own family's standards, ideologies, and religious observances—a truly personal-cultural matter.

So the boy had conformed in school to restraints and rules, and in fact reported that the family as a whole had made many concessions to society, detailing some of them. The issue, therefore, really was not that of conforming and making concessions to other restraints and rules. He had a clear membership in his own family and social group, hence, did not demonstrate idiosyncratic ideologies and behavior. Thus there appears no indication that the boy was personally ill. He had on the whole, it seems, made a rather good adjustment to two wholly different worlds. Doing so is one of the central issues and problems of our society today.

So it would seem that the counselor well understood the boy's honor and integrity and his need to maintain his own beliefs, while striving simultaneously to adjust, insofar as possible, to the school's needs. The counselor, however, in expressing her view of the matter, did it defiantly, rather than sympathetically: she was attempting to help others to understand and educate them in the process. The note was brief, defiant, and somewhat hostile rather than truly helpful.

It is clearly true that the teacher who told the student he was disgusting, had problems of her own. It would probably not be helpful to reprimand the teacher. A better course of action would be to help her attain tolerance, to broaden her understanding, and enable her to receive training in basic human relations, perhaps through sensitivity groups or other available means. There are two somewhat distinct matters in our teacher's behavior; first her thinking *disgusting* and second, saying "disgusting." In order to prevent statements that are deleterious to others, it is necessary first to recognize and then deal with such biases. Then come the controls regarding expression. Flexibility in relation to change, changing mores, and changing customs is vital in present-day dealings with young people.

John's family's preoccupations are an additionally interesting matter. It seems from what was said that their religion is probably not a unique one. Part of the evaluation has to do with whether their beliefs and practices are isolated and individualistic or whether others share them. With the present trend toward mysticism and Far East philosophies and religions, their theme would seem not to be very deviant in the present culture.

HOWARD PARAD

This is a fascinating incident because it portrays a problem as ubiquitous as it is troublesome; namely, the extent to which the school child should be obliged to follow school rules that pertain neither to the rights of others nor academic performance. A fundamental related question is what role the school counselor plays in the struggle between child and the school system. Is the counselor on the side of the child, or does he side with authority? Should he mediate between the child and school authority? Is he his own man, beholden only to the imperatives of his own conscience?

John is probably an adolescent. We assume the only point at issue is the length rather than the cleanliness of John's hair. Were the school to raise questions about the cleanliness of hair, this would be a legitimate concern of the rights of others—not to endure unpleasant body smells. Hence, the length of John's hair becomes a question of esthetics.

Let us begin with the counselor's questions.

1. He asks whether he failed John by not helping him to face the fact that restraints are inevitable in any society and that one must learn to conform, at least up to a point. It is important to recall that John did not request help. He was told to see the counselor. The vice-principal, while probably not as uptight as the woman teacher who finally brought the conflict to a head, wanted John to conform to the school system, albeit if only in a symbolic way, by cutting "just one-eighth of an inch" of his hair. So the counselor obviously had to deal with the problem as presented one way or the other.

After exploring the situation, the counselor comes to the conclusion that John should not be forced to knuckle under. Thus he sides with John against authority. Usually, in such predicaments, youngsters are probably in rebellion against their own family. Curiously enough, in this situation the child is conforming to his family's values. He would truly be in a dilemma if he obeyed the school; to do so would be to run counter to his family's teaching. For the counselor to attempt to make

John cut his hair, would have been unfair to the child as well as to the counselor's own strongly held principles.

On the other hand, inevitably John will encounter situations even more conflicting because of the fundamental cleavage between his family's way of life and that of the larger society. Instead of preaching to John about the disparity between his family's values and those of the outside community—which, in my opinion, would have been worse than useless—I wonder whether the counselor should have focused on John's personal misery. We are told that school was a "nightmare." He was criticized, ridiculed, and harassed. Could there have been a follow-up discussion to explore the extent of John's alienation from the system and whether, apart from the length of his hair, there were other ways in which he provoked and received ridicule? The counselor's "positive and unconditional regard" for John is unmistakably clear, so for him to see John again would not put the counselor on the side of the harassing authorities, but rather would give John someone he could turn to for sympathetic discussion of future problems that may arise due to a conflict between his ways and those of the school system.

2.   The counselor asks us whether utilizing the family's eccentricities as "guidelines for school practice may mean the perpetuation and contagion of a pathological condition." The question is phrased too strongly, since the assumption is that John and his behavior will become objects for identification by other students. The background of the problem presents no evidence for such an assumption, since we are told that John is isolated and apparently without many friends. Hence, it seems highly unlikely that he will attract a strong following from the student body.

3.   Does the school have a right to make rules pertaining to non-academic matters for which there are no legal prescriptions? Is any behavior not expressly forbidden by law permissible within the school? If so, this means only behavior which clearly jeopardizes persons or property could be forbidden. The reality is that every organization, to maintain its integrity as a social system, has rules about various aspects of interpersonal behavior. The question is not the school's right to establish such rules but, rather, whether these rules are reasonable and justifiable. We cannot explore here the intricacies of school policy decision-making, but we should remember that there is tremendous variation from school to school. In some school systems detailed policies concerning dress and social behavior exist. In other schools, the principal is given enormous leeway in deciding which norms shall be operative. In a growing number of schools a liberal, permissive atmosphere prevails, characterized by an irreducible minimum number of rules to govern a child's behavior in matters not directly related to his academic performance. For example, smoking cigarettes in the schoolyard may be ignored in these schools, while in others it may constitute sufficient reason for summary dismissal.

4.   This leads us to the counselor's next question: Should the school be a tool of some segments of society? That is, should the squares be able

to inculcate their philosophy on the hippies? The school, like all social systems, must have rules and norms for its own survival. The school is a prime socializing agent of society; a great deal of school time is spent on what is vaguely called "character building" or "preparation for life" rather than on formal teaching. So the issue is not whether the school has a right to inculcate values, but which values and how shall these values be taught.

Few would quarrel with the school's responsibility for teaching values such as honesty, responsibility, and concern for one's fellow man. While I agree with John's school counselor that the primary purpose of the school is to impart knowledge, yet there are questions of social convention that cannot be completely ignored. In some schools, democratically-elected student-faculty councils exist for the development of codes of social behavior that generally maximize opportunities for personal choice and freedom.

5. Should the teacher who was "disgusted" with John's hair be reprimanded? My inclination would be to urge this teacher to participate in the faculty discussion concerning whether or not the school had any right to regulate the length of hair. I would hope that the most effective reprimand would come from her own peer group, who would disapprove of her behavior. It would be far better to help the teacher with her attitudes—through peer group pressures—on the assumption that if she continued to have a stereotyped negative disposition toward John, her revulsion and disapproval would continue to have an abrasive effect on him and on other long-haired students, overtly or covertly.

There were two dramatic incidents which contributed to a crisis atmosphere within the school setting: the teacher's expression of disgust (the original precipitating event), and the school counselor's official response that those members of the school staff who object to John's appearance should come for counseling, not John. The counselor's provocative reply stirred up a healthy debate and the problem was effectively resolved when it was agreed that long hair and beards were no longer taboo.

But were there other less provocative approaches available to the counselor? If the counselor saw his role as that of consultant to the school he might have asked the vice-principal to call a faculty meeting for policy discussion regarding matters of personal grooming. We cannot say, on the basis of the information available, whether such an approach would have been as effective as the counselor's trenchant memo to the vice-principal. The school counselor, even though he won his point probably became *persona non grata* to those in disagreement with him. If so, the counselor's usefulness probably diminished.

This is not to say that a school counselor should become an organization man, but if one wishes to serve as a school counselor or consultant, he may well have to find ways of being true to his conscience that involve disciplined uses of consultation rather than confrontation. If the school counselor has a larger image of his role than that of seeing individual students, he may see himself as an agent of change for the betterment of the school social system, as well as an advocate of the rights of the individual student. The risk that the militant school counselor takes in this situation is that he may lose the war even though he has won the battle.

E. LAKIN PHILLIPS

The counselor in this incident was put in a compromising situation by the flow of events and by his general philosophy. While the counselor is probably right in thinking that the person who should be seen for help is the one objecting to John's appearance, this is probably not a useful or gainful tactic to employ.

One cannot force rules or values upon another person, at least not under the circumstances described here. What the counselor can do is to discuss with the client how his behavior may be perceived or evaluated by society, or by various segments of society, and help him to face the consequences of his actions. This is not to say he is either right or wrong; but to help him elucidate the outcome of his conduct on others.

I see no gain in describing the family as "sick." Although this is probably an eccentric family, many important and useful individuals have come from families with many peculiar beliefs and practices.

My inclination would be to side with the counselor's opinion that the school has no basic right to dictate values and behavior to students other than those expressly related to the scholastic or academic situation. This is often a hard line to draw, to be sure, but it is a lot easier than trying to legislate dress and other matters of personal conduct.

E. G. WILLIAMSON

I cheered when I read the note to the vice-principal, that the counselor should have seen the one who objected to John's appearance, rather than John. I might not have put it that sharply; certainly those who object ought to have sympathetic hearing from a counselor.

It is almost a miracle that after a faculty meeting with such vigorous visceral reaction, beards and long hair were deemed permissible. I have long felt we have made too much out of the revolt of the younger generations, particularly with respect to their eccentric dress, and that we should just ignore it. We can talk to each other about it if it bothers us, or to the students, but we should not publicly scold the individual or take advantage of authoritative relationships to impose our standards on dress. There is no question that some students will try us out for size and be as provocative as they can to see if they can get a reaction from us. This is the essence of the revolt of the adolescent today—resistance to what he considers to be imposed authority. I understand his antipathy and I sympathize with the adolescent. I think it is rather foolish on his part, however, and hope that he will grow out of it and forget such childish antagonisms that manifest themselves in long hair, and things of that sort which irritate adults so much.

In this case I think the counselor was right in his procedures and ideas, although I think there are times when a counselor can be wrong in going against the system for objectives and values that are just not that important. Refusal to kowtow has got to be justified in terms of *what* you are refusing to do. The mere act of refusal is not necessarily virtuous. There is no question in my mind that John will have to learn in the long run that he will have to conform to society to some extent by trimming his hair if he wants to work. It may be that John comes out of a sick family but I don't think that you can affect the family except in the way that the counselor did in this case.

The counselor asked the question: "How does one differentiate between the wholesome expression of man's uniqueness and a neurotic display of his syndromes?" All I can say is: "Wow! What a question!" This kind of either-or bipolarity is simply insoluble. All of us must learn to compromise and this present generation has not yet learned that they have to accept some of the restraints of external society, including the curtailment of freedom of self-expression on an impulsive basis. After all, we do have to live with each other. But how to teach John or any other person how to differentiate between the point at which he should be his unique self or conform is the question at issue, and I don't think we have even begun to think about it. We have been beset by proponents of pervasive permissivism—whatever an individual wants to do is to be permitted. I just simply can't accept that for an organized society. I can't agree with the counselor in trying to differentiate between the right of the school to dictate academic matters and in non-academic matters. It seems to me that the whole child goes to school, as the progressive education people used to say, and that you have to deal with the whole child. A certain amount of eccentricity should be tolerated. Those who conform should learn to tolerate this degree of eccentricity—not just counselors, teachers, principals, but everybody! I do not take any comfort in the division between what is legal and what is not legal. Mores, to me, are just as important as laws in controlling human behavior in an organized society. I don't agree that the school should be a tool of some segment of society; we are all mebers of society. It is just a question of trying to mediate among the competing elements throughout the whole range of any society's points of view, going forward with the maturing process that the school is dedicated to. This is more than academic subject matter; it is teaching students how to live in a civilization.

Nor can I agree that the teacher should be reprimanded for telling the student that his appearance was disgusting. I would counsel her but not reprimand her. She needs some understanding and some help in extending her range of tolerance of individual differences. She has to learn that individuality sometimes brings out eccentricities, some of which irritate us. We can look the other way, go around the block, or move out of town, but we can't go around forcing other individuals to conform to our own little mid-Victorian middle-class standards of taste and dress.

Now the argument starts: Where does tolerance end and conformity begin? That is what this whole issue is about. The school curriculum doesn't have anything to say about it, although I suspect that a good many of the social science teachers who have studied the sociology of primitive tribes would have something to say relevant to this whole problem. That is: how do you learn to live in an organized society and still have your own uniqueness? This question should precipitate endless discussions in teachers' meetings every year. But instead of an open discussion of such a vital issue as this, the bureaucratic rigidity of the school system permits—in fact, encourages—the principal to issue an edict as though he were Zeus on Mount Olympus. That is the law of the school! All teachers are now supposed to enforce it. This concept is equally silly and undemocratic as the childish concepts of some adolescents and some adults today who assume that freedom means to do what they damn well please without any external restraints.

You cannot "either-or" this question. You have to somehow or other find some kind of workable compromise between these two extremes —and this is the fun of counseling. At least it can be fun if you don't get too worked up about it!